Brennon

CW00822011

Microsoft®
Expression Blend™

UNLEASHED

SAMS | 800 East 96th Street, Indianapolis, Indiana 46240 USA

Microsoft® Expression Blend™ Unleashed

Copyright © 2008 by Pearson Education, Inc.

All rights reserved. No part of this book shall be reproduced, stored in a retrieval system, or transmitted by any means, electronic, mechanical, photocopying, recording, or otherwise, without written permission from the publisher. No patent liability is assumed with respect to the use of the information contained herein. Although every precaution has been taken in the preparation of this book, the publisher and author assume no responsibility for errors or omissions. Nor is any liability assumed for damages resulting from the use of the information contained herein.

ISBN-13: 978-0-672-32931-9
ISBN-10: 0-672-32931-X

Library of Congress Cataloging-in-Publication Data available upon request.

Printed in the United States of America

First Printing June 2008

Trademarks

All terms mentioned in this book that are known to be trademarks or service marks have been appropriately capitalized. Sams Publishing cannot attest to the accuracy of this information. Use of a term in this book should not be regarded as affecting the validity of any trademark or service mark.

Warning and Disclaimer

Every effort has been made to make this book as complete and as accurate as possible, but no warranty or fitness is implied. The information provided is on an "as is" basis. The authors and the publisher shall have neither liability nor responsibility to any person or entity with respect to any loss or damages arising from the information contained in this book.

Bulk Sales

Sams Publishing offers excellent discounts on this book when ordered in quantity for bulk purchases or special sales. For more information, please contact

> **U.S. Corporate and Government Sales**
> **1-800-382-3419**
> **corpsales@pearsontechgroup.com**

For sales outside of the U.S., please contact

> **International Sales**
> **international@pearson.com**

Editor-in-Chief
Karen Gettman

Executive Editor
Neil Rowe

Development Editor
Mark Renfrow

Technical Editors
Amir Khella
Chad Carter

Managing Editor
Kristy Hart

Project Editor
Anne Goebel

Copy Editors
Harrison Ridge
Services
Mike Henry

Indexer
Publishing Works Inc.

Proofreader
Linda Seifert

Publishing Coordinator
Cindy Teeters

Cover Designer
Gary Adair

Composition
Jake McFarland

The Safari® Enabled icon on the cover of your favorite technology book means the book is available through Safari Bookshelf. When you buy this book, you get free access to the online edition for 45 days.

Safari Bookshelf is an electronic reference library that lets you easily search thousands of technical books, find code samples, download chapters, and access technical information whenever and wherever you need it.

To gain 45-day Safari Enabled access to this book:

- ▶ Go to http://www.informit.com/onlineedition
- ▶ Complete the brief registration form
- ▶ Enter the coupon code JUCL-YZBE-QCHU-Z9EE-IEM2

If you have difficulty registering on Safari Bookshelf or accessing the online edition, please email customer-service@safaribooksonline.com.

Contents at a Glance

Table of Contents

Microsoft Expression Blend Unleashed

Loading an External Skin File 468
Summary 474

17 Working with Windows **475**

Window Elements 475
Setting a Window to Show as Transparent 477
Creating Multiple Windows 480
Switching Between Windows in Code 480
Summary 486

Part VII Advanced Topics

18 Creating a Custom Control **489**

Things to Consider 489
    Level 1—FrameworkElement 491
    Level 2—Control 491
    Level 3—Inherited Control 491
    Level 4—UserControl 491
Where to Start 492
Building the Control 492
Testing the Control 501
Summary 508

20 Using 3D in Blend **511**

Viewport3D 511
    The Selection Tool 513
    The Camera Orbit Tool 514
Importing 3D Objects 515
    Materials 516
    The Camera 518
    The Lights 518
Summary 522

20 Controlling Media (Music or Video) **523**

Creating the Project 523
    XAML Requirement 524
    Player Controls 528
    Code Requirement 532
Summary 553

Index **555**

About the Author

Brennon Williams is among the top .NET developers in the UK, consistently contracted by leading consultancies for cutting edge development projects. He has an extremely wide skill set as a hybrid designer/developer, with experience in Flash, 3D Object Modeling, and DirectX based development. Brennon's UK company X-Coders Limited is the preferred Blend/WPF training and development provider for some of the World's largest companies.

For almost 15 years, Brennon has worked in several countries as a consultant software developer. He is currently employed as XAML Architect for SmithBayes in the UK and Dev Lead/XAML Architect for Motorola's WPF project in the United States and Sri Lanka. He is also creating his ExpressTrain video tutorial network online at www.learnexpressionstudio.com. When he schedules an hour or two of free time, he enjoys nothing more than having a BBQ with his wife and kids in the backyard.

Dedication

It was always for you, Jane, my gorgeous wife...

*Your love and support, as well as your
dedication to our little family, inspires me.*

*With all my promises thus far fulfilled,
I will make you one more now:*

*I won't take any more projects on without first understanding
how they will affect you and our girls. How you all put up
with grumpy old me and my relentless work schedule is
a mystery—I know it hasn't been easy.*

I will try harder.

Acknowledgments

First, I must say a huge thanks to Adam Ulrich: The Microsoft Design Tools Test Manager has continually furnished me with Blend builds as soon as he possibly could, and made sure the issues I came across were dealt with. I am indebted to you, kind sir.

As you read through the book, you will see where I have relied heavily on the talents of Mr. Stephen Barker. Steve has courteously allowed me to use several pieces of art that he has created, along with numerous hours of advice on all things graphical about Expression Design, ZAM 3D, and everything else that needed an expert opinion. You are first class in my book, Steve, and thank you for being so very patient with me. Sooner or later it all gets done.

I would like to also thank former Blend development team member, Amir Khella, my first technical editor. Your amazing, positive outlook on everything you are involved with makes for a refreshing view of the world. Thank you.

Microsoft Designer Tools Program Manager, Steve White, was kind enough to create the foreword for this book, and you can tell by reading it that Steve has a very poetic way with words. Steve has on countless occasions assisted me with issues and advice. Thank you, Steve—there are few people in this world that will go out of their way to help others as you do.

For anyone who has spent any time in the Microsoft Expression Blend newsgroup, you would have at some stage come across the expert advice of Blend Program Manager, Unni Ravindranathan. Unni has a unique way of explaining concepts and has certainly taught me a great deal over the last few years while interacting with him. Thank you for your support and encouragement, Unni—it means a great deal to me.

I must also mention the huge support and advice given to me by Corrado Cavalli from Italy. Corrado provides me with an outpost to check thoughts and share concepts regarding Blend and WPF. Thank you for the reviews and advice you have given to me during the course of writing this book, Corrado. You are a good friend indeed.

My hat is also tipped to Mr. Brad Becker, Microsoft Group Product Manager for Rich Client Platforms, who was instrumental in introducing me to Microsoft staff and pointing me toward the right people to help me with this book. Cheers, Brad.

My boss at SAMS, Neil Rowe. Neil must certainly be the most patient man on the planet. Your guidance and understanding have made this task as easy as it possibly could be. Thank you, Neil—for not giving up on me.

Anne Goebel, who keeps me on my feet with production and assists me to no end to get the reviews back in one piece, as well as Mark Renfrow for keeping me on the straight and narrow with an authoritative tone!

I would also like to pay special tribute to Linda Harrison who had to endure my original musings. It doesn't help that I can't spell, have particularly poor grammar, and am slightly dyslexic. Thank you, Linda, for understanding me.

There are numerous other people that have made this book a possibility. Without their support and encouragement, I would not have continued, for I know it would have been a fruitless effort.

Thank you to everyone who has sent me well wishes and advice, and especially thank you for being so patient whilst waiting for me to finish. I hope I don't disappoint!

I guess I owe a lot of people...a lot of beers!

We Want to Hear from You!

As the reader of this book, *you* are our most important critic and commentator. We value your opinion and want to know what we're doing right, what we could do better, what areas you'd like to see us publish in, and any other words of wisdom you're willing to pass our way.

You can email or write me directly to let me know what you did or didn't like about this book—as well as what we can do to make our books stronger.

Please note that I cannot help you with technical problems related to the topic of this book, and that due to the high volume of mail I receive, I might not be able to reply to every message.

When you write, please be sure to include this book's title and author as well as your name and phone or email address. I will carefully review your comments and share them with the author and editors who worked on the book.

Email: feedback@samspublishing.com

Mail: Neil Rowe
Executive Editor
Sams Publishing
800 East 96th Street
Indianapolis, IN 46240 USA

Reader Services

Visit our website and register this book at www.informit.com/title/9780672329319 for convenient access to any updates, downloads, or errata that might be available for this book.

Foreword

You're a user of things—we all are. You have an experience with every *thing* you interact with. And, it better be a *good* experience, too; otherwise, you'll change the thing, avoid interacting with it, or suffer.

It could be that basking in the color of your bedroom walls is a therapeutic experience. Conversely, you might have a frustrating experience with a hammer whose head keeps falling off (or which, to keep you and those around you safe, asks you to confirm every blow). On the other hand, an object may be perfectly well-designed, but not necessarily designed for you. Even if you could fit in it, a child's chair would be too short for you. As anyone who has seen the movie *The Forbidden Planet* will know, Krell-sized doorways would be a needlessly extravagant use of space in a human home! In each of the previous examples, the experience depends, to some degree, on the person doing the experiencing.

Let's talk about software—the kind of software *you* create. That's why you have this book in your hands, right? Good software is concerned with the emotions of the person using it. It can excite the user from time to time, but it should never frustrate the consumer. When it's working effectively, good software's unobtrusive usability brings only a faint smile of satisfaction to its user's lips, not grumbles. The value of software is the value of the experience that flows from it.

This book is for anyone interested in designing usable and beautiful software. It's about a framework for helping you do just that. It's about a platform and toolset that do the heavy lifting so you can focus on the art, the usability, the experience. You'll learn how it's possible to separate the tasks done by the designer and developer roles so that you can work in an independent, yet complementary way. You'll see how you can avoid a potentially lousy translation step from comp to user interface. You'll see how to customize controls, bind to data, create artwork with vectors and brushes, and represent user interface and data in declarative markup that is kept separate from the application logic.

WPF, Silverlight, and Expression are instruments: Artists create with them. The tools have a user experience of their own—and that experience will improve as they mature. Expression Blend, for instance, is suited to designers with esthetic talent, to be sure—but those with a taste for a little technology will find a lot of additional possibilities. Soon, Blend will adapt to an even greater diversity among designers. Making that happen is the daily preoccupation of the development, test, program management, technical writing, product design, product development, support, and evangelism members of the Blend product group.

Jimi Hendrix asked: "Are you experienced? "A Hendrix album or concert *was* an experience that went beyond the everyday to provide astonishing sounds, virtuosity, charisma, psychedelia and theatrics. What makes *your* consumers enthusiastic about—and return to—your software and design is the quality and nature of their experience. For the most part the experience you provide is dependent on your talent and imagination. However, *some* of your success is due to the tools you use and how well you know them.

I hope you enjoy using WPF and Expression. I hope they give you what you need and make you successful. You can communicate with the Blend product group at http://expression.microsoft.com.

In the meantime, there's a lot for you to learn. I'll let Brennon tell you the rest!

Steve White
Program Manager, Microsoft Expression Blend

PART I

Overview

IN THIS PART

Introduction to Expression Blend

Taking aside the technical aspects of learning how to use Microsoft Expression Blend, there are many areas that are often disregarded within discussions about how Blend is—and should be—used in a real-world project sense. You may be a single person business or employee that needs to fill all the roles that Blend is best used for; or, you may be part of an enterprise size team.

Knowing, why a tool should be used in a certain way sometimes makes it easier to apply the options provided. This chapter talks about areas within project teams, their roles, and their perspective.

The Next Generation User Experience

One of my favorite pastimes is watching movies. I don't care how old they are or if I have already watched them 10 times. I find that watching movies relaxes me; it allows me to escape my own thoughts for an hour or two, and most of the time they inspire and motivate me in some way.

I especially enjoy watching movies in which computers are used in the plot in some way. I guess that is the geek coming out in me, but there is something special about the user interfaces, and in some spectacular cases the visual and interactive design, that are also explored in such movies.

Minority Report, with Tom Cruise, is a great example of what we want to be moving toward in providing an outstanding user experience and interface. That interface (and indeed the entire process that encompasses Tom's user experience) is custom made for its application in assisting the user to scrub video feeds and visualize complex data. Without having actually used such an interface, we can only assume that it is ideal because of the efficiency it gave Tom's character in performing his job's functional requirements.

The applications functional playback of simultaneous multimedia streams gave Tom's character the ability to visualize and analyze complex data, but it is the user interface and "light glove" device that provided the cohesive, relevant, and intuitive movements; allowing the application to work with him, flow with him, and ultimately deliver for him. The input hardware is not quite ready yet, but by the time we collectively perfect our interfaces, we should start to see additional hardware flow into the market place.

Next Generation Hardware Is Coming!

Already hardware changes are being made to accommodate Vista-specific features like Windows Sideshow. This technology allows next generation laptops (code named Newport) to show a second, smaller screen on the laptop lid. This system runs even while the main laptop power has ceased, providing email, calendar and a whole host of other features. However, it appears that the implementation has been slow to gather momentum in this particular case.

Will Vista deliver this? Or more accurately, will Vista allow us, as software designers and developers, to deliver perfect user interfaces? Gartner Inc. analyst Michael Silver believes that the year 2009 should see a noted shift in worldwide Vista installations, already predicting it to eclipse Windows XP. According to Microsoft (Securities and Exchange Commission Microsoft Corporation Quarterly report #0-14278), an estimated 80% of all new PC-based computers sold will be pre-installed with Vista and a steady upgrading through business will occur as the security models improve and business requirements for security of personal data increases.

Microsoft predicted (or just told anyone who would listen): Vista will be the quickest adopted operating system in history. I'm not so sure that this adoption wave is the reality at the moment; however, designing and developing better applications through improved user experience is the one thing that could push users into upgrading.

All the predictions are based on the maturity of the Internet as an information delivery mechanism. If you observed the Internet and the changes that occurred when dynamic rich content first began showing itself, you would have seen how companies were able to expand their business offerings to online customers in areas that were previously thought to be too complicated for the average nontechnical user to follow. Suddenly, holiday booking engines and online flight ordering businesses were able to provide live pricing data that enabled potential customers to shop for the best deal and a myriad of other business sectors could engage their current and potential customers by explaining their processes more clearly (visually as opposed to verbally by a sales person on a telephone) and in a nontechnical way.

From a user experience point of view, given the choice between two websites, even the most nontechnical users will opt for the more professional looking website, because subconsciously they believe that if a company has put great efforts into making things easier to view, the company must be more professional in their approach and will almost certainly treat personal information and security details with the same high quality of care. Of course, this is not always the case, and is a reason phishing attacks are so successful—but that's another story.

This does, indeed, prove the case that the best product with the most features does not always guarantee success for a business. You need a door opener, a way of first attracting the customer. Then you can educate them on the features and benefits of a given product or service. The main thing is that you got them interested in your offerings first, before that of your competition.

So, why would people continue to use desktop applications over web-based applications? The features and abilities of any given web or desktop application are directly linked to the code accessibility permissions of the client. The web will continue to be a delivery mechanism for partially trusted applications, whereas the desktop will continue to provide unrestricted high speed features, unbound by prohibitively expensive bandwidth limitations that still exist in countries like Australia and Ireland, to name two.

Where Is Your Stuff?

The level of trust the proponents of online applications place in the companies providing such services is interesting. Take any online application, such as a word editor, that also saves your work online. Do you really know where your material is? What happens if the company goes broke? Even the biggest companies go broke—anyone remember Enron? Don't be fooled into thinking it can't happen again!

How This Book Will Help You

The use of Blend in real-world environments has been a topic that not many people have wanted to discuss. Maybe that's not true, but it is difficult to find others that think about it in depth. On the surface, the discussions have been all about the nice flashy demonstrations, the eye candy side of the promise that Blend brings—the Kool-Aid—as one of my U.S. associates refers to it. The promise I am talking about is designer/developer collaboration.

It's one thing for people, even Microsoft, to talk about designer/developer collaboration, but actually making it work in the real world can be quite difficult. I thought that, aside from helping people (both designers and developers) to use Blend, I might also be able to provide some instruction in using the tool(s) so that others don't get the headaches I did when implementing Expression Blend in projects for the first time. You will still get some headaches—that's just a given!

The Tools

When I talk about the tools, I am talking about the classification of tools that I see as being necessary to implement the collaboration promise for creating User Interfaces.

▶ **Expression Design** or other graphic design packages that are capable of exporting Extensible Application Markup Language (XAML, pronounced "zamel")

▶ **Visual Studio** for solution architecture and .NET code requirements

▶ **Expression Blend** for the interactive designers and XAML architects

These three tools (along with the right workflow), not just one tool by itself, allow this promise to be delivered. Of course, people have their own preferences in their choice of tools, so feel free to insert your favorites. This tool package, however, is the focus of this book.

The best advice is to embrace as many designer/developer tools as you can, and then decide which ones are good and which ones are not. As a result of trying each tool, you will know which are best suited for a particular purpose when it comes time to deliver.

Expression Blend is a designer's tool because it has no true development language within it (it has a script but not a language). This does not mean that only designers should use it. Yes, you use .NET code in the form of C# and VB.NET to create the backend functionality for your controls and objects, but inside Blend it's all about XAML. The Blend UI serves as a visual aid in creating XAML scripts.

Before going any further, it is important to clarify the term *designer*. It is just too broad to be used often when discussing Expression Blend. There are many types of designers: interactive, graphic, and industrial to name a few. These individuals may see the term in relation to what they know of the product and think that Blend really isn't aimed at them at all. Blend can be used by most, if not all, classes of designers. However, it is most suited to the interactive designer—the designer who creates the workflow and user processes that are intended to create an experience.

Blend certainly provides several excellent services in real-world projects:

▶ **Prototyping**—By creating a functional prototype using Expression Blend, properly constructed UI solutions are available to the production cycle immediately, providing a massive productivity gain and reducing development lifecycles. Prototyping also removes an additional layer of interpretation that is traditionally performed by developers that can radically change the end user's experience if incorrectly implemented.

▶ **UI process development**—User interface processes can mean the difference between high and low application productivity. Involving potential end users in the design and development process is always advisable. Being able to modify the interface to suit the users' requirements with Blend is certainly a benefit to the end solution. Previously a designer may have needed to report end user feedback and changes that were needed to a developer. At that point, the whole "interpretation" issue was raised again.

▶ **Animation production**—Blend provides a simple, easy-to-use storyboarding mechanism for animating object properties that allows designers to control motion and workflow while, at the same time, giving developers a simple reference to execute when the specific animation is required.

- **Visual asset creation**—While not a primary role for Expression Blend, the application is stocked with enough tools to allow graphic designers to create exceptional visual assets. Using the built-in resource management system also allows those assets to be shared and reused with minimal work, increasing productivity and ensuring visual continuity within the solution.

- **Resource file management**—Expression Blend allows you to create, modify, and utilize templates and resources stored in the working files, the application, and/or a XAML file called a *resource dictionary*. This means that one designer could create a certain style or a specific functionality of a certain object, a button for example, and then provide that same group of styles and functionality to everyone else working on the solution. This is perhaps one of the most powerful features of Expression Blend.

- **XAML architecting**—This is how Blend is used in a real-world project—a role to which Blend is particularly well-suited. XAML architecting is about taking all the assets from both designers and developers and putting them together. Visual Studio plays a big part in this process as well; but, without Blend combining assets would be a very difficult job indeed.

Why the Architect Title?

By definition, an architect is someone who creates a solution. That is a pretty broad description. In software terms, object structure and communication are not the only parts of a solution that need to be architected; interaction and workflow should also be designed. Because there was no term describing the role that constructs those parts of the solution, I created one—XAML architect.

Of all the roles previously mentioned, the XAML architect (XA) is the role which embodies the prescribed collaborative process—the best in a real-world scenario.

The day-to-day process surrounding the XA is asset designers mocking up and creating beautiful pieces of art and coders implementing required functionality that brings said art to life. If these designers don't understand .NET development and the coders have no idea about animation, then without the XAML architect to bring their contributions together in a meaningful way, no collaboration can exist. Neither the designer nor the developer can understand or appreciate the requirements of the solution as a whole.

It is the job of the XAML architect (XA) to own and control the design and development of all XAML-based assets. The XA understands the creative vision of the graphic designer, the user experience and workflow concepts of the interactive designers, and how to implement functionality in .NET code to ensure animations, binding, and other pieces of the functionality work with the user interface (UI) specification and the user experience (UE) expectation.

This is where the power of Blend can be exploited to its capacity. The name says it all, really. As an XA, you blend the code and visual assets to produce the UI and UE.

This blending of design and development is the most important concept you should take away from this book.

The great scientist Louis Pasteur once said, "Chance favors the prepared mind." That means: If you expand your knowledge and gain experience that covers all the angles, then there is no such thing as luck—just opportunities. While a Zen Monk may disagree with this interpretation, no one could argue that keeping an open mind in today's world isn't a good approach.

Now is the time to gather experience, understand the potential, and prepare for the opportunities. This book is not going to give you all the answers, but it should make sure your head is screwed on the right way before you start your journey. I have tried to change the dialog you see in most technical books, because I want you to think of the two of us sitting in a pub somewhere having a chat over something cold, may be a beer, whatever suits your fancy!

The chapters are in the order in which a non-developer (but still technically astute) designer should be learning the skills necessary to use both Expression Blend and Visual Studio. There is no escape from Visual Studio if you want to use Expression Blend for anything more complex than creating XAML-based visual assets. Another reason for the chapter sequence is that there were moments during my initial experiences with Expression Blend and XAML that I wish I knew some things earlier. This chapter sequence addresses the concerns I had.

Unlike the rest of the book, this first chapter is one big rant. If you continue to read it, you will understand why it is important for you to grasp the new technology and how you might begin to change your working vision to become one of the new breed of XAML architects that is required to make the technology work successfully in enterprise level development. Of course, you may just want to continue to be a designer of a certain discipline or a developer—that's fine. I have tried to cater to diverse needs.

If you are just itching to get into the code, please be patient. Shortly you will be up to your neck in code and markup, but you will understand why you are doing certain things, and more importantly, what you are doing. You will understand the mindset of others in your working arena and should then be ready to climb this very steep learning curve.

Above all, remember: We are dealing with interfaces, user experiences, coding concepts, architecture, and how to bring this all together to capture, amaze, and empower your end users.

The Business Mindset of the End User

Think back to *Minority Report* for a moment. Visually speaking, those UI's are amazing. When you think about it, however, we are not too far away from that right now.

In my experience over the last 15 years working in several countries on projects of all sizes and budgets, the single biggest issue facing the development of these UIs in mainstream applications is a time/cost ratio that rarely has enough time or money assigned to the commercial development lifecycle. The one exception to this rule is the game/entertainment industry. They understand the importance of visual perception.

Visual perception is the awesome use of a designer's imagination, where he or she envisions user interfaces that are tailor-made to provide an immersive, state of the art navigation system that engages users so that they are excited about what they are doing. Although these navigation menus often don't provide any more functionality than could be achieved with the good old File menu ribbon system that is available in simple applications like Notepad.exe, the users' visual perceptions are that the interface is more engaging. These UI's actually draw upon the users emotional pool.

Most of the bigger companies are now starting to pick up on the fact that if you engage your user, make him or her feel good about what they are doing, the user's productivity goes through the roof. Regardless of whether another product has more features, higher productivity outweighs the lost feature benefits. High productivity is like a virus. If you walk into a room and everyone is smiling, you will naturally feel better. Similarly, in an office environment, if some staff are productive and excited, more people tend to get onboard and feel productive and excited. This is a huge benefit to business.

Companies like Microsoft have always tended to place particular importance on the standardization of interfaces. Using certain user interface items such as the *Ribbon* in Office products even have strict guidelines that must be followed to comply with the end user licensing. For most there is a Vista User Experience Guideline document that provides for requirements on such things as menus, control layouts, accessibility, and more. The logic here was that people would be more inclined to want to learn and continue to use an application if it had a familiar feel. That logic is still partly true today.

Familiarity is a strange sense. Just the other day I was helping a relative discover the joys of modern day computing. He happened to mention to me that the staff in his office use Classic settings in Windows XP. He had no idea what this meant. It was just something he heard them say once—it is their preference, or simply what they are comfortable using and feel most familiar with.

As an experiment, I showed him the standard Windows XP interface and explained where things were. Then I switched the view to Classic view. His response was that it looked dull, didn't really give him much in the way of the Start Menu, and that he would find it much easier to remember the pictures (he meant icons) as opposed to just the names of items in the control panel application, for example.

In the 21st century, the general population in most developed and technically advanced countries is becoming more tech savvy than ever before. People do not need to be coddled and can understand that moving a mouse and clicking on a button has repercussions. They don't need a paper clip (see Figure 1.1) telling them they have just clicked the button!

FIGURE 1.1   Just in case therapy helped you to forget!

People are going to ask the question "Why should I upgrade to Vista if it doesn't give me anything new?" I respond: It is not about getting anything new. Vista and the software designed for it help users work smarter, faster, and more efficiently by providing a framework of *smart* common controls and a more visually intuitive user interface. Together these elements ensure that all applications provide a familiarity while at the same time making the responses to choices that the end user makes much clearer.

It is certainly fair to say that while technology has continued to improve and advance, the opportunity to improve user experiences in software has not kept pace until now. Compared to the Internet, which has seen a huge rise in back-end technology as well as user interface design tools and standards in the last decade alone, application user experiences are far behind. Think of all the new languages that have come along to facilitate web applications: the more frequent use of Ajax to improve user experience and perhaps the biggest advance—the introduction of Adobe Flash and the shockwave format (.swf).

This improvement in technology is now affecting desktop applications, through user interface design. The power of the desktop application will always surpass that of the web application, primarily due to security; but, until now all of the desktop applications have been a tad boring and deployment has been nothing short of a nightmare. In the coming years ever more importance will be placed on the user experience, which is directly linked to the quality of the user interfaces that we will be building for our end users.

Vista and .NET Framework 3.0/3.5 (Formerly WinFX)

"Where is my *Minority Report*?" I hear you say. Well like Tom, you do not have a *Minority Report*. You can be 100% sure of what your future holds (hopefully not murder!) but it will contain Vista, high definition (HD) and high fidelity content, glass and gel interface objects, Expression tools and .NET programming languages. Microsoft is betting the house on it, so to speak, and they usually get what they want—eventually.

There are other companies out there producing products for designers and developers that are XAML based, like Aurora by Mobiform Software Inc. Regardless of what advanced features they have implemented, I can tell you that Microsoft are working a few years ahead so Expression Blend and their other products should ultimately work more efficiently with other integrating technologies that will become fulfilled with Vista, and even further ahead with Windows 7 and beyond.

If you have used Microsoft Vista, you will have noticed how Microsoft appears to have finally gotten an outstanding balance with their product with respect to familiarity, visual appearance, and general feel. As you go deeper into Vista, you will see that some of the dialogs have much the same content and layout as they did in Windows 2000 and XP. Figure 1.2 illustrates the similarity. There are slight differences in the user workflow in some cases, but the visual continuity is always the same throughout the operating system.

Vista also brings an outstanding addition to the operating system control base, the use of Bread Crumb controls. These controls have several features that make the task of navigating more flexible and more intuitive. Let's take a look at the file explorer application window (see Figure 1.3).

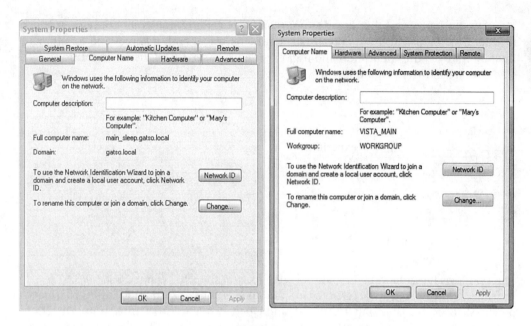

FIGURE 1.2   The Windows XP and Vista Computer Properties applications.

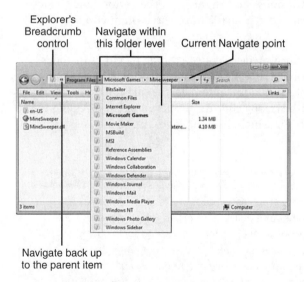

FIGURE 1.3   The Vista File Explorer with Bread Crumb control.

You can now navigate from within any hierarchical level along your path instead of getting repetitive strain injury (RSI) hitting the back button way back on the first level. You can enter a path directly as you have always been able to do, complete with history. You will also get visual feedback as to the status of your navigation from the control being used as a progress bar in the background. That is most handy when navigating large file sets or across really slow networks.

There are lots of controls like Bread Crumbs and Navigation Services that have been added to Vista. The important thing to realize is that better use of both graphics and functionality has improved the application and user experience tenfold. The Vista navigation elements are shown in Figure 1.4.

FIGURE 1.4   Vista application Navigation buttons.

The Windows Presentation Foundation (WPF), part of the .NET Framework 3.0/3.5, provides us with hardware-accelerated graphics power for standard applications that have previously been available only to DirectX and OpenGL applications. Integrating DirectX into a standard desktop application certainly has some great benefits, if not interesting results, but the development time is enormous—not to mention the performance issues designers and developers face when dealing with such a huge variation of end user machine specifications.

Increased visual performance through hardware-accelerated graphic pipelines includes more than just getting glass window borders in your applications. It includes the ability to apply transforms and animations to objects and use automated layout and true scaling with vector images that don't decay with size. By shifting all this graphic processing to the GPU, a huge load is removed from the CPU which, in itself, gives rise to massive performance increases.

A Developer's Note: Vector Graphic Versus Bitmaps

The difference between vector and bitmap graphics is the formats they comprise. A bitmap graphic contains thousands, sometimes millions of pixels, which represent the actual image. When scaling, the number of pixels is either decreased for reducing or increased for enlarging the image. The problems come into play when enlarging an image beyond its original size. The computer essentially has to guess what pixels should contain what color because when an image is increased in size, the pixels do not enlarge; more are merely added to the image to fill the required space.

Vector graphics, on the other hand, are instructions on how lines, points, and curves should be drawn to form complex shapes, rather than what these shapes should look like. The advantages are that the image can be increased in size or scaled without loss of quality. The disadvantage, however, is that while vector shapes can be complex, they are no match when it comes to producing an image with high-quality photo realism, which is best suited to the bitmap.

The key to all this interactive magic is XAML (the Markup script-language supported in Expression Blend) and its integration with the development language base of the .NET Framework 3.0 and 3.5. Visual Studio 2005 with extensions from the product code named Cider was a preview of Visual Studio 2008, which is now available. This tool is home to developers, allowing them to modify XAML as well as UI elements within a design surface.

XAML is the only reason designers and developers—and you as an XA—will be able to work together as a team . The XAML markup is the common component that binds all parties together, the glue, if you will.

So, why use Expression Blend if Visual Studio contains a design environment? The design environment in Visual Studio is simple at best at this stage. It contains no methods for applying animations through a timeline interface, nor does it have a control template editor. In other words, it is a limited design interface made for developers and not for animators or designers—and certainly not for an XA who needs a clear understanding of the end user workflow. Conversely, Blend is a designer's environment that switches between both XAML markup and .NET code in Visual Studio to allow you to apply CLR coding requirements. Both Visual Studio (or the .NET Framework to be more accurate) and Expression Blend share common UIElements. That is why we want to look at Expression Blend as an XA's tool. Understanding UIElements visually is far easier than looking at a heap of XAML markup and trying to picture it in your head, although in time you will be able to do this as well.

What I am trying to say is that with these new tools and pseudo languages you will be able to quickly create a "Minority Report" type of interface for Vista or XP. You, most likely, already have the majority of the core skills required. I am going to show you how to use those skills to give you a head start for getting into the new technology.

Getting your hands dirty is the only real way of understanding and perfecting your use of XAML and integrating it with the .NET languages. We will use only C# in this book because it is the language used most commonly for this purpose at the time of writing.

Does It Really Matter What You Use?

There is always a lot of conjecture about which language is best: C#, VB.NET, C++, or any of the other .NET-compliant languages. The fact is that all these languages still compile to almost identical MSIL code. Performance differences between them are negligible. Learn, at the very least, both C# and VB.NET to a professional level. This will increase your value as well as increase the number of jobs you could be qualified for when time comes to move on.

You do not have to be a coding guru to get great results from WPF—but it always helps. I am going to assume that you are a beginner programmer or designer. It would be helpful if you understand some of the core functionality provided by the .NET Framework within client application development terms. Don't worry if you haven't opened Visual Studio before, though. Chapter 10, "Visual Studio: C# Primer," provides a designer's view of coding to help you on your way.

If you are a developer, note that I am not going to try to convert you into a designer (which is more of a natural skill). Conversely, I am not trying to magically turn designers into developers. Instead, this chapter is intended to show you a little of how the other half lives, so to speak, so you understand and can liaise with teammates with other skill sets. The first half of the book is more oriented toward designers, focusing on Blend and XAML. The second half is more focused on developers, bringing in the concepts of the .NET coding requirements that will greatly extend the functionality of your applications.

Windows Presentation Foundation (WPF)

Windows Presentation Foundation (formerly code named Avalon) is a collection of display technologies—or a display level subsystem—that allows developers to take advantage of the latest graphic card hardware acceleration features. WPF is the father of XAML; it is what allows the XAML language to be used in a declarative way. The term declarative means "to describe" so XAML allows you to describe your applications UI functionality and components.

Through learning Expression Blend and a little .NET code, you will have the ability to compile your solutions into either a Silverlight or desktop deliverable. Technically, there are slight differences to some of the methods you use, but for the most part you will understand how both Silverlight and executable-based WPF applications are created.

Silverlight enables your applications to be viewed in a browser-hosted environment like Internet Explorer on any operating system that has the Silverlight plug-in installed. This gives the user the same experience they would get if they were using your application from a compiled .exe file running on a Windows desktop—or so the theory goes. There is some reduced functionality in Silverlight, such as the ability to create hardware-accelerated 3D visuals for example, so care must be taken to understand the construct you are ultimately deploying to and the users you are working for.

Microsoft describes WPF as *"a unified API, allowing developers to present high definition media content from within their application constructs, as well as providing extensibility to the .NET Framework for Vista specific technologies."* This, in reality, means that the best of both WINForms applications and web applications are available to you in WPF applications running on either Windows Vista or Windows XP (with Service Pack 2 and the .NET Framework 3.0/3.5 installed).

It has long been a nightmare for the UI Developer to ensure that content and visual assets were being managed in terms of layout. Before a generic entry level set of graphic cards (8Mb) came along, changing screen resolutions and color settings all pointed to early retirement for a vast number of us. Things have been getting better, certainly since .NET came along. Now WPF has once and for all sorted out such issues; never before has it been so easy to create an application that can adapt its content layout entirely based on the runtime environment.

I am writing this book on a laptop with a 17" widescreen display running a resolution of 1920 × 1200. Even though it is one of the most powerful laptops on the market, some of the biggest companies in the world have managed to produce software that does not layout correctly on it. One of the biggest joys I have found in creating applications with Blend is that the layouts work—perfectly every time.

It may take a little while to get your head around using Blend because most of the time you no longer need to specify a control's width and height. You are now working with dynamic flow and elements layout and positioning that is based on relevance to its parent and the construct it (the parent) provides. You can still specify width and height, but in most cases this will be a minimum width and a minimum height value. See Chapter 5, "UIElement: Control Embedding" for detailed information.

Silverlight

Microsoft unveiled the plans for Silverlight in the second quarter of 2007. Along with Silverlight comes the promise of a cut down, cross platform CLR plug-in that would make creating and distributing XAML-based applications across differing operating systems and devices simple. At the time of writing, Microsoft has just released a preview version of Expression Blend 2.5, which also showed the intended functionality that Blend will be providing in future for this new technology.

Silverlight delivers a subset of the WPF core and will allow loose XAML-based applications to run as pseudo web-based application or WBA. You can write the functionality for your application in your choice of .NET-compliant languages and/or JavaScript. So, Silverlight applications differ completely from another type of Internet-delivered XAML application called an XBAP.

XBAP applications run as a compiled application in a browser that supports additional features such as 3D, where Silverlight applications don't. There are many more differences that will change before the final incarnation of both these technologies are ratified.

In either scenario, though, you must consider that when your application (Silverlight or XBAP) runs in a browser type environment, it is running in what is known as a partial trust sandbox. In geek speak, that means the application is not installed on the end user's machine (although the plugins and other delivery mechanisms are).

Partial trust has some rules that you must follow. It is essential that you be aware of your application requirements before deciding to try and deploy your application in this manner, in either format. The rules are simple rules that govern whether an application is able to run based on the user authentication level and assigned roles or code privilege that is required by certain tasks, controls, and objects.

The essence of the partial trust sandbox is that it has been developed using the same security model that is available to all .NET developers using Code Access Security (CAS). This means that varying levels of an "application code" can demand and must obtain the correct security privileges before that code can execute.

In the XBAP deployment scenario, you will find tight controls on File read and write permissions and registry actions, as well as the inability to call and execute most areas of unmanaged code. From an application-specific point of view, you can't launch new windows from your application. You can't have application-defined dialogs present; you can't even apply BitmapEffects within your application. However, at the time of writing, the biggest concern is that you can't access all the features of Windows Communication Foundation Web Services. In other words, you are still restricted to only using data from within the same executing domain. Undoubtedly, Microsoft is working very hard to change these restrictions, and you should always seek the latest information from Microsoft with regards to such restrictions.

Exceptions to the Rules

There are exceptions for some forms of data, like video, for example. Your application will be able to display a video file hosted in another domain, but your application will not be able to access the raw data from the file that is playing.

Silverlight allows you to deliver streaming video content very efficiently through the browser. Expression Media Encoder assists you in packaging your video for streaming and creating Silverlight templates that are ready to go.

What Are BitmapEffects?

BitmapEffects allow you to apply effects to resources used in WPF applications such as Shadows or Ripples, similar to the types of effects you get with graphic applications like Adobe Photoshop. There are several effects that come as standard; and you can even write your own, although this is very convoluted at present. Companies such as Atalasoft are already producing libraries that you will be able to import and use. Technically though, at present BitmapEffects use software rendering in Windows; so they don't use the power of the graphics card, which will inhibit the performance of your application. The greatest concern, though, is the performance hit they place on Expression Blend in the design environment. It's your choice to use BitmapEffects or not.

Microsoft has indicated that hardware accelerated BitmapEffects will be available for the release of .NET Framework 4.0 possibly in late 2008 or early 2009.

I have described what has been slated at the time of this writing. Be sure to check with Microsoft to see if any of the restrictions have been lifted, or if more have been added. It's all about security, so it is important to understand it.

There are still many areas within an application that can run without issue, so don't be put off by the restrictions. Instead, look at it as a greater challenge to your initiative. After all, you can still incorporate 2D, 3D, and full animations in XBAPs, 2D in Silverlight, and image and audio features, flow documents and much more in XAML-based offerings—not to mention that your controls are no longer the clunky old CLR based controls.

Silverlight is exciting and it's fast. By learning Expression Blend and a little .NET development you will be able to create rich Internet applications (RIAs) that will become a standard in future development scenarios.

Expression Blend Versus Visual Studio

Expression Blend and Visual Studio are not really in competition with each other; instead, they are being developed to work with each other. Think of Blend being the intermediary between a designer-specific application like Expression Design or Adobe Illustrator and Visual Studio.

There is much rhetoric as to the potential for Blend being slowly merged into the Visual Studio environment. I would see this integration as a blow to the workflow that will exist between designers and developers if you start forcing designers to try and navigate the Visual Studio IDE. If you implement the role of a XAML architect, there is no need for a designer to ever worry about Visual Studio, and a developer needs only to concentrate on data structures and logic.

In the end, I believe Microsoft will see the value of the two products as they stand alone but in support of each other—and as the only tools fit for the purpose of the XA's role. Only time will tell, but for now, using both products simultaneously is workable, although a little clunky.

Is the XA a New Role?

At the time of this writing, the XA role was an area very few people understood, even those at Microsoft. I did find a few people that understood and had come to this conclusion themselves. Two such people are Darren McCormick and Jon Harris of Microsoft, both User Experience Evangelists. Both could see a clear need for the role to be defined and promoted.

It's not really a new concept. Most large design agencies have, for quite some time now, implemented such a role with projects involving Flash, in which designers were not always competent in Action Scripting.

There are indeed pros and cons to both environments. As it stands, I, personally, could not spend any great length of time trying to design an application experience in Visual Studio. At the end of this book you will make your own decision on how you like it.

Visual Studio does not provide for some of the functionality that Blend provides, such as an easy to use storyboarding tool to create animations and define triggers. Blend also handles data binding elegantly, which is a very important area of most applications. One of the biggest pros for Blend is that it will always give you an accurate depiction of the XAML (and code to some degree) live in the design-time environment, something that Visual Studio (in WPF solutions) continues to struggle with.

An Introduction to Expression Blend and XAML

If you believe that Expression Blend is an application best suited for a role like an XA, then you also understand and appreciate that its goals are to allow the rapid creation of user interfaces (UI's). Perhaps the area that you may have heard about is XAML.

Terminology

Throughout the book, XAML code is referred to as *markup*. This is common with most XML-derived languages.

The term *code* is used when referring to .NET developer language code like C# or VB.NET.

Expression Blend is itself written with XAML and WPF application development technologies such as Cider extensions for Visual Studio. Although there are marked improvements on the performance of the Blend application compared to the very first preview versions, the overall concept is starting to be accepted by the wider development/designer communities as a whole. They understand that performance will improve as the technology matures, which has been proven now with the release of Visual Studio 2008 and the .NET Framework 3.5, both improving the ability to develop for the platform.

You will find out pretty soon, if you like working with XAML. The Blend design interface may take a little longer to get into, simply because it is a different tool with a similar ideology as other timeframe-based design environments (or so it may appear).

When I began using the Expression Interactive Designer Community Technology Previews, I was excited at first. This was finally justifying everything I had been saying to development managers and others who couldn't grasp the importance of a great user interface—and more importantly, a great user experience—for years.

When I had been using it for a few days, I got angry with certain elements of it. It just wasn't working like Adobe Flash does. I couldn't understand why designers would *want* to use it, considering the complexities it would bring to their lives and how their confusion with .NET code and the application features would eventually turn into hostility toward the lowly developer who just wanted to provide the data for a list box and not have to worry about how it looked. It all came together for me a few days later (well at about three in the morning actually) during one of those rare moments of absolute clarity.

The combination of (Designer, Blend, and Visual Studio) is not about how a control looks, it's about how collections of visual and logical assets look, function, and ultimately perform as a singular unit to provide the overall user experience. Blend is not just for designers (or dare I say developers), but it is the head of a toolset aimed at bringing both parties together with a technology that can facilitate stunning designs with awesome .NET application performance.

I can't reiterate enough how important the glue—XAML—is! Graphic designers indirectly use it to make visual assets; interactive designers mold it with Blend; and together they create UIElements that integrate and use specific functionality that adds to an overall visual perception. Developers can use it to implement the designed functionality with additional feature sets.

An example of how XAML allows applications to be created better is when a designer produces a storyboard that shows a gorgeous list box that has glass highlights and rounded borders. The next storyboard shows that when a user clicks on an item in the list box, the selected item flies across the screen. There are very few instances where a conventional WINForms developer would take the time to try and produce this result as per the storyboards in a WINForms environment. But, by working together as a team, the XA makes this entirely possible with Blend and Visual Studio, using the XAML visual assets created by graphic designers. It is also extremely quick to build applications compared to the development time on other existing platforms. The following equation says it all:

$$(developer + designer) / time = speed = pub^2$$

The remainder of this chapter is an overview of XAML, complete with explanations of some primary levels of the XAML structures, how they relate to each other, and how it relates to code classes produced in .NET. In Chapter 4, "XAML for Beginners," you will study XAML in a far greater depth.

Before you look at some XAML, there is another issue that struck me when using Blend in the early stages. There is no Source Safe integration. Enterprise developers instantly shy away from products that don't have such integration. But then again, it could make you think a little more about the architecture. In a strict sense, your development environment should always contain some sort of source protection system. That is when the use of multiple client-side application layers came to me. By using this architecture, you can still implement a source protection system that will not affect the UI development.

Layered Understanding

From now on, when you think about the front end of your application, you need to think about layered development, similar to multi-tier or N-Tier development in which you have specific application layers that perform specific tasks for the entire application to function and perform in the manner in which it was designed. Think about your front end having, at the very least, two layers which I describe in detail for clarity.

The Graphical UI Layer

As the name suggests, this layer is where your user interface objects function within their own scope. You, as the XA, now take XAML markup provided by a designer or the design team and make it into a button or other required object in Blend. Previously, if you wanted this button control to have a rollover effect when the mouse moved over it, you would need to provide all the programming that not only created the button in the first place, but also the code to animate it or make it interact with other objects.

The designer creates the visual asset in a design tool like Expression Design that exports XAML. You, as the XA, put all the pieces together; in fact, as you will see, XAML is merely a representation of a .NET code class. As such, it has the power to set properties and apply resources and data binding to-from objects, UIElements, plus much, much more. Putting the design XAML together with the functional XAML is simple.

Let's say, for example, you have made a simple calculator application. When the user clicks the = button on your form, the buttons click handler method goes about taking the inputted values from other controls and or members in the form and then displays the output directly on a textbox control. There is nothing wrong with this; but to get my point across, now we are not going to provide this method of application logic to your simple calculator application.

In your new Blend applications, you or your developer team would go off and write a logic layer that receives inputs and provides outputs back to your graphical layer (see Figure 1.5).

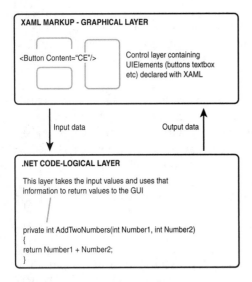

FIGURE 1.5   Data flow between the layers.

The Logic Layer (Class Library)

This layer is where developers author the code to interact and sometimes control the UIElements that will appear in the scenes, by way of events and property change notification. So, to continue with the previous example of a simple calculator, the logic layer (I prefer engine or wrapper) provides public methods with which each click of a button simply adds numbers and symbols for the underlying engine to deal with. The UI layer is free to carry on with any animations or UI-derived actions without the sequential hassles of also trying to deal with the application logic.

Now when the user clicks the = button, the engine is called by the UI graphics layer and goes to work with all the various inputs it has received. It then fires a result out through an event or property change notification where the graphics layer (which has subscribed to this event and or notification) then does what it needs to do in order to display the result.

You may choose to have the graphical assets flash red or go semi-transparent, who knows? The point is that the two layers remain completely separated, which allows developers to easily add unit testing with NUint or a similar tool, as well as gives you a complete set of functionality that will be the same regardless of the front end UI or OS on which you are running the code. The biggest advantage to this method, it has to be said, is from the developer's point of view. When they need to fix bugs or make maintenance changes, they only need to make them to a single code library before testing and redistributing the application. The advantage from the designer's point of view is that they may change the XAML style template applied to the buttons to give them a different look, but the user experience is maintained by you, the XA, controlling the collaboration between the developer and designer in Blend.

XAML Representations

So what exactly is XAML? People may be confused to learn that XAML does not contain objects, shapes, UIElements, animations, or transforms for that matter. XAML is simply an instruction set, and definitely not a programming language.

What Is the Difference Between a Scripting and Programming Language?

It's hard to answer this question without the thought of being skewered by certain people who definitely have very strong views on the subject. My defining characteristic is that a script provides a means to drive an application, while a programming language provides for a script to drive it.

I searched high and low, and still could not find a definitive answer. I did find out that the debate is very much alive on compiler newsgroups!—Freaks.

When these instructions are parsed to the WPF presentation engine, they are then converted to an object tree in memory. So you can think of XAML as being a type of serialization format for WPF, taking all the settings that you specify and then producing your application as the result.

Assuming that you understand the concept of XML formatting and you also grasp the concept that XAML is an XML representation of .NET code objects, take a minute to let the following settle into your mind.

.NET classes are represented in XAML as tags. For example:

```
<MyClass></MyClass>
```

Object children and or complex properties are represented by nested elements. For example:

```
<MyClass>
        <MyClass.Child> Additional Children </MyClass.Child>
</MyClass>
```

Attributes are properties or event handlers, for example:

```
<MyClass Property="100" Click="Click_Event">
        <Child> Value </Child>
</MyClass>
```

To put this into better perspective, let us look at a simple application example.

XAML/CLR Example

We are going to examine the same application (shown in Figure 1.6) twice, once in C# and then in XAML.

FIGURE 1.6   The simple button application.

As you can see, we have a simple window with a single button shown. The button contains text, but you should bear in mind that we could have used an image or another control (UIElement) as the content of the button if a designer required it. Listing 1.1 provides the C# code for this application.

LISTING 1.1   C# Example Application

```
public partial class Window1 : Window
{
    public Window1()
    {
        InitializeComponent();
        //button1 declared within the partial class initializer
        button1.Width = 100;
        button1.Height = 100;
        button1.Content = "Window Licker";
        button1.Click += new RoutedEventHandler(button1_Click);
    }
    void button1_Click(object sender, RoutedEventArgs e)
    {
        MessageBox.Show("Simple as that");
    }
}
```

In the code example shown in Listing 1.1, we are setting the properties of the button shown in Figure 1.5, just as a developer would do in a WINForms application. The text is applied by setting the Content property of the button.

Don't worry too much about following the specifics of the code if you are not familiar with C#. Just compare it with the XAML code shown in Listing 1.2, particularly with reference to property names like Width and Height that XAML sets at design time.

LISTING 1.2   XAML Example Application

```
<Window x:Class="Chapter_01_XAMLReps.Window1"
    xmlns="http://schemas.microsoft.com/winfx/2006/xaml/presentation"
    xmlns:x="http://schemas.microsoft.com/winfx/2006/xaml"
    Title="Chapter_01_XAMLReps" Height="300" Width="300"
    >

    <Button
        Name="button1"
        Height="100"
        Width="100"
        HorizontalAlignment="Left"
        VerticalAlignment="Top"
        Content="Window Licker"
        Click="button1_Click"/>
</Window>
```

You will note the property names are exactly the same. You may also note there are some layout directives in the form of VerticalAlignment and HorizontalAlignment that we will look at in future chapters.

This is a very simple example, but one I hope gives you a little insight into the core usage of XAML. You can certainly do a lot more than just declare and set up a button with XAML. As we go through the examples in the book, you will also be looking at both C# and XAML markup to cement your understanding of the XAML/C# relationship.

Code/Markup Integration

When we talk about integration, we are referring to how objects and resources are controlled within an application using either C# or XAML—or both. The key here is to remember that XAML is declarative and can only be applied to those objects and UIElements that are created in the design-time environment.

Although you can apply property setters to objects as well as data binding and dynamic layout instructions, you have to remember that once the application enters runtime mode, you need to apply any new dynamic integration through code alone. This is not to say that you can't add dynamic instructions in XAML; after all, the majority of all animations, trigger events like IsMouseOver for buttons, or even the "Click" event that we used in the Listing 1.2 example, will be declared and set in XAML.

A simple but powerful benefit of the XA role is that because the XA puts all the pieces together, designers and developers are not constrained by timeframes to deliver assets to each other. The XA can add buttons to the scene and apply the style template when the designer is finished. The developers can just get on with writing functionality based on inputs and outputs. Overall the deliverable time of an application is dramatically shortened.

I would like to think that after seeing the brief examples provided in this chapter you are now starting to recognize the purpose of XAML as a declarative script, how simple it will be to use, and how easy it will be for designer/developer collaboration under this workflow. Although some XAML scripts do get quite complicated to follow, once you have a grasp of the core concepts you will be able to follow any of them.

Another point of interest is that Microsoft has tried very hard to ensure that the XAML produced by the Blend designer does not become a mash of utter garbage that you need a deciphering wheel to understand it. You should be able to add a UIElement to your application, change some properties in the property palette within the Blend designer environment, switch to XAML view, and still understand exactly what you have just done. Of course, you can test this by running in Split View mode and seeing the XAML being added as you "draw" controls onto the design surface and vice versa.

The Benefits of Expression Blend

Besides working with a really cool product, you will probably inadvertently start using more and more cutting edge applications to keep in line with the requirements of not only Visual Studio, but also the changing landscape of the .NET Framework and the various operating systems.

You will also pick up new, fresh ideas for designs and methods of working because you will see how working with Blend and WPF has inspired others to reach for new ground in ease-of-use control designs. Expect to see user experience discussions increasing. Those discussions should also generate greater understanding of what *is* important, as opposed to what was never perceived to be so.

Blend will have different levels of engagement for the different types of roles played by those who use it. Interactive designers will use it for one purpose, while a developer will use it in an entirely different manner. In the following sections, try to see how Blend may or may not work for you in some areas and how it might be well-suited to helping in others.

The XAML Architect's View

The XA will get most of the praise from the commissioners of a project. After all, they (the commissioners) don't care if an application can split a call into 16 threads to speed up a data return by 0.0005 milliseconds. Most of the time, the big boys and girls (e.g., managers and directors) have no fundamental understanding of what it is you are doing or how it will help with their business. The most important issues to them are higher productivity within their workforce, a strong presence of professionalism, and brand projection. Higher productivity brings enormous cost benefits, which can, by themselves, justify the cost of development.

Perhaps the biggest benefit to a XAML architect is greater responsibility in projects which usually (not always) end with the XA earning more money then a standard developer or designer. XAs need to be able to speak different languages (designer and developer) effectively and act as a mediator between the designer and developer camps. Translating requirements and understanding the designers' vision will enable an XA to make sound architectural judgments about the requirements of the user interface layer.

In any environment in which the power base changes from designer to developer and back, the XA will have the benefit of being in both camps. Even if the XA can't perform as a developer, just understanding their language and concerns is enough. As long as the XA can appreciate and ultimately implement the visual goals of an interactive designer, the XA will see his or her Christmas card list expand!

Blend, along with Visual Studio, will absolutely be the tool of choice for the XA because the workflow between the two products will enable him or her to make quick decisions, test updates, and merge new resources into a solution. Blend becomes more of a XAML management tool for the XA than a visual design interface.

An Example of Power

To test how much of a benefit it is to have a producer/director-like figure (the XAML architect) calling the shots on a project, crack open a game of *Call of Duty 4* and take careful note of the way in which the application has been produced. The game illustrates an immersive, state of the art design at its best. You have no confusion as to what you are—or are about to be—doing.

These games are developed by teams of designers (interactive and graphic) and developers, but are ultimately produced by one or two people that act in the same capacity that an XA would for a WPF solution. Immersive, emotionally driven applications should be the end result that we strive for in standard application development.

The Interactive Designer's View

Some day designers and developers will recognize the fact that unless the user sees it happen on the screen, they will never be 100% sure it actually has happened. What I am talking about is simple user psychology. As an example, I ask you: How many times have you clicked on the Add to Basket button on a website and then had to go check the basket because you were not entirely sure your goodies went in there? With Blend, you can show the user, the item actually flying across the screen and into the basket to dispel any concerns, negative thoughts, and bad experiences that the user may ordinarily have.

I know that is a very simple example—and one that could be overcome using some special DHTML or something else wonderful. But this problem has been part of the user nightmare that interactive designers have been trying to stem, with only moderate success, for years, mainly due to project budgets (time/cost ratio).

An interactive designer might want to get down and dirty with some coding, not so much that the vein in her head will pop, but just enough to make sure the control(s) and/or UIElements perform as they are designed to.

That same designer might want to show some empathy and allow users to apply different control schemes and colors to allow them to *feel* where they are and how they are doing with the application. With Expression Blend, the interactive designer has the freedom to design a control that can show, for example, an ordered list of movies in thumbnails, ensuring that the listing is displayed in the application so that it fits with the overall continuity and visual perception of the project and the vision for the application.

The interactive designer also wants to be able to use his or her favorite graphic design package to create masterpieces of style and then export them into Blend. In this way he or she can ensure that design elements actually look like they are supposed to instead of having to ask a developer to try to make the elements look like the image the interactive designer just printed out.

Designers want to be involved much more in the lifecycle than they are at present. With the power to create fully functioning prototypes with Blend, which therefore expedites production lifecycles, the importance of the interactive designer's role is moved much higher up the food chain.

Going back to the games industry, interactive designers and graphic artists are the super stars, not so much the coders. Interactive designers take a leading role to ensure that the entire application is smooth in its appearance and that every animation, the music, and the fonts in the menus all come together as a perfect match of design integrity.

The Coder's View

I am sure that some of you reading this book as developers have, at one time or another, been told by a project manager or IT director that the application you have slaved over just does not look like the application they envisioned or were sold on. Another common concern is that test users complain about the time it takes to perform a certain task after taking numerous steps in order to navigate a complex screen. It's possible that your application has used controls from various third parties and that they just don't fit the overall visual perception because you can't modify the appearance or style of those controls. Even Microsoft still distributes controls like the CLR TreeView control that doesn't support transparent background colors. These are all very common issues relating to large application development solutions where designs are always changing to address functional, presentational, or usability issues.

Such issues most often occur in Agile environments, because development cycles are short, fluid, and incremental. Developers are often hamstrung by strict adherence to timelines in which they must provide functionality and maintainable levels of bug fixing. As a result, the user interface often gets the least attention, which leads to the poor user experience I keep talking about.

Blend means that developers can finally just focus on making sure that code functions as it is required to in a specification. Their objects get a value in, and then they make sure the correct value goes out. It's as simple as that. The developers can even test the object code to make sure someone else doesn't change the designed functionality. You can be guaranteed a format or a value type every time. The interface can either be designed around that format, or, preferably, the coder's objects can be designed by what they are required to input/output.

A lot of middle tier and backend developers will be extremely pleased that they no longer have to think about the user interface—nothing scares them more. They can just get on with coding and even help with the logical client layer, all without ever seeing the UI that they are developing for. They also have the added bonus of being able to apply unit testing to the logical layer, which fits in well with the psyche of the nonUI developer.

The Workflow

Traditional workflow in the development lifecycle has always depended on the development company's work practices and is based on whether they use standards to ensure quality products. Not all businesses do, and some even think they are not big enough to go to the trouble. As a single developer, I always use standards in my everyday work to ensure that I can provide not only quality results, but also auditable paths of my work to my clients.

You may, at present, be involved with designer and developer teams. Perhaps a move to a new job at a new company in the future will put you in this position. Either way, it is important to understand how this designer/developer workflow is supposed to work.

I have previously stated how Blend will significantly reduce the production time on solutions; but until you understand the time periods that will be removed, it is hard to see that becoming reality. Many interactive designers have their own methods of producing mock-up applications or prototype designs. Some choose to use animated environments such as Flash, some use PowerPoint, some use Visio, and others like to create traditional storyboards to indicate how they see the interface working. End users are then brought in to give initial feedback. Refinements are then made based on this research.

This design process allows the interactive designer to spot user workflow issues and other process improvement opportunities that are vital to an application being accepted by the end user. The process, called the blueprint, may also require a variety of diagrams: a structural diagram (or application map), a process diagram to provide architects an essential view, and sometimes a wireframe diagram to illustrate how different screens will appear.

The only problem with the blueprint now is that almost all the work done during its creation process is wasted when it comes time to actually develop the solution. Developers may (and it's not always the case) be able to use some of the visual assets created, the static images and the color palettes; but they certainly won't be able to use any animation sequences or event-driven reactions that are so crucial to informing the user of what has occurred. Remember the Add to Basket scenario?

Applications like Flash, Visio, and PowerPoint, when used in the interactive design context, are purely conceptual, whereas Expression Design, Expression Blend, and Visual Studio are production tools. Using the production tools, you can reach the end goal a lot quicker and the integrity of the design can be controlled and maintained by the designers instead of the developers.

Using Blend to deliver the blueprint now means that the interactive designer is creating the actual user interface that will be present in the end product. Blend provides all the tools necessary to deliver the animation of objects, providing the rich user experience end users crave; and perhaps more importantly, Blend provides a separate layer of development that the code developers never really need to modify or be involved with.

The workflow between Blend and Visual Studio allows the interactive designer to quickly test object implementations in the data binding scenarios and customized controls that are present in many applications.

The interactive designer along with the XAML architect, then, have the ability to accurately describe the required object model to the development team, which will, in most cases, provide a base object model with testable methods. That allows the interface to provide data, as well as test data being returned, all before the majority of the backend code is written.

The Importance of an Accurate Test Object

We will look at creating CLR data bound objects in Chapter 13, "Data Binding," where we will look at a method for creating test data. It is important to do this so the templates we design in Blend show real-world data and so we can make adjustments to either the data object—or the presentation of that data—without having to involve a developer, a data source such as a database, or a valid connection to a data source to do it. Methods such as these also speed up the development process by removing the reliance of one team on the other.

The End User or Client

End users always want simplicity. The Chinese discovered thousands of years ago that it was simpler to remember topics or points of interest when those topics were displayed as a picture or icon. The old adage, "A picture is worth a thousand words," rings true with today's marketing gurus who believe they can sell you anything if they can show it to you. People need to see vivid imagery to give themselves perspective.

According to George A. Miller (founder of the Center for Cognitive Studies at Harvard), we mere mortals tend to have a memory capacity of 7 + –2 items (Nelson Cowan revised this to 4 + –1 in 2000); yet, we can recall large collections of images, especially those that form part of our habits, which our brains are particularly fond of.

Why would you give the end user a static image button when you could show them an animated response to their choice? Why would the end client be happy having to rely on old data when they could be viewing the information live and in a graphical representation? The quick answer is they won't be happy. If your company's competition provides a better user experience in their products, you shouldn't expect to keep your job for much longer.

When designed correctly and composed with perfect harmony, a WPF application will give users an extremely positive experience. In some cases, people will forget they are using a computer and feel at one with the application. I have witnessed people who are single finger typists who suddenly discover extra fingers. The positive experience has added to their productivity.

You would have at one time or another experienced these really high levels of positive flow and productivity because the most common side effect is losing track of time. Time flies when you are having fun and enjoying yourself.

Again, when applications are built with the cooperation of the designer and the application developer, the end user will have no doubts as to what they are doing, what has just occurred, and how they should proceed next. With WPF there is simply no excuse for not delivering fantastic user experience. If you become a XAML architect, you could ensure the application delivers the appropriate user experience.

Having a well-designed product in terms of usability and visual appeal will ensure that your company earns development costs back in the long term because of the loyalty that a professional, easy to use, and fun application brings. Positive feelings are also transferred to a brand so, in the case of a publicly released piece of software, happy users are much more inclined to use new, different, and simple applications. Most importantly, they are likely to tell their friends and colleagues about it.

The end user demands perfection. We (the collective industry) can't expect them to keep shelling out for new hardware every 18–24 months if we are not going to make them feel good about their purchases by giving them a positive experience.

Would you buy a sports car if the seats where uncomfortable, the suspension was rubbish, and the driving experience was not up to the level that you expected—even if the motor was an absolute beast? Maybe...maybe not.

Maybe next time, instead of buying a PC, the user will go with a *fruitier* choice of computer, to see what it has to offer. If this happens too often, you and or I may lose our jobs.

Summary

Throughout the Interactive Designer CTP's and subsequent Blend 1 and Blend 2 preview releases, people from differing sides of the designer/developer roles have argued about what Blend is and who it is actually for. Maybe they only looked at it from their angle, without taking or trying to experience the other side's arguments and requirements. Either way, it is difficult to create a truly collaborative environment and, perhaps even more difficult, to implement the tools used to facilitate it. Expression Design, Expression Blend, and Visual Studio represent a real step ahead in the right direction to achieving this by speeding up the design/development process and allowing the original designers of a solution to maintain ownership of it.

Blend, used by a XAML architect, allows the collaboration to work in a real-world scenario, be it a small or large solution team. Only experience in working on WPF solutions will bring this requirement forward into discussions in future.

Blend offers you, the graphic or interactive designer, a way to decrease your delivery times while maintaining all your hard work throughout the solution development lifecycle and on to the end user. In other words, what you originally design is what you can now deliver instead of letting developers interpret and implement your visual requirements.

It doesn't mean you will never again need to use any of the tools you have used previously; it just means you will have the option to create, control, maintain, modify, and own your designs—instead of just hoping that someone else will.

CHAPTER 2

Welcome to the New World

The secret to working with Blend lies in understanding the relationship between XAML, CLR code, and object-orientated architecture. Unless you can integrate all three of these elements, your applications won't perform as you or, more importantly, your end user would expect. This chapter is about understanding that relationship and that everything you can do in XAML, you can do in code—and a whole lot more.

Your First Look at Expression Blend 2

I know that you must have seen a demonstration somewhere and instantly thought, "Whoa...I want to build that!" That means that you are highly motivated from the start; a good thing. You have to remember that, for some of you, the learning curve is going to be huge. So, let's crawl before we try to run.

The "Hello World" Application

Let's go through the old standard of creating something that says, "Hello World." Before you quickly jump to the next chapter with a sigh, let me assure you that we are going to do a few things differently than the traditional application. We are going to take a brief glimpse into the designer/developer roles and the collaboration workflow to create a WPF application and hopefully change the world along the way!

1. Start Expression Blend. On the first load of Blend, you may see a Welcome Screen, which you can close (opting to either run at start up or not using the checkbox) or create a New Project by selecting the Projects tab.

2. If you closed the Welcome Screen, select the File menu and then select New Project...

3. Select the WPF Application (.exe) option when you are presented with the New Project dialog as shown in Figure 2.1. You should ensure that Target is set to .NET Framework 3.5.

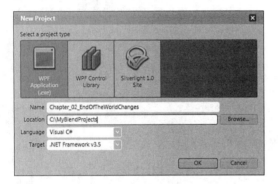

FIGURE 2.1   The New Project dialog in which you should always set the name of your application and location. These properties are difficult to edit later.

Do You Need to Set the Language and Target at the Start of a Project?

Note that in Figure 2.1 you have the option to set the Language and Target. Trying to change this later is almost impossible. Ensure that the Language you choose is the language you want to work with in Visual Studio should you have any coding requirements. The Target .NET Framework will also determine the feature sets available to you. Please see MSDN for further information on the differences in both .NET languages as well as a comparison of the Frameworks available.

Unless you have a specific reason (such as backward compatibility), you should always select the highest available .NET Framework version.

4. Give your new application a suitable name (different to the default UntitledProject) and set the location to your local drive—somewhere you can remember.

5. Click OK when you are happy with your choice.

6. You should now have a large white window in front of you with Window1.xaml at the top and a little tag-type item below it that says None selected. This is the control breadcrumb navigation system that you learn in greater detail a little later in the book. The white square on your screen is referred to as the artboard or work surface and is a representation of how your Window will render when you run this application.

Live Artboard!

As you make changes to your application, you will see the live representation in the Blend UI. This is to say that the artboard represents a runtime view of your application for almost all controls and components that you add to your application. This live view lets you see how your controls will appear to the end user on the form, which is especially important when you start making your own controls and/or use some complex layout scenarios.

Because Blend allows you to use a Split View, in which you can see both XAML markup screens and the artboard, you will see live changes reflected in both screens. Add some XAML and the artboard changes to reflect it; or, draw a button on the surface and you will see the relevant XAML markup added.

7. Don't be too concerned with how Blend has laid out the panels or what they all mean at this stage. Of course, some things should be almost familiar to you. Designers probably understand the icons, and developers probably understand the Project tab and subsequent hierarchy. Some familiarity is better than scratching your head with no clue. But, if you *are* scratching your head, don't panic! On the left side of the Blend application, you should see a strip of icons. That is the ToolBox panel.

8. In the ToolBox, scroll down until you see the icon highlighted in Figure 2.2.

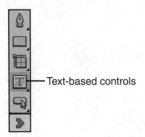

FIGURE 2.2   The standard TextBox icon from the ToolBox panel.

9. When you mouse over the icon, the tooltip should tell you that the item is a TextBox. Double-click the icon and you should see a TextBox appear on the artboard, in the top-left corner of Window1.xaml.

Can't See the TextBox?

If you can't see the entire Window area in the center of Blend, you may need to zoom the artboard out a little. Press the Control (CTRL) key and the – or minus key at the same time to zoom out. You can also use CTRL + + to zoom in or CTRL + 0 to fit the selected control to your screen.

10. If you see your cursor blinking inside the TextBox, you are in the text editor mode of the TextBox control. This is the default behavior when adding the control. It allows you to change the value from TextBox to something more meaningful for you or to remove the text altogether. If you are in the text editor mode, you might as well delete the word *TextBox* and type in **Hello World!** If you do not appear to be in the text editor mode, Press F2 or right-click on the TextBox control, and you should be able to find the Edit Text menu option in the context menu. Select this to return to the text editor mode.

11. While still in text editor mode; as you move the mouse over the rest of the artboard, notice that your cursor is a cross. Click anywhere on the artboard to exit Text editor mode, or press the escape (ESC) key on your keyboard.

12. The top-left corner of the parent control is the default position of the TextBox and all other controls are added by double-clicking their respective icon. That would be great if we wanted that to be the TextBox's final resting place—but it is not. We want to center the TextBox. To do this locate the Properties panel (which by default is located between the Project and Resources tabs) and ensure that it is selected to show its categories as illustrated in Figure 2.3. If you can't find the panel, select the Window menu item from the top of the Blend menu items and check whether the Properties menu item is checked as shown in Figure 2.4.

FIGURE 2.3   The Properties panel.

13. If no properties are visible, you are still in Text edit mode, so either click on the artboard somewhere in the white space or click on the Selection tool icon located at the top of the ToolBox icon panel.

14. Collapse all the property categories, if they are open, by clicking on the category heading labels so as your Properties panel resembles Figure 2.3 (I just don't want you confused by the new property types...yet). There are a lot of categories and properties for each control that you use in Blend. For now you are going to use the Property Search box to find the specific properties required.

The Check indicates that the panel is visible

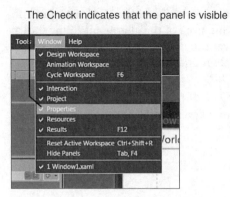

FIGURE 2.4   The Properties panel should be on the screen.

Property Searches

Figure 2.3 also shows you where the Property Search box is. This is a very handy work-flow tool that you should get used to using. Some property collections get pretty big, and using the Property Search box will cut down on a lot of clicking to open and close categories. The search phrase you enter is not case sensitive.

15. In the Property Search box, type **align** and you see the property categories shown in Figure 2.5.

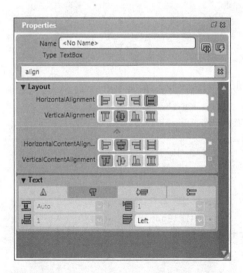

FIGURE 2.5   The results of the align property search.

16. Find and set the HorizontalAlignment property to Stretch and the VerticalAlignment property to Center as shown in Figure 2.5, taking note of the alignment terms shown in the tooltips when you move your mouse over them. For the moment, don't be too concerned with the alignment property values and what they mean. They are fairly self-explanatory, but as you will see in Chapter 5, "UIElement: Control Embedding," they have a big impact on the way controls are laid out on the screen.

17. Press F5 to run your first WPF application using Expression Blend.

Viewing XAML Elements

So far we've dealt with fairly simple material; but, before you fall asleep, let's examine the XAML that has been added by Blend and try to get a little understanding of what has happened in the application.

If you press F11, Blend will cycle through the View modes, from the artboard (Design view) to the XAML editor (XAML view) and then to the Split view mode—so you can see both the artboard and the XAML markup. If you examine the XAML markup you should see a listing very similar, if not exactly the same as the code shown in Listing 2.1.

My Windows Don't Cycle with F11

Only Blend2 December preview and later versions use F11 to cycle the workspace. You can always use the tabs on the side of the Blend artboard to switch between the available view modes. Blend1 doesn't have a Split View mode.

LISTING 2.1   Hello World Blend Style

```
<Window
    xmlns="http://schemas.microsoft.com/winfx/2006/xaml/presentation"
    xmlns:x="http://schemas.microsoft.com/winfx/2006/xaml"
    x:Class="Chapter_02_EndOfTheWorldChanges.Window1"
    x:Name="Window"
    Title="Window1"
    Width="640" Height="480">

    <Grid x:Name="LayoutRoot">
        <TextBox HorizontalAlignment="Stretch" VerticalAlignment="Center"
Text="Hello World!" TextWrapping="Wrap" HorizontalContentAlignment="Center"/>

    </Grid>
</Window>
```

Bold Markup

Throughout the book, you will see many markup examples. Most of the time those examples will start with the **<Grid x:Name="LayoutRoot">** line. You should assume that you need only replace your existing markup (as shown in the bolded area of Listing 2.1) to that point. If you changed the values in the <Window tag shown in Listing 2.1, you would receive errors because of possible name differences between your project and the version shown in the book.

If you are unfamiliar with XAML, in the sense that you have never seen it before, you are either sweating right now or you are thinking, "This looks like XML."

XAML is an XML-based markup language with some quirky additions to make it a suitable scripting language to work with .NET. You don't need to know anything about it at the moment—other than to know how to view it in Blend. We are going to go through some basics right now, but in Chapter 4, "XAML for Beginners," we go through XAML structures in detail.

For now, start with the first line:

```
<Window
```

This is a declaration of a Window class. The lines immediately following it are various settings that act in basically the same way as if we had declared a Window class (maybe a Form in .NET) and supplied the settings to the object constructor.

If you are a designer and don't understand the previous paragraph, then just think of that line of markup as being similar to how developers would normally create an instance of an application "Window" object in .NET code.

The next interesting line of markup is a few lines down:

```
<Grid x:Name="LayoutRoot">
```

This, again, is the declaration of an object (a Grid type), which in this case acts as a panel construct and allows you to add child elements to the Window object. You may have seen this panel object in Blend already named as *LayoutRoot*. This line of markup is added by default when you start a new project or add more Windows to your project.

Next you see the indented line:

```
<TextBox
```

Again the markup shows an object declared. Remember the values that you set in the Properties panel (e.g., HorizontalAlignment)? The corresponding values are now shown in this markup line.

I am guessing that you are nodding your head at the moment, and all that information is locked into your brain. As you can see, elements have closing tags like </Grid>. They take the same validation as a standard XML document.

Changing the "World" with XAML

So we are not entirely happy with what we have created: a TextBox in the middle of the application Window. A TextBox control is not the best control for the requirements of this application because no user input is required. The use of a TextBox, then, may confuse the user, creating a negative user experience. In this instance, a label control would be more appropriate.

While still in XAML view, find the following markup block (known as an element in XAML):

```
<TextBox
    HorizontalAlignment="Stretch"
    VerticalAlignment="Center"
    HorizontalContentAlignment="Center"
    Text="Hello World!"
    TextWrapping="Wrap"/>
```

You Could Just Search for It

Clicking on CTRL + F will open the Search panel for your markup. F3 will attempt to find the next instance of a highlighted value.

You are now going to change the control type declared (TextBox) to a Label.

1. First, change the object type. Replace the word *TextBox* with the word **Label**.

2. Change the property name from *Text* to **Content**. The Text property is not supported in the Label object. You should be able to see the squiggly line underneath the unsupported attributes and their values.

Content or Text?

The concept of Content will be explained over the next few chapters, but for now, understand that both the Text property of a TextBox and the Content property of a Label control both accept a string as a property value. A string is a block of letters, numbers, or symbols inside double quotations.

3. Change the property value from *"Hello World!"* to **"This is my World!"**

4. The label class does not support the TextWrapping property, so find the TextWrapping ="Wrap" element and remove it. Make sure you leave the element terminator (the />) at the end of the line.

5. Press F5 to test the application.

Manipulating the XAML has an immediate effect. To be honest, you really didn't need to test and run the application. The Design view in Blend shows you the same thing without rebuilding the application. Remember, the view on the artboard is live. It's good to get your hands dirty though, isn't it?

Using XAML in Visual Studio

Much has been made of the XAML editor that appears in Blend, or to be more accurate, what doesn't appear in the XAML editor in Blend. At the time of this writing, I am using a private release of Blend 2. Even at this stage, nothing has been done to implement so much as a context menu for copy and paste in the editor—let alone any form of IntelliSense that almost an entire user base has been requesting since early CTP releases of what was known as Expression Interactive Designer. I only hope that by the time you are reading this that it has been implemented in some way, shape, or form.

Visual Studio 2008 provides a good mix of XAML editing ability along with .NET code behind page editing—not to mention a much stronger debugging and stack tracing facility. So, the question may be: Why would you use Blend?

The answer to this will come later on in this book, when you move toward template and style manipulation, animations, and binding, which are extremely well-supported in Blend, which also offers many other features that would have you pulling your hair out in other environments, including Visual Studio. At the end of the day, you may not have those requirements (animations, style manipulation/creation) and can make up your own mind about using Blend, Visual Studio, or other tools that are available.

Changing the "World" with Code

We will now have a look at the effects of using Blend with code, which should tie a few concepts together for you.

The following gives you a brief glimpse at Blend/Visual Studio interactivity:

1. Return to Design View and using the Selection tool (the top icon in the toolbox or click V), click on the Label in the center of the Window.
2. Open the Properties panel again and study Figure 2.6 before continuing from here.
3. If you still have the word align in the Property Search box, remove it or click on the X to clear the search.
4. You must give a name to any object you add to the artboard that you want to access in code. By default, all new items are unnamed, and you will see the <No Name> in the Object Name box in the Properties panel. In the Name input box enter **ChangeWorld**.

   I will harp on naming controls throughout the book. At some stage you will, inevitably, forget to name your element and be unable to find it when you are adding code in Visual Studio—and then proclaim the whole thing to be worthless—when you really just need to remember to name things.
5. You should also note from Figure 2.6 what object type we are using, which is more than relevant later in the book. In this case the object type is Label. We want to change this type, though, to something more suitable for our purposes. Change the type again, this time to a button.
6. Just as you previously changed the type from TextBox to Label in the XAML editor, this time you are replacing the tag Label with Button.

Object Type   Object Name

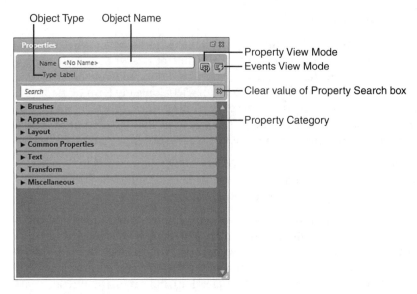

FIGURE 2.6   Important areas in the Properties panel.

7. After switching to XAML view, add a new attribute to the Button element: Width="125"

   You are about to generate an event handler (or let Blend do it for you). Before you begin, check to see that your settings are correct for the version of Visual Studio that you have installed. Go to the Tools menu item, select Options from the list, and when the Options dialog is presented as is shown in Figure 2.7, select the Event handlers button on the left of the dialog to review your settings.

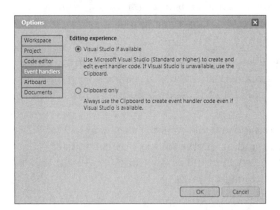

FIGURE 2.7   The Options dialog in which Visual Studio integration is enabled.

Visual Studio Compatibility

Note that in order to have the best user workflow scenario, you should have a Standard or higher version of Visual Studio installed. That installation is assumed in the examples throughout this book. If you are using an Express Version of Visual Studio, you should choose the second item in the Options dialog, which will copy the event handler code to the clipboard for you to manually add to your code behind page.

You can open your application project file using Visual Studio Express while you have the project open with Expression Blend; however, you will need to manually navigate to the correct code behind page and manually paste the event handler code as it is created.

8. Before invoking Visual Studio, you must save and build the project for the XAML to be parsed and all your objects to be accessible.

What Does the Term "Build" Refer To?

Before you run your application, Visual Studio or Blend will "build" the application, which takes any changes you have made to code and or markup as well as the application structure. It all gets compiled into the .exe that you will eventually run in order to see your application onscreen. When you build an application, you simply do everything previously mentioned with the exception of running the .exe at the end.

Save and Build

From time to time you will not be able to find newly added objects within the Visual Studio environment. You can switch back to Blend and select Save All from the File menu at any time. Or, you can build your project before returning to the Visual Studio environment. I suggest that you make it a habit to save any changes you have made within the Visual Studio environment before returning to Blend to ensure that both environments remain synchronized.

You can also build the application from within Visual Studio, which is covered later in this book.

9. Open the Properties panel and locate the Event viewer mode icon (see Figure 2.6—the icon has a lightning bolt on it.) Clicking this icon provides a list of available events for the currently selected control on the artboard.

10. Select Events Viewer mode in the Properties panel and, at the top of the event list, find the Click event. Double-click the input box to the right of the event name to generate an event handler named ChangeWorld_Click.

11. You should now be able to access the Button object using the name you gave it, and change some of the properties directly. Unlike XAML, .NET code can be called many

times during the course of the application running (called "runtime"), so changing property values here means that you can change the value of the object properties at "runtime" as opposed to "design time" when entering XAML markup. Duplicate the code shown in Listing 2.2. Save the changes in Visual Studio by clicking the File menu and then Save All.

First Time Saves in Visual Studio

When you first save an application in Visual Studio, you may be presented with the Solution Save dialog. Your application will always be accessible from either Visual Studio or Expression Blend via the project file (.csproj). However, in the event that you add other projects to your application solution, those events will only be available in Blend and Visual Studio when you open the solution (.sln) file. You can find more on solutions in Chapter 10, "Visual Studio: C# Primer."

12. Staying in Visual Studio for a moment, press F5 to build and test the application.

LISTING 2.2   Changing the World

```
private void ChangeWorld_Click(object sender, RoutedEventArgs e)
{
    this.ChangeWorld.Content = "My Changing World!";
    this.ChangeWorld.Background = new SolidColorBrush(Color.FromRgb
➡(0, 0, 125));
    this.ChangeWorld.Foreground = new SolidColorBrush(Color.FromRgb
➡(255, 255, 255));
    this.ChangeWorld.Width = 350;
    this.ChangeWorld.FontSize = 32d;
}
```

Now you should be able to marry up the concept of objects being declared in XAML and accessed in code for runtime manipulation and or management.

Yes, you can declare everything in code if you wanted to. But why would you when you have the power to apply animations, transformations, bindings, and much more to objects in XAML in a design time environment?

Why would you use Visual Studio to assist with the declaration of these objects when, clearly, Expression Blend provides a very fluid way of doing it—and more importantly, as you will see in later chapters, Blend allows you to re-style controls and create templates that can be applied to other objects of the same type within differing scopes of an application or an entirely new application all together.

The Best of Both Worlds or Not?

This next little area is a bit of a hot topic in some circles because it has implications for the way in which you design and build your applications. I am talking about adding .NET code directly to the XAML file. While your initial thoughts are probably positive toward the feature, there is more than just coding simplicity at stake here.

I try not to get too anal about this when I talk to others on this very topic, because I've always believed that every coder works in ways that they find most efficient. Who am I, or anyone else for that matter, to tell them that they are not doing it (coding) right?

If it works, in my book, it's the right way to do it—well, most of the time.

If the code works and is really elegant, if it is efficient in performance, secure, testable, easy-to-maintain, and easy for others to understand, it should be considered the right way to do it in everyone's book!

I am talking about coding standards here, and while I personally would never add code to XAML, I can understand why others might. If you choose to add code to XAML, you should understand a few important points.

- ▶ If you have previously added code in Visual Studio, you have seen the IntelliSense popping up all over the place. When applications get really complex or large, that IntelliSense is invaluable to help you work efficiently. When you add code to markup, you have no IntelliSense, so you can expect to have code issues because of the complexity of some objects.

- ▶ In the commercial world of application development, most of the time testing is a very important requirement for code. Special code is used to do what is called *unit testing*. This ensures that a block of code does exactly what it is supposed to in terms of the functions it performs. I have yet to see someone successfully apply unit testing to any code that is embedded in XAML markup. So, there is no guarantee that the code will continue to function as expected in a logical sense.

- ▶ Adding code to XAML makes the application layers messy, where they should be clearly separated. This has an impact on the designer/developer workflow. Even though Blend is about implementing collaboration, a secret to collaboration being successful is that designers need to know what they own in terms of code and markup. Similarly, developers need to know what they can and cannot touch. Code inside the markup means that sometimes developers will be interacting with the UI layer when they really should not have any right to do so.

- ▶ This method does not support partial class integration. This is a little technical at this point, but developers will understand the impact it has on coding. In a simplistic example, partial classes allow more than one coder to be writing code for the same object at the same time. That ability is imperative in large development team environments.

▶ No source code security integration for XAML files is available at present. I don't mean to be presumptive at this point as to your working requirements as a designer, but the vast majority of designers have never worked in an environment in which "things" get locked down so only certain people can modify them at a time. This is a major area of concern in commercial development projects because without being able to control who has access to what code and when, a change made by one person may totally conflict with a change in the code made by someone else. Such a situation generally results in an application neither building and or running, which is (of course) bad.

Again, it's not for me to hide this feature from you just because I don't condone it. I'll show you how to do it, and you can make up your own mind. Just make sure you aren't working for me when you try it!

Changing the "World" with C# Code in XAML

We are going to add another event handler to our project, but this time you are providing the handler inside the XAML markup. Before you can do this, though, you need to add another property attribute to the existing XAML so it calls your event handler during runtime.

The following walks you through adding C# code to XAML:

1. Press F11 to cycle the View mode in Blend and return to the XAML editor. Add the following line inside the Button element.

   ```
   MouseMove="MouseMove_Handler"
   ```

2. Locate the </Grid> closing tag. Directly after it, add the markup/code shown in Listing 2.3.

LISTING 2.3   CDATA C# Code in XAML

```
<x:Code><![CDATA[
private void MouseMove_Handler(object sender,
     System.Windows.Input.MouseEventArgs e)
{
    LayoutRoot.Background = Brushes.Green;
}
]]></x:Code>
```

3. Save the project and press F5 to build and test the application.

Reading back through the markup and code that you have added, you can follow what your code instructions are: When the mouse moves over the window surface, make the background green.

Right about now you are starting to think that this XAML stuff is a replacement for .NET code. That isn't exactly true.

While you are declaring objects and setting properties (e.g., Button or Label or TextBox) in XAML in the same way developers do in the .NET coding environment, XAML does not allow you to manipulate these values during runtime. Sure, you can call events and even react to them being raised or properties being at a certain state or value, but you can't perform standard logic switching (code execution flow) or declare new instances of objects in XAML after you start the application. All these are functions that are usually required in an application of any complexity greater than showing a MessageBox. That is why you still need .NET code.

XAML is awesome, though, for what can be achieved with very little markup; binding and animation, especially, are extremely well-suited to the format that XAML uses.

If you have time, open Notepad.exe and type in the 25 lines of XAML markup included in Listing 2.4. When you are finished, save the file using a .xaml extension in a location that you can navigate to easily.

Remember that all the code and markup you have created in Blend is larger than 25 lines, so double-click your .xaml file. It should open in Internet Explorer 7. If it doesn't, you will need to right-click on the file and select Open with..., and choose Internet Explorer 7+. You will see just how powerful WPF can be, considering we just declared a single object and changed a few property values in a text file!

LISTING 2.4   Simple XAML

```
<Label
    xmlns="http://schemas.microsoft.com/winfx/2006/xaml/presentation"
    HorizontalAlignment="Stretch"
    VerticalAlignment="Stretch"
    HorizontalContentAlignment="Center"
    Content="This is my World!"
    Margin="0,0,0,0"
    FontFamily="Papyrus"
    FontSize="48"
    FontStyle="Normal"
    FontWeight="Bold"
    VerticalContentAlignment="Center">
    <Label.Background>
        <RadialGradientBrush>
            <GradientStop Color="#FF300EF7" Offset="0.327"/>
            <GradientStop Color="#FF000000" Offset="0.543"/>
        </RadialGradientBrush>
    </Label.Background>
    <Label.Foreground>
        <LinearGradientBrush EndPoint="1,0.5" StartPoint="0,0.5">
            <GradientStop Color="#FFFF0000" Offset="0"/>
            <GradientStop Color="#FF4CFF00" Offset="1"/>
```

```
            </LinearGradientBrush>
        </Label.Foreground>
</Label>
```

Blend Versus Visual Studio Project Types

The four types of projects that are primarily used in WPF development are described in Table 2.1.

TABLE 2.1   Project Types

Expression Blend Name	Visual Studio Name
WPF Application (.exe)	WPF Application
WPF Control Library	WPF User Control Library
Silverlight Site*	
	WPF Browser Application**
	WPF Custom Control Library

*Silverlight Site is dependent upon the version of Silverlight installed. At the time of this writing Silverlight 2.0 was not released and Blend 2 was not going to support it initially either.

**WPF Browser Application was initially called an XBAP application.

Three project types are available from Expression Blend (see Figure 2.8) and four are available from Visual Studio 2008, as shown in Figure 2.9.

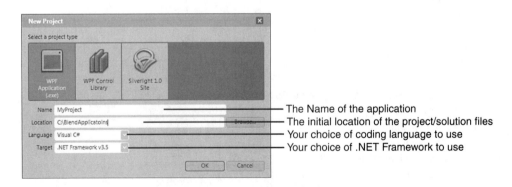

FIGURE 2.8   Blend project types.

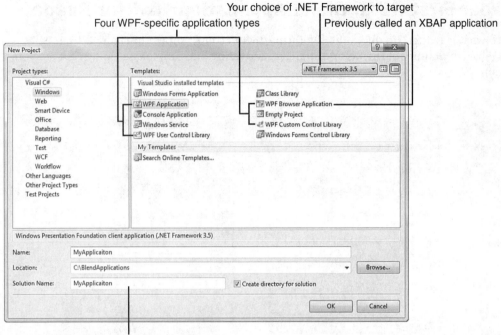

FIGURE 2.9   The Visual Studio Windows project types, as well as the XBAP project type now named WPF Browser Application.

There are subtle differences in the project types supported by both applications. We will look at them in greater depth as we move to Visual Studio to architect a solution in a later part of this book.

Should you start new projects in Visual Studio? The short answer is: It doesn't matter if you use Blend or Visual Studio. If you open the project files for the same project types created by both applications, you will immediately see the differences that could be a concern later on in your development life cycle. Projects that are created in Visual Studio have the full implementation of ClickOnce security applied to them. This feature is also available to Blend-created solutions when they are opened in the Visual Studio environment and the relevant deployment settings for the solution are set. Visual Studio projects also allow for varying build configurations, whereas Blend doesn't provide support for this; and, depending on the size of your application and the overall solution complexity, the development team may require varying build configurations.

This lack of build configuration options is a downside to creating your application architecture with Expression Blend; however, because of the interactivity between Blend and Visual Studio, there is nothing stopping you from creating the solution in Visual Studio and then importing it into Blend for additional work. If you are working as a XAML architect, you may wish to create a solution shell first (or get your development team to do it if no XAML architect is present). Then, open the solution in Blend.

Your First REAL Blend Application: Twitter Reader

So what is twitter? To quote the site (http://twitter.com/), shown in Figure 2.10, it is, "A global community of friends and strangers answering one simple question: What are you doing?"

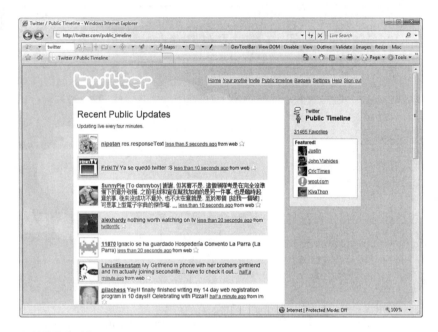

FIGURE 2.10   The twitter site and the mashup of people posting stuff.

It's one of those strange social networking phenomena that I was introduced to briefly by Dave Malouf in New York when I went to assist him with some Blend application training. People sign up and just post stuff back and forward about what they are doing, something they heard, or maybe something they just ate. It's a bit loopy, I know; but the simplicity of it all lends itself to some great samples in Blend.

That being said, the first application we are going to write is a simple RSS reader hooked into a twitter service to show us what we and our twitter friends have been writing...err...doing.

The first step is to go to the twitter website and sign up for an account. It's free and takes about 48 seconds to complete. You will need to do this to get an RSS address, which I will explain as you proceed with this example.

Creating the New Project in Blend

Open Expression Blend and close any screens that have popped up wanting to show you help files or other items. Next, select the File menu and then select New Project. Give the project a name and select the location in which you want to create the application. From now on in this book, I will simply ask you to create a new application.

Building the UIElements

Being one of the first applications you create using Expression Blend, we are going to take things easy. We want to create a simple RSS reader with a Refresh button.

The following steps guide you through the process of creating the application, but you should pay very close attention to the instruction on how to create a twitter account.

1. Find the Objects and Timeline panel and double-click on the LayoutRoot element. This should add a yellow border around the element, which is called activating the element.

Selecting and Activating Elements

In the Objects and Timeline panel, you can single-click on elements as they are shown in the visual tree. You will see the Properties panel update to reflect the element you have selected. You should also see the bounding box of the element on the artboard. What you need to be constantly aware of is what element is the currently activated control. That element appears in the Objects and Timeline panel with a yellow border around it. The importance of element activation is that when you add child elements, they are, by default, added as children to the currently activated element as opposed to the currently selected element.

2. Find the Grid element icon in the Tools menu on the left side of the Blend UI, as shown in Figure 2.11. Double-click the icon to place a Grid as a child of the LayoutRoot element as shown in Figure 2.12.

FIGURE 2.11   The Grid element icon selected.

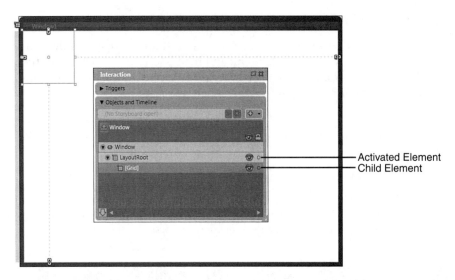

FIGURE 2.12   The LayoutRoot as the activated element and the Grid as a child of it. In the background is the Grid elements bounding box.

3. This Grid element is going to play host to our Reader panel; so setting the layout of this Grid's position is important. We don't set the Grid's position by modifying the properties of the Grid itself. Instead, we set its parent's Layout properties. In this case, the parent is the LayoutRoot element. Select the LayoutRoot element again and then depress the V key on your keyboard. You should note that you no longer have the Grid icon selected and the top icon on the toolbar (the Selection tool) should now be highlighted.

4. If you look at the artboard carefully, you should see an icon that looks like a Grid at the top left of the Window. Beside this grid to the right (Horizontally) and directly down (Vertically) from this icon you should see a faint semi-transparent, light blue rectangle that is just outside of the white background of the Window, as shown in Figure 2.13. These rectangles, known as adorners, allow you to create Columns and Rows to help control the layout of any child controls added to this Grid. All Grids have the same facility, not just the LayoutRoot.

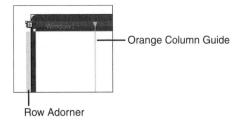

FIGURE 2.13   The bars that allow you to add Rows and Columns.

5. You are going to create a Row on the LayoutRoot, which is actually called a RowDefinition. Remember the name, because you will use a lot of these in the future. Figure 2.14 shows an approximation of what you need. When you move your mouse over the definition adorner bar on the left side, you will see an orange guide appear. When you are satisfied with your positioning, click the left mouse button once. If you need to move the Row up or down, simply move your mouse over the RowDefinition bar on the line, and you should see your mouse change to indicate that it can be moved.

GridUnit Type (See Chapter 5)

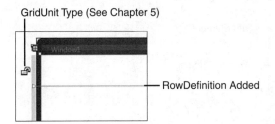

RowDefinition Added

FIGURE 2.14   The creation of a RowDefinition.

6. Now you should have two Rows in the LayoutRoot: one above the line representing the RowDefinition and one below. You want to make the Grid element, which will show the RSS reader, fill the bottom Row of the LayoutRoot. If you click on the Grid element in the Objects and Timeline panel, you should see the Grid element's bounding box reappear.

7. Select the Grid element in the artboard (not in the exact center, but just inside the Grid's bounding box). Hold down the mouse and drag the grid slowly into the bottom row area of the LayoutRoot element. When you try to position the top-left corner of the Grid into the Row, you should see a pink border (see Figure 2.15), which also runs along side the RowDefinition. If you don't see the Pink border, turn on Snapping to Snaplines, which is also shown in Figure 2.15). This guide is controlled by the default artboard padding, which is set in the Tools-> Options -> Artboard menu. It is set to 8 pixels by default.

8. Grab the bottom-right corner of the Grid's bounding box and drag it to the bottom-right corner of the white background until you see the pink border again, this time running along the bottom and right sides of the Window.

9. Ensuring that the LayoutRoot element is still activated and has a yellow border around it, find the Button element in the Tools menu on the left side of the application. This icon should be two icons down from where the Grid icon was. Once you have located it, double-click it to add it to the artboard as a child element of the LayoutRoot. The Grid element and the Button element should be on the same level of depth in the Objects and Timeline category under the LayoutRoot element.

10. You should now have a Button in the top-left corner of your artboard. If you don't have Blend set to show both the artboard and XAML editor at the same time, click

F11 a few times to cycle through the views until you can see both. This is called Split view and is probably the most convenient of all the views, most of the time.

Row Definition

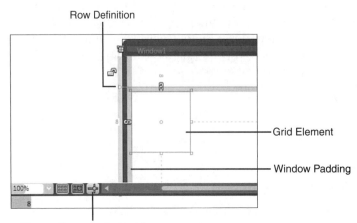

Grid Element

Window Padding

Turn on Snapping to Snaplines

FIGURE 2.15   The Grid and the pink border padding.

11. Search for a line of XAML markup near the bottom, (approximately line 15) that looks like the following:

```
<Button HorizontalAlignment="Left" VerticalAlignment="Top" Content="Button"/>
```

12. Add the end of the markup line, change Content="Button", to read "Refresh". You should notice that the text inside the button on the artboard has also changed. You could have made this change in the Property panel just as quickly, but it is important that you keep moving in and out of the XAML to cement your understanding.

13. Head back to the web and sign in to your new twitter account. It is very important that you add some content (one or two posts will be sufficient) so the RSS feed contains the fields we need. If you don't do this, the following steps won't work. Consult the twitter website help documents, if you need to, in order to post some content.

14. When logged into twitter, you should be able to find a hyperlink on the page that says RSS. Click on this to obtain your user feed URL. It should look similar to the following:

http://twitter.com/statuses/friends_timeline/3885401.rss

15. Keep this URL handy. You will need to use it in a minute. Now back to Blend. The next thing you need to do is double-click the Grid element in the Objects and Timeline panel to set the Grid as the activated control.

16. Look for the Project panel on the right side of the Blend application. You may need to click on the tab item that says Project to make it visible. If you do not see a Project tab, then open the Window menu at the top of the application and make sure Project is checked.

17. At the bottom of this panel, you should see a category called Data. Underneath it is a button with the text +XML, as shown in Figure 2.16.

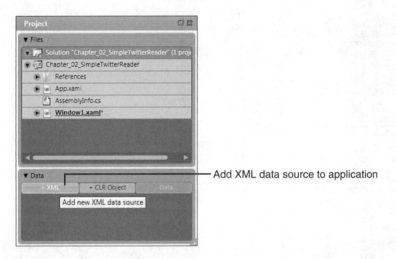

— Add XML data source to application

FIGURE 2.16   Click the +XML button in the Data category of the Project panel.

18. Click on the +XML button, which launches the Add XML Data Source dialog. Don't worry too much about these dialogs at the moment. We will view them later when discussing data binding.

19. In the Connection Name property box, in the dialog box, type **rssDS**.

20. In the URL for XML data, you can now paste the RSS URL you got from the twitter website in step 14. Then click OK.

21. You should end up with a Data category. You can drill-down into the rss area item, then the channel, then the item if required, as shown in Figure 2.17.

What If You Don't See an "Item" Category in the Data?

If no "item" category appears when you drill-down into the data, this is because you need to add at the very least two entries recently to the twitter feed. Log into twitter and add a few test entries. Click "-Data" to remove the XML data source and attempt again to add the source as shown in step 18.

22. Now comes the easy part. You can drag and drop elements onto the artboard, and the data binding will all take place for you thanks to Blend. First, click on the title tag inside the data source (in the data category) and, with your mouse, drag it on top of the Grid element.

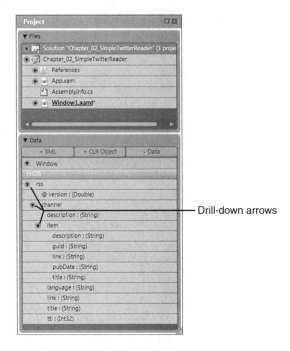

— Drill-down arrows

FIGURE 2.17   The drill-down mechanism provided, enabling you to view the data structure.

What Does Binding Really Mean?

When we use the term *binding*, we are referring to a relationship that is being created between two objects, values, widgets, etc. There is usually a source and a target. Depending on how the binding is specified, when a source value changes, the target reflects the change. Or, it is possible that the source could use the target value to change its value. See Chapter 13, "Data Binding," for more detailed information on binding and the options that are available in Expression Blend.

23. A Data Binding context menu displays, showing you some of the options you have in terms of the type of control you want to use to display the value. Select Label, which will then produce a Create Data Binding dialog for you (see Figure 2.18).

FIGURE 2.18   The list of controls suitable for displaying your bound data.

24. The Select Field property should read Content. Click OK. This produces an even bigger dialog called the Create Data Template dialog, which is shown in Figure 2.19. We will not go into the details of this dialog at this stage, but it should at least show you some data in the preview area to the right of the dialog as the one in Figure 2.19 does.

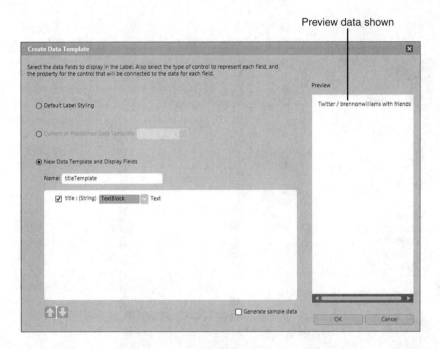

FIGURE 2.19   The Create Data Template dialog, complete with preview data.

25. Click OK. You will almost certainly have a large square Label element sitting in the center of your Grid, which is great. Manually resize this element so it sits neatly in the top left of the Grid layout. Again, use the pink border as a guide.

26. Now add your twitter post content using the item (Array) field from the Data category on the Project panel. Select and drag the Item (Array), specifically, to the center of the artboard. Notice that the element options have changed. All the elements shown are capable of presenting collections or arrays of fields. If you don't see Item (Array), then you need to go back to twitter and add some more posts. If you still don't see it, find the public timeline and look for the rss link for it, which should most definitely have an item array.

27. Select Listbox from the given choices and then make sure that ItemsSource is the property value shown in the Create Data Binding dialog and click OK.

28. Things look a little more complicated in the Create Data Template dialog than they did previously. Nevertheless, we will work with the dialog in the same way. You may notice in the preview box on the right side of the dialog that some of the values

look as if they have been duplicated. You will remove some bindings and change the order of others.

In Figure 2.20, notice how some of the fields have been unchecked. I have also used the re-ordering buttons to put the pubDate field at the top and have changed the content type from a TextBlock to a Label.

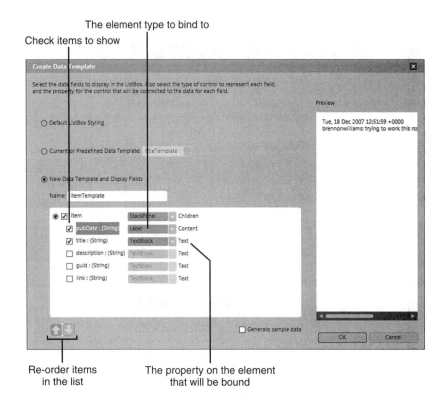

FIGURE 2.20   Fields that are required.

29. After clicking OK to return to the artboard, you should now have a Listbox with the chosen data fields showing as an item in your list. You are now going to perform some basic styling to move the elements into place on the artboard.

30. Making sure that the Grid element is still activated (has a yellow box around it) and that you have the Selection tool chosen in the toolbox (remember to press the V key if you need to make sure), add a Row to the Grid element. Add the RowDefinition comfortably below the title label, as shown in Figure 2.21. This figure also shows you how the Label needs to be laid out.

31. In the Objects and Timeline panel, right-click on the Label element that you added previously showing the title. If you are in Design view mode, from the context menu that appears, select View XAML, otherwise, when you select the Label you should see the corresponding XAML become highlighted in the XAML editor.

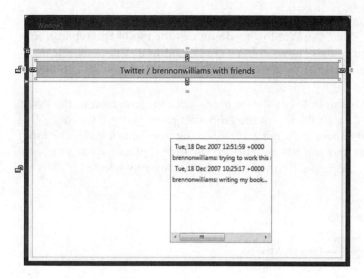

FIGURE 2.21   The position of the new RowDefinition.

32. You should now change or add some of the values in the Label elements line of markup to be:

    Width="Auto"

    HorizontalAlignment="Stretch"

    Margin="8,8,8,8"

    Add the following values and attributes to the same elements markup line:

    HorizontalContentAlignment ="Center"

    FontSize="16"

    Background="#FFFFC600"

33. Return to the Design view. The artboard should resemble Figure 2.21. If it doesn't, check your Label element markup against the following:

```
<Label Margin="8,8,8,8" Content="{Binding Mode=Default,
Source={StaticResource rssDS}, XPath=/rss/channel/title}"
        ContentTemplate="{DynamicResource titleTemplate}"
        Width="Auto"
        HorizontalAlignment="Stretch"
        HorizontalContentAlignment="Center"
        FontSize="16"
          Background ="#FFFFC600"/>
```

34. Select and then manually drag and stretch the Listbox element so that it fills the remaining space, using the pink padding guides to correctly align the element.

35. In the Objects and Timeline panel, find the button element you added to the project with the *Refresh* label. Double-click the element in the visual tree to activate it.

36. On the right side of the Blend application, find the Properties tab and select it. If you can't find the tab, select the Window menu item at the top of the application and then in the list, verify that *Properties* has a check next to it. You can check and uncheck it a few times, making sure it remains checked. This should display the Properties panel.

37. If the Properties panel is still in Event Viewer mode, click the icon next to the Event icon (shown in Figure 2.6). At the top of the Properties panel you will see the Property Search box, as shown in Figure 2.22. It has the word *Search* inside the input box. Enter the text **mar** and you will be returned the Layout property category containing the Margin properties for the button that is currently selected.

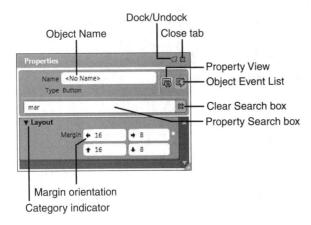

FIGURE 2.22   A quick overview of the Properties panel elements.

38. Enter the number **16** as the left and top margin property values and **8** as the right and bottom margins. You should now see that the button has moved on the artboard, aligned with the title Label and the Listbox element.

39. In the Object Name area of the Properties panel (shown in Figure 2.22), type **btnRefresh**.

40. Click on the Object Event list button (shown in Figure 2.22) and right at the very top you should see an event labeled *Click* with an empty field next to it. Double-click in the empty field next to the event label.

IMPORTANT:

If you have not installed Visual Studio 2005/2008 Standard Edition or above, you will receive a notification saying that a Click Event handler has been copied to the clipboard. You should open the Project tab next to the Properties tab and navigate to the file named Window1.xaml. You should be able to drill-down on that file to find another named Window1.xaml.cs. Double-click on this file to open it and insert the clipboard code directly after the following block of code:

```
public Window1()
{
    this.InitializeComponent();
    // Insert code required on object creation below this point.

}
```

Coding Up Your Twitter

You have completed the very simple layout of our twitter reader elements. Now you are going to add just a few lines of code to add a refresh capability to the application. Don't be too concerned about what this code actually means at this point; just know that the code is referring to the object we created in Blend that is responsible for getting the data feed. We are simply telling it to refresh when the button is clicked.

We continue on with the last four steps:

41. You should now have your click handler code pasted or automatically inserted into your code file, which looks like the following:

```
private void btnRefresh_Click(object sender, RoutedEventArgs e)
{


}
```

42. Inside the curly braces, add the code shown in Listing 2.5.

LISTING 2.5   Refreshing the Data Source

```
private void btnRefresh_Click(object sender, RoutedEventArgs e)
{
    XmlDataProvider myRSSBinding =
this.FindResource("rssDS") as XmlDataProvider;
    myRSSBinding.Refresh();
}
```

43. In Visual Studio, select the File menu at the top of the application, then select Save As. If you get a dialog asking whether you want to save the solution, leave the name and the location as it is shown, and click on the Save button to close the dialog.

44. Return to Expression Blend and press F5 to run the application.

I am hoping that you are able to see some posts in your twitter reader. Try adding some new posts in the twitter browser (in your web browser), then after a few seconds hit the refresh button.

If you cannot see any posts, all is not lost. You need to understand why this application can't function as a personal twitter reader, realistically only as a public list reader.

The twitter API (Application Programming Interface) specifies that only the public list is retrievable without authentication. Because adding authentication is a little beyond the scope of this chapter we should really set the data provider source to point to the public list to further test the application and ensure that the code works for the Refresh mechanism.

If you press F11, you should eventually switch back to XAML viewer mode, where you can search and find the <XmlDataProvider tag, which should be relatively close to the top of the page. Along the line of markup you will see an attribute (property) called *Source*. Replace the text inside the inverted commas with:

http://twitter.com/statuses/public_timeline.rss

Press F11 to return to the artboard and then F5 to test the application again. Give it about 30 seconds and then click on the Refresh button. You should eventually see the list change to represent the latest public twitter feed (see Figure 2.23).

FIGURE 2.23   The completed application with a running twitter RSS reader.

Summary

OK, the application isn't going to be a saleable item; but it was never meant to be. Of course, you can try your luck on eBay by all means.

A goal of this chapter was for you to move around the Blend application and start getting used to where things are. Start using the shortcut keys. They will speed up life for you and also give you a glimpse of the workflow between Expression Blend and Visual Studio. Earlier on you did manage to "change the world," even if it was only your world. It's a start! You can move on to conquering the rest of the world as you learn more skills throughout the rest of this book.

A great many of you reading this are designers. You are probably wincing at the thought of having to write a lot of code? The idea of Blend and using the declarative markup, XAML, is so you only have to write code that is necessary. Chapter 10 goes into the coding requirements that I believe all user interface/interactive designers will be required to know when using Blend in the Interactive Designer and XAML architect context. Master the code side of things to that level, and you will find working with Blend and Visual Studio a breeze.

The chapters leading up to Chapter 10 will be quite light on code, but it is present none the less. Don't be afraid of it—and don't expect to understand a concept right away. You'll grasp it once you've had some experience.

2

Expression Blend Panels

The Panels in Expression Blend would appear vaguely familiar both to designers and developers. Collectively, they are a mix of tools and property panels that assist in controlling UIElements, storyboards (for animations), events, properties, and Resources.

Some of the panels have hidden areas that contain more advanced features, and some do exactly what they say on the screen.

In this chapter you take a brief view of all the panels and their contents so that you know where you need to look in order to perform given functions.

Panels

Upon opening Expression Blend for the first time, you might be intimidated by the number of panels that fill up the Blend user interface. Don't be. These panels have a lot in common with applications you may have used before, both designer and developer orientated; and after a while, their use will become second nature.

Figure 3.1 shows the two panel layout modes that exist: design and animation. At the time of this writing, user modification of these panels is limited to undocking and resizing, which is quite limited in certain scenarios.

In either mode, you can select to show or hide any and/or all panels from the current view by using the Window menu. In design mode, the Results panel is hidden by default.

Pressing the Tab or F4 key hides or shows all panels in design/split view and F4 in XAML view only achieves the same. (Tab in XAML view inserts tabs in the editor). In design/split view, the Tab and F4 keys collapse the Properties panel to a ToolBox style menu located on the right side of the screen, as shown in Figure 3.2. What is also interesting about this view is that now when you click an Icon to view a property category, the entire set of properties—including advanced property options—are also shown, so it could be thought of as being an advanced view.

Design workspace   Animation workspace

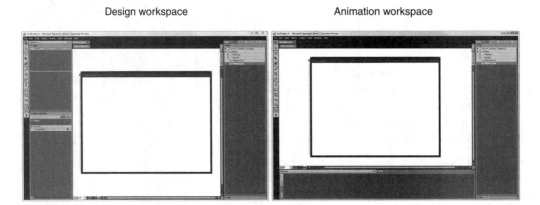

FIGURE 3.1   The design and animation modes, respectively.

FIGURE 3.2   The collapsed Properties panel.

When Tab Means Tab

If you select XAML editor view and your cursor is active on the screen, you can't use the Tab key to hide or show panels because the Tab key becomes part of the key down sequence used in text editing. The size of the Tab space used in the XAML editor is also adjustable from inside the Options panel, which will be covered shortly.

Are the predefined layouts the best layout for the purpose of animating and designing? "Not always," would be my answer, but for every user out there like me who doesn't think so, you may find a user who disagrees. It's about personal preference. Give them both a try, and you will make up your own mind fairly quickly. I personally stay in animation mode 99% of the time; it's just the way that I prefer to work.

In the next section you look at the most common elements of the panels and their uses so that you can find your way around the samples provided in the rest of this book.

Interaction

The Interaction panel contains a lot of functionality that is the subject of several chapters. Primarily used for element selection and the creation and modification of Storyboard animations, you need to know where specific items are to increase your productivity with Blend (see Figure 3.3).

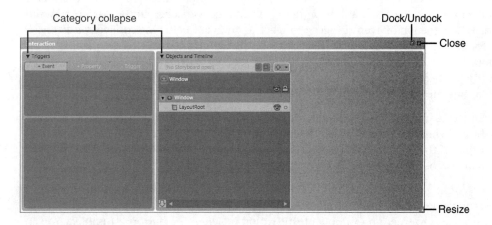

FIGURE 3.3   The panel areas that provide user customization and usage choice.

Category Collapse
Indicated by a triangle icon, when clicked the category area of the panel collapses. Selecting any part of the collapsed item expands the panel again.

Dock/Undock
This option is present in all detachable panels, allowing you to dock the panel to its predefined layout position or undock the panel for manual relocation.

Resizer
This is the only area of the panel that you can select and drag to resize the panel to a custom requirement.

The Interaction panel contains the Triggers category and the Objects and Timeline category.

Get to Know Two Panels Better Than the Rest

The Objects and Timeline and the Properties panels are probably the two you are most interested in and certainly will be the two main panels that you will work with. Take some extra time to get to know where everything is in these panels to increase your productivity.

Triggers

Triggers are predefined sets of property values (property trigger) or event listeners (event trigger).

The term *Trigger* realistically means that an action (or series of actions) will begin when either a property condition evaluates to true or an event is raised.

Imagine, if you will, that you have a button element in your project; and when the user clicks the button you want that button to slowly change its background color from White to Red. This is the job of event triggers; to react to an Event being raised. Event triggers listen for all the events being fired by all the objects within the scope of the parent Window. When the button is clicked and the subsequent Button_Click event is raised, the event trigger then goes about performing its series of actions, which in this case would be to call a timeline that changes the background property of the button from White to Red.

A similar trigger (defined as a property trigger) is watching the property values of the specified object. When the property change notification fires, the trigger evaluates its settings against that of the object. In this case the button property IsMouseDown would be true, so you could also begin a timeline that changes the background color of the button.

Trigger recording is also switched on when editing a property trigger, which means you can set the values of any other properties for that object that will be applied when the trigger evaluates to true. An example of this would be when the button is disabled. You can record all the property values (text color = grey, background = grey) so that they are applied directly to the object. Conversely, you would have a property trigger for when the button becomes active to set its property values to give the appearance that the control is active.

Triggers become clearer as you get your hands dirty to create them, first shown in Chapter 8, "An Example Control Using Just the Tools Palette," and then in detail in Chapter 14, "Animations with Storyboards" (see Figure 3.4).

Trigger Types

Two types of triggers are supported at present within the Blend UI: Event and Property triggers (see Table 3.1). When enabled, these buttons provide a pop-up box list with the relevant events or properties available.

Remove Trigger

Removes the active trigger and its actions from the collection.

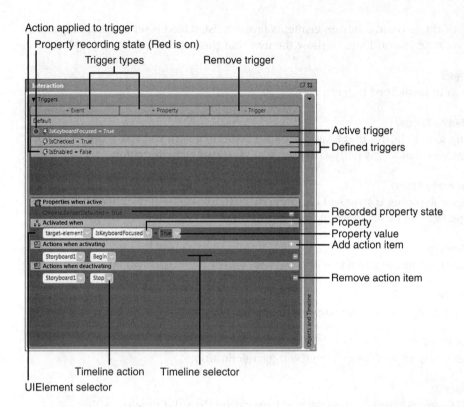

FIGURE 3.4   The areas that make up the Triggers category inside the Interaction panel.

TABLE 3.1   **Trigger Types**

Trigger Type	Description
Event Trigger	Event triggers provide a method of listening and acting upon the specified event being raised.
Property Trigger	Property triggers provide a method of implementing actions when a property evaluates the specified condition as true. The code IsMouseOver = False evaluates the trigger to be true when the mouse is not over the property owner.

Active Trigger
The currently selected trigger that defined actions and or recorded property states will be applied to.

Property Recording State
When a property trigger is the active trigger, a Red circle indicates that Property Recording is on while an empty circle indicates Property Recording is off.

Property Recording means that any property values changed for any object will be recorded as the required state of the object, when a property evaluates to true.

An example of this is when a Button elements property IsEnabled is set to false. Properties change the way the button looks to show the user that the button is, in fact, disabled.

Defined Triggers
The collection of predefined triggers.

Action Applied to Trigger
The lightning icon indicates that a valid action is associated with the active trigger, either a recorded property state or a defined action, such as starting an animation.

Recorded Property State
When Property Recoding is switched on, property changes will be shown here as the state that all properties will be set to when the trigger is fired.

UIElement Selector
Selects the element in the visual tree of objects for which the trigger will be applied.

Timeline Selector
All timelines available within the scope of the parent object will be available to select.

Add/Remove items
Add or remove actions and items from the trigger definition.

Timeline Action
Begin, Stop, Pause, Skip to Fill, Resume, and Remove are the valid timeline actions.

Property
The property that will be evaluated. When an event trigger is specified, this will be the event for which to listen.

Property Value
Only available for Property triggers, which is the value that the property must equal in order to fire the trigger. In event triggers, the term *raised* is automatically applied.

Objects and Timelines

The Objects and Timelines panel is where you direct the animation sequences recorded as storyboards in your application (see Figure 3.5a). It is important to note that Blend uses the predefined layout style of Animation workspace to enable you to work more productively with a timeline by placing the Objects and Timeline panel horizontally, allowing you to view more information about your Timeline.

The Objects and Timeline category is one of the most used areas of any of the panels, because you are continually switching between UIElements, activating parents to add children, and so on.

As Figure 3.5a shows, this category has a lot going on. With large collections of UIElements spread throughout the visual element tree, you are advised to group as many

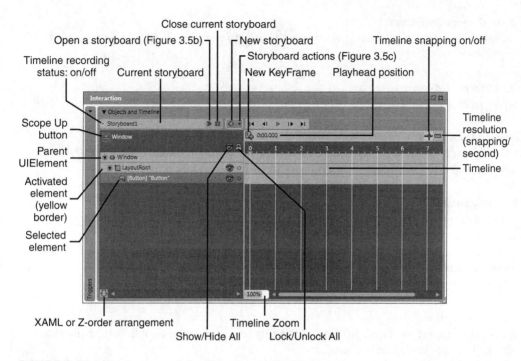

FIGURE 3.5A   The features of the Objects and Timeline panel.

controls as possible and where practical. Element naming also plays an important part here, because elements are not named by default when added to the project. You can imagine if you have 10 button objects on the screen and you want to find a specific one, you are going to get RSI trying to find it.

This panel category plays an important role in both design and animation, because you will also use the Timeline functions of the panel to define animated property changes. See Chapter 14 for a detailed look at timelines.

Timeline Recording Status On/Off

When Timeline recording is On (default), property changes are recorded as KeyFrames. These recorded property changes will transition as an animation. When Timeline recording is off, modifications made to the control properties are not recorded in the Storyboard as animated changes.

Open a Storyboard

All timelines created within the current scope will be available via the Storyboard Picker dialog box (see the next section, "Storyboard Picker").

Current Storyboard

The current storyboard with which the user is working. To change the name of the storyboard, double-click in this panel and edit the present value.

Close Current Storyboard
Closes the current storyboard and returns the user to the normal editing features of the application.

New Storyboard
Select to create a new storyboard.

Storyboard Actions
Allows you to choose actions associated with the current storyboard, such as duplication and reversal. The Storyboard Actions drop-down menu is shown in Figure 3.5c.

Timeline Snapping
When turned on, the playhead position snaps to equal incremented values specified by the resolution (default is 10).

Timeline Resolution (Snapping/Second)
Allows the user to specify the snapping increment value.

Playhead Position
Shows the current playhead position of the timeline. You can manually adjust the timeline by double-clicking in this area.

New KeyFrame
Select to add a new KeyFrame at the current playhead position and on the currently selected element.

Timeline
Shows KeyFrames and animated property changes.

Lock/Unlock All
When enabled against all (or individual) elements, the Element properties are locked completely, so you cannot change the element's colors or the location. Unlocking the set or single element returns the element to the normal usage state.

Timeline Zoom
Zoom the timeline in or out to control the accuracy of time values and the playhead position shown.

Show/Hide All
Select to hide or show the element of choice or above the parent element to hide or show all child elements.

XAML/Z-Order Arrangement
View the visual element tree either in order of appearance or in the order that the XAML markup lists elements.

Selected Element

A single mouse click sets an element as the current element to which KeyFrames and animations apply.

Activated Element (Yellow Border)

Additional elements added become children of the currently activated element. Double-click to activate an element.

Parent UIElement

The parent element within this scope.

Scope Up Button

When editing templates, the Scope Up button returns the user back up the scope tree.

Storyboard Picker

See Figure 3.5b for the Storyboard Picker.

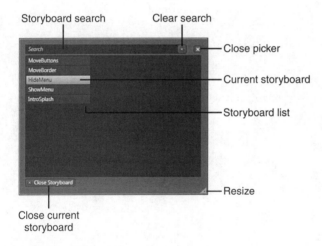

Storyboard search   Clear search

Close picker

Current storyboard

Storyboard list

Close current storyboard

Resize

FIGURE 3.5B   The Storyboard Picker.

Storyboard Search

This is a case-insensitive search box for your list of defined storyboards.

Clear Search

Clears the current search results.

Current Storyboard

The active storyboard.

Close Storyboard

When a storyboard is open, as shown in Figure 3.5b, this button becomes enabled, allowing you to close the current storyboard.

Storyboard Actions

See Figure 3.5c for storyboard actions.

FIGURE 3.5C   The storyboard actions as they appear in a pop-up.

Storyboard actions are available only if you have a storyboard currently selected. If you haven't chosen one, the only enabled option in the pop-up is the New function.

New

Creates a new storyboard.

Duplicate

Duplicates the active storyboard.

Reverse

Creates a new instance of the current storyboard, but with the entire timeline collection reversed.

Delete

Deletes the current storyboard.

Rename

Renames the current storyboard.

Close

Closes the current storyboard.

Resources

Figure 3.6 shows all available Resources for the application with no Filter present.

Create New Resource Dictionary

Creates an external XAML file in which to store resources.

Filter Resource List

By selecting an element in the Objects and Timeline panel, and then selecting that element again in the Resource List, clicking on the Filter button shows only those resources available to the selected element.

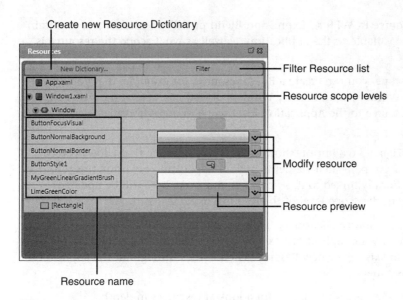

FIGURE 3.6   A look at some of the Resource panel features.

Resource Scope Levels

Scopes include the following:

▶ Application level. Resources you designate as being available to all Windows, Forms, and so on.

▶ Document level (Window). Resources stored here are available only to the Window in which they are created.

▶ Object level (element). Resources are available only to a specific object.

Various resources will be shown at one or more scoped levels.

Resource Name

The name of the resource.

Resource Preview

A thumbnail preview of the resource, which can be represented by icons, images, and text.

Modify Resource

If available, the Resource property viewer shows to enable live changes to the selected Resource. Any changes are visible instantly in the live UI environment of Blend.

Resources are an integral part of WPF applications and can be made available to other applications by saving resources in a Resource Dictionary (.xaml file).

A resource takes many forms, from a Brush type object, a Style collection, a 3D object material, or even an opacity mask. Almost anything can be created, modified, applied, or consumed as a resource in WPF, so Expression Blend provides a nice way of maintaining what is currently available to the application, as well as what scope the resource is available to.

When talking about scope, you can create a Brush resource, for example, that you want to use only in a specific Window, so that other Window objects can't see and or use it. You could also add that resource to the Application level scope to make it available everywhere within the project.

You will also note in Figure 3.6 a button showing next to a resource that allows you to modify the base resource type. When elements in your application are using this resource, they are usually dynamically linked to it, so changes you make here will be updated immediately throughout the scope level of the resource usage.

As briefly mentioned, a Resource Dictionary file is an external .xaml file that contains the same XAML you write in your applications as a method of distributing resources. You can create and add items to existing or new Resource Dictionaries throughout the application and not just from this panel.

See Chapter 16, "Using Resources for Skins," for a look at resources in depth.

Project Panel

Just as other panels (such as the Properties panel) contain separate categories, you can collapse and expand either or both the Files and Data categories. As shown in Figure 3.7, the Data category allows you to import and maintain data sources in your application.

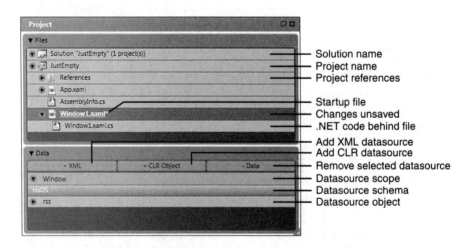

FIGURE 3.7   The Project panel with the Files and Data categories.

Files
Solution Name   The name of the current Visual Studio Solution (which is a collection of 1 or more projects). If requiring editing the application in Visual Studio, you are advised to

right click on the item and select Edit in Visual Studio. This will ensure you have the entire solution available to you as well as proper IntelliSense help.

Project Name   The name of the current project.

Project References   Valid references may be added to or removed from the context menu of this item. References are connections to .NET .dll or .exe files that contain referable objects (such as class types) inside them.

Startup File   The current file that starts when you run the application. You may also set a different file as the "Startup" by right-clicking on the item and selecting Startup from the context menu. The Startup object is always shown underlined.

.NET Code Behind File   The partial class file associated with the parent XAML file.

The Files category is not dissimilar in layout to that of the Visual Studio Project panel, although you will find a distinct lack of features by comparison. You can add references and so forth, but you have no control over build configurations and real project properties.

Can Blend Handle Larger Projects and Solutions?

The short answer is Yes. Blend 2 by default uses the same solution structure as Visual Studio, whereas Blend 1 created only projects but could still open full Visual Studio solutions. You can use and view full solutions, but creating multiple project types in Blend is something of a pain in present versions.

When creating large solutions from an architectural point of view, you should become proficient at using Visual Studio.

Visual Studio allows you to create an empty solution and include only the projects required for that part of the application. This sometimes makes it easier when working in a team, because the team members then are looking only at the areas of the solution that are required for a particular task.

Visual Studio also allows you to specify pre- and post-build events which are currently not supported in Expression Blend.

You can edit a given file by selecting Edit externally from the context menu, or you can opt to edit the entire solution in Visual Studio, which is the recommended practice as you will then receive full IntelliSense for your solution.

In Blend 1, editing a file externally opened up Notepad.exe, whereas Blend 2 supports full Visual Studio integration.

Changes Unsaved   Whenever you make changes to a Window or User control, you will see an asterisk (*) appear to the right of the name of the file indicating that changes have not yet been saved.

Data

Add XML Datasource   Select to browse and add a valid XML Datasource. You can manually change the settings and add X-Path Definitions in the resulting dialog box.

Add CLR Datasource   Select to browse for a CLR object from referenced assemblies to be used as a Datasource.

Remove Selected Datasource   Removes a selected Datasource from the project.

Datasource Scope   Refers to the level of object(s) that can reference and use the Datasource.

Datasource Schema   Can be specified or inferred.

Datasource Object   The valid Datasource object containing node definitions for drag-and-drop functionality.

A lot of work has been done to ensure a simple yet feature-rich databinding environment in Expression Blend. The Data category allows you to control your databinding to a very fine degree and has a superb drag-and-drop function where you can drag Datasource nodes directly onto the artboard to be shown presentation options based on the data collection type. Blend works out if the data should be shown in a ListBox type control or a Menu type control and gives you the option to choose.

See Chapter 13, "Data Binding," for a detailed look at data binding.

Properties Panel

Object Name

The default name for elements added to your artboard is <No Name>, (Window is shown in Figure 3.8 for the selected type) which results in the element not being accessible from the code behind page. When objects are used in a storyboard, they are given a new default value—for example, button1—but you wouldn't want to rely on this naming convention in an application.

You should try to ascertain which elements need to be named for use in code and agree on a naming convention before you start creating your application.

Object Type

The assembly type is referenced within the class namespace.

Case Insensitive Search

Type a search phrase or combination of letters into the input box to see a list of properties and their categories.

Property View Mode

Shows the selected object's properties.

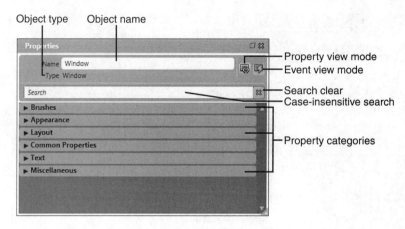

FIGURE 3.8   An overview of the comprehensive Property panel.

Event View Mode
Shows the selected objects available events.

Search Clear
Clears the search phrase from the input box.

Property Categories
All available property categories for the selected object. These categories change depending on the object definition.

The Property panel and contained categories do take a little while to get used to. Once you consistently use the property search facility, you will be wondering how you ever lived without. The same facility is not present for events, but it is slated for future versions.

Depending on the property categories that are defined by the element/control, the developer(s) determines how many and the type of categories visible. It would be prudent investment of your time to add controls to a blank project and then familiarize yourself with the categories available.

An overview of the most common property categories follows with the most detailed commentary located in those chapters that deal specifically with the category at hand.

Brushes
Properties   The property types are determined by the control type being modified. To modify a particular property, select it and then set the brush type. As shown in Figure 3.9, a Window element is selected and the relevant Brushes properties are shown.

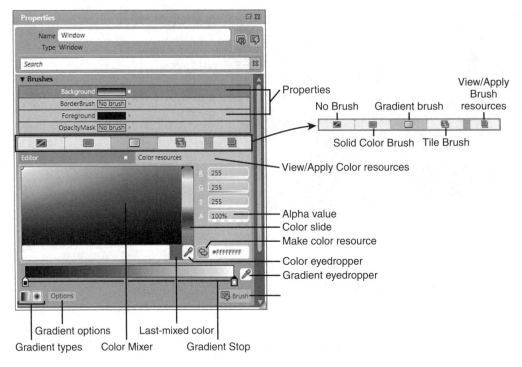

FIGURE 3.9   A Gradient Brush being created, along with descriptions of the major parts of the Brushes category panel.

No Brush   No brush is different from just having an invisible brush filling a property. This is equivalent to specifying null or nothing in the code for this property.

Although you will receive better rendering performance for elements that have No Brush applied to them as opposed to an invisible or transparent brush, you should also understand that mouse events are not raised against elements that have No Brush applied to them. In the case of a Button style, you will need mouse events to understand when the user has clicked on the button.

Color Mixer   The standard color mixer workspace.

Gradient Stop   You can drag these Gradient stops to create differing effects. To create additional stops, click on the gradient bar. To remove stops click, hold, and drag your mouse off the gradient bar.

Gradient Types   At present only Linear and Radial exist in the Blend UI.

Gradient Options   Allows you to control the applied gradient visual effect, from Pad, Reflected, or Repeat.

Last Mixed Color   The last color "mixed" in the workspace.

Color Eyedropper   Selecting and moving this eyedropper grabs any color in any Window that you can view.

Make Brush Resource   Converts the specified Brush to a resource, either locally within the applications scope levels or in a resource dictionary file.

Gradient Eyedropper   A strangely cool tool that allows you to click and hold the eyedropper tool and then drag it across to a given point in the artboard. Every color and the distances between them are re-created as a gradient pattern and applied to the current object property.

Make Color Resource   Converts the currently created color to a color resource, either locally within the applications scope levels or in a resource dictionary file. This is different from a Brush resource, because you can use two Color resources to specify two Gradient stops.

Alpha Value   The Alpha value of the current color, which controls the color opacity of the brush, as opposed to the entire object's opacity, which is a property in the Appearance category.

View Color Resources   Views local and system color resources.

View Brush Resources   Views local and system brush resources.

Tile Brush   A strange brush that allows you to apply brush resources as a property and then control their pattern settings. That is, you can Tile, Fill, or UniformFill a specified property with the resources brush.

Gradient Brush   As shown in Figure 3.9, the Gradient brush allows you to specify multiple colors to be applied to a brush. There are two types of Gradient brushes available in Blend, RadialGradient and LinearGradient brush types.

Solid Color Brush   Applies a solid, singular color to the property.

Color Slide   Modifies the mixing palette base color.

Appearance
Object Opacity   Controls the entire object's opacity—0% is invisible, 100% is opaque as shown in Figure 3.10.

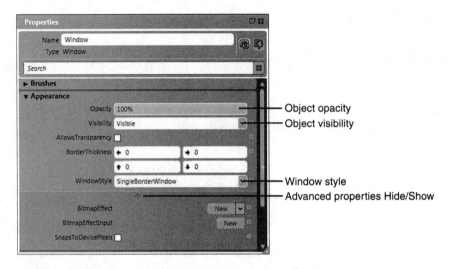

FIGURE 3.10   The appearance properties of a Window object.

Object Visibility An object can be either the usual visible or hidden values, but in Blend, an object can also be collapsed. This is particularly important not only when you want an object to be invisible but also when you don't want it to take up any screen space.

Window Style You can choose one of the following four options:

1. None (used for borderless windows)
2. SingleBorder
3. ThreeDBorder
4. ToolWindow

Advanced Properties Hide/Show Most property categories contain extended properties, with some containing dozens of additional options. This is another good reason to get used to working with the property search box.

Even though in Figure 3.10 you see only three properties, if you add a Rectangle to your artboard (and select it), you will see 10+ additional properties in the Advanced Properties drop-down. You should review all the Advanced Properties of as many controls as possible to familiarize yourself with additional control functionality.

Layout

Set to "Auto" Sizing When you need an object to use its Margin and Alignment settings to ascertain Width, or allow a parent to control the object's Width value, set a Width and or Height property to Auto. The property type is a double, so if you need to set this value in code, you must set the value as double.NAN. NAN stands for "not a number." It is important to try to set all element Width and Height properties to Auto should you intend to localize your application. For example, label values can vary tremendously among languages, so you want your element(s) to grow or shrink based on their content as opposed to a fixed Width that may truncate their value(s).

Stretch Alignment   Alignment determines how the objects align within their parent containers. Stretch fills the available area, and the actual width is controlled by any additional margin settings.

Margin Settings   The Margin values determine how far the edge of an element sits from its parent boundary. It is important to understand the "boundary" meaning, particularly when an element is placed inside a row or column of a parent Grid. The margin determines the distance from the cell boundaries, as opposed to the entire Grid element boundaries. (This is discussed in detail in Chapter 5, "UIElement: Control Embedding.")

Content Alignment   If this object is to contain additional objects, you can control its alignment by default from this property. As shown in Figure 3.11, many controls have a default HorizontalContentAlignment set to Left and VerticalContentAlignment set to Top.

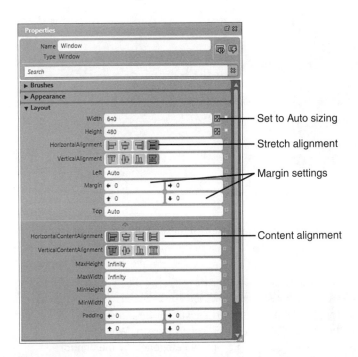

FIGURE 3.11   The standard Layout properties for a Window object.

Common Properties
Application Icon   You can either navigate to an icon stored on your machine or use the drop-down arrow to select an image asset that is already stored as a resource in your application. Interestingly, in previous development platforms you were only allowed to use

images in a specific *.icon format. In Blend you can select any image type that is supported (such as BMP, JPEG, TIFF, and so on) from any location, and the image will be used as the icon for the application.

As shown in Figure 3.12, by default no value is assigned to the icon property. Your application will use the default application icon defined by your operating system if you leave the property blank.

Application icon

Window title

FIGURE 3.12   The most common properties for a Window object.

Window Title   The title of the Window as shown in the taskbar and at the top of the Window when the application is running.

Properties Change Based on Type

At this point, you can probably tell that all these properties will not be the same as a different type of object if selected in the Objects and Timeline category. When you create a control or object, the properties are assigned property categories by the control author, so it is a good idea to open all the properties of all the controls to familiarize yourself with any specific properties that exist in only a single control type.

Text

Various text-based controls allow you to control different property settings for the text that is contained within them, such as a Label control, which has different properties available in the advanced property area compared with a RichTextBox control. The Text property category also allows you to modify the displayed text in controls such as a Button or ListItem (see Figure 3.13).

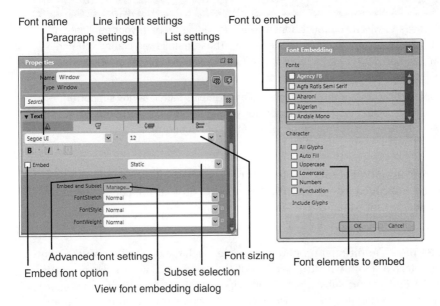

FIGURE 3.13   The standard Text properties category and the related Font Embedding dialog box.

Font Name   Simply drop down the list to choose the appropriate font or begin typing the font name in the input area of the combo box. Segoe UI is the default font used by Expression Blend when installed on the Vista operating system. Tahoma is the default for Windows XP.

Paragraph Settings   Within this tab you can set line heights and text spacing properties with controls that support such actions.

Line Indent Settings   Set left and right indents from this tab for controls that support such actions.

List Settings   For the creation of bulleted lists and for controls that support such actions.

Font Size   Sets the size of the applied font from this drop-down list.

Embed Font Option   False (unchecked) by default, this option embeds the selected font face into your application.

Can Any Font Be Embedded?

Fonts have licenses to which you must adhere when including them in your application. See each font's license information for more details. Those details will clarify whether you are allowed to use the font if the application runs in Windows XP, for example, as opposed to Windows Vista.

WPF also supports only certain font face types. For example, Sahali is not supported, so if you intend to provide localization support for your application, consult the Windows SDK or MSDN for information on which fonts are supported.

Subset Selection   This option allows you to specify if only the characters used in this element should be embedded into the application (Static) or if all the characters of the selected font should be embedded (Dynamic).

Advanced Font Settings   Additional properties become available depending on the control that is currently selected. From with this section of the category, you can also click the Manage button for Embed and Subset, which will open the Font Embedding dialog box, as shown in Figure 3.13. This dialog box is also accessible by clicking the Tools menu and then choosing Font Embedding.

Font to Embed   The listbox contains all the fonts available to your application. You can scroll through the list and select which fonts to specifically include.

Font Element to Embed   A font is a collection of various parts that make up the entire font. For example, most (but not all) fonts have both an uppercase and lowercase version of characters. These options allow you to specify exactly which parts (or all) of the font that you wish to embed. Why is this important? Some fonts are very large (20+ MB), so you if you intend to embed that font, your application executable footprint will grow to accommodate it. If you are using only a specific font for numbers, for example, then it makes much more sense to embed only the number parts of the font.

Miscellaneous

This particular property category varies greatly from control to control and is the default placement of properties that are not given a specific category when they are created. The following is a look at a specific property set for a button control object (see Figure 3.14).

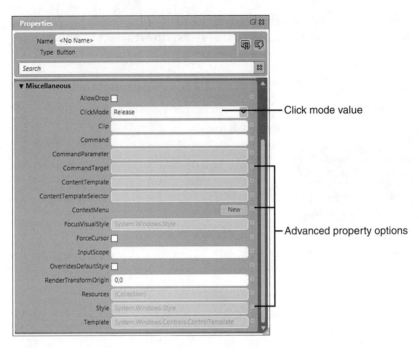

FIGURE 3.14   Different sets of properties that are categorized by the control author as being Miscellaneous.

Click Mode Value   This property is specific to a Button object and lets you decide how to tell when a user has clicked on a button. You could set it to Pressed or Hover, which will raise the click event when true.

Advanced Property Options   Right about now, you might be thinking that there appears to be two places for the Advanced property. Well, there is a difference. I believe that one should have been called Additional property collections, while this particular area I am talking about now should remain as Advanced property options.

Next to every property in every category, there is a little square box. This box allows you to specify advanced property values for the specific property you are modifying.

This is discussed further in the next section.

Advanced Properties   Depending on the property type and level of access that you are currently in, these options become available; for example, when you are editing the template of an element, the Template Binding can be used. Chapter 13 covers Template Binding.

As previously stated, every property has a little box to the right of the property. When you click on this box, the Advanced property dialog box, as shown in Figure 3.15, displays.

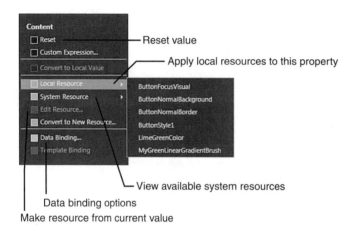

FIGURE 3.15   The Advanced property dialog box.

Reset   This handy option resets a property to a default value. An example of this is when you modify any (or all) of the margin property values. Instead of selecting each margin input area to return it to 0, simply select the Reset menu option and all of the inputs will be returned to 0.

Apply Local Resource   Similar to when you set a local resource brush or color to a background property in the Brushes category, clicking here when enabled presents all the matching resource types for the property you are viewing, as shown in Figure 3.15.

View System Resources   Similar to local resources, Blend gives you the ability to apply preset system value resources to a property. This is important if you intend for your application to apply user-specified settings for their entire system, which may assist with such things as accessibility.

Convert to New Resource   You can make just about any property value into a resource. For example, if you want a button's Tooltip property value to match that of the buttons content (string only) property, you could make the content property a resource by selecting this option, giving it an appropriate name. Then, when you select the Tooltip's Advanced property options, you will see the resource you just created in the Local Resource list to which you can then apply.

Data Bind Element   If you need to bind the value to a data provider or even a corresponding value type on another object, click here to view the data binding dialogs. See Chapter 13 for more details on data binding.

Properties in General

The more you use the properties panel and category panels, the easier they become. Optimized workflow elements, such as advanced properties and property searches, are outstanding additions to the property dialog. Use these as often as possible.

Results

The Results panel is one of those panels that you don't know is there until something goes wrong. At the time of this writing, Blend had improved with how it delivered bad news, but it still has no serious debugging features incorporated. Visual Studio is the tool of choice when errors arise. F12 hides or shows the Results panel.

Output

The most important part of Figure 3.16 is seeing the statement at the bottom: The build has successfully completed.

FIGURE 3.16   The Results panel delivers compiler information as a project is being built.

Errors

At the time of writing, the error output did little to realistically help in a time of great crisis. I would expect this functionality to improve dramatically as the XAML editor improves. I would not take the Line number value as gospel (meaning they are not always accurate). As previously stated, if you find that you can't track and trace an error quickly in Expression Blend using this error panel (shown in Figure 3.17), open your project in

Visual Studio and build it from there. You will be able to accurately determine build issues in the Visual Studio environment. When an error does show, however, the first thing to do is double-click the error in the Results panel, which most of the time will take you directly to the offending line of XAML for you to fix.

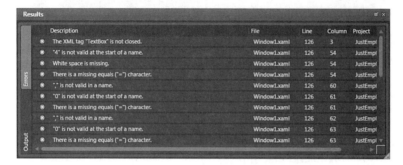

FIGURE 3.17   Almost as exciting as Figure 3.16.

You can dramatically improve the debugging information shown in Visual Studio 2005 by adding an Exception option that is specific for XAML errors as shown in the following steps.

1. Open Visual Studio. You will need to open a solution as well.
2. Select Debug from the top menu.
3. Select the Exceptions menu item.
4. The Exceptions window should now appear.
5. Click Add.
6. In the type drop-down list, select Common Language Runtime Exceptions.
7. Add the name System.Windows.Markup.XamlParseException and click OK.
8. You should now see the new Exception highlighted with a check box to the right of the Thrown column. Check this box.
9. Click OK to exit the dialog.

Asset Library Panel

The Asset Library panel contains a lot of functionality that you will use quite often within your application UI development. Predefined, referenced, and custom controls are all available from this panel (see Figure 3.18).

Search Library
Case-insensitive searching of all the controls in the current Control Collection. Control collections are selectable from the Control collections and Style libraries panel.

Control Collections and Style Libraries
System controls represent standard WPF controls that have had a degree of styling or animated properties added to them. As you create Style templates for controls, if you add

or define those styles inside a Resource Dictionary, that Dictionary will appear in this panel under Simple Styles.

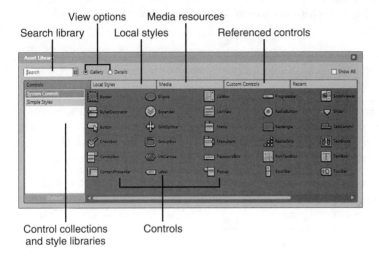

FIGURE 3.18   The versatile Asset Library panel.

Local Styles

If you create a control template and define it inside the local file instead of a Resource Dictionary, that Style template will appear in the Local Styles tab.

Controls

Each resource dictionary contains collections of controls that have specific styling or templates applied to the base level of these controls. You can select a control directly and drag it onto the artboard, or double-click it to make it available from the Recent Controls button on the toolbox (just above the button you click to view the Asset Library Panel).

Referenced Controls

When, and if, you create user or custom controls, once referenced to the project, they will be available in this tab for you to view and select from. You can also reference existing controls from third parties or other projects, and those controls will also be available in this tab.

Media Resources

Any resources that you add to your project are available in this tab for you to select and reuse. You will see resources created and added from style templates you add as well.

Views

You can modify the method used to display the Control Collections to you by selecting either Gallery or Details.

Summary

You have now seen your fair share of Blend panels and the categories that reside within them. Take every opportunity to explore the panels, in particular, the Properties and Object and Timeline panels.

Some objects can contain hundreds of properties, so getting accustomed to using the property search box is a habit that you should quickly form. Just remember to clear the search after you have used it!

Also, take considerable note of the property names as you change them. These names are exactly the same regardless of whether you are entering them into a line of XAML or from code in Visual Studio. For example, the property Width in the Blend Property panel (Layout category) is the same as Width="100" in XAML or Button.Width =100 in code.

Obviously, you explored only certain property groups in this chapter, because it would have taken forever to detail each and every control type and property type. You can find more detailed information on control properties in the Windows SDK or MSDN online. You use quite a few different controls throughout the rest of the book, so you will see more and more property types as you progress.

CHAPTER 4

XAML for Beginners

In this chapter you take a look at XAML, where it is from, and how it relates to .NET code. While you will gain a basic understanding of the markup, remember that one of the goals of Expression Blend is to remove the need for a user to actually have to create large amounts of hand-coded XAML. I obviously recommend learning XAML to a very detailed level. There are scenarios in which WPF and XAML support certain actions, but the Blend UI does not yet implement those scenarios, such as Ancestor Template binding. The good news is that most of these scenarios are advanced, so understanding the base level of XAML and the XAML that Blend produces is certainly a great starting point.

XAML Syntax

In order to perhaps appreciate XAML, we should take a look at how its great granddaddy XML came along and changed the world of computing.

I bet a lot of you didn't know (including me until I researched it...) that XML (in its initial format) was actually created back in the late 1960s. It was called GML (General Markup Language) back then, but was used only for documentation systems in IBM.

Apparently when it was brought into use by the ISO standards people in 1986, they named it SGML, and away it went from there. HTML, the cornerstone of the web is a derivative of SGML as it was universally agreed to be one of the best ways of sharing text-based data.

XML is a descendent of the original SGML, taking some three-quarters of its functionality, but also reducing the complexity of the SGML structure by around 80%. XML was designed (as was SGML) to allow the creation of other derived language scripts, but realistically the format stayed very similar regardless of which derivative you use today. XML, HTML, XHTML: They all use a tag system to declare objects and/or elements, or in the case of XAML, to declare objects in design time as well as providing a mechanism to set the properties and event handlers of those respective objects.

So if you hate looking at XML, then you are going to wince when you go to do some hand cranking of your XAML markup because that is what XAML really is. Still, despite all my original views about working with an XML derived script, I must admit that XAML is starting to win me over.

Maybe it's just that I like all the possible syntax colors of the Visual Studio coding environment—who knows?

XAML Elements

When we talk about elements in XAML, we are looking at the complete block of markup as it refers to an object.

For example, the markup listing in Listing 4.1 shows the declaration of a button, with some properties set as well as a reference to the Click event. Figure 4.1 illustrates how the coding appears in the Objects and Timeline panel.

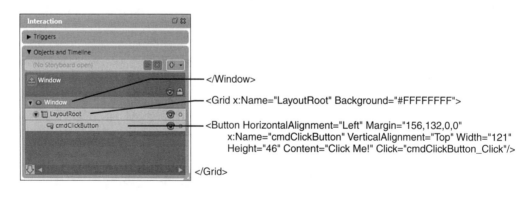

FIGURE 4.1   The Button element as it appears in the visual element tree exposed by the Objects and Timeline panel.

LISTING 4.1   XAML Button Declaration

```
<Button
    HorizontalAlignment="Left"
    Margin="156,132,0,0"
    x:Name="cmdClickButton"
    VerticalAlignment="Top"
    Width="121"
```

```
Height="46"
Content="Click Me!"
Click="cmdClickButton_Click" />
```

Finding Elements in XAML

A nice little work flow addition to Expression Blend is that you can select any element in the Objects and Timeline panel, right-click it for the context menu, and select View XAML, which will switch you to the XAML viewer with your selected element highlighted.

This workflow is only available when you are not in Split View mode.

Note, in Figure 4.1, how each element in the Objects and Timeline category is related based on its position within the parent element; for example the entire Button element is inside the <Grid ...> and </Grid> tags.

The very first element is the Window, which is referred to as the Root element of type System.Windows.Window. The Root element is where all the reference declarations for this XAML file are added, which enables the rest of the file to adhere to specific formats as well as to contain references to other objects, including CLR objects (via their namespace) that you may create.

Two important areas within the Root elements XAML markup (which are not shown in Figure 4.1) are the default namespace and the referred namespaces that are specified in the following attributes:

```
xmlns="http://schemas.microsoft.com/winfx/2006/xaml/presentation"
xmlns:x="http://schemas.microsoft.com/winfx/2006/xaml"
```

These two declarations, the first being the default (no colon after xmlns) tells the compiler that all the elements within this XAML file are WPF elements. The second is a special namespace that ensures certain XAML utilities are included before compilation is attempted. It also allows other child elements (like the button element in Listing 4.1) to use these special features, for example, object naming.

If you look closely at Listing 4.1, you should be able to see the properties that have been set, as well as the declaration of the Click Handler event. In point of fact, if we wanted to create this same button in code it would look similar to Listing 4.2.

LISTING 4.2 The .NET Equivalent to the Previously Shown XAML Button Declaration

```
Button cmdClickButton = new Button();
        cmdClickButton.HorizontalAlignment = HorizontalAlignment.Left;
        cmdClickButton.Margin = new Thickness(156, 132, 0, 0);
        cmdClickButton.VerticalAlignment = VerticalAlignment.Top;
        cmdClickButton.Width = 121;
```

```
cmdClickButton.Height = 46;
cmdClickButton.Content = "Click Me!";
cmdClickButton.Click +=new RoutedEventHandler(cmdClickButton_Click);

this.LayoutRoot.AddChild(cmdClickButton);
```

Nested Elements

When an element block is added inside another element block (such as the Button element inside the Grid element in Figure 4.1), the outermost element (the Grid, in this case) is referred to as the Parent element.

The term *Nested* means that a tag is placed between the opening < and terminating /> of an element, so for example:

```
<Tag1>
    <Tag2/>
</Tag1>
```

You would say, in this example, that Tag2 is a nested element of Tag1; Tag1 is the parent.

In Listing 4.3 you can see that a Button element is added inside a Border element, which, in turn is inside a Grid element, which also has a parent Grid element.

LISTING 4.3   Nested Elements

```
<Grid x:Name="LayoutRoot" Background="#FFFFFFFF">
    <Grid Margin="130,130,130,130" Background="#FFB7F8FF">
        <Border Margin="100,20,100,20">
            <Button Content="Button"/>
        </Border>
    </Grid>
</Grid>
```

Child Elements

So does this mean that a control, such as a Grid, can be either a Parent or a Child? Certainly. Control types, such as Grid, allow other controls to be embedded inside them. This is generally referred to as a *child collection*. Other controls, such as ListBox, have specific child elements. For example, ListBoxItem controls can be used as the child items to display in the ListBox.

For children to be accepted by the .NET compiler, the parent object must implement either the IAddChild or ICollection interface or an error will be raised when you go to build your project.

If you go back to Listing 4.2, notice the last line of code:

```
this.LayoutRootAddChild(cmdClickButton);
```

The AddChild method is defined by the IAddChild interface for the Window object, which is implemented within the inherited class System.Windows.Controls.ContentControl, from which the System.Windows.Window class inherits.

The Required Child Interfaces

The IAddChild interface implements two methods, AddChild and AddText, which are most commonly seen in controls that inherit from ContentControl or the ContentControl base class itself. AddChild takes an Object type as a valid child, while AddText requires a string. Some objects, such as the ContentControl, expose a Content property, which asserts that only a single control may be added to the child collection. (See Chapter 9, "Using the Blend Asset Library," for more details on ContentControl.)

The ICollection interface allows for child elements to be added directly to the collection.

Examine the markup in Listing 4.4. From it, you will get the complete picture of the parent/child/children scenario, where the Grid is the parent, the ListBox is the child and the ListBoxItem(s) are the children. The result is illustrated in Figure 4.2.

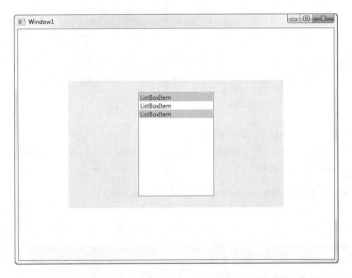

FIGURE 4.2   The parent/child/children scenario created as a result of the code in Listing 4.4.

LISTING 4.4   Creating a Simple Embedded ListBox

```
<Grid
    Margin="100,100,100,100"
    x:Name="gridParent"
    Background="#3ACCCCCC">
    <ListBox
        HorizontalAlignment="Center"
        x:Name="listBoxChild"
        VerticalAlignment="Center"
        Width="150"
        Height="200"
        IsSynchronizedWithCurrentItem="True">
        <ListBoxItem
            x:Name="listBoxChildren_1"
            Content="ListBoxItem"
            Background="#FFC8C8C8"/>
        <ListBoxItem
            x:Name="listBoxChildren_2"
            Content="ListBoxItem"/>
        <ListBoxItem
            x:Name="listBoxChildren_3"
            Content="ListBoxItem"
            Background="#FFC8C8C8"/>
    </ListBox>
</Grid>
```

Because we named all the items (the parent, the child, and all the children), we can now refer to them directly in code to set properties during runtime in the following manner:

```
this.listBoxChildren_1.Content = "The first item";
```

By default when you add new objects within Expression Blend, those objects are not named; but this does not stop you from referring to the index item from the collection of children held by the ListBox object as is shown in the following:

```
(this.listBoxChild.Items[0] as ListBoxItem).Content = "The first item";
```

Accessing XAML Objects in Code

You must name your objects to have access to them from your code-behind files. You can do this by adding the x:Name attribute and giving it a meaningful value (for example, x:Name="MasterGrid").

Object Properties and Events

Attributes within XAML either refer to object properties or events as we have seen in Listing 4.1. Object properties and events are usually shown without any such qualifiers such as x: and are interpreted by the compiler as being relative to the elements that they reside in.

Now, you may be thinking that so far we have set pretty basic property values and wondering what you would do if your property was something other then a string, as it would appear that we are using strings exclusively to set the properties. The truth is that XAML uses the .NET TypeConverter extensively to ensure that the value of a string can be and is converted to the required value type.

Examine the markup in Listing 4.5 and compare it to Listing 4.4. Note the changes made to the Background property of listBoxChildren_1—the Brush type is set to a gradient.

LISTING 4.5   The Nested Element Syntax Required for More Complex Properties

```
<ListBox
    HorizontalAlignment="Center"
    x:Name="listBoxChild"
    VerticalAlignment="Center"
    Width="150"
    Height="200"
    IsSynchronizedWithCurrentItem="True">
    <ListBoxItem
        x:Name="listBoxChildren_1"
        Content="ListBoxItem">
        <ListBoxItem.Background>
            <LinearGradientBrush
                EndPoint="1,0.5"
                StartPoint="0,0.5">
                <GradientStop
                    Color="#FF828282"
                    Offset="0"/>
                <GradientStop
                    Color="#FFFFFFFF"
                    Offset="1"/>
            </LinearGradientBrush>
        </ListBoxItem.Background>
    </ListBoxItem>
</ListBox>
```

The interesting area to look at in this listing is the line:

`<ListBoxItem.Background>`

It shows the dotted (or period) notation, which tells the compiler that this is a property and not a nested child element, for example:

`<Object.Property>`

Markup Extensions

Markup extesions play a very important role in XAML as they allow you to specify how the compiler should handle more complex property values.

Typically, the curly braces {} are used to implement an extension, and the type of extension is what is declared directly after the opening brace. Markup extensions allow you to add references to *other* objects so the value provided to attributes (such as an item's text value or color) can be dynamic in nature, as opposed to a hard-coded value.

There are a number of extensions available, with the most common being located in the XAML namespace. So, you use the extensions with the x: prefix. Listing 4.6 shows a common extension in action—the Static extension.

Although in this case, we know what the value is, static or dynamic values supplied in the extension enable you to supply value types to your properties in the scenario in which you don't actually know what the runtime value will be.

LISTING 4.6   Setting the Grid Background Color to a Static Resource

```
<Grid Background="{DynamicResource {x:Static SystemColors.WindowFrameBrushKey}}"/>
```

`DynamicResource` is also an extension type and is used here to specify that the property value should change as the value changes. Because the markup specifies a `SystemColor`, when the user changes the system colors via theme or additional settings, this Grid's `Background` property will change to match any new value.

The following markup again uses an extension to specify that the property will be set to `Null`.

```
<Grid Background="{x:Null}"/>
```

As another example, you may create a brush (using the Blend interface or directly in XAML) that you want to apply to every visual elements Background property throughout your application (see Listing 4.7). Instead of having to type out all the `Brush` properties for each element, a method is needed to refer to the `Brush` object and apply it to the elements as a resource.

LISTING 4.7   Using Period Notation to Add a Brush to the Window's Resource Collection

```
<Window.Resources>
    <SolidColorBrush Color="#FFFF0606" x:Key="RedBrush"/>
</Window.Resources>
```

You can clearly see that the markup has defined a brush of type SolidColorBrush and set the Color property value. You will also note that we have given the resource a Key value (x:Key="RedBrush"), which we will refer to shortly.

When applying this resource to a grid, use the following markup extension:

```
<Grid Background="{DynamicResource RedBrush}"/>
```

To apply this resource in code, first find the resource by Key value, and then apply it to the property as shown in Listing 4.8.

LISTING 4.8   Creating a New Grid During Runtime

```
//Define a new Grid object
Grid GridTest = new Grid();
GridTest.Height = 100;
GridTest.Width = 100;
GridTest.Margin = new Thickness(20, 20, 20, 20);

//Add the new grid to the LayoutRoot
this.LayoutRoot.Children.Add(GridTest);

//Apply the Brush Resource
Brush ResourceBrush = Window.FindResource("RedBrush") as Brush ;
GridTest.Background = ResourceBrush;
```

Without going into too much detail at this stage, let's take a look at the Binding extension, which enables powerful data binding within XAML and WPF. Chapters 12 and 13, "Templates" and "Data Binding," respectively, go into more detail about how to use data binding in your applications.

Add the markup in Listing 4.9, and then run the application. Your result should resemble Figure 4.3.

You should replace all the markup in your application from "<Grid x:Name="LayoutRoot"/> on down, with the code in Listing 4.9.

FIGURE 4.3   The simple application created in Listing 4.9.

LISTING 4.9   Binding Example

```
<Grid
    HorizontalAlignment="Stretch"
    Margin="0,0,0,0"
    Width="Auto">
    <Grid.RowDefinitions>
        <RowDefinition Height="0.5*"/>
        <RowDefinition Height="0.5*"/>
    </Grid.RowDefinitions>
    <Slider
        x:Name="TestSlider"
        HorizontalAlignment="Center"
        Margin="0,0,0,0"
        VerticalAlignment="Center"
        Width="150"/>
    <StackPanel
        HorizontalAlignment="Stretch"
        Margin="0,0,0,0"
        Width="Auto"
        Grid.Row="1"
        Grid.RowSpan="2">
        <Label
            HorizontalAlignment="Center"
            Margin="0,0,0,0"
            Content="Slider Value"/>
        <TextBox
            HorizontalAlignment="Center"
            Margin="0,0,0,0"
            VerticalAlignment="Stretch"
            Width="Auto"
            Height="Auto"
```

```
            Grid.Row="1"
            Text="{Binding ElementName=TestSlider , Path=Value}"
            TextWrapping="Wrap"/>
    </StackPanel>
</Grid>
```

The important piece of markup here is

```
Text="{Binding ElementName=TestSlider , Path=Value}"
```

The Binding extension allows you to specify a source element—in this instance, a Slider control—named TestSlider and a source value path, which is the Slider's value property.

You should be able to see the power of this simple technique. By now you may also appreciate just how little coding was actually required to achieve the desired result—98% of the XAML was created by Blend.

Summary

The aim of this chapter was to show you the basics or core of XAML and how the various attributes refer to properties and events that make up your objects. If you understand this, then you are well on your way to understanding any XAML you encounter in future. It all revolves around what you see here.

If you are interested in learning more about XAML, then I would strongly recommend that you purchase a copy of *Programming Windows Presentation Foundation* by Chris Sells and Ian Griffiths. The .NET SDK also provides a great (if not very technical) overview of XAML and can be found at http://msdn2.microsoft.com/en-us/library/ms747122.aspx.

PART II

Going with the Flow

IN THIS PART

CHAPTER 5

UIElement: Control Embedding

If you have created user interfaces previously in Microsoft .NET, Adobe Flash, or any other visual tool, you probably have come across situations in which you have spent hours—if not days—trying to get controls to look, feel, and function the way the designers and architects of the application intended.

For developers it was not impossible to embed many controls within controls—and then within more controls— to create a single custom control. But what you almost always ended up with was a hard-to-maintain control, which bubbled events through multiple control managers. And in some cases, you ended up with the inability to deep clone the object (because of the lack of ICloneable interface support from certain controls that were used), no serialization, or poorly constructed interior object references.

The more you work with XAML-based controls, the more you will come to enjoy the freedom and power that you now have when delivering the requirements of the designers and architects of a given interface specification. You can build UIElements that easily inherit parent item properties through the power of Dependency Properties (see Chapter 16, "Using Resources for Skins," for more information), and you can apply templates or styles to your controls to ensure visual continuity. Best of all, you can embed your controls inside other items or embed other items inside your controls with unprecedented ease.

There are always exceptions to the rule, but I struggle to find any situation that cannot be overcome within a matter of an hour or two, thanks to the flexibility that the control base supports.

Of course in an ideal workflow, a designer will be defining the UI and a developer will be coding up the functionality of the application, which greatly reduces the level of replication. Developers can sleep better at night now.

UIElements

Technically speaking, you should refer to any visual objects that you use within an interface environment as a UIElement. The distinction is important later on when it comes to class design for custom control creation. Elements are how you refer to controls when declared in a block of XAML, whereas a UIElement could be a group of elements to form a single control, such as an Image element embedded inside a Button element.

Managing Embedding

When you first heard the statement, "UIElements support the embedding of other UIElements," or if you have just read it for the first time, what did this really mean to you as a developer or designer?

Some of you might have thought, "So what? I can already put a button in a panel, which is in another panel." Others might have thought, "Great, I can finally play a movie in a textbox!" Still others might have thought, "What does this really mean?"

It means that you can add a ComboBox control to your application window, and inside that ComboBox you can add an image, a radio button, or a standard button as items in just a few lines of markup, which is unbelievably quicker than how long it previously took in WINForms. If you do not believe me, try to do that in any other visual development environment/language.

I will give you a head start; then I will read the paper and maybe take in a movie or two. When you are finished, come back to the book and read on.

To prove just how easy it is to embed UIElements, Listing 5.1 shows the XAML markup needed to achieve the goal previously mentioned.

LISTING 5.1   UIElement Embedding

```xaml
<ComboBox x:Name="ComboBox" HorizontalAlignment="Center" VerticalAlignment="Center">
    <ComboBoxItem x:Name="ComboBoxItem">
        <StackPanel x:Name="StackPanel">
            <Image x:Name="Blend_gif" Source="Blend.gif"/>
            <RadioButton x:Name="RadioButton" Content="RadioButton"/>
            <Button x:Name="Button" Content="Button"/>
        </StackPanel>
    </ComboBoxItem>
</ComboBox>
```

Reference Required

You will need to add a reference to an image in your project for this markup to work.

This ease means so very much to those of us who are developers and have always pulled our hair out, trying to overcome the limitations of CLR controls that we have had to use in our standard toolbox, but it also means that for those of us who implement the visual design of the UI that we have absolute freedom to think of new ways of displaying items on the screen.

If you are a developer, think about it for a minute. How many times in the past have you wanted to embed a control within another control (and I mean truly embed a control) and just realized in the end that it was not worth all the hassle? Think about that amazing visual on that Flash-based website you visited, when you clicked the button and the vector graphics animated around the page while simultaneously loading the corresponding screen of your choice. Did you ever try to replicate something like this in your desktop environment? Sure, they were achievable; but again we come back to a time/cost ratio for which most commercial projects don't allow.

Most designers I know stopped trying to design interfaces like this for the desktop as well. They just gave up after the controls could never be implemented.

Now you can create these interfaces for your desktop applications by using Expression Blend and Visual Studio, but it would not be possible if the application base did not support object embedding with such flexibility. When you build several interfaces using the new technology, the one thing that will become quickly apparent is the roles that Margins, Alignment, Size, Layout Spans and Panel type choice plays. (See Chapter 6, "Panel-Based Containers," for a more in-depth look at panel-based controls.)

Positioning Properties

One of the most important areas of thought you should give to your application is how the UIElements that are embedded in various panel-based constructs will react when the page(s), window(s), or parent UIElements are resized, maximized, scaled, or localized. We are talking not only about embedding UIElements inside each other but also embedding UIElements into your page construct.

Have you ever navigated to a website only to find that the menu items don't line up properly or that an embedded image on the page has caused the text to move to a weird position? Most of the time that isn't much of a problem, and you can live with it. But imagine if you wanted to read that information or had to interact with that site all day. Your rating of the site would be pretty low, regardless of how good the content is. This is why user experience is so important in a XAML-based application. The same sorts of issues can and do occur with WPF applications.

Why does positioning sometimes get messed up?

It comes down to the flexible layout system that WPF uses to place your controls in the correct position, regardless of the screen size, resolution, Z-order, and so on.

What Is Z-Order?

Z-Order occurs when you have overlapping controls or elements and you want one of them to be either in front or behind of the other.

Although layout in WPF is extremely flexible in its approach, as with all things powerful, great responsibility is also present. Your responsibility is to ensure that the settings are correct and accurately reflect the environment that the controls(s) are being used in.

When you create a new Standard Project in Expression Blend, you will note that a Grid UIElement is used and named as the LayoutRoot, a child of a Window base element. Visual Studio also uses a Window as its parent container and provides a standard empty Grid as the base panel container.

Adding controls via drag and drop is simple enough in either environment. How these controls are shown in Blend, however, is not always how they will be interpreted in the Visual Studio design environment, and the resulting layout functionality can be impaired.

You will find this occurs sometimes when you switch between the two environments. Most of the time, you can repair the problem simply by looking at the column and row span requirements of the controls in question (see Figure 5.1).

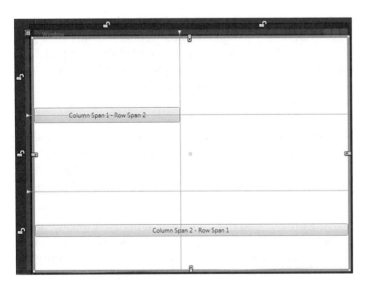

FIGURE 5.1   UIElement span differences are apparent.

In Figure 5.1, the same Button element is used twice. Everything (including the properties) is identical in both the top and bottom buttons, with one slight change to the layout property on each. The top button has its Row Span set to 2 and Column Span set to 1, whereas the bottom button has its Row Span set to 1 and its Column Span set to 2.

Although this is a simple example, it does demonstrate just how different your UIElements will appear if you are not careful about properties such as the margins and the spans.

You may be wondering why it is necessary to bring up such a simple issue, but you would be surprised by the number of times that you will miss this. This is especially true if you are embedding child UIElements in code only, because you will not get any visual verification until runtime.

You may also be using UIElements that have been built by other developers, XAML architects, or designers; and you may not understand the intended span logic used within the various embedded objects.

As a demonstration of how margins and size can cause you grief with embedded UIElements, use the following steps to create a small application that will display a red grid in the center, with a yellow rectangle embedded in it for visual effect and a block of text centered in the grid.

Even though this scenario may cause you a headache (which may not appear to be a good incentive to actually doing the following steps—you still should), it is very important that you understand how you may find yourself in the following situation so that, in your future design experiences, you can work around the same potential problems.

1. Create a new Standard Application in Blend.

2. Find the Grid element in the ToolBox panel (or locate it in the Asset Library) and double-click the icon to make the Grid element a child of your LayoutRoot element.

3. Double-click the Grid in the Objects and Timeline viewer to ensure that the Grid element is the active element. When the Grid element is active, it will display with a yellow border.

4. In the Properties panel, name this element "Grid."

5. Open the Layout category of the Properties panel. Make sure that both Width and Height are set to Auto and that the HorizontalAlignment and VerticalAlignment properties are set to Stretch.

6. Set all four margins to be 100.000 px.

7. Set the Grid background color to a Red Solid Color Brush in the Brushes category.

8. Add a Rectangle element as a child of the Grid.

9. Name this element "Rectangle" in the Properties panel.

10. Then go to the Layout category in Properties.

11. Again, make sure that both Width and Height are set to Auto and that the HorizontalAlignment and VerticalAlignment properties are set to Stretch.

12. Set all four margins to 50.000 px.

13. Set the Rectangle background color to Yellow.

14. Select a TextBlock element from the ToolBox panel (or locate it in the Asset Library). Draw the TextBlock in the center of the Rectangle.

15. You are now in the Text Edit mode of the TextBlock control. Either press ESC or click on the Selection tool in the Toolbox to edit this mode.

16. Name this element "TextBlock."

17. Select the Layout category in the Properties panel. Set Width and Height of the TextBlock to Auto and set the HorizontalAlignment and VerticalAlignment to Center. Set all four margins to 0.000 px.

    You should end up with something similar to what is shown in Figure 5.2. While this design might look bad, it highlights the problem.

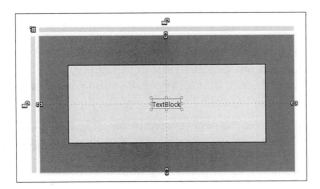

FIGURE 5.2   The TextBlock is centered in the application Window.

18. Double-click the LayoutRoot element to make it active. Put your mouse over the lower-right corner grab box, and then press and hold your left mouse button so that you can resize your LayoutRoot.

19. Move your mouse up and notice that the yellow Rectangle element starts to disappear. This is the result of the margin settings. You will also observe that the yellow Rectangle is disappearing altogether but the TextBlock UIElement remains visible, which is unprofessional.

This example highlights how incorrect settings within the margins of the embedded UIElements can cause some ugly results. (Okay, it was always going to be ugly.) The point is, who knows how your application users will resize and move your application window(s)?

It's important to be aware of this and not just go slapping controls all over the place, hoping that it will all work correctly when the application is launched, because 99.9% of the time, it won't work how you wanted it to. Understanding how to set up controls properly will make the difference between a great user experience and a poor one.

So, how do you fix it?

You should define, within your application design specification, the minimum size that the application can run at. You will restrict the application Window from becoming so small that elements disappear, which is what currently happens.

You could modify the properties of the Window in the Properties panel to restrict the minimum Width and Height, so that, regardless of how your user changes the size of the parent Window, the elements will always show. However, in this example, you will fix it by modifying the properties of the Window in the code—after all, you can fix anything in code (you should always tell your boss this if you are a developer).

> **When Not to Modify**
>
> As a general rule, you should avoid modifying the original XAML of a control or UIElement unless you understand what the repercussions of doing so may be. Just because a control does not present in your scenario, it does not mean that control was not purposely built this way for a different one. Setting properties of a control at run-time will enable you to change a control's appearance without being concerned about breaking it.

1. Open your Project panel and find the code page of your Window, which should be Window1.xaml.cs, as shown in Figure 5.3.

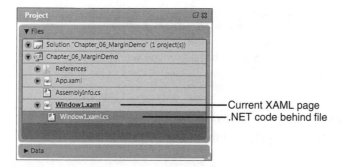

FIGURE 5.3   Finding the Window code behind page.

2. Double-click the .cs file. The corresponding code behind page for your XAML Window should appear within Visual Studio when it loads.

3. With any luck, you will now be looking at the default constructor for your scene. Enter the following code to modify your Window1 behavior:

```
public partial class Window1
{
    public Window1()
    {
        this.InitializeComponent();

        // Insert code required on object creation below this point.
        this.Loaded += new RoutedEventHandler(Window1_Loaded);
    }

    void Window1_Loaded(object sender, RoutedEventArgs e)
    {
        this.MinHeight = this.ActualHeight ;
```

```
            this.MinWidth = this.ActualWidth;
        }
    }
```

4. Save the file in Visual Studio and return to Blend.

5. Build the application from the Project menu and then press F5 to test.

You should now be able to stretch your application both horizontally and vertically, and the child elements will continue to resize dynamically. You will note that the Window is now restricted to resizing below the initial startup Width and Height of the Window.

These sorts of issues will occur many times during your application development lifecycle, at least until such a time that all the people involved with the design and development are 100% accustomed to sizing controls and UIElements with layout properties instead of straight measurements and anchors. This is a strong claim to make, but I have witnessed it firsthand working with teams of designers (and developers) who are new to Blend.

Good Habits

As a rule of thumb, activate the parent UIElement and manually change values until you have the correct functionality in your application or control every time you add a new UIElement to your scene, page, or window.

When using the Grid (which is the most flexible layout panel and, therefore, quite often the most used), there are really three main Layout properties that you need to make sure are correct:

1. The Width and Height property values determine if

    a. Your element will grow and shrink (Auto) based on

        i. The parent boundaries if Alignment is set to Stretch.

        ii. Taking Margin settings into account.

    b. Your element will be a fixed size if

        i. Positioned according to the Alignment settings.

        ii. Offset by the Margin settings.

2. The Alignment property setting relates to the control's relational setting given its parent's boundaries.

    a. Stretch directly affects the Actual Width and Actual Height controlled by Min/Max Width and Height property values.

        i. Control bounding box ignores Min/Max and Width/Height settings, but the visible content of the Control is affected directly.

    b. Controls with Width and Height set to Auto, and Alignment other than Stretch, will not show on the screen unless Min/Max Width and Height are also set to a value greater than 0.

3. The `Margin` property determines the distance between the outer edges of a control's bounding box to that of its parent construct.

  a. When Alignment (Horizontal or Vertical) is set to Stretch, Left/Right and Top/Bottom margins determine the distance between the outer edge of the control bounding box and the parent construct.

    i. Min/Max Width and Height affect the visual content of the control but not the bounding box of the control to which the margins are applied.

  b. When Alignment is set to Center (either Horizontal or Vertical), the margin properties are an offset value from center of the Parent.

  c. When Alignment is set to Left, the Left margin is the only value that affects the position of the control from the Left edge of the parent.

  d. When Alignment is set to Right, the Right margin is the only value that affects the position of the control from the Right edge of the parent.

  e. When Alignment is set to Top, the Top margin is the only value that affects the position of the control from the Top edge of the parent.

  f. When Alignment is set to Bottom, the Bottom margin is the only value that affects the position of the control from the Bottom edge of the parent.

Adding Child Controls

You may have previously added additional controls at runtime to an application by adding a control to the controls collection of the parent control (generally a form- or panel-based construct in .NET). You add XAML elements in much the same way to a parent `UIElementCollection` property, generically named as `Children`, for controls that inherit the Panel base class.

The generic `Children` property has an Add method that accepts a UIElement type. For example, the following code adds a Button UIElement to a Grid UIElement:

```
this.Grid1.Children.Add(myNewButton);
```

The `Children` property also has an Index accessor that returns a `UIElement`:

```
Button myButtonReference = (Button) this.Grid1.Children[0];
```

Those controls that inherit from ContentControl (Button, CheckBox, Frame, Label, and so on) have a `Content` property that accepts a single object as a child and is assigned like the following:

```
myNewButton.Content = myNewGrid;
```

(See Chapter 9, "Using the Blend Asset Library," for a detailed look at the ContentControl.)

The same traditional rules apply when you want to add elements to subelements of a UIElement. As long as the UIElements are publicly accessible, you can call the Children.Add method and pop an element in there. Some XAML UIElements use an ItemCollection property called *Items*, although these are generally used for elements that are designed to take multiple child elements as part of the design functionality.

A TreeView is an example UIElement that has an ItemCollection. It takes an object of type object to display as a node in the tree. This object (of type TreeViewItem) can then contain child elements in both the HeaderedItemsControl collection and the ItemsCollection collection, which could be another TreeViewItem, UIElement, or even another TreeView control element.

.NET Tree Versus WPF Tree

.NET 1.0 and 2.0 trees allow only for single nodes to be inserted onto a tree, which forms a hierarchical visual metaphor. Added functionality in the .NET Framework 3.0 allows you to insert a header and then add multiple nodes as grouped children of the node. As mentioned, each node and, indeed, the header can contain other nodes, groups of nodes or additional trees if necessary.

You may find that some developers add child elements directly to the XAML. Sometimes this occurs automatically when you develop a control element with a visual helper such as Blend and when the developer or designer uses the drag-and-drop method to create the UIElement tree. The benefit to this is always that the controls can be visualized during design time. You also have access to the element properties and events to respond to, as well as manipulate in Timeline animation options.

Workflow Tip

The quickest way to add a generic TreeViewItem to a Tree is to find the Tree control in the Objects and Timeline panel, right-click, and select Add TreeViewItem.

Adding additional elements to a parent in design time XAML is simple but you will find that a number of controls have larger initialization requirements then others and working in XAML can be cumbersome for some. I advise against this if you suffer from nose bleeds.

The following code shows a button as a child UIElement of a parent grid:

```
<Grid Name="ParentGrid">
    <Button Height="23" Margin="233.8,164.8,301.6,0"
      Name="ChildButton" VerticalAlignment="Top">Child Button</Button>
</Grid>
```

You probably wouldn't type this yourself, because you can just drop the control straight onto the grid in the design time editor, but sometimes you may need to "hand crank" the

XAML in order to get your UIElements into the parent. (See Chapter 4, "XAML for Beginners," for more information on XAML structures.)

The TreeView control element was mentioned previously, so the following example runs through using a TreeView control to display various information and UIElements.

Looks Like an Apple But Tastes Like a Peach

Before you disregard going through the TreeView sample because you consider yourself to be a TreeView guru in .NET, be aware that the .NET 3.0 + WPF TreeView control works differently from the previous .NET 2.0 CLR (and earlier) versions of the control. Many WPF controls function the same way but are completely different when it comes time to code them.

First make a simple TreeView display page.

If you are a developer, you are probably thinking that we are going to create a class that inherits from TreeViewItem as we would do normally. In this case, however, we are concentrating on UIElements, so we are going to create two custom controls:

1. An element to insert into the TreeViewItemHeader
2. An element to insert into the TreeViewItem collection

Previously, you may have been limited to the types of information you could show in a node within a TreeView control in .NET. If you had a little time on your hands and you didn't have a project manager wanting a build every six hours, you could add some other features to your nodes. Unfortunately, I've never found an easier way to add other controls, such as a progress bar, another button, or a sub TreeView control, to the node.

You can use a third-party GridView control to show hierarchical data, because it allows you to contain embedded grids within grids. Obviously, however, it will always be primarily determined by the amount and type of information that needs to be shown.

Tree Control Sample in C# and XAML

The following steps begin your application by creating a base of functionality within your Window. You will then move on to creating a User Control where the TreeView control functionality will be added.

1. Create a new project of type WPF Application .exe in Blend.
2. Copy Listing 5.2 into the XAML editor, replacing the existing LayoutRoot element. Your window should look similar to the one shown in Figure 5.4.

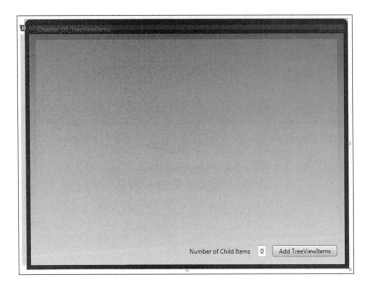

FIGURE 5.4   This listing provides a nice base to work from, by adding a TreeView control to the window.

LISTING 5.2   Tree Control Sample in C# and XAML

```xml
<Grid x:Name="LayoutRoot">
    <Grid.Background>
        <LinearGradientBrush EndPoint="0.5,1.203" StartPoint="0.5,-0.203">
            <GradientStop Color="#FFFFFFFF" Offset="1"/>
            <GradientStop Color="#FF005FC4" Offset="0"/>
        </LinearGradientBrush>
    </Grid.Background>
    <TreeView HorizontalAlignment="Center" VerticalAlignment="Top" Width="600"
Height="375" Background="#2DA4EFFF" BorderBrush="{x:Null}" Margin="0,10,0,0"
x:Name="tvMain"/>
    <Grid HorizontalAlignment="Stretch" VerticalAlignment="Bottom" Width="Auto"
Height="52">
        <Grid.ColumnDefinitions>
            <ColumnDefinition Width="0.478*"/>
            <ColumnDefinition Width="0.23*"/>
            <ColumnDefinition Width="0.058*"/>
            <ColumnDefinition Width="0.109*"/>
            <ColumnDefinition Width="0.106*"/>
            <ColumnDefinition Width="0.019*"/>
        </Grid.ColumnDefinitions>
```

```
        <Button HorizontalAlignment="Stretch" Margin="3,0,3,0" x:Name="btnAdd-
Child" VerticalAlignment="Center" Content="Add TreeViewItems" Grid.Column="3"
Grid.ColumnSpan="2"/>
            <TextBox HorizontalAlignment="Center" x:Name="txtItemCount" Verti-
calAlignment="Center" Grid.Column="2" Text="0" TextWrapping="Wrap"/>
            <Label HorizontalAlignment="Right" VerticalAlignment="Center" Con-
tent="Number of Child Items" Grid.Column="1"/>
        </Grid>
    </Grid>
```

3. Select the File menu and then New Item to view the Add New Item dialog box.

4. Select UserControl and rename the item TreeHeader.xaml. Click OK when you are done.

5. Don't be concerned about the default Height and Width properties at the moment; you will fix them later. Open the Objects and Timeline panel and select the LayoutRoot element.

6. Open the Properties panel and select the Brushes category.

7. Verify that the Background property is set to No brush.

8. Select to add a Solid Color Brush object and set the panel color to White by dragging your mouse cursor through the Color palette to the upper-left corner.

9. Open the Asset Library, search for Border, and select to use it.

10. You should see the icon appear above the Asset Library button. Double-click the Border icon to add it as a child to your LayoutRoot element.

11. Open the Properties panel and find the Layout category.

12. Set both the HorizontalAlignment and VerticalAlignment properties to Stretch.

13. Set the Width and Height properties to Auto by clicking the button with an X-type icon, to the right of the Width/Height property input boxes.

14. Find the Border element in the Objects and Timeline panel. Double-click it to set the element as active (the yellow border around the element).

15. Open the Properties panel again and type **pad** into the property search box.

16. Set each of the padding values to 5.

17. Open the Asset Library and find the Grid control, or locate the Grid control in the Panel Based Control collection on the ToolBox panel.

18. Double-click the Grid icon to add it as the singular child element of the Border control.

19. Double-click the Grid element in the Objects and Timelines panel to make it the active element. You should see that the Grid fills the border but has a nice little gap between it and its parent thanks to the padding property you set previously.

20. Find the Rectangle icon on the Toolbox panel and double-click it to add it as a child element of the Grid control.

21. Open the Properties panel again. In the property search box, type **rad** to reveal to radius properties.

22. Set each of the Radius properties to 15.

23. Clear the Property search box and type the search word **height**. Set the Height property to 30.

24. Now search for the Width property and set it to Auto also.

25. Clear the property search box.

26. Open the Brushes category of the properties panel and select the Fill property, which should have a White Solid Color Brush object assigned to it. Set this property to No brush.

27. Select the Stroke property, which should have a Black Solid Color Brush object assigned. Change this color to a deep Blue color. (You could use #FF02378E as the hex value.)

28. Set both of the HorizontalAlignment and VerticalAlignment properties to Stretch.

29. Open the Asset Library again and locate the ViewBox control, and then select the control to add it to the ToolBox.

30. Double-click the ViewBox icon to add it as a child control of the Grid. (Remember that the Grid is still the active control.)

31. Open the properties panel, Layout category and then set both the HorizontalAlignment and VerticalAlignment properties to Stretch.

32. Set the Height property of the ViewBox to 20.

33. Set the Width property to Auto.

34. Locate the Margin property in the Layout category and set the Left and Right Margin properties to 10. The ViewBox should be comfortably within the borders of the Rectangle element now.

35. Double-click the ViewBox control to make it active.

36. Locate the Label control either in the ToolBox or from the Asset Library.

37. Double-click the Label icon to add the control as the singular child of the ViewBox.

38. Click the Escape button to exit the Text edit mode of the Label.

39. By default the Label control is not named, so you need to name it in order to have access to the control from the .NET code behind file. Name the control labItemInsertedValue.

40. Select the Label element in the Objects and Timeline panel; then search for the Content property in the properties panel.

41. Clear the Content property so that no text shows in the Label.

42. Select the LayoutRoot element in the Objects and Timeline panel.

43. Open the Brushes category of the Properties panel and set the Background property to No brush.

44. Locate and activate the UserControl element in the Objects and Timeline panel.

45. Open the Layout category of the Properties panel and set the Width and Height properties to Auto. Your results should look similar to those shown in Figure 5.5.

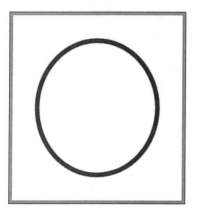

FIGURE 5.5   The HeaderItem on completion of the styling.

The XAML in Listing 5.3 allows you to verify your markup created in the previous steps.

LISTING 5.3   The XAML Representation of the Tree Control

```xml
<Grid x:Name="LayoutRoot" Background="{x:Null}">
    <Border HorizontalAlignment="Stretch" VerticalAlignment="Stretch"
Width="Auto" Height="Auto" Padding="5,5,5,5">
        <Grid>
            <Rectangle HorizontalAlignment="Stretch"
VerticalAlignment="Stretch" Width="Auto" Height="30" Fill="{x:Null}"
Stroke="#FF02378E" RadiusX="15" RadiusY="15"/>
            <Viewbox HorizontalAlignment="Stretch" VerticalAlignment="Stretch"
Width="Auto" Height="20" Margin="10,0,10,0">
                <Label Content="" x:Name="labItemInsertedValue"/>
            </Viewbox>
        </Grid>
    </Border>
</Grid>
```

Now you need to add a public method to the control, allowing you to set the `Content` property of the Label control with a string value, when the TreeHeader control is used.

Open the Project panel and within the Files category, locate the TreeHeader.xaml file. Expand the node to reveal the code behind page for the control as shown in Figure 5.6.

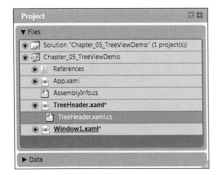

FIGURE 5.6   The selected TreeHeader code behind file.

1. From the Project menu, select Build to ensure that everything is as it should be with the control and that no errors are raised. Should you receive any errors, please go back through the steps carefully.

2. Right-click on the TreeHeader.xaml.cs file to reveal a context menu. Click on Edit in Visual Studio to launch Visual Studio, showing the constructor of the TreeHeader control.

No IntelliSense?

A common complaint throughout the Expression Blend release cycles of CTP to Beta has been that there is a loss of IntelliSense functionality in Visual Studio. You should expect that if you double-click to open a single code file in Visual Studio, you will not have any IntelliSense, because you have opted to edit the file only and not the solution, which means it would be the same as editing the file in Notepad.exe.

Expression Blend 2.0 now opens the entire solution in Visual Studio when you opt to edit any file in Visual Studio from the right click context menu. If you still find no IntelliSense functionality, rebuild the solution from within Visual Studio by using the Build menu and then selecting Build Solution.

3. Add the code from Listing 5.4 to your C# file, just below the closing curly brace "}" of the constructor that is already shown:

```
public TreeHeader()
{
    this.InitializeComponent();

    // Insert code required on object creation below this point.

}


}
```

LISTING 5.4   The Public Method Required to Set the Label Content Value

```
public void SetLabelContent(Object LabelValue)
        {
            if (LabelValue == null)
                this.labItemInsertedValue.Content = string.Empty;
            else
                this.labItemInsertedValue.Content = LabelValue;
        }
```

4. Save the file, exit Visual Studio, and then return to Blend.

5. Build the application from the Project menu once more.

6. Close the TreeHeader.xaml file.

Naming Conventions

Throughout the rest of the book, you will notice some consistencies in how I named certain controls and elements. For example, a button will always have the name btnButton or similar. The button name will always contain the prefix "btn," which is short for button. By using this naming convention in code, I (or any other designer or developer) can instantly know what the control is without having to rely on intellisense of a visual guide. It also helps group control types in Visual Studio IntelliSense, which display in alphabetical order.

Other prefix naming conventions include gd for elements, such as Grid, pb for progress-bar, and lab for labels.

In the following steps, you create the next control that will serve as the TreeViewItem Items content.

1. Press Ctrl+N to launch the Add New Item dialog box.

2. Again, select UserControl and rename the control to TreeItem.xaml.

3. Select the LayoutRoot element in the Objects and Timeline panel; then open the Properties panel.

4. Find the Brushes category and select the Background property. Set this to show a Solid Color Brush object of color White.

   To make this a little more interesting this time and to demonstrate the embedding capability of WPF control elements, you will add a Label control, a Button control, and a ProgressBar control.

5. With the LayoutRoot element activated in the Objects and Timeline panel, find the Grid control again, either in the Asset Library or within the Panel Base Controls located on the ToolBox panel.

6. Add the Grid as the singular child control of the LayoutRoot element.

7. Open the Properties panel and locate the Layout category.

8. Set both the Width and Height properties to Auto and then set both the HorizontalAlignment and VerticalAlignment properties to Stretch.

9. Select and activate the Grid element in the Objects and Timeline panel.

10. Open the Properties panel. In the search box, type **def**, which should present you with the Column and Row Definitions for the Grid.

11. You want to add three columns of equal width, so click on the ColumnDefinitions property button three times, as shown in Figure 5.7.

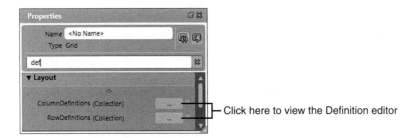

FIGURE 5.7   Click the button with the ellipse to open the ColumnDefinition Collection Editor.

Figure 5.8 shows the ColumnDefinition Collection Editor with three items added to the collection. You will notice that the items have a Width property set to 1 *. If you quickly look at the XAML for the Grid element, you will see that the Grid Column Definitions are declared but are completely empty of property attributes. This will ensure that the distances are equal between all the Collection Items (representing the Columns).

1. Ensuring the Grid element is activated in the Objects and Timeline panel, find and add a Label control as a child of the Grid.

2. Press the Escape key to exit Text Edit mode of the Label control.

3. Name the Label control labChildName.

4. Clear the Property search box.

5. Open the Layout category of the Properties panel and set the HorizontalAlignment and VerticalAlignment properties to Stretch.

6. Search for the Content property of the Label and remove the text Label.

7. Find and add a ProgressBar control from the Asset Library.

8. Name the control pbRunner.

9. Set the Column property to 1, which should move the ProgressBar to the second column of the Grid.

10. Set the HorizontalAlignment property to Stretch.

11. Set the VerticalAlignment property to Center.

12. Set the Width property to Auto.

13. Set the Left and Right Margin properties to 10.

FIGURE 5.8   The ColumnDefinition Collection Editor.

14. Find and add a Button control as a child of the Grid.

15. Name the control btnIndeterminate.

16. Open the Layout category of the Properties panel and set the Column value to 2.

17. Set the HorizontalAlignment property to Stretch.

18. Set the VerticalAlignment property to Center.

19. Set the Width and Height properties to Auto.

20. Set the Left and Right Margin properties to 10.

21. Find the Content property and set the Text to show Not Determinate.

22. Activate the UserControl element in the Objects and Timeline panel.

23. Set the Width and Height properties to Auto.

24. Select the LayoutRoot element and set the Background property, located in Brushes to No brush.

25. Press Ctrl+Shift+S to save all the files in this project and then select Build from the Project menu.

You are about to add a Click Event handler for the Button control you added to the UserControl. This is the reason that you just saved and built the application to ensure that you have access to all the controls from the Visual Studio environment.

1. Find and select the Button control in the Objects and Timeline panel.

2. Next to the control name property of the Properties panel is an icon with a little lightning bolt on it. This icon shows you a list of all available events for the currently selected control. Click this icon now to view the list.

3. The very first event at the top of the list should be Click. Double-click in the input box to auto-generate a Click handler method. If you have Visual Studio Standard or higher installed, Visual Studio should be launched and automatically add the code for your event handler method. If you are copying the methods to the clipboard, open the project now and add it to the code behind file.

4. Above the event handler method just created, add the code from Listing 5.5. This code creates an enum for the Button state as well as a property to store the current state in.

LISTING 5.5   Creating an Enum for the Button State

```
/// <summary>
/// Button State choices
/// </summary>
public enum ButtonState
{
    NotDeterminate = 0,
    Determinate = 1
}

//Default set
private ButtonState _currentState = ButtonState.NotDeterminate ;

/// <summary>
/// Get or set the current button state
/// </summary>
public ButtonState CurrentState
{
    get { return _currentState; }
    set { _currentState = value; }
}
```

5. Listing 5.6 shows the Click event handler, which controls the ProgressBar control. Add this code now.

LISTING 5.6   Controlling the ProgressBar Depending on the CurrentState Value

```
private void btnIndeterminate_Click(object sender, RoutedEventArgs e)
    {
        switch (CurrentState)
        {
```

```
        case ButtonState.NotDeterminate:
            this.CurrentState = ButtonState.Determinate;
            this.btnIndeterminate.Content = "Determinate";
            this.pbRunner.IsIndeterminate = true;
            break;
        case ButtonState.Determinate:
            this.CurrentState = ButtonState.NotDeterminate ;
            this.btnIndeterminate.Content = "Not Determinate";
            this.pbRunner.IsIndeterminate = false;
            break;
        default:
            break;
    }
}
```

6. Now you create a method for setting the Label Content property, which is shown in Listing 5.7.

LISTING 5.7   Setting the Content of the Child Name Label

```
public void SetLabelValue(String ValueToShow)
    {
        this.labChildName.Content = ValueToShow;
    }
```

Select to save the project in Visual Studio and then "Build" the solution choosing the Build Solution menu item as you did previously. You can now return to Blend.

Listing 5.8 shows the XAML for the control should you have any issues with the previous steps.

FIGURE 5.9   The TreeItem control is ready to go.

LISTING 5.8   The XAML for the Entire Control

```
<Grid x:Name="LayoutRoot" Background="{x:Null}">
    <Grid HorizontalAlignment="Stretch" VerticalAlignment="Stretch"
Width="Auto" Height="Auto">
        <Grid.ColumnDefinitions>
            <ColumnDefinition/>
            <ColumnDefinition/>
            <ColumnDefinition/>
        </Grid.ColumnDefinitions>
        <Label HorizontalAlignment="Stretch" x:Name="labChildName" Verti-
calAlignment="Stretch" Content=""/>
        <ProgressBar HorizontalAlignment="Stretch" Margin="10,0,10,0"
x:Name="pbRunner" VerticalAlignment="Center" Width="Auto" Height="10" Grid.Col-
umn="1" IsIndeterminate="False"/>
        <Button HorizontalAlignment="Stretch" Margin="10,0,10,0" x:Name="cmdIn-
determinate" VerticalAlignment="Center" Content="Not Determinate" Grid.Column="2"
Click="cmdIndeterminate_Click"/>
    </Grid>
</Grid>
```

You should be ready to continue on with the TreeView sample application that you first started with, using the two controls you just built to display the required information. You added the Button control and ProgressBar controls to the TreeItem control to show that the control can and will maintain its own functionality, independent of its parent.

The majority of the work remaining is carried out in Visual Studio, so as per good working practices, save the project in Blend, and then Build it from the Project menu before continuing.

1. Close all UserControls in Blend and leave only Window1.xaml showing.
2. Find and select the btnAddChild button control in the Window by using the Objects and Timeline category.
3. Open the Properties panel and show the events available for the control.
4. Again, locate the Click event at the top of the event list and double-click the input box to create the Click handler method.

Listing 5.9 shows that you are looking at the Number of Child Items to add value, which is located in txtItemCount, and basing your additions on it.

LISTING 5.9   Adding Children of Children

```
private void btnAddChild_Click(object sender, RoutedEventArgs e)
    {

        int LoopCount = Convert.ToInt32(this.txtItemCount.Text);
```

```csharp
//Make sure we have at least 1 to add
if(LoopCount == 0)
{
    this.txtItemCount.Text = "1";
    LoopCount = 1;
}

//Create a new TreeItem to add to the control
TreeViewItem TempItem = new TreeViewItem();

//Create a single Header that will show the time it was created
TreeHeader MyHeader = new TreeHeader();
MyHeader.SetLabelContent("Item added: " + DateTime.Now.ToLongDateString
() + " " + DateTime.Now.ToLongTimeString());
MyHeader.MinWidth = 300;

//Add the header to the control before we start to add child items
TempItem.Header = MyHeader;

//Add child elements
for (int LoopValue = 0; LoopValue < LoopCount ; LoopValue++)
{
    //Create and add an item to our TreeViewItem
    TreeItem TempTreeItem = new TreeItem();
    TempTreeItem.SetLabelValue(Convert.ToString(LoopValue + 1) + " of "
+ LoopCount.ToString() + " children");
    TempTreeItem.MinWidth = 500;
    TempItem.Items.Add(TempTreeItem);

    TempTreeItem = null;
}

//Add our item to the TreeView control. If an item or header is selected,
//add our item as a child of it
if (this.tvMain.SelectedItem != null)
{
    if (this.tvMain.SelectedItem is TreeItem)
    {
        TreeViewItem SelectedItem = (this.tvMain.SelectedItem as
TreeItem).Parent as TreeViewItem ;
        this.tvMain.BeginInit();
        SelectedItem.Items.Add(TempItem);
        this.tvMain.EndInit();
    }
```

```
            else if (this.tvMain.SelectedItem is TreeHeader )
            {
                  TreeViewItem SelectedItem = (this.tvMain.SelectedItem as Tree-
Header).Parent as TreeViewItem;
                  this.tvMain.BeginInit();
                  SelectedItem.Items.Add(TempItem);
                  this.tvMain.EndInit();
            }
            else if (this.tvMain.SelectedItem is TreeViewItem )
            {
                  TreeViewItem SelectedItem = this.tvMain.SelectedItem as Tree-
ViewItem;
                  this.tvMain.BeginInit();
                  SelectedItem.Items.Add(TempItem);
                  this.tvMain.EndInit();
            }

      }
      else
      {
            this.tvMain.BeginInit();
            this.tvMain.Items.Add(TempItem);
            this.tvMain.EndInit();
      }
}
```

If you study the previous Add methods, you will see how you must now manage child objects and their header and child items compared with just child items in .NET TreeView controls.

Before you send emails telling me that I should have broken the code in Listing 5.9 into multiple methods, know that I was thinking that some of you reading this book may not have used any code previously. The concept of methods (functions) is covered in Chapter 10, "Visual Studio: C# Primer." By all means, refactor away if it makes you feel better!

Now add the code to your .NET code behind page, return to Blend, and build and test your application. Your results should be similar to Figure 5.10.

This is a simple sample, but you are probably already thinking about the possibilities this dimensional embedding provides developers. It also lets designers get away with some pretty amazing concepts.

Before you finish with embedding controls, you may be wondering why you had to add a Grid in places where you would normally just add multiple control elements as children. Cast your mind back, and you will remember that you had to do this when building the

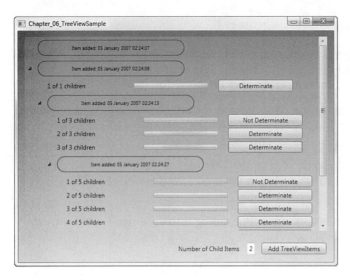

FIGURE 5.10   The finished product.

TreeHeader control when you added a Border control. The only Child element of the Border is a Grid. Everything else under it is a child of the Grid.

The explanation for this pertains to a special control that handles content, aptly called a *ContentControl*.

Limitations with ContentControls

The first time I started playing with some of the controls within Blend, I could not under-stand why my child elements kept disappearing. I thought that this was a huge oversight by the developers and that I was going to have a field day with them all on Microsoft Connect! But I thought before I did that and looked like a proper idiot, I'd better check what the WPF SDK said about content controls.

There it was in black and white (as well as that pale blue border), staring me in the face and telling me that I could only have one child UIElement for any control that inherited from the base ContentControl.

Content is not a collection, it is simply a property that can hold a UIElement or String *type*, essentially being what is held inside the content property owner and what is rendered when the control is drawn on the screen.

To get around the issue of having just a singular object embedded into controls Content property, you can embed controls that themselves contain a child collection; for example, a Grid control.

Summary

In this chapter, you learned how important it is to think about the relationship between the parent and child elements when determining the layout of such elements in an embedded scenario, an issue that is bound to come up in the future.

You also witnessed the flexibility of the TreeView control, which is a shining example of the embedding power now provided in WPF controls via ContentControls and child collections. That should be what you take most from this chapter.

Even though you got a look into some code in the later part of this chapter (which you may not fully understand), hopefully you saw how important it is to give your controls public accessor methods.

The next chapter is really an extension of this one, going into each panel and trying to understand when and where to use each one.

CHAPTER 6

Panel-Based Containers

As a developer, when you first step into the world of Blend and WPF, one of the biggest changes from WINForms that can be hard to adapt to is the use of different layout scenarios inflicted by your choice of panel-based containers/controls/constructs (PBCs). Some designers might see the layout scenarios as being almost restrictive because each layout container has rules, in terms of how the child elements are laid out as opposed to free-moving controls (which are possible as well).

In this chapter, you learn all about when and what to use as you look at the most common PBCs and the features specific to each type. This chapter gets you working with the panels and understanding the repercussions for your child elements, in terms of their layout positioning.

Where Are the Anchors?

If you're a developer, you probably got used to working with anchors in your WINForms developments. If you became really proficient with them, then likely, at some stage or another, you came across their limitations as well. If you come from a designer-orientated background, this might not make much sense. In essence we are talking about how controls/elements are positioned in relation to their parent. That parent could be the main form, another control in the same panel, and so on. It's been time consuming and not very dynamic in the past.

To overcome the limitations, I used fewer margins and was more concerned about end-client screen resolutions than I was about how far away my button was from the edge of the screen. Now I look back and wonder how I managed to flounder through without a layout system like the one WPF provides.

In this layer scenario I keep going on about, it's key to always remember that the element you are working on will most likely be the child of a control that has its layouts defined for certain purposes.

Almost all of the common controls in this chapter inherit the System.Windows.Controls. Panel class, which is the base class for all elements (or controls) that support the Layout features of WPF. The Panel class has some very specific features, such as the following:

- ▶ Content can be one or more UIElement(s).

- ▶ The primary property for accessing content is Children.

These features become more important with the development of custom controls and in understanding how your control fits (Layout) in relation to the other controls that are sharing the screen space (or real estate) with it.

Add to the mix the idea of Grid spans, rows, and columns, and you can sometimes find yourself in an unfortunate predicament, where your control just won't position as you want because the parent control requires that it be organized in a specific manner. On the other hand, you may be creating the parent control, and you may be the one who specifies how its children will be laid out.

A simple example of this was shown in Chapter 5, "UIElement: Control Embedding," which goes into further detail about how spans can become a problem if you do not consider them when designing your applications and or controls.

Z-Order

When rendered to the screen, objects display relative to their Z-order, which you can change both in code and by the order in which the element appears within the XAML markup.

When you select an element in the Objects and Timeline viewer, you can right-click to display the context menu, which allows you to specify the order in which the selected object appears.

Grid Element

The Grid element is arguably the most commonly used panel-based control, because it is the LayoutRoot element added to all new projects by default.

Because the Grid has a number of Layout possibilities, you will now work with the settings of the grid, changing them one at a time to note the effect each has on child elements. Until such time as the rules of the different PBCs are firmly implanted in your mind, you may find that trial and error serves you best, with quite a bit of both being used during your initial design attempts. With some understanding, however, hopefully it will be less error than trial.

You can create a static-sized object by setting Width and Height to a nominal value and setting the margins to 0. You can also set Width and Height to Auto and set the Margins to arbitrary values so that the grid resizes with its parent. Finally, you can set width height and margin properties to ensure the element stays in the same position and size.

In the following steps, you run through several trial scenarios to get you in the zone of using panel-based controls:

1. Open a new project in Blend.

2. Select and activate the LayoutRoot element, find the Rectangle control in the toolbox, and double-click it to add a new Rectangle element to the top-left corner of the LayoutRoot parent element. The Rectangle control has a default Width of 100 and Height of 100.

3. Set the Background property (located in the Brushes category of the Properties panel) to a Red SolidColorBrush.

4. Type "ali" (short for alignment) into the property search box to reveal the HorizontalAlignment and VerticalAlignment properties. Set these both to Center to center the Rectangle element.

    If you select the Window element in the Objects and Timelines panel, you should note the resizing grab handles appear at the corners and the centers of each side along the Window. Take a moment to play around with resizing the Window (by dragging the bottom-right grab handle) to see the effect that the current settings have.

5. Double-click the Rectangle element in the Objects and Timeline category of the interaction panel.

6. Clear the property search box and enter **mar** (short for margin) to show the four margin positions that you can set.

7. With your Red Rectangle centered in the LayoutRoot parent, change the margin values for each, by clicking and holding the left mouse button and then dragging the mouse in a direction of your choice.

    You should see that the Rectangle stays the same size but moves around the parent to comply with the margin settings. When the alignment is set to center, the margin value is offset from center.

8. Clear the property search box and collapse of the category parts except for the Layout category so that you can clearly see the Height and Width properties as well as the Margins.

9. Double-click the LayoutRoot element to activate it. Select the Rectangle element (so that the LayoutRoot displays with a yellow border around it and the Rectangle is highlighted).

10. Set the Width and Height properties to Auto.

11. Set HorizontalAlignment and VerticalAlignment to Stretch.

The Rectangle should completely cover your artboard. Try changing the margins again, as well as selecting the Window element and changing its size to see how these properties have changed the layout logic applied to your grid.

You can probably see that when you set the Width and Height properties to Auto, the Margin and the Alignment properties control both the positioning and sizing of the child element (in this case the red Rectangle) in relation to its parent.

When both Width and Height properties are Auto, the child element shows only when you set both the HorizontalAlignment and VerticalAlignment properties to Stretch or when you set the Min/Max and Width/Height properties to a value greater than 0.

The last setting to look at here—Margin—can be confusing. The following steps demonstrate the effect margins can have on your elements.

1. With the Rectangle selected, ensure that both the Width and Height are set to 100.

2. Set HorizontalAlignment to Left.

3. Set VerticalAlignment to Top.

4. Set the Left Margin value to 172.

5. Set the Right Margin value to 317.

6. Set the Top Margin value to 130.

7. Set the Bottom Margin to 0.

   All looks fine?

8. Finally, set the Right Margin property to 400.

The Right Margin property now controls the right edge of the Rectangle in relation to the Parent construct. The bounding box does not change size, however, so in this scenario, the Actual Width of the Rectangle remains unchanged.

Now set the mouse on the Left Margin value and drag it down (or left) to reduce the Left Margin value and move the Rectangle to the left.

By default, the LayoutRoot element, which is a Grid, is set to Grid mode, which means that your Red Rectangle is laid out according to the Margins and Alignment properties. But sometimes you may need to use absolute positioning values.

Mode Switch button

FIGURE 6.1   Clicking the Mode Switch button switches between Canvas and Grid modes.

Activate any Grid to see the Button located in the top-left corner of the Grid element (see Figure 6.1). Switch to Canvas mode, and then take a moment to play with the Margins and the Width and Height properties. This time, when you select the Window element and change the size, you should notice different behavior from your Rectangle. Because in Canvas mode the Margin property values act as absolute positions, the Rectangle no longer dynamically changes size and position based on the Parent.

If you want, you can set Grid or Canvas mode as the default by using the Options menu. Open the Tools menu, select Options, and then select Artboard. Here you find a setting under the heading *Layout*.

Grid Mode Applies to All Grids in Your Application

Changing the property changes every Grid element you already have defined, so it's best to set this value at the start of a project rather than in the middle of it!

Now that you have an understanding of Layout modes, it's time to take a look at how the Grid panel defines layout constraints for its children by using Rows and Columns.

Reset your LayoutRoot by removing the Red Rectangle and ensuring that it is using Grid Layout mode. Double-click on the Red Rectangle to activate it.

To add rows and columns to your Grid during design time, you have three methods from which to choose. Plus, you can always add more row and column definitions during runtime in code.

The first method is to add a dividing line directly on the Grid during design time. Simply move the mouse over the Grid definition line, as shown in Figure 6.2.

FIGURE 6.2 The mouse hovers about the Grid and the column definition line, which is displayed in orange.

Although this method is not highly accurate, it allows you to define the row or column definitions and then manually adjust the values in XAML, as shown in the Listing 6.1.

LISTING 6.1   The Star Sizing Value Type

```
<Grid Margin="76,68,90,90" Background="#FFFFE2E2">
    <Grid.ColumnDefinitions>
        <ColumnDefinition Width="0.456*"/>
        <ColumnDefinition Width="0.544*"/>
    </Grid.ColumnDefinitions>
</Grid>
```

As you can see, the Width property values add up to 1 in this case. The reasoning behind this is that the star (GridUnit type) represents a proportion of the available screen area. Therefore, a value of 0.500* would be half, with a value of 3* being three times the available screen area.

Another method of adding rows and columns to your Grid is found in the properties of the Grid itself. You access these properties by selecting the Grid, opening the Properties panel, and typing **def** into the property search box, as shown in Figure 6.3.

FIGURE 6.3   The ColumnDefinition Collection Editor has a lot of properties that you can assign to each column/row.

How Many Halves Make a Whole?

You need to add a minimum of two row or column definitions for the column or row to become available. This makes sense because you are essentially creating two columns or rows by splitting the Grid down the middle or at an arbitrary point. Each definition you add results in a defined column or row.

When designing controls, or perhaps building a new control template, laying them out first on a Grid parent element enables you to check whether everything scales as it should, which saves you a lot of problems down the road.

Canvas Element

Experienced WINForms developers probably feel most at home when using this type of panel because it acts the same as CLR forms. This is not a negative feature of the element, however, because sometimes you need to place UIElements in an absolute position. The positioning properties include the following:

- Left
- Right
- Top
- Bottom

Retrieve Child Positions

Instead of accessing a method directly on an element to return a position value such as Left or Top, you must call a static method from the Canvas object itself. For example, the code `Canvas.GetLeft(ChildElement)` returns the required value. This happens because an element's parent controls its layout positioning. This type of property value is called an *attached property*, which you can also "set" and "get" in XAML by using the following markup:

```
Grid.ColumnSpan="2"
Grid.Column="0"
```

ClipToBounds Property

Another property worth mentioning is the `ClipToBounds` property, which is set to False by default. This comes in handy if you want to restrict elements from being drawn outside of the Parent region—and, conversely, if you do.

The Canvas is not the only panel that allows you to draw outside the panel bounds, as shown in Figure 6.4.

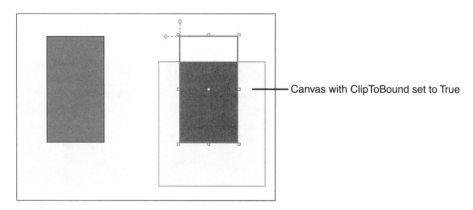

Canvas with ClipToBound set to True

FIGURE 6.4   The two Canvas panels. The one on the left had no Clipping (so you can see the entire Rectangle child), and the one on the right has Clipping turned on, so you can see only the outer boundaries of the Rectangle child.

Stack Panel

The Stack panel is extremely useful for controlling tight linear positioning layout of child controls either in a Horizontal or Vertical manner, accessible through the Orientation property of the Stack panel.

The Orientation property of the Stack panel does not control the child alignment in any situation. Alignment remains controlled by the HorizontalAlignment and VerticalAlignment properties of each child, as shown in Figure 6.5.

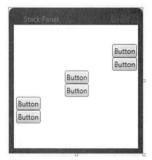

FIGURE 6.5   A ListBox with three Children that each contain a Stack panel with two child controls, each with an individual alignment setting.

The control is commonplace in WPF applications because the panel reapplies stack layout principles to its children whenever the panel changes size. If you use a Stack panel as a

ListBoxItems' child, rest assured that the Stack panel content always aligns correctly, considering that the child elements have identical layout properties applied.

The XAML in Listing 6.2 demonstrates this by showing a ListBox with three ListBoxItem children, each containing a Stack panel control and two child button controls stacked identically. The child buttons have different alignment settings, but as you can see in Figure 6.5, the items all align.

LISTING 6.2   Performing Child Element Alignment

```
    <ListBox IsSynchronizedWithCurrentItem="True" Margin="0,30,0,30"
BorderBrush="{x:Null}">
            <ListBoxItem HorizontalAlignment="Right" VerticalAlignment="Stretch"
Height="Auto">
                <StackPanel RenderTransformOrigin="0.5,0.5"
HorizontalAlignment="Stretch"
VerticalAlignment="Stretch" Width="Auto" Height="Auto"
Grid.IsSharedSizeScope="False"
ScrollViewer.CanContentScroll="False">

                    <Button Content="Button" HorizontalAlignment="Right"/>
                    <Button Content="Button" Width="Auto" Height="Auto"
HorizontalAlignment="Stretch" VerticalAlignment="Center"/>

                </StackPanel>
            </ListBoxItem>
            <ListBoxItem Height="Auto" HorizontalAlignment="Center"
VerticalAlignment="Center">
                <StackPanel RenderTransformOrigin="0.5,0.5"
HorizontalAlignment="Stretch" VerticalAlignment="Stretch" Width="Auto"
Height="Auto" Grid.IsSharedSizeScope="False" ScrollViewer.CanContentScroll="False">

                    <Button Content="Button" HorizontalAlignment="Right"/>

                    <Button Content="Button" HorizontalAlignment="Stretch"
VerticalAlignment="Center" Width="Auto" Height="Auto"/>

                </StackPanel>
            </ListBoxItem>
            <ListBoxItem Height="Auto" HorizontalAlignment="Left"
VerticalAlignment="Top">
                <StackPanel RenderTransformOrigin="0.5,0.5"
HorizontalAlignment="Stretch" VerticalAlignment="Stretch" Width="Auto"
Height="Auto" Grid.IsSharedSizeScope="False" ScrollViewer.CanContentScroll="False">

                    <Button Content="Button" HorizontalAlignment="Right"/>
```

```
                    <Button Content="Button" HorizontalAlignment="Stretch"
VerticalAlignment="Center" Width="Auto" Height="Auto"/>

                </StackPanel>
            </ListBoxItem>
        </ListBox>
```

Wrap Panel

The Wrap panel is handy for displaying large groups of elements that you are certain will fill the available space of the parent container but are unsure what the exact number of elements will be in each row or when your content is dynamic. The Wrap panel detects when content elements will touch the outer edge and automatically moves them to the next line in the panel.

Being a dynamic control, you can also see the effects of the Wrap by adding the control to your project. After inserting several child elements, simply resize the parent and watch as the Wrap panel takes care of everything!

Add the XAML in Listing 6.3. Select the Window element to enable resize grab handles and then change the form size.

LISTING 6.3   A Simple WrapPanel Example Showing Wrapping Functionality

```
        <WrapPanel Margin="120,100,120,100">
            <Button Margin="5,5,5,5" Width="125.623" Height="104.96"
Content="Button"/>
            <Button Width="125.623" Height="104.96" Content="Button"
Margin="5,5,5,5"/>
            <Button Width="125.623" Height="104.96" Content="Button"
Margin="5,5,5,5"/>
            <Button Width="125.623" Height="104.96" Content="Button"
Margin="5,5,5,5"/>
            <Button Width="125.623" Height="104.96" Content="Button"
Margin="5,5,5,5"/>
            <Button Width="125.623" Height="104.96" Content="Button"
Margin="5,5,5,5"/>
        </WrapPanel>
```

Dock Panel

Developers are likely already familiar with the concept of docking, because of their use of WINForms and dock properties. But in case you're a designer and haven't used docking before, or as a developer you didn't use the feature much, this section takes a quick look at exactly what this style of panel offers.

The Dock panel, as the name suggests, forces its child controls to dock to an edge of its container or to fill the entire remaining panel region, which includes the panel in its entirety when there are no other child controls. After a control is added to the child collection, the control defaults to "left" dock, which you can change by searching for the Dock property of the embedded child. This property appears only when the child is added to a DockPanel parent.

Interestingly, another property available on the Dock panel itself is LastChildFill. This property is set to False by default (contrary to what the Windows SDK says). If you check this or set the property to True in code, it simply means that any other children that you add to the Dock panel will fill the remaining available space.

ScrollViewer Control

Because the ScrollViewer control is a container built specifically for—you guessed it— scrolling, it contains several properties designed to assist you with the layout of the singular child in presenting the Child-Parent relationship.

When you use a word-processing program, such as Microsoft Office Word, and you want to create, view, or edit a document, you see the document as a child explicitly of the containing area. This allows you to visualize the exact look of a page.

Figure 6.6 demonstrates this exact usage by clearly defining the look of the ScrollViewer container control with a Black background brush and the singular Child (in this case a Grid with a RichTextBox control as its child) as a text-based display item.

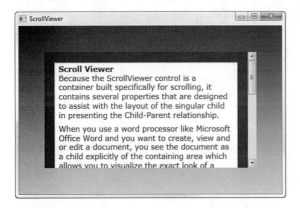

FIGURE 6.6   The Parent-Child explicitly contained within the ScrollViewer's bounds.

Border Element

The Border element means different things to different people. This is evident between me and my friend, Amir Khella. Amir thinks the Border element doesn't deserve to be in a chapter about panel-based controls. Your view probably depends on whether you intend to use the Border as a panel, controlling child layouts, or adding cosmetic effects.

The panel-based controls include the Border control because it allows for a single child to be added to its ContentControl. In a previous chapter, you may recall that a suggested good usage for the Rectangle tool is to create rounded rectangle borders for controls. But that would mean adding a rectangle to that control's child collection (if indeed it had one) or creating a Grid control group with both the Rectangle and the Control added as children.

Hypothetically speaking, what if you want to add a border to a Rectangle element? You could go through the steps listed previously, but why do that when you could use the Border control and then add the Rectangle element as its child? Of course you can always add another panel as the child and then go nuts with content, as well.

Within styles of almost every control that comes with Blend, you find heavy use of the Border control. As you continue the UI creation process and restyle more controls, the more you will work with it.

Uniform Grid

The Uniform Grid is often overlooked for the functionality that it provides. That functionality includes displaying all its child controls in uniform proportion to each other based on the Grid Row and Column property settings of the parent Uniform Grid (see Figure 6.7).

When added via the Asset Library or Common Controls category of the Toolbox palette, the Uniform Grid defines no Rows or Columns by default. Instead, the Uniform Grid assumes dynamic sizing is required of children as they are added.

You can declare the Row and Column properties initially, which constrains the child element sizes regardless of their settings or the number of children that have been previously added to the Uniform Grid.

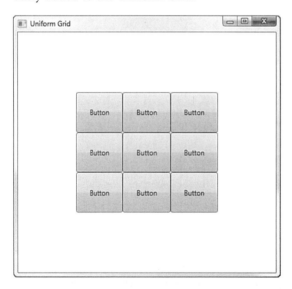

FIGURE 6.7   The simplicity of the Uniform Grid control.

ViewBox Control

ViewBox is a useful control that stretches the content of its single child and any children of its singular child. Set the StretchDirection property to control how the stretch is applied within the Vertical space of the container. Figures 6.8 and 6.9 show just one use for the ViewBox control, which in this case is creating a Page Heading that dynamically renders the text font depending on the size of the form. The font does not actually change size; the font merely renders according to the layout properties of the parent.

FIGURE 6.8   The original implementation of a label added as the ViewBox Child.

FIGURE 6.9   The same ViewBox and child labels after the parent window control changes size.

The XAML shown in Listing 6.4 re-creates Figures 6.8 and 6.9.

LISTING 6.4   The Viewbox Effect on Child Elements

```
        <Viewbox Margin="50,5,50,50" VerticalAlignment="Stretch" Height="Auto"
Stretch="Fill" StretchDirection="Both">
            <Label HorizontalAlignment="Stretch"
            Margin="5,5,5,5"
            VerticalAlignment="Stretch"
            Width="Auto"
            Height="Auto"
            FontFamily="Arial"
            FontSize="10"
            FontStyle="Normal"
            FontWeight="Bold"
            HorizontalContentAlignment="Center"
            Padding="0,0,0,0"
```

```
        VerticalContentAlignment="Center"
        xml:space="preserve">This is a Heading
        </Label>
    </Viewbox>
```

Panel Type Switching

Here's a quick usability tip. When using Blend, if you find you chose the incorrect panel type, you can select the panel-based element in the element tree located in the Objects and Timelines panel. Right-click to reveal the context menu and then search for the menu item Change Layout Type, which quickly switches between panels without you needing to move around children.

Summary

As you can see from the vast array of panel-based containers, you can—and should—make a specific choice of which one to use based on the anticipated children of that container.

Obviously some containers are better at displaying items such as Thumbnail images, like the Uniform Grid or Stack Panel; and some of the other controls are better at displaying things like child Label Controls. The ViewBox or the Wrap panel are good choices here.

You will make mistakes about which panel is best suited for the job until you use each one and then instinctively know which one will get you home in your chosen task.

Hopefully, you now understand that having multiple panel types is indeed a good thing. The responsibility is yours to ensure that the correct type is utilized for the given scenario and will take time to get used to.

Perhaps the biggest lesson to be learned is that scaling sometimes throws up ugly results that you just don't expect and, therefore, Grids in Canvas mode become a danger. Personally, the biggest problems I have faced with scaling relate to embedded multi-point path elements in Blend 1, which did not support animated paths.

A general rule of thumb should always be to look for the simple solution to your panel-based container needs. Don't overlook the features and benefits that some PBCs have instead of using a Grid or Canvas just because it appears easier to do so at first.

PART III

Using All the New Stuff

IN THIS PART

CHAPTER 7

Using the Blend Toolbox: Tools and Common Controls

At first glance, you might mistakenly think that the tools supplied with Expression Blend through the Tools palette are slightly on the skinny side. It's not until you start to see how all these tools can be used together, as well as the special features included with some of them, that you come to understand that the opposite is closer to the truth. The toolset is quite complete. Figure 7.1 shows the Toolbox palette as it appeared in the Beta versions of Blend 2.

In this chapter, you will look at each of the tools in detail and you will also see most, if not all, the actions of each tool as well as the special functions that some of them possess. In Chapter 8, "An Example Control Using Just the Tools Palette," you use these tools to create a Button UIElement. While it contains complex representations, it is ultimately simple to construct thanks to the Tool palette. In Chapter 9, "Using the Blend Asset Library," you will look at the controls that are also found on the Toolbox palette. They are not described in any great detail here because they are simply added to the Toolbox as a shortcut selection area.

To get you warmed up for Chapter 8, throughout this chapter you use some of the tools to create a nice little piece of vector graphic artwork.

Practice Makes Perfect!

Take the time to go through these tools and practice with them. You will surely see that some of them could save you literally hundreds of hours of development time due to the automated Markup additions. This is just another reason why I believe developers should understand and learn to use this tool.

FIGURE 7.1   The Blend Toolbox.

Tool Categories

Note in Figure 7.1 that several of the tools have a small dark (or light depending on the theme that you are using) triangle in the bottom-right corner of the Tool icon. This indicates that the tool is part of a Tool collection or category.

Toolbox Categories

Throughout this chapter, you will use several tools, but the order that they are explained unfortunately is not always in the order in which Microsoft's developers have added them to the Toolbox.

It would appear that the positioning of these tools has now stabilized (along with the shortcut keys which have also changed over the last few releases).

Here is a quick explanation of the categories.

Usability Tools (Environment)

Usability tools are included to assist you with either moving around the application or moving around your work surfaces and/or objects, controls, and UIElements. Light on features, these tools usually serve a very specific function that you can access by using keyboard shortcuts.

Path Tools

The term *Path* refers to a specific *type* of UIElement that is used in the creation and manipulation (sometimes animation) of vector-based graphics. These tools are invaluable if you have a need to incorporate vector graphics in your application. Once you have mastered them, you can save considerable development time. The vast majority of this chapter is focused on the Path element because I believe it to be one of the most confusing areas when first starting with Blend. Figure 7.2 shows the Category submenu in the Toolbox.

FIGURE 7.2 The Path submenu.

Shape Tools

Three tools are part of this category: Rectangle, Line, and Ellipse (see Figure 7.3). Essentially, these tools work hand in hand with the Path tools. We look at two of them during the construction of our sample.

FIGURE 7.3 The Shape submenu.

Panel-Based UIElements

As of this writing there were nine panel-based UIElements available from this category, as illustrated in Figure 7.4. Each element has a specific purpose. Together they are responsible for the superb layout features found with WPF applications. As previously mentioned, some of these UIElements are discussed in detail in Chapter 9.

Text-Based UIElements

Six controls are available in this category and represent the most commonly used text-based controls. Notice that there are several other similar controls that don't appear on the Toolbox palette (see Figure 7.5). They differ in their performance and handling of certain types of content, but feel familiar once you understand the concept of FlowDocuments.

Flow document-based text controls refer to those controls that contain specific properties and features designed to assist with the formatting and pagination of page elements and content. They are generally sorted from lightest weight to most robust in the following order:

1. Textblock
2. FlowDocumentScrollViewer
3. FlowDocumentPageViewer
4. FlowDocumentReader

FIGURE 7.4   The Panel submenu.

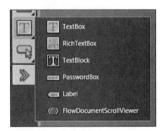

FIGURE 7.5   The Text submenu.

RichTextBox

While the RichTextBox supports the FlowDocument object model, it is generally considered as a heavyweight control, providing an extremely large and flexible property set that includes support for displaying images.

See Chapter 9 for more detailed information.

Common Controls UIElements

A list of nine common controls is available in this category (see Figure 7.6). Each of the controls can also be found in the Asset Viewer (see Chapter 9 for more detailed information on the controls). Having them available from the Toolbox is convenient. The more controls and elements you have available in the Asset Viewer, the longer the control or element takes to become active after you have selected it.

FIGURE 7.6   The Common Controls submenu.

Recent Control Elements

Almost a usability item, the Recent Control Elements area on the Toolbox shows the most recently used controls from the Asset Viewer and allows you to add additional controls to your screen more quickly by selecting from previously selected controls. Your own custom controls also appear here when you add them to your scene; but, be aware that if you change your control, the icon representing your control will become disabled.

Tools in Detail

Let's investigate the tools, and along the way create a sample. In this process you will be introduced to several tools but they are not in the order (from top to bottom) as they appear in the Blend ToolBox. In this process, you will attain a basic familiarity with most of the tools. Open a blank application to begin and don't forget to save your application at regular intervals.

Pan Tool

The Pan tool is a usability tool added to assist you when you are working with an extremely large artboard (the work surface). It is also useful when you are zoomed into your work at a very high ratio and need an easy way to move around your UIElements.

Pan is simple to use. Just select the tool from the Tools palette and a hand icon will replace the standard mouse cursor, allowing you to click and hold the artboard. Now drag your mouse to reposition your viewable area.

A handy feature of this tool is that if you double-click the Pan icon in the Tools palette, your artboard will center itself in your current view.

Zoom Tool

The Zoom tool is another usability tool that most designers are familiar with, as is just about anyone else that has used a computer for more than two days. By selecting the Zoom tool, you can click and hold your mouse down on the artboard, drag a zoom region, and zoom to a specified region of your work. You can click your mouse and zoom in instead of using the region; and if you hold down the ALT key and click, you will zoom back out.

The tool has a few more features as well:

▶ If you double-click the Zoom icon on the Tools palette, your artboard will zoom in or out to center and show your artboard at its actual size.

▶ If you have a scroll mouse, you can hold down the control (CTRL) key and scroll your mouse to zoom the artboard in or out.

▶ If you hold down the Shift key, you find that the artboard pans from left to right and back again as you scroll your mouse. If you hold down the ALT key and scroll, you will find that the artboard pans in a vertical fashion.

 Line Tool

The Line tool is a Shape tool that creates a vector object. As the name suggests, it is just a line between two points; but interestingly enough, it does not create a Line element. The Line tool actually creates a Path.

I know it isn't very sexy, but when you look a little deeper, it livens up. Think in geometry class terms. There are two classes: Geometry and Shape. It is important to note that a Path and a Line are *types* of Shape.

With a Line, you must specify a Stroke (line thickness) value, or it will be invisible and the Fill property is not valid. I am unsure why the Line is not actually a line, but I am guessing that it might have something to do with some of the other tools and their features. I say this because while you can create a line using a Path, as is done by the environment, if you declare a line as *typeof* Line you can never add curves to it, whereas the Path element does give you this ability whenever you choose to use it—plus much more. Perhaps this is the answer to my earlier question bout a line not being a line.

Path elements are extremely flexible in comparison to Lines, as you can create complex items from a Path element base by adding Geometry groups to the Data property of a Path.

The Path element can be created with as little XAML Markup as shown in the following:

```
<Path Stroke="Black" Data="M 10,50 L 200,70" />
```

While looking at all the tools, keep an open blank application available in Blend so you can experiment. Start now!

Open your blank application, select the Line tool from the Tools palette, and draw a line in your application. From here on, I will refer to the resulting Path element as a line. Take a look at the XAML produced by Blend. It will resemble Listing 7.1.

LISTING 7.1   A Simple Line: Path Element

```
<Path Fill="#FFFFFFFF"
    Stretch="Fill"
    Stroke="#FF000000"
    Margin="153.9,129.3,297.1,166.5"
    Data="M154.4,129.8 L336,281"/>
```

Remember the Bloat?

Microsoft has promised it would not create excess Markup, which can be a positive or a negative, within this environment. Nonetheless, the basics are there for you to manipulate, animate, or translate. Of course, doing this manually would be unnecessary and quite time-consuming. Authoring in Blend and using its many palettes (Transform, Timeline, etc.) allows you to achieve the same results in a much shorter timeframe.

A Path is extremely flexible in what it offers. You can add curves to your Path lines at any point, creating closed shapes, open shapes, or even multiple shapes.

While still in XAML view, find the Data tag within the Path declaration. Replace what you already have within the quotes in your Data tag with the following values:

```
Data="M270,315.6 L402,217.2 238,218 375.6,316.4 326.8,154.8 z"
```

Notice the Data property tag and the letters that appear in it: M,L and z in this case. This is referred to as *mini-language* syntax and is used to reduce the amount of XAML required to perform an operation or set a value property on certain areas of certain elements. We don't know whether Microsoft will continue to support these mini-languages in coming versions because they have already removed them from several other areas of the XAML specification.

TABLE 7.1   Some Mini-Language Commands Used by Path

Data Code	Description	Information
M (x,y)	Move to	Used for the start of an object where location x and y are given
V (y)	Vertical Line	Draws a vertical line from the current position directly to the location of y
H (x)	Horizontal Line	Draws a horizontal line from the current position directly to the location of x

TABLE 7.1   Some Mini-Language Commands Used by Path

Data Code	Description	Information
L (x,y)	Line	Draws a line from the current position to location x and y
Z	Close Path	Specifies that the object created should be a Closed Path, so the last point is connected directly to the first point

Some of the path-compliant codes are shown in Table 7.1.

At the time of this writing, getting some form of documented instruction for these commands was almost impossible. Several other commands exist, including Bezier curves represented by *C*; smooth Bezier curves, which are represented by *S*; Arcs represented by the *A*; and even a quadratic Bezier command represented by *Q*.

Relative Commands Exist

In most cases a relative command is also available as the lowercase representation of a command. As an example, with the Line command, the uppercase *L* refers to Line, while a lowercase *l* refers to a relative line.

Let's say that the current position is X=50, Y=50. By adding L20,20 to your data property, you would draw a line to the location X=20,Y=20. If you were to use l20,20, you would, in fact, be extending the line 20 pixels to the current X position and 20 pixels to the current Y position.

The purpose of mini-language is to reduce the amount of markup. Without it, you can imagine just how much markup would be required just to draw a line.

We have only touched on the Path element here; but as you will see, there are several other tools in the Tools palette that are also involved in the creation and manipulation of Path elements.

 Direct Selection

The Direct Selection tool is a usability tool that is particularly handy at allowing you to manipulate vector objects, as well as their contained lines and curves.

The two main areas of use are

1. It allows you to select individual vector-based shapes contained within a larger complex whole.
2. It allows you to very accurately control the shape definition by providing grab handles on the shape/path curve (see Figure 7.7) that you are operating on.

To get a feel for this tool, create a new application in Blend and add the XAML declaration in Listing 7.2.

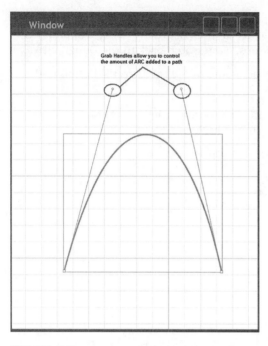

FIGURE 7.7   The grab handles are the unfilled circles on the end of the antenna-looking lines.

LISTING 7.2   Sample Application

```
<Path
    Stroke="#FF000000"
    Fill="#FFFFFFFF"
    HorizontalAlignment="Stretch"
    VerticalAlignment="Stretch"
    Margin="25,25,25,25"
    Width="Auto"
    Height="Auto"
    x:Name="Path"
    RenderTransformOrigin="0.5,0.5"
    Stretch="Fill"
    Data="M25,95 L75,45 135,45 175,95 135,155 75,155 z">
    <Path.RenderTransform>
        <TransformGroup>
            <TranslateTransform X="0" Y="0"/>
            <ScaleTransform ScaleX="1" ScaleY="1"/>
            <SkewTransform AngleX="0" AngleY="0"/>
            <RotateTransform Angle="0"/>
            <TranslateTransform X="0" Y="0"/>
            <TranslateTransform X="0" Y="0"/>
        </TransformGroup>
    </Path.RenderTransform>
</Path>
```

Find the Window tag at the top of your XAML page, and then find the width and height properties that are being set within the initial declaration. Set the width to **315** and the height to **390**. This is important for scale reasons. Now switch back to the Design view.

Yes, I know it isn't pretty, but that is why we are going to use the Direct Selection tool, to make it look pretty—or at least try to.

1. Name all sides of the object starting at the 9:00 position on a clock. Move clockwise around the object to name the sides as shown in Figure 7.8.

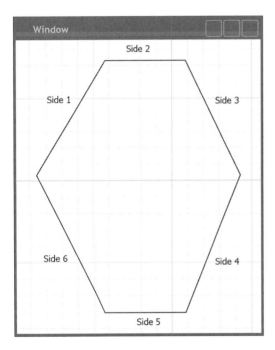

FIGURE 7.8   Ugly hexagon sides.

2. Select the Direct Selection tool from the palette. Make sure you have the UIElement Path selected in the Objects and Timeline palette (sometimes referred to as the Timeline viewer). All the connecting points (unfilled squares at each line end point) of our pathetic, ugly hexagon should be visible.

3. Place the mouse in the center of the hexagon. Don't click anything yet, just put it there. Now, slowly move the mouse toward Side 1. Notice the cursor changed from having a four-pointed icon below the arrow cursor (drag cursor) to having a semi-circle (arc cursor) when you moved within a few millimeters of the side. This indicates that you are within range of the Path element and are now free to work on it. If you move outside of the closed shape, the cursor does not show an icon, which indicates that you can use the mouse to make an individual element selection, similar to the Pointer tool.

4. Move your mouse so it sits right on top of Side 1, about halfway up the line. If your mouse is right on top of the line, left click it to select Side 1. This is what we call a line segment.

5. When you hold down the ALT key on your keyboard, the mouse cursor changes to a weird upside down looking V with a semicircle icon to the right of it. If you don't see the same thing, you are most likely not on top of the line or have not selected the Side. You may need to zoom in some more to make sure that your cursor is properly positioned.

Zoom in for Greater Clarity

You will always get a more accurate result the more you zoom in on your chosen object. Manipulation of Path elements can sometimes get out of control if you are not very accurate with your mouse movements.

6. Now, hold down your left mouse button and press the ALT button to display some grab handles. You can ignore them for the moment. Move the cursor toward the top left point of your artboard, just enough to create a nice-looking curve as shown in the Figure 7.9.

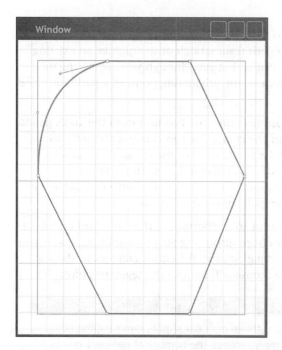

FIGURE 7.9   The path curve and the resulting grab handles.

7. Continue around each Side, pushing each straight line of the path until it forms a nice circular curve. You don't have to be accurate here, just get the rough shape.

This is what I like to call the *developer's circle* or *DC*. Not exactly round in shape, it is similar to the artistic efforts of a five-year-old, in some cases not even that. If you are from a designer background, I would expect perfection here! You can think of it as the *designer's circle*!

If you have the DC, go ahead and refine it a little more by using the grab handles. To get started, go back and select the curved line that used to be Side 1. Remember, the grab handles appear at the beginning and the end of the line segment.

1. Select either one of the grab handle points (small circles) and, while holding down the left mouse button, move the grab handle in various directions, which results in either a smoother circle or a really big mess. If you have the mess result, that is not really a problem. You can safely press, CTRL + Z to undo the last action and return to your starting point.

2. Move your way around your DC, but don't spend too much time on this task. You probably won't create a perfect circle using this method. Still, it should give you a good understanding of the use of the Direct Selection tool.

Now we are going to continue using the Direct Selection tool, but add the simultaneous use of the Pen tool. They go hand in hand, really. In fact, all path tools can be used in conjunction with one another to get a desired result.

Pen Tool

The Pen tool is a path tool that allows us to add or remove arbitrary points from a path object. You can use the Pen tool to create a path from scratch or to enhance an existing path. What is important to note about the Pen is that even though you are adding or removing point segments, you can also return to the originating point of a path and close an object to form a complex shape.

Continuing on from our Direct Selection sample, select the Pen tool from the Tools palette and move your cursor toward the bottom of the circle. The Pen cursor is the same as the icon shown in the Tools palette with a small x to the right of the cursor. That small x means that if you clicked the left mouse button, you would be creating a new Path element. If the cursor shows no x, then the next click of the mouse button would add an additional line segment to the newly created path (more on this later).

For now, notice that when you move the cursor to the bottom of the circle and on top of an existing line segment, the cursor changes from displaying an x to displaying a +. If you move the cursor over a segment end point (small square) the cursor changes to show a small – sign, which means that clicking the mouse will remove the segment point.

Removing a Segment Point

If you are removing a segment point that is within a complex shape, removing the point will not *break* the shape, so to speak. It simply reduces the number of segment points available. Any curvature applied to the previous segments will be re-applied to the single segment left by the removal action.

We want to add two additional segment points to our circle, as shown in Figure 7.10.

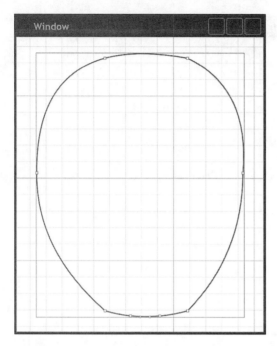

FIGURE 7.10   New segment points added to the circle.

Now that we have the two new points added, select the Direct Selection tool again and drag each of the points vertically below the circle as shown in Figure 7.11. This may require a little manipulating of the existing Path points in order to give the height required.

Just a Little Tip

It is far easier to move the bottom line segment before you add the additional points.

When you select one of the points with the Direct Selection tool, you now have grab handles. Use the grab handles to manipulate the curves until you have an object that looks similar to Figure 7.12.

It might take you some time to get your shape to look like the one in Figure 7.12. Be patient and you will get it eventually. Remember to use the undo (CTRL + Z) feature if you are beyond saving at any point. When you are satisfied with your shape, then you can move on.

The following steps continue on with the sample, filling in the shape to add some context:

1. Select the LayoutRoot in the Objects and Timeline palette. Then go back to the Tools palette and select the Pen tool. You are going to add several points here that follow a part of our original shape. The important thing is to be as accurate as possible; so zoom in again if it helps.

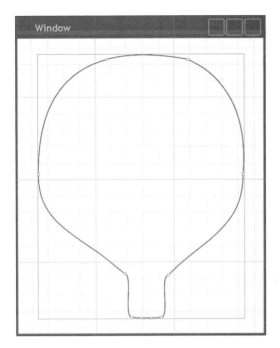

FIGURE 7.11   Repositioning the newly added points.

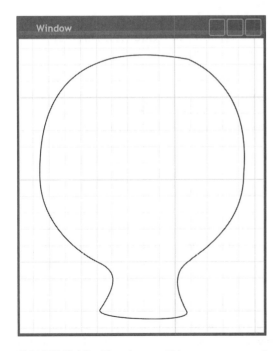

FIGURE 7.12   The shape will become apparent soon enough.

2. If you look at the shape as it stands and imagine a top half and a bottom half, the top half has the shape of a semicircle. Follow that path (the semicircle), adding new points along the way, and finally close the new complex shape by returning to the starting point. With the Pen tool selected, move to the 9:00 position on the imaginary clock or the start of the semicircular top half. With the Pen cursor showing an x on the icon, click your mouse button to add a new point directly above the line of our original path.

Path Secrets

The secret to creating paths is that the more points you add, the greater the accuracy of the end result. But don't go overboard or the shape will be too unmanageable to allow you to smooth the curves.

Notice in Figure 7.13 that when the shape moves back across the middle of the original shape it dips down slightly to form a V shape. We did this on purpose. When you are working on the shape and move the Pen tool back to the first point you created, notice that the cursor changes to show a small circle next to the Pen icon. This indicates that a closed complex shape will be created by the last connecting point.

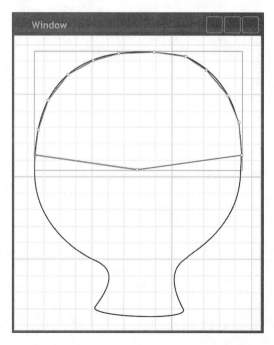

FIGURE 7.13   It's a fine line between not having enough points and having too many.

When you have finished adding new points and have successfully closed the shape, you can then go around with the Direct Selection tool and perfect the smoothness of the curves. Remember to use the ALT key when selecting line segments to view the grab handles and to push the segments into a curved position. That bottom line that was shaped like a V should also be pushed into a nice smooth downward curve. With any luck you should end up with two path objects that resemble something close to Figure 7.14.

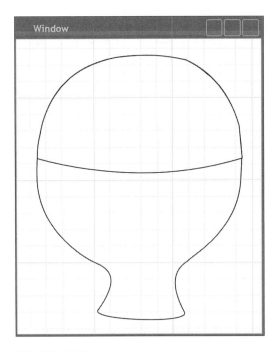

FIGURE 7.14   The path after smoothing.

When completed, your objects panel should show a similar object tree to that as shown in Figure 7.15.

FIGURE 7.15   The object tree.

Now let's give some life to the shapes. The shape you created in this exercise will be recognizable to most of you.

1. Select the element named *Path* in the Timeline palette.

2. Open the Brushes palette and select the `Fill` property. Make sure you have the Solid Color Brush selected. With the color selector, change the color to show a nice bright yellow.

3. Select the visual element named [Path] in the Objects and Timeline palette. Go to the Brushes palette. Again, using the `Fill` property, select the *Gradient Brush* type and ensure you have *Linear Gradient* selected. The palette should change to show a color control widget (see Figure 7.16) in which you can set appropriate gradients (see Chapter 3, "Expression Blend Panels," for an in-depth look at the Brushes palette). Set the left color controller to a nice deep orange color and the right color controller to white.

FIGURE 7.16   The Linear Gradient selection of the Gradient Brush on the `Fill` property.

4. Set the Alpha (Opacity) channel to 75% on both the left and right Gradient stops.

We continue to work on this sample next with the Pencil tool.

Pencil Tool

Similar to some of our previous path tools, the Pencil allows us to create a Path element. In this instance, however, the path we create will be entirely freehand. This tool is used predominantly to add highlights and small path additions because without the use of a "pen and tablet" input device it is sometimes very difficult to control.

The following steps provide a very small usage scenario for the Pencil tool, but it is the master stroke to emphasise what the object is.

1. Select the LayoutRoot element in the Timeline palette and the Pencil tool from the Tools palette.

2. Starting at the top-right side of the previous path elements, create a zigzag path object, as shown in Figure 7.17.

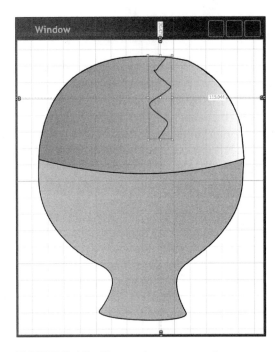

FIGURE 7.17   The cracks are appearing.

3. Open the Brushes palette, select the Fill property, and set it to *No Brush*.

4. Select the Stroke property, and then select Gradient Brush. Set the Gradient type to Radial. On the left Gradient stop, set the color to a pale cream type color and the right Gradient stop to white.

Ellipse Tool

The Ellipse tool is part of the Shapes class provided within the Presentation Framework. Interestingly you may note that the Line, Path, and Rectangle elements are as well. There are, however, two others that are not shown as tools. Polygon and Polyline are also part of the Shape class. So why are they not shown as individual tools? The answer is that they are both combined as part of the Pen tool.

The Polyline element is a Path of connected points that results in an open shape. Remember clicking all those points around the semicircle top part of the previous path element? You were, in essence, creating a Polyline element when you were doing it.

The Polygon is basically the same, except that the resultant shape is a closed object, the same as when you closed the shape by returning to the original point you added with the Pen tool.

The following steps have you using the Ellipse tool to create a shadow effect:

1. Select the Ellipse tool from the Tools palette and draw an ellipse with similar appearance to the one shown in Figure 7.18.

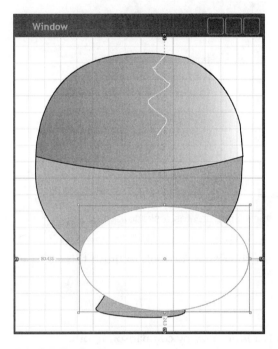

FIGURE 7.18   Using an ellipse as a shadow object place holder.

2. Open the Brushes palette again and select the Fill property and the Radial Gradient Brush. This time, set the left Gradient stop to black and the right Gradient stop to white. Select and hold the mouse over the left Gradient stop and move it to the right—toward the center of the color gradient to create a very dark spot in the center of the Ellipse with a nice gradient leading to the outer edge.

3. Make sure the Stroke property is set to No Brush, and then open the Timeline palette to view the visual element tree.

4. Find the [Ellipse] element in the tree and then right click on it, bringing up a context menu in which you see the menu item I. Move your mouse over this item, and then from the next menu that appears, select Send to back.

Your work should resemble Figure 7.19.

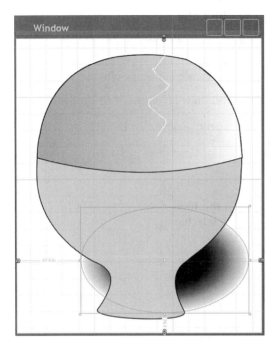

FIGURE 7.19   With the appropriate shading, the ellipse creates a shadow.

It doesn't quite look right does it? Time to use the rest of the tools to finish this exercise off.

Eyedropper Tool

The Eyedropper tool is a usability tool and is a little crazy by comparison to other Eyedroppers that I personally have used in the past. I am used to being able to view the colors that I have selected with this type of tool and then decide whether I want to use that color in some way, shape, or form.

Things are a little different in the world of Blend—as I am sure you have already realized. Find the Ellipse element in the Timeline palette and make sure it is the selected element.

1. Select the Eyedropper tool from the Tools palette. Then click on the bright yellow base object.

2. Press CTRL+Z to undo this color and use the Eyedropper to select the gradient pink/brown object above.

3. Again press CTRL+Z to undo it.

I suppose I have been fairly harsh on this tool as it is in reality quite flexible compared to other Eyedroppers. Furthermore, some of the features that it does expose are unique.

There is a second Eyedropper tool with Blend. What? Two Eyedroppers? There must be a mistake! If you open the Brushes palette, there is a Color Eyedropper tool the bottom of the color picker. The difference in the tools is that this Color Eyedropper allows you to visualize what the color on the element is going to be before you actually apply it, whereas the Eyedropper in the Toolbox requires you to click the color that you want to apply.

Paint Bucket

As crazy as the Eyedropper would appear, the Paint Bucket usability tool works in a reverse manner. Find and select the Path element in the Timeline palette. Now select the Paint Bucket tool from the Tools palette and amuse yourself by clicking on other elements on the artboard.

Remember to press CTRL+Z to get back to the yellow object.

As with the Eyedropper tool, you can right-click on the Toolbox icon and select which properties the Paint Bucket tool will apply to on the selected objects.

Brush Transform Tool

The Brush Transform usability tool is a particularly handy tool for getting the fine details that we sometimes require when playing with the color and lighting settings of our objects.

Look at your work. It is starting to take shape, except that the yellow object is flat where all the other objects show some degree of lighting effect or 3D appearance.

We want to make this yellow object worldlier. Let's apply a gradient brush to give us the desired effect.

1. Find and select the Path element in the Timeline palette. Open the Brushes palette and select the Fill property. It was set to Solid Color Brush when we created it; but now we would like to use a Linear Gradient Brush. Don't worry about the colors changing because, by default, they will always show the last selected color pairings, regardless of the object selection.

2. Set the left Gradient stop to a nice bright yellow, and then set the right Gradient stop to a slightly darker shade of yellow or gold. Make sure they are noticeably different, but so similar that they blend if you cross your eyes.

3. Select the Brush Transform tool from the Tools palette. An arrow appears on your screen that is representing the adjustment layers of the gradient. When you place your mouse over the ends of the arrow, your cursor changes to indicate a rotation ability, which is one part of what you will need to do. You can also shorten or lengthen the arrow by selecting the ends of the arrow object and dragging them to the desired length.

Control the Rotation with Accuracy

If you hold down the Shift key while rotating the arrow object, you will notice a snap-to type of action, which will control the rotation increments by 15%. This can be particularly useful when you are trying to re-create an accurate shading model on several objects.

1. Shape and move the arrow until your figure looks something like Figure 7.20.

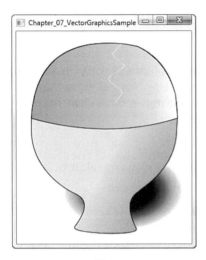

FIGURE 7.20   The finished product.

2. Select the LayoutRoot element in your Timeline palette and stand back to admire your creative work. Press F5 to view your application.

What is it? It should resemble a boiled egg in a cup!

Although you haven't created a museum quality piece of art, you have worked with the most useful parts of many of the tools—particularly those related to Path elements. With a little work, you will find that the tools, for the most part, become easier to use and cut down the amount of raw markup you need to enter.

Without these path tools you would spend perhaps hours, if not days, sketching points on a grid notepad trying to work out where each point should be placed.

One tool that you have not looked at yet is the Camera Orbit tool. It is used when working with 3D objects, more specifically for controlling the camera positioning when viewing 3D objects on the artboard.

 Camera Orbit

In Chapter 9 we go a little deeper into some of the controls and elements that are included with Expression Blend. One of the controls that is very interesting is the Viewport3D control, which lets you display and control 3D content that, for the most part, is created in other 3D modelling applications.

ZAM3D: Built for XAML

ZAM3D, created by Electric Rain, is a tool that allows you to create 3D models and export them to XAML, which is very handy. I would suggest you check out this tool (still in CTP as of this writing and free to try) because it will give you a good idea of some of the more powerful elements involved with using 3D. This application has been specially designed and built for use with XAML. The company has partnered with Microsoft to ensure that the end results work just as well in both environments. There is more on the ZAM3D tool in Chapter 9 along with a more detailed explanation of the Viewport3D.

For now, we want to use the Camera Orbit tool, which is a usability tool. To do that, we must have a Viewport3D control to use it with. We are going to create a very basic version of the control and add a simple object to it that allows us to use the tool.

As the name Camera Orbit would suggest, this tool allows us to manipulate the camera object that we are going to add as a requirement to the control.

Open a new application in Blend and insert the XAML markup in Listing 7.3, replacing everything that was already present.

LISTING 7.3   A Simple 3D Scene Using Viewport3D

```
<Grid
    xmlns="http://schemas.microsoft.com/winfx/2006/xaml/presentation"
    xmlns:x="http://schemas.microsoft.com/winfx/2006/xaml"
    xmlns:mc="http://schemas.openxmlformats.org/markup-compatibility/2006"
    xmlns:d="http://schemas.microsoft.com/expression/interactivedesigner/2006"
    xmlns:c="http://schemas.openxmlformats.org/markup-compatibility/2006"
     c:Ignorable="d"
    Background="#FFFFFFFF"
    x:Name="LayoutRoot"
    x:Class="UntitledProject1.Scene3"
    Width="640" Height="480">



  <Viewport3D x:Name="SimpleViewport3D" ClipToBounds="true" Width="400"
Height="300" >
     <Viewport3D.Resources>
       <ResourceDictionary>
         <MaterialGroup x:Key="SimpleSquare_Material" >
           <DiffuseMaterial>
```

```xml
                <DiffuseMaterial.Brush>
                  <SolidColorBrush Color="#555592" Opacity="1.000000"/>
                </DiffuseMaterial.Brush>
              </DiffuseMaterial>
            </MaterialGroup>
            <MeshGeometry3D x:Key="SimpleSquare"
              TriangleIndices="0,1,2 2,3,0 "
              Normals="0,1,0 0,1,0 0,1,0 0,1,0 "
              Positions="-0.5,0,-0.5 -0.5,0,0.5 0.5,0,0.5 0.5,0,-0.5 "
                    />
          </ResourceDictionary>
        </Viewport3D.Resources>

        <Viewport3D.Camera>
          <PerspectiveCamera x:Name="Front"
          FarPlaneDistance="10"
          LookDirection="0.32,-0.92,-0.21"
          UpDirection="0.17,0.60,-0.77"
          NearPlaneDistance="1"
          Position="-0.32,0.92,1.05"
          FieldOfView="39.59" />
        </Viewport3D.Camera>

        <ModelVisual3D>
          <ModelVisual3D.Content>
            <Model3DGroup x:Name="Scene" >
              <AmbientLight Color="#999999" />
              <DirectionalLight Color="#555555" Direction="-0.07,-0.08,-0.9" />
              <Model3DGroup x:Name="SimpleSquare_Model">
                <GeometryModel3D x:Name="SimpleSquare"
                Geometry="{DynamicResource SimpleSquare}"
                Material="{DynamicResource SimpleSquare_Material}" />
              </Model3DGroup>
            </Model3DGroup>
          </ModelVisual3D.Content>
          <ModelVisual3D.Transform>
            <Transform3DGroup>
              <TranslateTransform3D OffsetX="0" OffsetY="0" OffsetZ="0"/>
              <ScaleTransform3D ScaleX="1" ScaleY="1" ScaleZ="1"/>
              <RotateTransform3D d:EulerAngles="13.5258889753983,-
22.5696102525033,14.8888734737036">
                  <RotateTransform3D.Rotation>
                    <AxisAngleRotation3D Angle="31.418218946377149"
Axis="0.515927492106696,-0.656404167690378,0.550411111376939"/>
                  </RotateTransform3D.Rotation>
              </RotateTransform3D>
```

```
    <TranslateTransform3D OffsetX="0" OffsetY="0" OffsetZ="0"/>
    <TranslateTransform3D OffsetX="0.093558293676071519" OffsetY="-
0.28066454973272076" OffsetZ="0.83244198066907094"/>
      </Transform3DGroup>
    </ModelVisual3D.Transform>
  </ModelVisual3D>
 </Viewport3D>


</Grid>
```

The camera object is created within Listing 7.3:

```
<Viewport3D.Camera>
  <PerspectiveCamera x:Name="Front"
  FarPlaneDistance="10"
  LookDirection="0.32,-0.92,-0.21"
  UpDirection="0.17,0.60,-0.77"
  NearPlaneDistance="1"
  Position="-0.32,0.92,1.05"
  FieldOfView="39.59" />
</Viewport3D.Camera>
```

If you have used DirectX before, you are aware that the properties we are setting here are basically identical to what is required with the Direct3D API. If you don't have a camera, you can't see anything. Remember, the control serves as a viewer to a 3D world.

When you get the markup into a blank scene, save it and then switch to Design view. Make sure you have the Timeline and Tools palettes visible.

1. From within the Timeline palette, expand the SimpleViewport3D element to show the child elements: Camera and [ModelVisual3d]. Notice that you cannot select the Camera element, but you can expand it to show the Front element, which is, in fact, our Camera object.

2. With Front selected in the Timeline palette, notice that most of the tools in the Tools palette have become disabled. They are not applicable to this control type. Select the Camera Orbit tool and move your cursor to the center of the object on screen.

3. Click and hold the left mouse button while moving your mouse to the left and right of the object. Do this slowly. What you are actually seeing here is the rotating of the Camera object itself.

4. Holding down the Shift key at the same time allows you a greater controlled rotation of the Camera. Holding down the CTRL key allows you to pan the Camera. Holding the ALT key provide tilt.

5. Press CTRL+Z to return the scene to its original state; or reload it if you saved it as instructed previously.

6. In the Timeline palette, select the [ModelVisual3D] element as the current activated element (double-click it in the Timeline palette) and again select the Camera Orbit tool. A large yellow frame appears around the object in the center of the Viewport3D control.

This is the Field Of View (FOV) setting for the Camera and relates to how near or far the Camera is to the object.

Again, simply move the cursor to the center of the object. Click and hold down the left mouse button and your FOV changes accordingly.

The CTRL and Shift keys give the same functionality as previously shown, but the ALT key does not. While holding down the ALT key, when you move the mouse the Camera's FOV changes to either increase or decrease your Camera's clipping area.

What you may have noticed before is that the Direct Selection tool is still enabled. This is a very cool feature of the control that allows you to set the starting position of the actual objects that are being displayed.

7. With [ModelVisual3D] still selected, go ahead and select the Direct Selection tool from the Tools palette, a control object similar to the one shown in Figure 7.21.

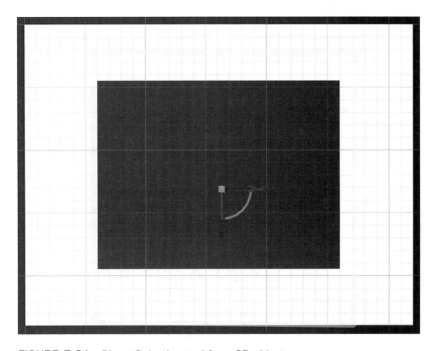

FIGURE 7.21   Direct Selection tool for a 3D object.

Now you may want to zoom in so the object fills the entire screen, which should assist you in making accurate changes to the shape you are working on.

This control object serves two purposes. First, it lets you reposition the 3D object along any of the three axes, as well as allowing you to rotate the 3D object around all three axes.

If you move the mouse slowly over the object, it shows you which axis you are working on and, if you are on a rotation point, the cursor changes to indicate that as well.

Play around with it, move and rotate the object, then switch back and change the Camera settings as well.

Until you work with 3D objects, this tool probably appears a little out of the ordinary. But believe me, when you do start using the Viewport3D control, this little tool is invaluable. As with some of the other tools we have looked at, this tool has been cleverly conceived and perfectly implemented.

Neil McGarry and Steve Barker from www.xamlexpress.com show in Figure 7.22 what real designer professionals can do with a Viewport3D control and simple Geometry shapes with their take on the world famous "Welcome to Las Vegas" sign. The elements and materials are free to be transformed or even dynamically retextured if so required. More importantly, you can make all these changes to the element properties with just a few simple clicks.

FIGURE 7.22   Welcome to Vegas.

It is difficult to provide huge details of samples in 3D in this book, because usually the required resources are quite large and most people hate having to type out huge amounts of code or markup at the best of times. Chapter 19, "Using 3D in Blend," provides a much more detailed overview of the 3D tools in Blend. I would recommend visiting the msdn.com website for in-depth discussions of 3D in WPF.

Summary

You now have a thorough grasp of the power that the simple looking toolset provides. Given the time and the head space, you are only limited by what you can think of as far as vector graphic content is concerned. You have also seen how the toolset provides for simple manipulation and animation of 3D content.

In the next chapter, you build on what you have learned here. Using only the Path tools available, you create a visually pleasing button that can be used in other projects and scenes.

CHAPTER 8

An Example Control Using Just the Tools Palette

My original plans for this chapter were that it be around 16 pages long, which was an estimate based on some of the first CTP's of what was called Expression Interactive Designer. Things have cleaned up a lot since those early days of the application but in saying this, there are a lot of new features that I want to show you. As a result, it may be a longer journey to Gel button utopia than was first planned, but with any luck you will have an even better experience.

Building a Gel Button from Scratch

It was a strange coincidence that when I first saw Expression Interactive Designer being demonstrated, I had just spent the better part of three days making what I thought was sure to be the most awesome Gel button making application in .NET. The application I was working on at the time called for a cutting-edge look and feel, and it was for one of those rare companies that didn't care how long things took as long as the results were mind blowing.

Three days. The results were brilliant because I had based the results on early Vista builds; but it took three days just to get to that point. I took a day off to go to a demonstration put on by Microsoft, and you can imagine my eyes when I saw a Gel button built from scratch in around 5 minutes. I knew then that what I had been asking for—for years—had finally arrived: an interface development tool built for designers but which, at the same time, allowed the developer to ensure functionality and maintain performance.

It was not even the fact that the Gel button shown in the Demonstration was that good, it was more about the fact that the results had been stored in a template and could be used at will on any other button object.

The thing to remember about Blend is that everything you see and do can essentially be saved as a template and can be stored and retrieved from what is known as a *Resource Dictionary*. So you can design a complete series of buttons, drop-down lists, Treeview controls—whatever you want—and store these templates in your application or one of your Resource Dictionaries.

The term *template* is being used here rather generically, and you may think that I should have said *Skin*. Remember, however, what I said about everything being able to be saved as a template? Well, that includes data bindings, styles, brushes (made from the color palette), and the list goes on. So, you can see how the term *Skin* is incorrect.

It does get confusing at first when you are trying to get used to the idea of templates, what certain templates are for, what the difference is between a style and a control parts template, and so on. We will get to all of this in a bit. But for now, let's just get on with building the button and worry about the finer points of the templating side of things later. (Chapter 12, "Templates," details the different template types and how to create and modify them.)

The goal is to design and build a button similar to the one shown as the Play button in Figure 8.1, which is actually the button control used in Windows Media Player 11. As mentioned previously, without the help of Blend, you could work for days just trying to get all the lighting effects right to try and replicate this, but thankfully you don't have to worry about that any longer.

FIGURE 8.1   The visually stunning controls of Windows Media Player 11.

Working the Layers

You are going to use just the tools found in the Toolbox, so it is nice and easy for you to take this sample and apply it to other areas of design without having to worry so much about how other controls will integrate. You may think the subtitle of this area is a little strange, but as you will see, you will be building this control using carefully constructed layers, one on top of the other to give the overall appearance.

Before you begin, take a moment to understand the Brush Suggestion tables presented in this chapter (begin with Table 8.1). They will provide a little bit of insight into working with the Brushes. After this chapter, however, you are on your own!

All the information shown in the above table and others like it, correlate directly to the Brushes and Appearance panels located within the Properties palette. Fill, Stroke, Foreground, and other brush properties are shown as a suggestion in this format.

TABLE 8.1   Sample 1 Brush Suggestion

Brush Property	Brush Type	Overall Opacity	Stroke Thickness		
Fill	Linear Gradient	55%	4		

Gradient Stop	Position	Red	Green	Blue	Alpha
1	50%	140	26	204	100%
2	100%	255	255	255	100%

XAML Listing (Sample 1):

```
<LinearGradientBrush EndPoint="0.5,1" StartPoint="0.5,0">
    <GradientStop Color="#FF8C1ACC" Offset="0.5"/>
    <GradientStop Color="#FFFFFFFF" Offset="1"/>
</LinearGradientBrush>
```

As you can see from the suggested Brush and in Figure 8.2, you are looking at setting the Fill property brush, using a Linear Gradient brush type, which has two Gradient Stops added to it, which is done by default.

FIGURE 8.2   All the relevant areas of the suggested Brush.

What if There Are More Than Two Color Selectors (Gradient Stops)?

In the event you see more than two Gradient Stops, you only need to click on the gradient display graph and another Gradient Stop will be created. To remove them, simply click and hold the Stop and then drag down and off the graph.

You should also note that individual Gradient Stops can have a different opacity value than the overall opacity, which is located in the Appearance panel. These individual Stops are also given a position that refers to the position on the color gradient graph, the far left of the graph representing 0% and the far right 100%.

As you can see in Figure 8.2, the first Gradient Stop is located approximately 50% along the graph, while the second remains firmly to the far right.

Also notice the Stroke thickness, which is again located in the Appearance panel. This panel also contains additional property settings for the Stroke property.

Lastly, if you do not see a value in the suggested Brush, it is safe to assume that you can use the default values that it has been given by Blend. In the case of a Brush being suggested as a Solid Color Brush type, you will not see Gradient Stops within the table because none are available with this type of brush.

Let's get into it!

1. Start by creating a new project in Blend. You can call it whatever you would like, but you are not going to be saving this application along the way. (You can always name the project if you are not confident of completing the chapter in one sitting.)

2. Make sure you have the Design Workspace selected by either depressing F6 (to cycle the workspace) or selecting it from the Windows menu.

3. Start by making the base of the button first. As you see, it is a circular shape, so select the Ellipse tool from the Toolbox and draw a shape of arbitrary size on your artboard. Make it nice and big, though, because it will scale how you want it to later.

4. The shading in this type of design is what gives the lighting effect, so pay close attention to it and your results should be even better than mine. Now, select the Ellipse element in the Objects and Timeline palette and right-click to display a context menu with the Rename option on it. Name this element ButtonBase.

5. Hopefully you have the Properties palette open; if not, select it from the Windows menu and find the Brushes area of the palette. First select the Fill Brush property. For now set it to a Solid Color Brush with a nice dark deep blue color. Take note of the color suggestions I make or change the color at will along the way (see Table 8.2).

   Next, you use the Pen tool in much the same way as you did in the previous chapter to create the shaded area that represents the gloss on the button. Be careful where you add the points, particularly the points along the center area of the button. The shape you create is critical to eliciting the correct effect. Figure 8.3 shows where I added points with the Pen tool, starting on the far left and eventually going full-circle and returning to that point to close the path object.

TABLE 8.2   Sample 2 Brush Suggestion

Brush Property	Brush Type	Overall Opacity	Stroke Thickness
Fill	Solid Color	100%	1

Red	Green	Blue	Alpha
0	25	158	100

XAML Listing (Sample 2):

```
<Ellipse HorizontalAlignment="Left" VerticalAlignment="Top"
Width="100" Height="100" Fill="#FF00199E" Stroke="#FF000000"/>
```

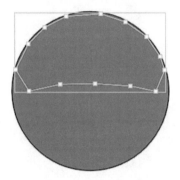

FIGURE 8.3   Add points with the Pen tool.

6. Now select the Direct Selection tool from the Toolbox palette and begin to smooth out the object. Use the image in Figure 8.1 as a reference. Remember, the goal is to create a nice-looking gloss object. At this point, your path object is most likely the same blue color as the ButtonBase element you created in the previous steps. You can leave it like that for the moment. I'll provide some brush suggestions a little later on. For now, rename this path element to Hood.

7. Next, add the Arrow element. Because you are enjoying using the Pen tool so much, you might as well get this part of the task completed. Select the Pen tool again and add the points for the arrow. When I created the arrow shown in Figure 8.4, I did not just add three points to make the arrow. Instead, I placed a point at the beginning and end of the straight line sections of the arrow, and then selected them to place a curve in the corners. Remember to select the first point with the Pen tool again to close the path element.

8. Rename the arrow element to Arrow. You have now completed all the shape elements required for the button. It probably looks like a blue blob at the moment; but remember that the magic is all in the colors and the shading. Figure 8.5 illustrates how mine turned out. Does yours look similar?

FIGURE 8.4   The completed arrow shape.

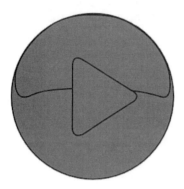

FIGURE 8.5   All the shapes completed.

9. Now, hide both the Arrow and the Hood elements by selecting the eye icon displayed next to the elements in the Objects and Timeline palette. Concentrate on each layer now, building the brushes as you go. Select the ButtonBase element in the Objects and Timeline palette and apply the following Brush suggestions in Table 8.3 to it.

TABLE 8.3   Sample 3 Brush Suggestion

Brush Property	Brush Type	Overall Opacity	Stroke Thickness		
Fill	Radial Gradient	100%	1		
Gradient Stop	**Position**	**Red**	**Green**	**Blue**	**Alpha**
1	50%	0	229	255	99%
2	100%	0	25	158	100%

XAML Listing (Sample 3):

```
<RadialGradientBrush>
    <GradientStop Color="#FC00E5FF" Offset="0.5"/>
    <GradientStop Color="#FF00199E" Offset="1"/>
</RadialGradientBrush>
```

10. Next, apply the Stroke property settings described in Table 8.4.

TABLE 8.4   Sample 4 Brush Suggestion

Brush Property	Brush Type	Overall Opacity	Stroke Thickness		
Fill	Linear Gradient	100%	1		

Gradient Stop	Position	Red	Green	Blue	Alpha
1	50%	255	255	255	100%
2	100%	29	37	194	100%

XAML Listing (Sample 4):

```
<LinearGradientBrush EndPoint="0.5,1" StartPoint="0.5,0">
    <GradientStop Color="#FFFFFFFF" Offset="0.5"/>
    <GradientStop Color="#FF1D25C2" Offset="1"/>
</LinearGradientBrush>
```

11. Select the `Fill` property again. This time select the Brush Transform tool from the Toolbox. Figure 8.6 shows how to manipulate the brush to place the highlights in the required position.

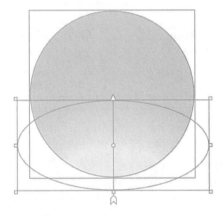

FIGURE 8.6   The Fill Brush Transform position.

12. With the Brush Transform tool still selected, change the property in the Brushes panel to `Stroke`. Manipulate the Brush highlights again to as close to the `Fill` property as possible. It is a little difficult because you do not get the bounding box that was supplied with the `Fill`, but you can just switch between the two properties to get a rough similarity.

13. Now make the Hood element visible again and apply the Brush suggestions included in Tables 8.5 and 8.6.

TABLE 8.5   Sample 5 Brush Suggestion

Brush Property	Brush Type	Overall Opacity	Stroke Thickness		
Fill	Radial Gradient	100%	1		

Gradient Stop	Position	Red	Green	Blue	Alpha
1	30%	20	71	206	12%
2	100%	255	255	255	95%

XAML Listing (Sample 5):

```
<RadialGradientBrush>
    <GradientStop Color="#1E1447CE" Offset="0.3"/>
    <GradientStop Color="#F2FFFFFF" Offset="1"/>
</RadialGradientBrush>
```

TABLE 8.6   Sample 6 Brush Suggestion

Brush Property	Brush Type	Overall Opacity	Stroke Thickness		
Stroke	Radial Gradient	100%	2		

Gradient Stop	Position	Red	Green	Blue	Alpha
1	55%	255	255	255	100%
2	100%	27	46	180	23%

XAML Listing (Sample 6):

```
<RadialGradientBrush>
    <GradientStop Color="#FFFFFFFF" Offset="0.55"/>
    <GradientStop Color="#3A1B2EB4" Offset="1"/>
</RadialGradientBrush>
```

Data Property Available in the Appearance Panel

Do you recall in Chapter 7, "Using the Blend Toolbox: Tools and Common Controls," I mentioned the mini-language used to create paths? You can see the syntax that has been applied for you in the Data properties located in the Appearance panel.

14. The secret to the Hood element is within the Brush transforms. Pay close attention to the following figures, which show you the Fill property transform (Figure 8.7) and the Stroke property transform (Figure 8.8).

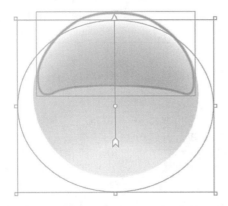

FIGURE 8.7   The Fill brush transform.

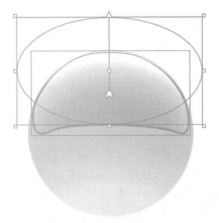

FIGURE 8.8   The Stroke property transform.

8

15. Make the Arrow element visible again and apply the Brush suggestion provided in Tables 8.7 and 8.8.

TABLE 8.7   Sample 7 Brush Suggestion

Brush Property	Brush Type	Overall Opacity	Stroke Thickness		
Fill	Radial Gradient	100%	1		
Gradient Stop	**Position**	**Red**	**Green**	**Blue**	**Alpha**
1	60%	255	255	255	100%
2	100%	186	186	186	100%

XAML Listing (Sample 7):

```
<RadialGradientBrush>
    <GradientStop Color="#FFFFFFFF" Offset="0.6"/>
    <GradientStop Color="#FFBABABA" Offset="1"/>
</RadialGradientBrush>
```

TABLE 8.8   Sample 8 Brush Suggestion

Brush Property	Brush Type	Overall Opacity	Stroke Thickness		
Stroke	Linear Gradient	100%	1		
Gradient Stop	**Position**	**Red**	**Green**	**Blue**	**Alpha**
1	0%	0	0	0	100%
2	100%	255	255	255	100%

XAML Listing (Sample 8):

```
<LinearGradientBrush EndPoint="0.5,1" StartPoint="0.5,0">
    <GradientStop Color="#FF000000" Offset="0"/>
    <GradientStop Color="#FFFFFFFF" Offset="1"/>
</LinearGradientBrush>
```

16. Now apply the Brush Transform for the `Fill` property as shown in Figure 8.9.

With any luck, you now have a gorgeous Gel play button. I hope you also now have more confidence in your ability to create this style of element.

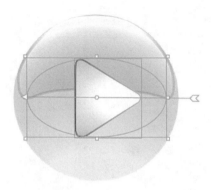

FIGURE 8.9   The Fill property transform.

If you haven't been able to re-create it exactly as shown, don't worry too much about it. You can always try again—and each time you do it, you will get better at placing the curves and the lines in the correct places.

If you want to cheat a little, which is fine by me, you can always just open a new project and type in the XAML provided in Listing 8.1 by hand. It might be quicker, however, to try to use the brushes again.

LISTING 8.1   Complex Button Shapes

```xml
<Grid x:Name="LayoutRoot">
    <Ellipse Opacity="1"
     StrokeThickness="1"
     Margin="249.746,123.849,245.592,188.287"
     x:Name="ButtonBase">
    <Ellipse.Fill>
        <RadialGradientBrush GradientOrigin="0.5,1.058">
            <RadialGradientBrush.RelativeTransform>
                <TransformGroup>
                    <ScaleTransform CenterX="0.5"
                        CenterY="0.5"
                        ScaleX="1.159"
                        ScaleY="0.535"/>
                    <SkewTransform AngleX="0"
                        AngleY="0"
                        CenterX="0.5"
                        CenterY="0.5"/>
                    <RotateTransform Angle="0"
                        CenterX="0.5"
                        CenterY="0.5"/>
                    <TranslateTransform X="0.005"
                        Y="0.306"/>
                </TransformGroup>
```

```xml
        </RadialGradientBrush.RelativeTransform>
        <GradientStop Color="#FC00E5FF" Offset="0.502"/>
        <GradientStop Color="#FF00199E" Offset="1"/>
    </RadialGradientBrush>
</Ellipse.Fill>
<Ellipse.Stroke>
    <LinearGradientBrush EndPoint="0.498,0.561"
        StartPoint="0.498,1.101">
        <GradientStop Color="#FFFFFFFF" Offset="0"/>
        <GradientStop Color="#FF1D25C2" Offset="1"/>
    </LinearGradientBrush>
</Ellipse.Stroke>
</Ellipse>
<Path Opacity="1"
    Stretch="Fill"
    StrokeThickness="2"
    Margin="251.733,123.478,247.072,0"
    x:Name="Hood"
    VerticalAlignment="Top"
    Height="69.625"
    Data="M252.42643,173.06279 C254.48207,164.32278 258.4611,157.86994
264.19778,150.36784 268.71292,144.67081 272.29185,140.86135 277.38975,137.28246
283.23859,132.40728 290.1125,128.65259 298.49689,126.44613 307.17547,123.79786
325.28673,122.76574 335.8403,125.83263 345.03072,126.9941 352.00882,131.50965
357.1504,135.03366 362.63063,138.47065 367.103,142.89265 370.95122,146.68778
376.39771,152.59304 378.77487,156.69182 381.30189,162.02215 383.24375,166.02556
385.00012,170.21081
   385.56368,173.88104 387.58732,189.00662 382.95216,194.52641 376.1114,192.02416
368.52424,189.64282 361.15644,188.11773 354.01074,187.45957 343.37655,186.04817
333.10954,185.37263 323.262,185.53773 312.98013,185.00436 302.89249,185.17094
292.9937,186.01819 281.67796,186.41552 272.4693,188.33731 265.36788,191.78369
255.86256,195.09834 251.16319,187.8839 252.42643,173.06279 z">
        <Path.Fill>
            <RadialGradientBrush GradientOrigin="0.501,0.685">
                <RadialGradientBrush.RelativeTransform>
                    <TransformGroup>
                        <ScaleTransform CenterX="0.5"
                            CenterY="0.5"
                            ScaleX="1.239"
                            ScaleY="2.049"/>
                        <SkewTransform AngleX="0"
                            AngleY="0"
                            CenterX="0.5"
                            CenterY="0.5"/>
                        <RotateTransform Angle="0"
                            CenterX="0.5"
```

```
                                        CenterY="0.5"/>
                            <TranslateTransform X="-0.002" Y="0.624"/>
                        </TransformGroup>
                    </RadialGradientBrush.RelativeTransform>
                    <GradientStop Color="#1E1447CE" Offset="0.268"/>
                    <GradientStop Color="#F2FFFFFF" Offset="1"/>
                </RadialGradientBrush>
            </Path.Fill>
            <Path.Stroke>
                <RadialGradientBrush GradientOrigin="0.5,0.677">
                    <RadialGradientBrush.RelativeTransform>
                        <TransformGroup>
                            <ScaleTransform
                                ScaleX="1.172"
                                ScaleY="1.277"/>
                            <SkewTransform AngleX="0"
                                AngleY="0"/>
                            <RotateTransform Angle="0"/>
                            <TranslateTransform X="-0.092" Y="-0.404"/>
                             </TransformGroup>
                        </RadialGradientBrush.RelativeTransform>
                        <GradientStop Color="#FFFFFFFF" Offset="0.55"/>
                        <GradientStop Color="#3A1B2EB4" Offset="1"/>
                    </RadialGradientBrush>
                </Path.Stroke>
            </Path>
        <Path Stretch="Fill"
            StrokeThickness="1"
            Margin="300.844,160.078,277.043,223.929"
            x:Name="Arrow"
            Data="M301.34447,218.38417 L301.51887,166.19908 C301.82203,160.49434
304.64037,159.30446 309.53978,161.85022 L351.5611,186.89926 C356.60548,189.32806
357.59647,192.21381 354.17685,195.5968 L310.58607,222.38521 C305.13799,224.84771
302.0932,223.45672 301.34447,218.38417 z">
            <Path.Fill>
                <RadialGradientBrush GradientOrigin="1.17,0.508">
                    <RadialGradientBrush.RelativeTransform>
                        <TransformGroup>
                            <ScaleTransform ScaleX="2.091" ScaleY="1"/>
                            <SkewTransform AngleX="0" AngleY="0"/>
                            <RotateTransform Angle="0"/>
                            <TranslateTransform X="-0.714" Y="-0.008"/>
                        </TransformGroup>
                    </RadialGradientBrush.RelativeTransform>
                    <GradientStop Color="#FFFFFFFF" Offset="0.573"/>
                    <GradientStop Color="#FFBABABA" Offset="1"/>
```

```
            </RadialGradientBrush>
        </Path.Fill>
        <Path.Stroke>
            <LinearGradientBrush EndPoint="1,0.5" StartPoint="0,0.5">
                <GradientStop Color="#FF000000" Offset="0"/>
                <GradientStop Color="#FFFFFFFF" Offset="1"/>
            </LinearGradientBrush>
        </Path.Stroke>
    </Path>
</Grid>
```

Now that you have the shapes needed for the button, what is missing is the functionality that a button is required to have. It would be a bit of a mess trying to move all these elements around from place to place. You also want to contain the design you have just slaved over and be able to apply it as a template to other button elements if you choose. To accomplish this portion of the task, embrace the magic of the Make Button tool.

Using the Make Button Tool

The Make Button tool does pretty much what its name implies. It turns UIElements into Button elements. It doesn't just rename the object type to achieve its goals; it adds triggers and declares events like *click*—all the things that you need for a button to function as you or anyone else using your button would expect.

You should (as good practice), test your elements to make sure they scale correctly. You should also Group all the elements together, using the *Group Into* option on the context menu of the Objects and Timeline category by taking the following steps:

1. Open the Objects and Timeline palette and select each of the three elements in the tree by holding down the Shift or Ctrl key. Make sure you only select the three elements you created.

2. Right-click on one of the highlighted elements. A popup context menu containing the Group Into menu item appears. Move your mouse over the item to reveal a further context menu with all the optional element types that you can select to contain your elements.

3. For this example select Grid. There are several reasons for this, but the most important is that the Grid element will allow the three elements to coexist with the same layout settings that they currently have. If you were to select Stack panel, you could find a fairly unique button being developed, so I wouldn't use that at this stage.

4. You now have a new element named [Grid]. The brackets indicate that it has child elements, namely your elements, contained within it. Rename the Grid element to MyGelPlayButton.

5. If you now select the MyGelPlayButton element, you can resize it at will and test the scaling ability of your element. Note that if you elongate the element, then the Hood doesn't look right—or the Arrow disappears all together if you make the MyGelPlayButton very thin. These design problems all need to be taken care of to

ensure that the button scales and still remains the same visually as it does at the original size you created it in. You can come back later and do this if you wish. Chapter 5, "UIElement: Control Embedding," for more details on Grid layout scenarios and Chapter 6, "Panel-Based Containers," for more information on object embedding. At this point, know that this type of combined element (Circular) is very hard to set correct scaling on, mainly because the center points of each element are in a different position.

6. With MyGelPlayButton selected in the Timeline palette, click on Tools from the main menu at the top of the application and then select Make Button. A dialog box displays that contains the information about the button as shown in Figure 8.10.

FIGURE 8.10   The Style Resource dialog box.

Notice that I changed the name of the button to *GelPlayButton1* in the Resource name (key) area of the dialog box. This is particularly important because, as you will find out soon enough, defining a manageable naming convention for Templates is half the battle to using them effectively.

Also note that you are defining the button element in this document only, which means that you can only apply this resource to other button elements in this window element. That is called *Scope*. You will see shortly how to put the button into a Resource Dictionary (RD) to enable you to use it anytime and at any place within your solution(s).

For now, make the changes as shown in Figure 8.10, and then click the OK button.

You should have noticed that a few interesting things have happened to the element. First, the text *Button* appears in the center of the button element. Second, if you look in the Timeline palette you will see that the Grid element is gone and has been replaced by the [Button] Button, which shows you that the type is now that of Button and the name is the default name of Button.

Why is there text in the center of the button? The Make Button tool applies default button elements within the button to ensure that the basics of a button are created. One of the default properties of a button (any button) is that it contains what is known as a *ContentPresenter* (see Chapter 6 for more details about content controls).

If you switch to the Properties palette for a minute, you should be able to navigate to the Common Properties panel. In here you will see a property named *Content* with the text Button displaying.

If you remove the text from this property, all is well and the button begins to resemble what it previously was. In the same area, just below the Content property is a property named *Cursor*. Select the drop-down list beside the label and look for the Hand cursor and select it.

Realistically, to make this button more reusable, you would probably make the button without the Triangle embedded and instead create the triangle as a separate path and add it as the Button's content property value instead of text. This way you could create different shapes to add to the Button without the need for re-creating the button for each symbol you wish to use.

Introduction to the Timeline and Timeline Events (Triggers)

You are now going to briefly see some features of the Animation Timeline as well as the timelines associated Event Triggers and Property Triggers, which are also collectively referred to as Triggers from time to time. Chapter 14, "Animations with Storyboards," provides more detailed information. You use these triggers to add the finishing touches that really set your button apart from other buttons.

Maybe you have used Flash previous to using the Blend application. In case you haven't, it is helpful to understand a little of what the Timeline does and how it ties in with any code you may wish to add to the object.

Timelines do indeed use measurements of time as an instrument of functionality. This really means that while you can create an animation of sorts with any object using the Timer class, you would realistically miss out on certain key points in time when the animation is meant to be applying certain property values like position or size or both for example. The Timeline-based solution provided in Blend is really simple to use; however, because of this simplicity, you also lose out on some of the functionality you either need to add within XAML or you can code the entire animation before you set it off in the .NET backend.

When you animate an element, you are, in point of fact, animating a certain property or set of properties on that element. For instance, if you animate the width of an element, you set the width property at the beginning of the animation to, perhaps, its current value of 50 and the ending point anywhere you wish, perhaps 150 wide. The animation backend uses an algorithm to work out exactly what width the element should be at all points along the duration of the animation to ensure that the end property value is met at the end of the specified duration. That provides a nice, smooth animated result.

Timeline events allow you to specify when an animation should start, pause, stop, resume, complete (skip to fill), or be removed. They are tied directly to a Timeline and are derived (for lack of a better word) from events available to the object or element that you are intending to animate.

Look at the process like this:

1. Figure out which element event will trigger your animation.
2. When your chosen trigger fires, what object(s) or element(s) do you want to animate?
3. Which Timeline will contain the animation?
4. What action will be performed on the animation?

Using this process you can say: "When the Window.Loaded event is raised, I want the Timeline OnWindowLoaded to Begin animating my Button element". You will shortly see how this intuitive action list is implemented in the Blend UI. It really *is* as simple as that.

You can create as many Timelines as you wish and animate any number of element properties as the animation progresses. There are different types of animation described in Chapter 14. For now you will be using what is known as the *Key Frame* technique (see Figure 8.11). This means that you will be specifying what values certain properties are to contain at a particular point in the animation lifecycle on the Timeline (using a KeyFrame).

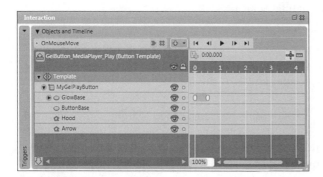

FIGURE 8.11   A Timeline with Key Frames set on it.

That is animation in a nutshell. You can only animate a property—and only certain types of properties. You can provide a start and/or end property value or values at arbitrary points in time; and last but not least, you specify a duration.

Animations can get quite complex. There are several other properties that can be set within the Blend animation set, but we will stick with using the Blend Timeline interface for animating the button.

Adding Animated Glow

Let's say that when the user's mouse moves over [the button], you want to get a glow to emanate from behind the button in order to provide a perception of depth as well as to provide valuable user feedback. You can create that effect using animation techniques.

Now that you have your button element viewable on the artboard, you have essentially created a template that the button visually represents (more on templates in Chapter 12). Follow these steps:

1. Select the button in the Objects and Timeline palette and right-click to display the context menu. Move your mouse over the Edit Control Parts (Template) menu item, which will bring up a submenu. In that submenu, select Edit Template.

2. You now can see the elements you created previously using the Make Button tool. There is also an additional element named [ContentPresenter] that was placed here by the Make Button tool. It is responsible for the text that is shown on the button. Select this new element, right-click on it and select Delete. There is no requirement to include text on this style of button.

3. It is now time to add an additional element to represent the Glow of the button. Because you want the glow to begin from the back of the button, you should select ButtonBase, right-click on it, and select Copy.

4. Now select and activate the MyGelPlayButton element so you can see the yellow bounding box around it on the artboard. Right-click on it and select Paste. The ButtonBase_Copy element is added, but it is the top layer of all the child levels. To remedy this, right-click the element and find the Order menu item, for which a submenu displays with an item named Send to back.

5. Rename the ButtonBase_Copy element to GlowBase.

6. The first action you are going to take with GlowBase is to resize it to the intended maximum size of the glow that the element will produce. Find the Properties palette and then the Layout panel. Make sure that both the HorizontalAlignment and VerticalAlignment properties are set to Stretch.

7. Just below the Layout Panel is the Alignment property called Margin with four input boxes representing the Top, Bottom, Left and Right margin values. Enter the value -50 in all four property inputs and you will create a fairly large Ellipse element. Do not be concerned that the Button will be this big. Regardless of any child element size or placement, the top level parent always maintains the Buttons footprint when being used in a scene.

8. Go back to the Timeline panel and select the eye icon next to the ButtonBase, Hood, and Arrow elements to set each to invisible. You need to have a clear image of the GlowBase element while still seeing the bounding box area of the Parent.

9. Make sure you once again have the GlowBase element selected in the Timeline palette and select the Brush Transform tool from the Toolbox. What you will see straight away is that the Gradient Brush needs to be re-transformed to make it work as a centered glow element.

10. Figure 8.12 illustrates how the brush gradient should be transformed. The main area of concern here is that the bottom of the transform arrow must be placed in the center of the active element bounding box. This will spread the gradient equally outward. Figure 8.12 has been purposely faded to show you the transform requirement; however, you should see a light blue glow in the center of the GlowBase

element and a darker blue outer area. You must ensure that the light blue area is inside the yellow bounding box.

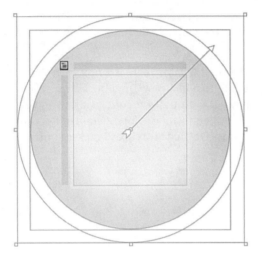

FIGURE 8.12   The Brush Transform requirement.

11. Return to the Brushes panel within the Properties palette and apply the Brush suggestions in Table 8.9.

TABLE 8.9   Sample 9 Brush Suggestion

Brush Property	Brush Type	Overall Opacity	Stroke Thickness		
Fill	Radial Gradient	100%	Set No Brush		

Gradient Stop	Position	Red	Green	Blue	Alpha
1	25%	6	196	227	100%
2	60%	255	255	255	0%

XAML Listing (Sample 9):

```
<RadialGradientBrush>
    <GradientStop Color="#FF06C4E3" Offset="0.25"/>
    <GradientStop Color="#00FFFFFF" Offset="0.6"/>
</RadialGradientBrush>
```

It is important that you remember to set the Stroke brush property to *No Brush*.

The next step is the animation requirements. If you do not already have your workspace configured for animation, select Window from the menu at the top of the screen and then select Animation Workspace or press F6.

At the bottom of the screen two palettes are displayed: an Interaction palette and a Results palette. Select the Interaction palette, which displays the Object and Timeline panel as well as the Trigger panel.

Figure 8.13 shows that just under the Objects and Timeline label there is a box with the words *(No Storyboard open)* written in it. You are going to add a new Timeline first so you have something to work with. Figure 8.13 also shows the drop-down control allowing you to create a new Timeline. See Chapter 3, "Expression Blend Panels," for a detailed description of the Objects and Timeline category as well as the related Storyboard picker control.

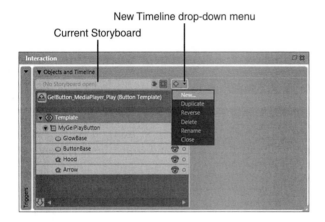

FIGURE 8.13   The areas of interest in the Objects and Timeline category.

A dialog box is displayed that asks you for the name of the new Timeline. Enter **OnMouseMove** and click the OK button. Your timeline appears to the right side of the visual element tree. You may also notice that the artboard now has a red highlighted border with a label in the top left of the artboard saying *Timeline recording is on*. This red light means that changes made now to any property of the element that is currently selected will be recorded in a KeyFrame on the timeline.

Knowing that you want to make the glow appear when the user moves the mouse over the button, you can determine that a Property Trigger, something like ButtonBase. IsMouseOver is in order. This property (when evaluated to true) lets you know when to start the animation. All you need to do now is define the OnMouseOver Timeline to show the glow effect.

Let's go through adding the correct trigger step-by-step.

1. Select the element in the Objects and Timeline panel for which you want to view the property values in order to start the animation. I suggest that you use the ButtonBase element.

2. Now switch over to looking at the Triggers panel. A number of predefined property events are already listed, as shown in Figure 8.14. All these predefined events are courtesy of the Make Button tool; however, for future reference, you can click on the button with the label + Property Trigger and then select from the Trigger display list the property you want to use.

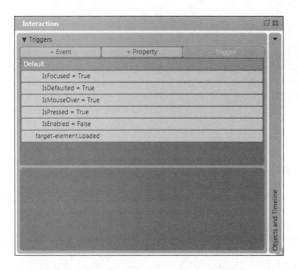

FIGURE 8.14   The Trigger list with predefined property events.

3. Search the Trigger list for one that has the label IsMouseOver = True and then click on it. You will notice the panel below called Properties when active shows a number of headings. The one named as Activated when should already have an entry with three fields, each indicating a drop-down list is available. When you select the first entry (target-element), you should see the ButtonBase element listed. Select ButtonBase from the list.

4. The next field is the property name, which is already set with the correct value, the IsMouseOver requirement. Ensure that the last field (actual property value) is set to True.

5. You are now ready to set the actions that you want to happen when the property value resolves. When activating, you should see a plus (+) sign next to the label Actions. Clicking the plus sign enables you to add a new action. Click on the sign and you add a new action with two available fields, which again indicate that a drop-down list is available. The first field represents the Timeline on which you want the action to be performed. You should see the name of the timeline you declared earlier: OnMouseMove. Also note that from this list you can create a new timeline if one is required.

   Figure 8.15 shows an example of where you are and the action options available to you. Because this is the first action planned, set the action to Begin. Notice that in the list of triggers in the top panel, there is now a lightning bolt next to the trigger. That symbol tells you there is a valid action assigned to this trigger.

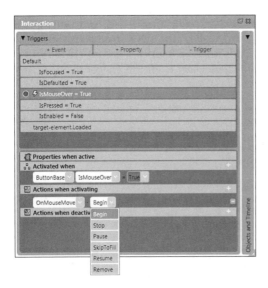

FIGURE 8.15   The timeline action options.

6. You may now want to think about what is going to happen to the button when the user moves the mouse away. You can't leave the animation at its end point, because that will leave the glow visible. You must add another Trigger representing the action to take when the IsMouseOver property value is False. Click on the + Property button at the top of the Triggers panel. A new trigger is added to the list below with a red circle next to it (by default, Timeline recording is on).

7. Set the target element, the property, and the value in the Activated when area of the Properties when active panel.

8. After setting the values to ButtonBase, IsMouseOver and False, add another action for the trigger. Remember to select the timeline OnMouseMove and then set the action to Stop. This will return the timeline to its first position ready to be executed again.

Now that you have finished adding the triggers, it is time to turn your attention to the animation area of the Object and Timelines panel and really bringing the GlowBase element to life. You should still have the MyGelPlayButton element activated. If not, then select and activate it now.

It is now time to add the animation of the GlowBase element:

1. If you only see the words No Storyboard open in the Object and Timeline category, select the previously declared timeline OnMouseMove using the Storyboard picker, which will automatically turn on Timeline recording. If recording has not come on, click Ctrl+R.

2. The timeline reappears in the right side of the Objects and Timelines panel, and you can clearly see the orange line representing the time position (also called the Playhead position). Above the orange line you should see another icon with a green

plus symbol. This adds a KeyFrame to the animation path for the element you are animating. Before clicking it, make sure you have the GlowBase element selected and that the timeline playhead position (the orange line) is on the position 0. When ready, add your first KeyFrame.

3. Adding a KeyFrame does a number of things:

   a. It ensures that the object or element containing the KeyFrame will look exactly as it did when the KeyFrame was added (not withstanding any changes to the element properties).

   b. Each time your timeline is returned to the beginning, any element(s) without KeyFrames will stay at their present settings, regardless of the changes being made to elements with KeyFrames. This is called Hand-off animation and is what enables you to link (or transition) between timelines, specifically when you don't know what the previous property state of the animated object(s) will be.

Figure 8.16 shows various elements of the Objects and Timelines panel. Study it and find the Timeline Zoom control. This tool enables you to view time at different scaled ratios so you may either add KeyFrames closer together or animate for a longer period of time, as is shown in the timeline window. The callouts on this image are discussed in detail in Chapter 3.

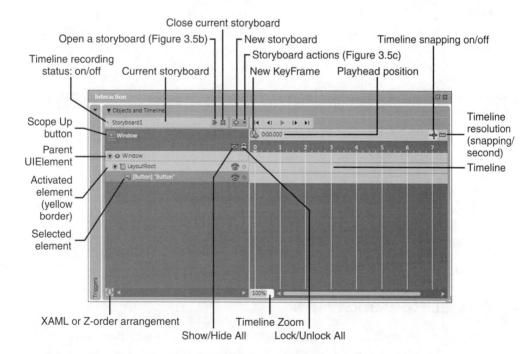

FIGURE 8.16   Various elements of the Objects and Timeline panel.

1. Apply the Timeline Zoom until you see the setting of 400% in the Zoom control and the Timeline markers show half-second intervals. You want the glow on the button to appear quite quickly. Drag the timeline position indicator (the orange line) to the position of 0.5. After making sure that the GlowBase element is still selected, add a second KeyFrame to the timeline. Next to the added KeyFrame button, notice the time indicator label, which shows the value of the Playhead position. After moving the position indicator to the required position, the Playhead position now displays 0:00.500. You can double-click this label and manually enter a position value, which is handy for those animations requiring greater levels of accuracy.

2. Now that you have added an additional KeyFrame, you need to set the properties of the element to the desired result. As this is the last KeyFrame position in this timeline, this KeyFrame is sometime referred to as the Fillframe; hence, the trigger action option to Skip to Fill. Open the Properties palette and select the Brush panel.

3. After selecting the `Fill` brush property, notice the color selectors that make up the gradient of the glow element. Move the left selector to the 45% position, making sure the solid area of the color gradient stays within the yellow bounding box of the parent element. Now move the right selector to the 95% position on the color graph. That was simple, wasn't it?

4. Last but not least, click on the Scope Up button to return to the design scene. You are now ready to test the button. Either select Project from the menu at the top of the screen, and then select Test Project from the menu that appears or depress the F5 button.

Did you notice that nothing happens if you move the mouse over the Hood or Arrow element? This is a serious issue that you must now address. Thanks to the elegant event structure employed by WPF, a very clean method exists to fix it.

Had This Problem Before with CLR Controls?

For those that have built a lot of controls before using pre-Framework 3.0 controls, especially complex controls, you may have come across this issue before. The solution was to capture the MouseOver event for every object on the control and then funnel the events to a singular method to handle it. If you have had this problem before, you are going to love this!

Before you get confused that all of a sudden I am talking about events when you just worked on Property triggers, understand the fact that an event fired somewhere in order to set a property to True or False.

A Look at RoutedEvents

RoutedEvents are very special to me for a number of reasons, but mostly because of similar issues facing large complex controls that I have constructed in the past that had similar issues. It was a situation that I dreaded every time I got a spec for a new control that essentially had layers of UIElements.

The name actually says it all. RoutedEvents move events along a Route until they reach their final destination—or until they are used by a subscribing handle.

RoutedEvents work in one of three ways:

1. Bubbling
2. Tunneling
3. Direct

Unlike CLR events (the events used by developers in previous .NET Framework versions) that only notify a specific subscriber, bubbling RoutedEvents, for example, travel along every node of the visual tree, right up to the root element. Tunneling RoutedEvents work in reverse, traveling downward through the element children until they find a subscriber. Direct RoutedEvents act almost identical to the old CLR events.

This means that you could subscribe to a MouseOver event at the root element of the tree (for an object embedded several items deep) and still get notified when the event is raised. How awesome is that? Well, it will mean more to developers....

So taking this into perspective, your IsMouseOver property is not True when you mouseover the ButtonBase element if the Arrow or Hood element is on top of the ButtonBase element. You need to be listening to the IsMouseOver property (set by the MouseOver event) deeper toward the root of the control itself.

I wonder: How many of you have thought far enough ahead to see another potential problem in this situation? Even though you can listen to the event on the root element, the GlowBase element is currently larger in size compared to the root element, so it effectively extends the boundary on which events will be raised.

What you need to do is make the initial size of the GlowBase element the same size or smaller than the parent root element. Then, when it is enlarged, listen for a mouse movement on it (the glow). This would indicate to you that the user has indeed moved the mouse off the button element, even though the mouse is still over the top of the GlowBase element. If you are lost, relax. It will all make sense shortly.

To make this work is fairly trivial. All you need to do is go back into the button template, change the element that the property triggers are listening on, and change the default size of the GlowBase element.

1. Select the button element in the Objects and Timelines panel. As previously described, you could right-click to bring up the context menu and select the Edit Control Parts (Template) menu item, and then the Edit Template submenu item to get into the template. But this time, direct your focus to the top of the artboard where you see a collection of tabs relating to your currently selected control.

   Because you have edited the template and/or Style of this control before, you now have access to a shortcut between the three viewable layers of the control, as shown in Figure 8.17. You can click on any of these layers at anytime from now on instead of having to scope up and do multiple selects to access the templates of the control.

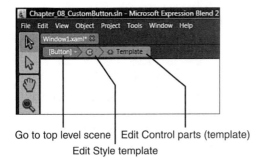

Go to top level scene | Edit Control parts (template)
          Edit Style template

FIGURE 8.17   The improved template access workflow.

2. Select the Control parts (template) from the template level tabs.

3. Select the GlowBase element in the Timelines panel. Open the Properties palette and find the Layout panel located within it.

4. No timelines are selected yet because you are changing the default property values for the element. Once you have found the Margin properties, notice that they are still set to –50, as they were when you initially created the element. Set these all to 0.

   Now select the OnMouseMove Timeline from the Storyboard picker.

5. You should select each one of the KeyFrames added and right-click to reveal the context menu, where you can select Delete.

6. Move the Playhead position back to position 0, and after ensuring the Timeline recording is on and the GlowBase element is selected, click to add a new KeyFrame.

7. Advance the Playhead position to 0:0.500 and again add a new KeyFrame.

8. Locate the Margin properties for this element and now add the value –50 to each property.

9. Open the Brushes panel within the Properties palette and select the Fill brush property. Move the second Gradient Stop to a position of 90%—or until you are happy with the level of glow showing from behind the Button.

10. In the Object and Timeline category, select and activate the parent element, MyGelPlayButton.

11. Scroll down the trigger list and find the two property triggers, each with lightning bolts next to their names.

12. Select the first trigger IsMouseOver = True, and notice that the property values and action reappear in the subpanel.

13. You only need to change the value in the Activated when area, which at present shows ButtonBase as the element of choice. By selecting the drop-down list item, the parent element, MyGelPlayButton, in the list below. Click this item to make it the value.

14. Now select the GlowBase element in the Timeline panel and select the second IsMouseOver = False trigger.

15. Change the element that will activate this trigger to GlowBase.

16. Click on the Scope Up button to return to the scene and test the button.

With any luck you are now the proud owner of a Button that looks pretty sweet and has a properly working mouse move trigger that causes a glow to emanate from behind the button element.

Creating a Control Template

As you will know by now, I am a huge advocate for the use of Resource Dictionaries (RD) and templates in general. They are used throughout the application. RD's will save a substantial amount of design/development time, not to mention enable the visual continuity of an application to be honed to an extraordinary degree.

To be truthful, I must say that you have already created a control template, but it is only available as a local template because of the way you first created it. I can tell you that the Microsoft development team has worked extremely hard to make the creation, management, and use of templates as easy as possible. I, for one, am very impressed thus far.

Take a quick look at putting this button template into a Resource Dictionary and making it available to every application you write from now on. You can simply add a button element to your application and then apply this control template, or you could derive new versions and again add them to the Resource Dictionary.

Chapter 12 goes into greater detail about Resource Dictionaries and the various templates that you can create using Expression Blend; so for now, let's take the most direct root to get the required result.

1. Open the Objects and Timelines panel on the Interactive palette and select the Button element.

2. Right-click to view the context menu and look for the Edit Control Parts (Template) menu item. When you put your mouse over it, a submenu appears. Select Edit a copy.

3. The Create Style Resource dialog is displayed. From here you can create a new Resource Dictionary to store this control template.

4. Within the Define in group box at the lower half of the dialog box, click the New button.

5. The Add New Item dialog shown in Figure 8.18 is displayed. Figure 8.18 also shows that I have named this RD, GelButttons.xaml. You can ultimately name your dictionary whatever you want; but, for now, just stick with the suggestion.

8

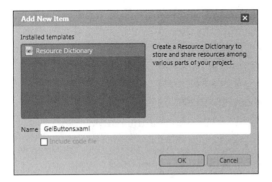

FIGURE 8.18   Creating a Resource Dictionary takes no special skills!

6. The Resource Dictionary is placed, by default, in the root directory of your project and is included in your open project resources. Back to the Add New Item dialog, notice that the Define in group box is already switched to use the RD you just created. The only thing left to do is to give the template a good name. Something like GelButtonMediaPlayerPlay perhaps? You can choose whatever you want, but do try to be descriptive.

Why Are Underscores a Bad Thing in Resource Names?

Resource names with underscores can cause confusion inside the Blend IDE. It appears that the development team did not switch off the mnemonics on the menu item template they used. When you go to view your list of resources, if you have named anything with an underscore in it, the first underscore will be missing and you will see an underscore under the first letter after where the underscore was originally created.

You can test this by naming a resource with an underscore and then applying that resource to a control such as a button. Then go back to the Edit Control Parts (template) menu item and view the Applied Resource list.

Considering that a designer could be creating the resource before sending it to someone else, any documentation may not reflect the correct name. This is a small issue, I know, but it can become annoying. I did report this to the team, but they only consider it to be an esthetic defect. For now, it is yet to be fixed.

7. Click OK and the interface will change dramatically in front of you. This is because you are now in resource-editing mode, which means you can only select and edit parts of the given template. You are all done with this at present; but later on, if you decide to enhance or change your button, you will see this same environment change. To leave and return to the scene, click on the Scope Up button within the Objects and Timelines panel or select the Go to top level scope tab, as shown in Figure 8.17.

And that, as they say, is the ball game! How simple was that? It used to be a lot more difficult than that, let me tell you.

You can now send that Resource Dictionary to other people who will be able to reproduce not only the button style, but also any functionality that you added to the template. In this case the Make Button tool did all the work. But it doesn't stop you from doing the exact same thing.

Now you are going to use the template in the next example to test that the template is valid and that the events that the button contains function properly.

Testing the Template and RoutedEvents

You are going to test the events of the Button element, but I also wanted to show you a little experiment that confirms the capability of the RoutedEvents, specifically the Tunneling and Bubbling events.

Tunneling events should always be named *Preview{event name}*; so, for example, the MouseDown event has an attached Tunneling event named PreviewMouseDown. Tunneling events are always the paired event of a standard counterpart. Their purpose is to be raised first, to enable parent elements to act on the event raised by the child before the child actually changes.

This could be handy if you wanted to validate some property after a button was clicked but before the Click event was raised and be able to handle the event if so required. The Bubbling counterpart always fires after the Tunneling event, unless an action causes the event to be cancelled.

1. Open a new project and add the XAML from Listing 8.2. Use only the markup from the "LayoutRoot" element down, but do note the Window dimension is 230 × 330.

LISTING 8.2   The Custom Button

```
<Window
... { Blend created definitions here }
    Width="230"
    Height="330" >

    <Grid x:Name="LayoutRoot">
        <Button
            x:Name="btnEventButton"
            VerticalAlignment="Top"
            Height="120"
            HorizontalAlignment="Center"
            Margin="0,10,0,0"
            Width="130"
            Content="Button"/>
        <ListBox
            Margin="0,144.8,0,0"
            x:Name="listBox_EventListener"
            IsSynchronizedWithCurrentItem="True"/>
        </Grid>
</Window>
```

2. You should end up with a Window containing two elements that looks like Figure 8.19. You are going to test the Resource Dictionary and control template with this button element. Find the previous example application and copy the Resource Dictionary file you created to the root or to a subroot folder of this project.

FIGURE 8.19   A simple test rig.

Managing Resources

It is a smart idea to create a folder somewhere in which you can store all your Resource Dictionaries. It does not take long to build up a number of these files, and it can be a nightmare trying to remember where each file is located and what each one contained.

3. Click on the Project menu item at the top of the application and then select Add Existing Item... or press Ctrl + I to add the Resource Dictionary to the project.

Why the Root Folder?

Expression Blend allows you to either add resources to the project or to link to existing files as a quasicopy-type method. If you link to an existing file resource, Blend creates a copy of the resource and adds it to the Root folder of the application.

If you try to link to a resource file that is already in the root of the application, you will receive an error dialog telling you that the file already exists in the location. For the type of file that a Resource Dictionary is, I would advise you to make a copy of the file, place it in the root or a subroot folder, but always add the file as a resource to the project rather than linking to the file.

The downside of linking is also that if the linked file is ever removed from the original path, the application will almost certainly fail with a file not found error.

4. Locate/Show the Resources palette, which is shown in Figure 8.20. You will see the layout of the application as it stands. Select the relevant scope for the resource, which in this case is the Window element. Right-click it to reveal the Link to Resource Dictionary menu item. From the submenu, select your Resource Dictionary.

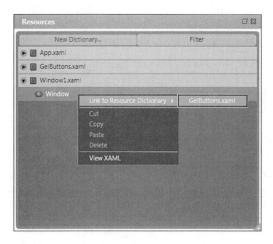

FIGURE 8.20   Linking to a Resource Dictionary.

5. Make sure you have the Selection tool chosen from the toolbox and click on the button element in the window on your artboard to select it. Open the Properties palette. In the Search box, type the word **style**. This returns only the relevant properties.

6. You are now going to apply the style template (from the previously created button) to the original standard button template that exists in this current project from the Resource Dictionary you just added. Notice that beside each property, a little square that is either filled (a white square denotes this property is applied in the xaml) or unfilled (default is assumed) is present. A click of the little box displays the Advanced property options menu for the associated property, as shown in

Figure 8.21. Figure 8.21 also shows how to select the template that was previously created and named GelButtonMediaPlayerPlay. Go ahead and select the template.

FIGURE 8.21   The Advanced menu for the Style property.

7. With any luck, your button looks similar to how it was at the end of the previous project, although you may have to tinker with the layout properties, width, height, and margins to get it back to just how you want it. After you have the button sorted out, make sure that it is still the selected item in the project and then open the Properties palette again.

8. You are about to add some events for the button element. Before you do so, save the project.

9. At the top of the palette, the name of the button element btnEventButton is displayed. To the right of this, are two icons. The one on the left, which is currently selected, allows you to see the properties for the selected element. The one on the right with the little lightning strike in the icon image represents the events that are available for this element. Select the event icon now.

10. Scroll down until you find the MouseMove event name, and then click into the input box beside it and type **BubbleMouseMove** and press Enter. Visual Studio launches with an open copy of the project and the event handler code shown in Listing 8.3 already inserted into the code editor.

LISTING 8.3   Sample Application

```
private void BubbleMouseMove(object sender,
 System.Windows.Input.MouseEventArgs e)
{

}
```

1. The first thing to do here is to build the solution from the Build menu or press the F6 button. Once done, the build should succeed and you are ready to add the event handler code. Add the code in the event handler method, as shown in Listing 8.4.

LISTING 8.4   The MouseMove Event Handler

```
private void BubbleMouseMove(object sender,
System.Windows.Input.MouseEventArgs e)
    {
        this.listBox_EventListener.BeginInit();
        this.listBox_EventListener.Items.Add("Bubble MouseMove");
        this.listBox_EventListener.EndInit();
    }
```

2. Now return to Blend. This time, scroll down the event list until you find the event named PreviewMouseMove and add the following event name: TunnelMouseMove.

3. Again, you should be able to see the event handler in Visual Studio. Enter the code as shown in Listing 8.5.

LISTING 8.5   Adding Items to the ListBox

```
private void TunnelMouseMove(object sender,
System.Windows.Input.MouseEventArgs e)
    {
        this.listBox_EventListener.BeginInit();
        this.listBox_EventListener.Items.Add("Tunnel MouseMove");
        this.listBox_EventListener.EndInit();
    }
```

4. Select Save All from the File menu in Visual Studio, and then return to the Blend environment.

Time now to test the application by pressing F5. Move your mouse over the button. If the application is working properly, the ListBox will fill up with messages in the order in which they fire, as shown in Figure 8.22. Scroll the ListBox to the top if necessary, and you can see that the Tunnel Event message is shown first and the messages continue on all the way down the list.

8

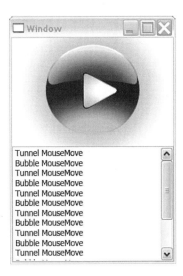

FIGURE 8.22   The event messages are added as they fire.

Summary

That was a simple demonstration of the effect of RoutedEvents, not to mention the application of a template stored in a Resource Dictionary. Creating buttons and other templates is a "fun" by-product of working with Blend. The very first question almost all designers ask when I introduce them to Blend is: How do I create a button? The next thing they want to know is how to put a rollover effect on it!

I cannot stress enough that using Resource Dictionaries is the method of choice for future development teams to embrace. It is one of the foundation features of the application to enable designers and developers to work together on the same project.

Teams implement their desired processes out of necessity to fulfill a project requirement. As a result, there is no *one* right way to enable collaborative solution development using Resource Dictionaries alone. But now you know how create and modify a template within one. After a little practice you will wonder how you ever worked without them. They are that powerful of a tool in WPF projects.

CHAPTER 9

Using the Blend Asset Library

The Expression Blend Asset Library is to be viewed—from the developer's perspective—as the replacement to the Visual Studio ToolBox palette. As you'll see in Figure 9.1, many areas are all neatly packaged within this one palette that allows you to transform your applications, from Styles to Controls to your own Custom Controls created in Blend or Visual Studio.

In particular is a search feature that can quickly narrow down the available toolset into library viewing based on full or partial item names. For example, type the word **grid**, and you will see only those controls with the word *grid* appearing within their given names.

This chapter contains overviews of the most common controls, because these controls enable you to work with most of the remaining controls as long as they are derived from the main PresentationFramework classes. Most notable are the Control, ContentControl, and FrameworkElement classes that encapsulate the majority of the control features among them.

This chapter also includes code snippets to assist you with common scenarios and some C# code snippets that prepare you for the next chapter, which deals completely with writing code. There is nothing too mind-bending at this stage; you're just getting your feet wet. So don't feel compelled to try and add the code in this chapter to a project while you are reading through it, but do read the code and try to understand the relevance of the elements, the markup, and the code working together.

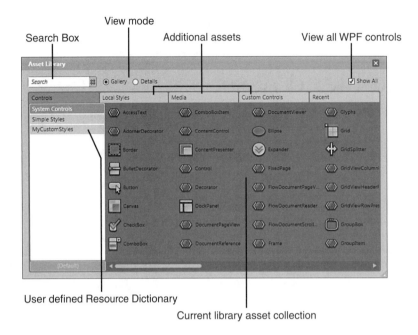

FIGURE 9.1   An overview of the Asset Library.

Asset Library Overview

As covered briefly in Chapter 3, "Expression Blend Panels," there are five primary areas of workflow within the Blend Asset Library, and each has varying degrees of usefulness depending on how you use the tool. For the most part, Controls and Custom Controls are the areas of primary concern, because the other panels provide views that are easily accessible from multiple areas within the Blend IDE.

Controls Tab

Figure 9.1 shows the default opening screen of the Asset Library. You will quickly become used to ducking in here to grab a quick control, whether you use it during the normal functionality of your application or whether you need a component to style. The search feature is invaluable for reducing the amount of time you trawl through the control set, whether you are searching for something specific or just looking to discover new control types.

Most functionality in the Controls tab is self-explanatory, but there is one nifty feature that appears to be fairly innocuous until you are in a situation where you need it. (And then, of course, you won't be able to find it!) At the bottom of the list of user-defined resource dictionaries is a button with the name *(Default)*. By default Blend uses the System Controls style directory, but this feature allows you to select your own Resource Dictionary as the default, just as you would expect. What you may not expect is that this feature also modifies the Toolbox so that you can use any control's styles you defined in your default style library. So if you have a button in your library, for example, every new button you add to your project contains your style by default.

Local Styles Tab

Figure 9.2 shows the Local Styles tab, which contains a complete list of all style templates that you created and saved locally to the currently selected file. Creating a Style locally is often the most efficient method of working with styles within Blend from a performance point of view, but you must remember that the availability of these styles is then contained to the local file.

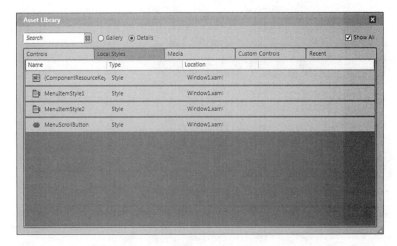

FIGURE 9.2   The Local Styles tab.

Media Tab

As you can see in Figure 9.3, the Media tab not only shows all different types of media linked and added to your application but also shows some resources (in this case brushes) that are part of the attached resources. This tab is one of those that becomes very important the more media assets you include in your application, allowing you to easily and quickly search and narrow your choices.

Custom Controls Tab

The Custom Controls tab's contents include all the custom and user controls that you defined within your application scope as well as any external .dlls or third-party controls that you referenced (see Figure 9.4). One interesting note is that only controls that build successfully are shown within this tab. At the time of writing, I could not confirm if this was a defect or done by design. If you are missing a control that you are sure should be there, check that the control is both without error in the design surface and builds correctly.

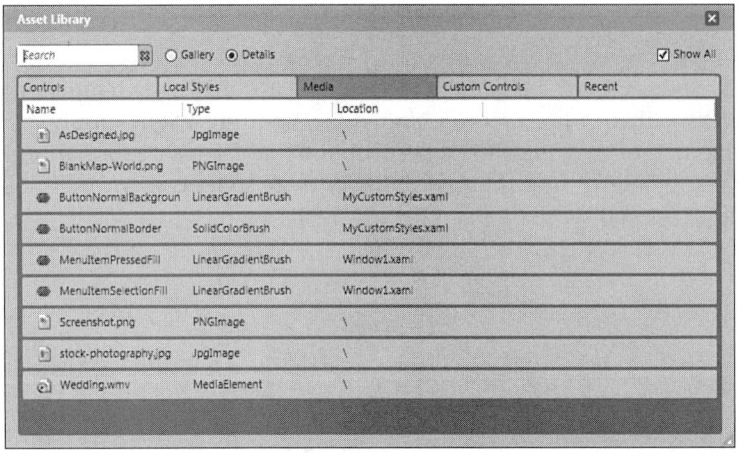

FIGURE 9.3   The Media tab.

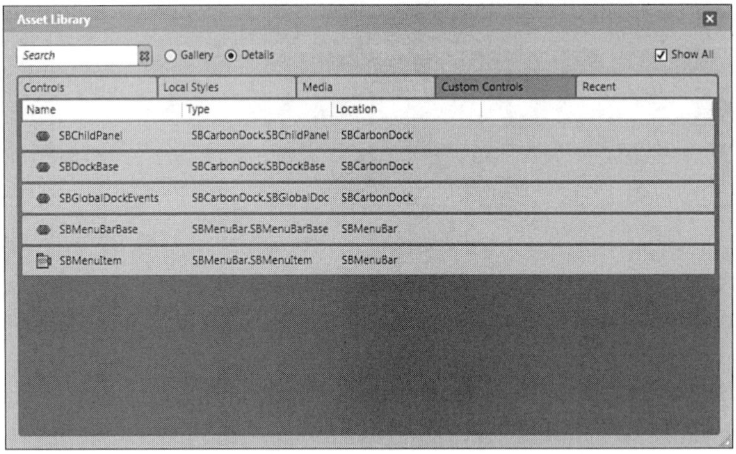

FIGURE 9.4   The Custom Controls tab.

Recent Tab

As the names suggests, the Recent tab shows recently used assets. It not only shows controls but also, as can be seen in Figure 9.5, presents all media types and styles. This is a great shortcut when you have those long, boring, and repetitive jobs to complete.

The Asset Library is a great workflow panel because it allows you to very compactly manage your applications resources and assets easily. I still don't understand why this panel cannot be permanently pinned or floated on another monitor, because surely its value would only further increase.

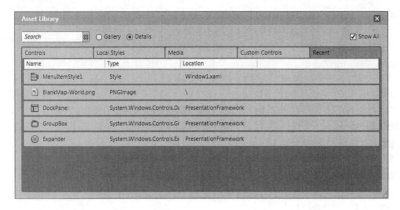

FIGURE 9.5   The Recent tab.

Familiar Windows Controls

For most developers, the controls included in WPF will sound, and in some cases function, similarly to those controls you previously used. If you are a developer, here is an important word of warning: the controls in Framework 3.0 and 3.5 are vastly different in some areas from the previous control types. Method names changed to become more standardized across the control types, and several control methods that previously were common may now return nullable types or have disappeared altogether.

For those of you who are designers, the control names in WPF are, for the most part, fairly descriptive. After you start to feel comfortable with the property and event types of most of the standard controls, you will find that you almost "know" how to use the others, because their familiarity and standardized names make it easier.

Take the time to go through the following control types to get a good basis of understanding with their most prominent features and the events they use.

Button Element

The ubiquitous Button control is arguably the most common control used to direct user workflow within an application. The control, however, can also go a long way toward providing positive user experiences by having non-ambiguous labels and being positioned and styled to match its surroundings.

Gone are the days in which you had four choices of style, one type of content (text string), and static responses to Click and various mouse events.

One of the most sought-after visual effects with Winforms applications is the capability to create and display Gel button types. As a developer, I never dared to dream past this point because I was always so limited by time, as well as the need to provide theme and accessibility support.

I have tried many different ways of creating Gel buttons with XAML-based applications, and let me tell you, the permutations are endless (which is a very good thing).

Listing 9.1 represents the fewest lines of XAML I could come up with to create a simple Gel button.

LISTING 9.1   A Simple Gel Button

```xaml
<UserControl.Resources>
        <Style BasedOn="{x:Null}" TargetType="{x:Type Button}" x:Key="SimpleGel">
            <Style.Triggers>
                <Trigger Property="IsEnabled" Value="False">
                    <Setter Property="Foreground" Value="#FFB9B9B9"/>
                </Trigger>
            </Style.Triggers>
            <Setter Property="Template">
                <Setter.Value>
                    <ControlTemplate TargetType="{x:Type Button}">
                        <Border  Margin="0,0,0,0" VerticalAlignment="Stretch"
➥Height="Auto" BorderBrush="#FF88D641" BorderThickness="1,1,1,1"
➥CornerRadius="18,18,18,18">
                            <Border.Background>
                                <LinearGradientBrush EndPoint="0.5,2.607"
StartPoint="0.5,-1.607">
                                    <GradientStop Color="#FF34FC00"
➥Offset="0.328"/>
                                    <GradientStop Color="#FFFFFFFF"
➥Offset="0.576"/>
                                </LinearGradientBrush>
                            </Border.Background>
                            <Border CornerRadius="18,18,18,18" Height="27.573"
Width="176">
                                <Border.Background>
                                    <LinearGradientBrush EndPoint="0.5,3.488"
StartPoint="0.5,-2.488">
                                        <GradientStop Color="#FF88D641"
➥Offset="0"/>
                                        <GradientStop Color="#4BFFFFFF"
➥Offset="0.645"/>
                                    </LinearGradientBrush>
                                </Border.Background>
                                <ContentPresenter SnapsToDevicePixels="
➥{TemplateBinding SnapsToDevicePixels}" RecognizesAccessKey="True"
➥HorizontalAlignment="Center" VerticalAlignment="Center"/>
                            </Border>
                        </Border>
                        <ControlTemplate.Triggers>
                        </ControlTemplate.Triggers>
```

```
                    </ControlTemplate>
                </Setter.Value>
            </Setter>
        </Style>
    </UserControl.Resources>

    <Grid x:Name="LayoutRoot">
        <Button Margin="30,15,30,15" Style="{DynamicResource SimpleGel}"
Content="Button"/>
    </Grid>
```

The code in Listing 9.1 provides for a simple button built using the Make Button tool. Although this code contains no extended functionality for event animations or focus styling, it does show that creating a button like this is both extremely quick and invaluable when needing to create a mock-up application commonly required by interactive designers.

The Button control (as well as any button created with the Make Button tool) contains a ContentControl that can contain strings, images, grids, and more Content controls. (See the "ContentControl" section later in this chapter for a detailed look at how to use this core control.)

As you are well aware of by this point, you can quickly draw on the artboard a standard button that is available from the toolbox. You can also enter markup directly with the Content property assigned a value:

```
<Button x:Name="btnMyButton" Content="Howdy"/>
```

As long as you name the button (in the Properties panel or in markup defined by the x:Name attribute), setting the Context value of the button in code to a string value, if that is the requirement; is as simple as the following line of code:

```
btnMyButton.Content = "Tester Text";
```

Bear in mind that the button also contains excellent functionality built in with its endless events and methods. You may want to style the button to look more like a label but still allow for the Click functionality.

The ClickMode property on the button allows you to specify exactly when a Click event should take place, be it a Release of the mouse, or the Press or Hover of the mouse that should raise the Click event.

Two other properties commonly used with the Button control include the IsCancel and IsDefault properties. When IsCancel is set to true, the user of the application can press the Escape (ESC) key to perform a button click. IsDefault enables the button to respond when the user presses the Enter key.

CheckBox Element

"How much different can a CheckBox really be?" you may be asking. There are two answers to that. The first answer is that you are correct; there are no significant changes to the control that warrant a five-page rant. The second answer (and possibly worth the five-page rant) is the capability to use the CheckBox control—and others like it—for the functionality that is already designed and implemented, not for the look or style of the existing control.

When you think about it, the CheckBox has great functionality built in for determining MouseOver, MousePressed, and MouseReleased events. Why not use that functionality when required instead of reinventing the wheel?

If you think of not only the CheckBox control but also most other controls as merely providing a form of styled container, you may then see that you can take the functionality and use it to your advantage. Listing 9.2 uses the built-in functionality of the CheckBox control to create a presentation menu. You can add the XAML from Listing 9.2 to a project to create the sample.

LISTING 9.2   A Simple Menu Created from CheckBoxes

```xml
<Window
    ... Blend created Window attributes
    Width="340" Height="500">
    <Window.Resources>
        <LinearGradientBrush x:Key="CheckRadioFillNormal">
            <GradientStop Color="#FFD2D4D2"
                Offset="0"/>
            <GradientStop Color="#FFFFFFFF"
                Offset="1"/>
        </LinearGradientBrush>
        <LinearGradientBrush x:Key="CheckRadioStrokeNormal">
            <GradientStop Color="#FF004C94"
                Offset="0"/>
            <GradientStop Color="#FF003C74"
                Offset="1"/>
        </LinearGradientBrush>
        <Style x:Key="EmptyCheckBoxFocusVisual">
            <Setter Property="Control.Template">
                <Setter.Value>
                    <ControlTemplate>
                        <Rectangle Margin="1"
                            StrokeThickness="1"
                            Stroke="Black"
                            StrokeDashArray="1 2"
                            SnapsToDevicePixels="true"/>
                    </ControlTemplate>
```

```xml
                </Setter.Value>
            </Setter>
        </Style>
        <Style x:Key="CheckRadioFocusVisual">
            <Setter Property="Control.Template">
                <Setter.Value>
                    <ControlTemplate>
                        <Rectangle Margin="14,0,0,0"
                            StrokeThickness="1"
                            Stroke="Black"
                            StrokeDashArray="1 2"
                            SnapsToDevicePixels="true"/>
                    </ControlTemplate>
                </Setter.Value>
            </Setter>
        </Style>
        <Style
            TargetType="{x:Type CheckBox}" x:Key="CheckBoxStyle1">
            <Setter Property="Foreground"
                Value="{DynamicResource {x:Static SystemColors.
ControlTextBrushKey}}"/>
            <Setter Property="Background"
                Value="{StaticResource CheckRadioFillNormal}"/>
            <Setter Property="BorderBrush"
                Value="{StaticResource CheckRadioStrokeNormal}"/>
            <Setter Property="BorderThickness"
                Value="1"/>
            <Setter Property="FocusVisualStyle"
                Value="{StaticResource EmptyCheckBoxFocusVisual}"/>
            <Setter Property="Template">
                <Setter.Value>
                    <ControlTemplate TargetType="{x:Type CheckBox}">
                        <ControlTemplate.Resources>
                            <Storyboard x:Key="Expand">
                                <DoubleAnimationUsingKeyFrames BeginTime="00:00:00"
Storyboard.TargetName="grid" Storyboard.TargetProperty="(FrameworkElement.Height)">
                                    <SplineDoubleKeyFrame KeyTime="00:00:00"
Value="50"/>
                                    <SplineDoubleKeyFrame KeyTime="00:00:01"
Value="100"/>
                                </DoubleAnimationUsingKeyFrames>
                            </Storyboard>
                            <Storyboard x:Key="Contract">
                                <DoubleAnimationUsingKeyFrames BeginTime="00:00:00"
Storyboard.TargetName="grid" Storyboard.TargetProperty="(FrameworkElement.Height)">
```

6

```
                                    <SplineDoubleKeyFrame KeyTime="00:00:00"
➥Value="100"/>
                                    <SplineDoubleKeyFrame KeyTime="00:00:01"
➥Value="50"/>
                                </DoubleAnimationUsingKeyFrames>
                            </Storyboard>
                        </ControlTemplate.Resources>
                        <Grid x:Name="grid" Height="50">
                            <Rectangle Stroke="#FF1438A7" RadiusX="10.7"
➥RadiusY="10.7" HorizontalAlignment="Stretch" Margin="5,5,5,5" Width="Auto">
                                <Rectangle.Fill>
                                    <LinearGradientBrush EndPoint="0.5,3.295"
➥StartPoint="0.5,-2.295">
                                        <GradientStop Color="#FF8EBDF3"
➥Offset="0.444"/>
                                        <GradientStop Color="#FFFFFFFF"
➥Offset="0.605"/>
                                    </LinearGradientBrush>
                                </Rectangle.Fill>
                            </Rectangle>
                            <ContentPresenter HorizontalAlignment="Center"
➥VerticalAlignment="Center" Width="100"/>
                        </Grid>
                        <ControlTemplate.Triggers>
                            <EventTrigger RoutedEvent="ToggleButton.Checked">
                                <BeginStoryboard Storyboard="{StaticResource
➥Expand}"/>
                            </EventTrigger>
                            <EventTrigger RoutedEvent="ToggleButton.Unchecked">
                                <BeginStoryboard x:Name="Contract_BeginStoryboard"
➥Storyboard="{StaticResource Contract}"/>
                            </EventTrigger>
                        </ControlTemplate.Triggers>
                    </ControlTemplate>
                </Setter.Value>
            </Setter>
        </Style>
    </Window.Resources>
    <Grid x:Name="LayoutRoot">
        <ScrollViewer HorizontalAlignment="Stretch" VerticalAlignment="Stretch"
➥Width="Auto" Height="Auto" Margin="15,15,15,15">
            <StackPanel Width="Auto" Height="Auto">
                <CheckBox Style="{DynamicResource CheckBoxStyle1}"
➥HorizontalContentAlignment="Center" VerticalContentAlignment="Center"
➥Content="Menu Item 1" Grid.IsSharedSizeScope="False" ClickMode="Release"
➥Cursor="Hand" ScrollViewer.VerticalScrollBarVisibility="Hidden"/>
```

```
                    <CheckBox Style="{DynamicResource CheckBoxStyle1}"
➥HorizontalContentAlignment="Center" VerticalContentAlignment="Center"
➥Content="Menu Item 2" Grid.IsSharedSizeScope="False" ClickMode="Release"
➥Cursor="Hand" ScrollViewer.VerticalScrollBarVisibility="Hidden"/>
                    <CheckBox Style="{DynamicResource CheckBoxStyle1}"
➥HorizontalContentAlignment="Center" VerticalContentAlignment="Center"
➥Content="Menu Item 3" Grid.IsSharedSizeScope="False" ClickMode="Release"
➥Cursor="Hand" ScrollViewer.VerticalScrollBarVisibility="Hidden"/>
                    <CheckBox Style="{DynamicResource CheckBoxStyle1}"
➥HorizontalContentAlignment="Center" VerticalContentAlignment="Center"
➥Content="Menu Item 4" Grid.IsSharedSizeScope="False" ClickMode="Release"
➥Cursor="Hand" ScrollViewer.VerticalScrollBarVisibility="Hidden"/>
                    <CheckBox Style="{DynamicResource CheckBoxStyle1}"
➥HorizontalContentAlignment="Center" VerticalContentAlignment="Center"
➥Content="Menu Item 5" Grid.IsSharedSizeScope="False" ClickMode="Release"
➥Cursor="Hand" ScrollViewer.VerticalScrollBarVisibility="Hidden"/>
                    <CheckBox Style="{DynamicResource CheckBoxStyle1}"
➥HorizontalContentAlignment="Center" VerticalContentAlignment="Center"
➥Content="Menu Item 6" Grid.IsSharedSizeScope="False" ClickMode="Release"
➥Cursor="Hand" ScrollViewer.VerticalScrollBarVisibility="Hidden"/>
                    <CheckBox Style="{DynamicResource CheckBoxStyle1}"
➥HorizontalContentAlignment="Center" VerticalContentAlignment="Center"
➥Content="Menu Item 7" Grid.IsSharedSizeScope="False" ClickMode="Release"
➥Cursor="Hand" ScrollViewer.VerticalScrollBarVisibility="Hidden"/>
               </StackPanel>
          </ScrollViewer>
     </Grid>
</Window>
```

Figure 9.6 shows how clicking on a Menu item expands the size of the item, which is simply an animation connected to the Checked event. Conversely, another animation is specified for the UnChecked event, which causes the menu item to contract.

The preceding XAML may be a time-consuming process to add to your project, but if you put in the effort, you will see quite a few interesting concepts, including styles and animation, each of which the book covers in future chapters. Don't let the size of the XAML put you off this way of thinking, however, because this demo application took about four minutes to create using the Blend application interface.

In code, the named CheckBox has the same properties as shown in the Property panel inside Blend. Setting the Checked state of the control, the code would look similar to the following:

```
myCheckBox.IsChecked = true;
```

When the user sets the state of the control to showing a Check, the CheckedEvent is raised, allowing you to react to this new state. Conversely, an Unchecked event is available. Listing 9.3 demonstrates these events in code by displaying a MessageBox on the relevant event being raised.

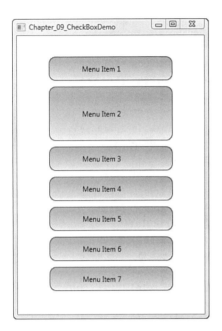

FIGURE 9.6   Using a CheckBox for something different.

LISTING 9.3   Example CheckBox Events

```
private void myCheckBox_Checked(object sender, RoutedEventArgs e)
{
    MessageBox.Show("The CheckBox is checked!");
}

private void myCheckBox_Unchecked(object sender, RoutedEventArgs e)
{
    MessageBox.Show("The CheckBox is un-checked!");
}
```

The CheckBox contains many similar features to of that of a button: a Click event as well as the capability to take different types of Content. In addition is a property called IsThreeState, which allows the CheckBox to either display a Check, no Check, or a Block representing the in-between state.

ComboBox Element

The ComboBox control takes its core functionality from the ancestors of pre-Framework 3.0 and 3.5 classes. This control contains a collection of ComboBoxItems, each with an index, and each programmatically selectable—and importantly—bindable to an XML or CLR Datasource, or even another UIElement property.

Perhaps the greatest exploitation of the ComboBox comes from the ability to nest child elements to an infinite number (well maybe, I didn't check the limit). The XAML shown in Listing 9.4 gives you proof of this by nesting three ComboBoxes, each with a Button child, and all in just 34 lines of markup!

To try it out, add the code in Listing 9.4 XAML to a new project.

LISTING 9.4   Nested Child ComboBoxes

```
    <Grid x:Name="LayoutRoot">
        <ComboBox Margin="13.8,8.6,15,0" VerticalAlignment="Top" Height="32.8"
Text="ComboBox 1" IsSynchronizedWithCurrentItem="True">
            <ComboBoxItem Height="37.277">
                <Button Width="246.483" Height="36.477" Content="Button"/>
            </ComboBoxItem>
            <ComboBoxItem>
                <ComboBox Width="232.6" Height="34.477" Text="ComboBox 2">
                    <ComboBoxItem>
                        <Button Width="221.683" Height="36.477" Content="Button"/>
                    </ComboBoxItem>
                    <ComboBoxItem>
                        <ComboBox Width="210.2" Height="34.477"
IsDropDownOpen="False" Text="ComboBox  3" SelectedIndex="-1">
                            <ComboBoxItem>
                                <Button Width="199.283" Height="32.477"
Content="Button"/>
                            </ComboBoxItem>
                        </ComboBox>
                    </ComboBoxItem>
                </ComboBox>
            </ComboBoxItem>
        </ComboBox>
    </Grid>
```

To add new ComboBoxItems in code, you need to create an instance of the item first and then assign it to the ComboBox. Listing 9.5 shows exactly this by creating two simple ComboBoxItems and then inserting them into the ComboBox's item collection.

LISTING 9.5 Inserting ComboBox Child Items

```
private void AddNewComboItems()
    {
        ComboBoxItem NewItem = new ComboBoxItem();
        NewItem.Content = "First Item";

        myComboBox.Items.Add(NewItem);

        NewItem = null;

        NewItem = new ComboBoxItem();
        NewItem.Content = "Second Item";

        myComboBox.Items.Add(NewItem);
    }
```

The properties in Table 9.1 are not exactly common properties but are very handy to know.

TABLE 9.1 Additional ComboBox Properties Available in Expression Blend

Property Name	Description
IsDropDownOpen	False by default (Unchecked in the Blend interface), this property sets the control either to display its contents by default or to keep them hidden until the user selects the control to display the child items.
IsEditable	False by default (Unchecked in the Blend interface), this property allows the user to edit the text shown in the control's header.
SelectedIndex	Set to –1 by default (no item selected), you can either set the value in design time or in runtime, which raises the SelectionChanged event.
MaxDropDownHeight	Set to 350 by default, this property allows you to contain the maximum visible drop-down area.

ItemsCollection Controls

The ComboBox control contains a collection of items. Each ComboBoxItem or element that you add to the ComboBox is contained within the ComboBox's "item" collection, which is also accessible in code.

Other controls, such as Listbox, also maintain item collections, so it is handy to know how to retrieve references to the item controls if you have not named them but still need access in code.

Listings 9.6 and 9.7 work together to demonstrate this principle. First, add the markup to a new project, to create a ComboBox with several unnamed child ComboBoxItem controls and a Button with an associated Click event. The code in Listing 9.7 (which is the Click event) shows how you can iterate the item collection to find an item control and perform functions on it (in this case finding Item 2 and changing its background color).

LISTING 9.6   Creating Unnamed ComboBox Items

```
<Grid x:Name="LayoutRoot">
    <Grid.RowDefinitions>
        <RowDefinition Height="0.266*"/>
        <RowDefinition Height="0.734*"/>
    </Grid.RowDefinitions>

    <ComboBox HorizontalAlignment="Center" x:Name="comboStandard"
VerticalAlignment="Top" Width="200" IsSynchronizedWithCurrentItem="True"
Grid.Row="1">
            <ComboBoxItem Content="Item 1"/>
            <ComboBoxItem Content="Item 2"/>
            <ComboBoxItem Content="Item 3"/>
            <ComboBoxItem Content="Item 4"/>
            <ComboBoxItem Content="Item 5"/>
    </ComboBox>
    <Button HorizontalAlignment="Center" x:Name="btnFindItem"
VerticalAlignment="Center" Content="Find Item" Click="btnFindItem_Click"
Grid.Row="0"/>

</Grid>
```

LISTING 9.7   Finding an Unnamed Child Item in a ComboBox

```
private void btnFindItem_Click(object sender, RoutedEventArgs e)
{
    foreach (ComboBoxItem currentItem in this.comboStandard.Items)
    {
        if (Convert.ToString(currentItem.Content) == "Item 2")
        {
            currentItem.Background = new SolidColorBrush(Color.FromRgb(185,
185, 185));
        }
    }
}
```

(Chapter 10, "Visual Studio: C# Primer" explains the for each looping C# syntax.)

Another important concept is that a collection contains additional functionality to enable you to sort, group, and filter the content that the item collection presents.

The combination of Listings 9.6 and 9.7 added, and therefore presented, the child items in sequential order (see Figure 9.7). However, as shown by the modifications in Listing 9.8 (which is a complete replacement for Listing 9.7) and with Figure 9.8, you can easily sort the items. If you intend to try this, add the following using directive at the top of the code page:

```
using System.ComponentModel;
```

FIGURE 9.7   The original ComboBox item collection, sequentially presented.

FIGURE 9.8   The modified sorted ComboBox, with the item's collection reversed.

What Is a Using Directive?

Using directives are covered in Chapter 10 but for now you should understand that they are simply telling .NET that you want to use some functionality that is included in the System.ComponentModel object (namespace).

You could think of these objects as being similar to a box, which happens to have functions inside it that help you perform a task. When you need to use a specific function, instead of trying to rewrite it yourself, you just "use" what is already provided.

LISTING 9.8   Reorder Child Items of the ComboBox

```
private void btnFindItem_Click(object sender, RoutedEventArgs e)
{

    foreach (ComboBoxItem currentItem in this.comboStandard.Items)
    {
        if (Convert.ToString(currentItem.Content) == "Item 2")
        {
            currentItem.Background = new SolidColorBrush(Color.FromRgb(185,
185, 185));
        }
    }

    //Sort the collection
    this.comboStandard.Items.SortDescriptions.Add(new SortDescription
("Content", ListSortDirection.Descending));

}
```

Using Images

Images take on many different formats, ranging from bitmaps to JPEGs and so on. You are most likely completely comfortable using a tool that you have spent many hundreds if not thousands of hours (and possibly the same amount of money) working with, so when Microsoft unveiled Expression Design, criticism was quick to flow about the so-called "lack of features."

Given some time and a little patience on learning the tool (Design), the workflow between Expression Design and Blend is really quite good, allowing you to provide visual assets to Blend in either XAML- or an image-based format such as .png, .bmp, or .eps, to name a few.

Be diligent in whether you choose to use XAML vector images over bitmap-based, because there is a point of performance where one has more benefit than the other. Complex XAML images can take up thousands of lines of markup. Unless you need the scaling benefits of vector images over the of photo-realism available with bitmaps, you should consider the following:

Use XAML vector images for

- ▶ Image assets that need scaling flexibility

- ▶ Small assets that need to be animated or potentially "morphed" during runtime

- ▶ Situations in which application skinning affects the appearance of the image

Use bitmap-based images for

▶ Complex shaded images

▶ Instances that require photo-realism

▶ Assets where the total kilobyte file size is approximately 75% smaller than that of the same amount of XAML required to produce the same or a similar image

You will inevitably need to make compromises of performance over quality in some scenarios, based on the capabilities of the end users' machines. That said, XAML vector images are fast to load and easily to modify in comparison to bitmap-based images in dynamic WPF applications.

To add an image to your project:

1. Click on the Add Existing Item menu option under the Project menu in Blend. The File Open dialog displays, allowing you to select an image file, which is then added to the Project hierarchy under the Project panel.

2. Right-click on the image and select "Insert" to see the image element appear on the artboard. Alternatively, select the image from the Media tab of the Asset Library and then drag the image onto the artboard.

Naturally, you can manipulate and rescale the image as needed. Something you may not expect, however, is the ability to convert bitmap-based images to 3D, which brings in a whole host of new capabilities.

To try changing an image to 3D, create a new project and add an image, as previously described by using the Add Existing Item menu option of the Project menu.

1. Locate the image in the Projects panel, Files category. Right-click the image and select Insert from the context menu.

2. The image now displays on the artboard. Manually reposition (center, center) the image using the HorizontalAlignment and VerticalAlignment properties inside the Layout category.

3. Select the Tools menu and then select Make image 3D.

4. The image is now inside a Viewport3D control, inside the Objects and Timeline category of the Interaction panel. Double-click the Viewport3D control to activate it. Notice that only the top four toolbox items are active.

   You can use these controls to reposition the viewport or the object inside the viewport.

5. Expand the Viewport3D control inside the Objects and Timeline category. You should see some child controls, one being a ModelContainer. Activate the ModelContainer control.

6. With the Selection tool (V) enabled, a series of red, green, and blue arcs and arrows shows over the image on the artboard. These allow you to control the item in the 3D view. Move your mouse over the center of the image. The cursor changes to an

arrow with what looks to be a forward slash running through it that points to the top left of the screen.

7. Press and hold the left mouse button and move the mouse in either the up or down direction to bring the 3D object closer or send it further away. In this scenario, you want to send the object away, making it appear smaller.

8. Activate the Viewport3D control again. The ModelContainer now appears to be scaled inside it (see Figure 9.9).

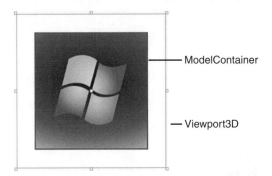

ModelContainer

Viewport3D

FIGURE 9.9   The Viewport3D and the ModelContainer control (housing the image).

9. Press the O key or select the Camera Orbit tool from the toolbox. Move the Arrow/Globe-looking mouse cursor over the center of the Viewport3D control. Hold down the left mouse button and drag the mouse around in several different directions to view the 3D position of the ModelContainer.

Another great feature of Blend is the capability to make images dynamically in the forms of visual and drawing brushes. These brushes can then be painted onto a UIElement surface to create effects such as reflection and thumbnails.

The following example shows you the differences between the two.

1. Create a new Standard application in Blend.

2. Activate the LayoutRoot element and add a Grid control as a Child.

3. Set the Background color property of the Grid to a very pale blue, center the Grid both horizontally and vertically, and change the size of the Grid to 150 for both width and height.

4. Set the bottom margin property to 150 to position the Grid in the center and near the top of the artboard.

5. Activate the Grid and, inside the Grid, draw a random selection of ellipses and rectangles as child elements, as shown in Figure 9.10.

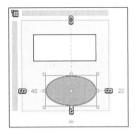

FIGURE 9.10 The Grid with an ellipse and a rectangle with different colors added.

6. Ensure that the Grid remains active and select it. Open the Tools menu and then select the Make Brush Resource menu item, which shows the additional child menu options of Make Drawing Brush Resource and Make Visual Brush Resource, as shown in Figure 9.11.

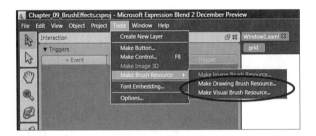

FIGURE 9.11 The Make Brush Resource menu items.

7. Select Make Drawing Brush Resource to open the Create Drawing Brush Resource dialog. Leave the name as DrawingBrush1 for this example.

8. Repeat step 7, but this time, select Make Visual Brush Resource, the default name of VisualBrush1.

9. Select and activate the LayoutRoot element. Add two child Grid elements in arbitrary positions at the bottom of the artboard, making their size the same as the first Grid: 150 by 150.

10. Select the first of the new Grid elements and then open the Brushes category of the Properties panel.

11. Select the Background property (which is No Brush by default) and then select Brush Resources as the brush type (see Figure 9.12). The DrawingBrush1 and VisualBrush1 resources display in the Local Brush Resources category.

12. Select DrawingBrush1, which is an exact copy of the Grid you created with the Ellipse and the Rectangle objects.

13. Repeat step 12, for the last of the Grid elements you added, but this time select the visual brush for the Background property resource.

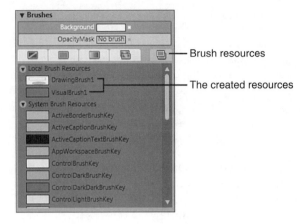

Brush resources

The created resources

FIGURE 9.12   The Resource collection.

14. Right about now, you might be thinking, "What is the difference?" Go back to the first Grid you created, with the Ellipse and the Rectangle elements. Select and activate it.

15. With the Selection tool (V), scale and move the Ellipse and Rectangle elements inside the Grid. These live results clearly show the difference.

You are not limited to just showing a Grid. You also can make a DrawingBrush or VisualBrush from any UIElement, even Viewport3D. See Figure 9.13. Table 9.2 provides for some additional properties of the Image element.

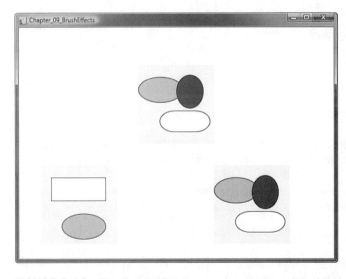

FIGURE 9.13   The DrawingBrush resource, as the original looked, and the VisualBrush resource showing the additional elements added to the source Grid.

TABLE 9.2   Additional Image Properties in Expression Blend

Property Name	Description
Stretch	Set to Fill by default, this property allows you to set the rate of stretch applied to an image inside the control.
StretchDirection	As the name suggests, you may set the direction (Up, Down, or Both) that the image element applies to its source.

BitmapImage Type

Another object type, called a BitmapImage, allows you to create an image from a source file in code and then convert it to an ImageBrush, which can then be painted onto UIElements that require a brush for the background fill property. The BitmapImage type is powerful, but you must remember that only properties set during the object's initialization period will be used.

Initialization Specification

To set properties on the object, declare a new BitmapImage object and then call BitmapImage.BeginInit(). Then set the properties of the BitmapImage, including the URISource property for the source location of the image file, and call BitmapImage.EndInit() to signal the initialization is complete.

In a new application, add the XAML shown in Listing 9.9.

LISTING 9.9   Creating the ImageBrush Example

```
<Grid x:Name="LayoutRoot">
    <Grid.RowDefinitions>
        <RowDefinition Height="0.106*"/>
        <RowDefinition Height="0.894*"/>
    </Grid.RowDefinitions>
    <Grid HorizontalAlignment="Stretch" Margin="20,20,20,20" x:Name="gdImage-
Board" VerticalAlignment="Stretch" Width="Auto" Height="Auto" Grid.Row="1"
Grid.RowSpan="1" Background="#FF8D8D8D"/>
        <Button HorizontalAlignment="Left" Margin="20,10,0,0" x:Name="btnFindImage"
VerticalAlignment="Top" Content="Find Image" Click="btnFindImage_Click"/>
    </Grid>
```

Listing 9.9 contains a button element that has a click handler declared. Open the Events list in the Properties panel, with the Button selected, then double-click the Click event input box. When you have the event handler code added in Visual Studio, add the code from Listing 9.10. Notice how the BitmapImage is converted to an ImageBrush.

LISTING 9.10   Making the ImageBrush the Background of a Grid

```
void btnFindImage_Click(object sender, RoutedEventArgs e)
{
    OpenFileDialog OFD = new OpenFileDialog();
    OFD.Filter = "TIF ¦ *.tif";
    OFD.ShowDialog();

    //Build the image to show in the scene
    BitmapImage NewImage = new BitmapImage(new Uri(OFD.FileName,
    UriKind.RelativeOrAbsolute));
//No properties set on the BitmapImage after the initialization work

    //Create a brush that we use to paint the UIElement with
    ImageBrush ImageToShow = new ImageBrush(NewImage);
    //Assign it to the scene object
    this.gdImageBoard.Background = ImageToShow;
}
```

Add the following two using directives:

```
using Microsoft.Win32;
using System.Windows.Media.Imaging;
```

You could use a specific Image UIElement, which requires you to set the Source property with an ImageSource value. You could use the same code as previous and instead set the Source of the Image UIElement as follows:

```
ImageElement.Source = NewImage as ImageSource;
```

Label Elements

The Label control provides a way to show simple labeling in an application. The control also allows you to specify the Content, which could be a string of text or an additional control, such as an Image or a Grid, with many more controls as children.

Labels also support mnemonics in runtime, so your users can press the Alt key to see an underline under a letter in your label.

```
<Label HorizontalAlignment="Left" Margin="66,48,0,0" VerticalAlignment="Top"
Width="229" Height="30" Content="La_bel" x:Name="use"/>
```

By default, the Focusable property is set to false, so when a user executes the mnemonic, focus goes to the next control in the tab order.

Setting Tab Order

All controls have a `TabIndex` property, which is a number that represents the order in which the control receives focus if the user continually presses the Tab key. Each control must have its Focusable property set to true in order to be included in the rotation. Simply change the `TabIndex` values from lowest value (1, for example) for the first item to be "tabbed to" to the highest for the last control.

Similar to the code syntax required to set the string value of a Button, you can set the display value of the Label by also assigning a value to its `Content` property:

```
labMyLabel.Content = "Howdy";
```

Listbox Element

The Listbox is a commonly used control to show the end user, collections of items in a scrollable container. You can activate the control by double-clicking on it in the Objects and Timeline category of the Interaction panel, and then draw any other control directly into it, a Grid for example.

The power of the Listbox comes in when it is data bound to a collection of items, because at heart, the Listbox is an ItemsControl (see the previous discussion in this chapter about ItemsControl). This means it is designed to effectively show a list of items. (See data binding in Chapter 13, "Data Binding," for more details on using a Listbox in the data-bound context.)

ListBoxItem

A ListBoxItem is a child item element of a ListBox control and can contain additional child elements as is required by the user interface specification. Listing 9.11 shows the XAML markup of a simple ListBoxItem.

The quickest way to add a ListBoxItem to a ListBox control is to select the ListBox control in the Objects and Timeline category and right-click to see the menu option to add a ListBoxItem. Listing 9.12 though, shows how to programmatically add ListBoxItem child elements using the items collection "Add()" method.

LISTING 9.11   Creating ListBoxItems in XAML Markup

```
        <ListBox Margin="149,107,265,72" x:Name="myListBox"
IsSynchronizedWithCurrentItem="True">
            <ListBoxItem Content="ListBoxItem 1"/>
            <ListBoxItem Content="ListBoxItem 2"/>
        </ListBox>
```

LISTING 9.12   Creating and Filling the ListBox with the Same Items

```
ListBoxItem Item1 = new ListBoxItem();
Item1.Content = "ListBoxItem 1";

this.myListBox.Items.Add(Item1);

ListBoxItem Item2 = new ListBoxItem();
Item2.Content = "ListBoxItem 2";

this.myListBox.Items.Add(Item2);
```

As you can see from the code in Listing 9.12, a new ListBoxItem is instantiated by the "new" call. The item is then "added" to the Listbox items collection.

Like the CheckBox, the ListBox control has fantastic functionality and can also be used as a Menu control. The items that appear in the List can be styled to any requirement. Additionally, the items collection gives you the flexibility to iterate the child item elements as well as sort, group, and filter, as previously shown with the ComboBox example.

Several events are used commonly with controls such as the Listbox, ComboBox, and ListView controls. The majority of the time you won't be using one of these controls simply to display items, but more often, you will use these controls to allow a user to actually select an item, which then dictates additional actions for which your interface provides. A master-detailview is a common scenario in many commercial applications, which implements this concept. This concept is discussed in detail when data binding is explained in Chapter 13.

The Selection_Changed event fires when the user makes his or her choice and either clicks or uses the keyboard to highlight a child item element in the control. The event allows you to discover which item the user selected by comparing and sometimes converting the object parsed through the event arguments, therefore giving you the selected item. An example of this functionality is discussed in the next section. You can apply the same methods to the ListBox and other ItemsCollection controls.

ListView Control

The ListView has a long history and a quite impressive pedigree in terms of user functionality. I personally think it took a wrong turn in the early days of .NET, because the ability to add images to multiple columns was a pain, to say the least.

All is not lost with the ListView, however, which makes a triumphant return as one the top controls provided by WPF. ListView allows for extremely flexible data binding, making multicolumn views simple.

ListViewItem

You can add ListViewItems to a ListView by using the method described with the ComboBox and ListBox. Select the element in the Objects and Timeline category of the Interaction panel, right-click, and then select Add new ListViewItem from the context menu.

To present multicolumn functionality, you must create a view for the ListView to use. The view represents an object that defines the style and organization of data in the ListView. WPF comes with a predefined view, called the GridView, which you will use in an example shortly. You may also create your own custom views.

Take a few minutes to create the simple XML file shown in Listing 9.13. Add the listing directly to a text file and then save it as Sample.xml in a location you can remember. Then work through the following example that demonstrates the view concept.

LISTING 9.13   A "People" Object Created in XML with Three "Person" Objects Added

```xml
<?xml version="1.0" encoding="utf-8"?>
<People>
    <Person>
        <Name>Bill Turner</Name>
        <Age>25</Age>
        <EyeColor>Blue</EyeColor>
        <Gender>Male</Gender>
    </Person>
    <Person>
        <Name>Steve Turner</Name>
        <Age>32</Age>
        <EyeColor>Brown</EyeColor>
        <Gender>Male</Gender>
    </Person>
    <Person>
        <Name>Jill Turner</Name>
        <Age>29</Age>
        <EyeColor>Green</EyeColor>
        <Gender>Female</Gender>
    </Person>
</People>
```

The following steps take you through the same simple binding you used in Chapter 2, "Welcome to the New World," with the Twitter reader, only this time you browse to a file instead of entering a URL for the source XML:

1. Create the XML file shown in Listing 9.13.
2. Open a new application in Blend.

3. Find a ListView control in the Asset Library and add a ListView to the LayoutRoot element.

4. Open the Project tab panel and click on the +XML button in the Data category.

5. Browse to the Sample.xml file you created.

6. Select the ListView control in Objects and Timeline category and then search for "view" in the property search box of the Properties tab panel. The property View(GridView) displays under the Miscellaneous category, as shown in Figure 9.14.

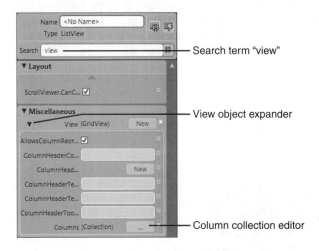

FIGURE 9.14   The hidden default view of the ListView.

7. Click on the Columns (Collection) editor button, as shown in Figure 9.14, to launch the GridViewColumn Collection Editor shown in Figure 9.15.

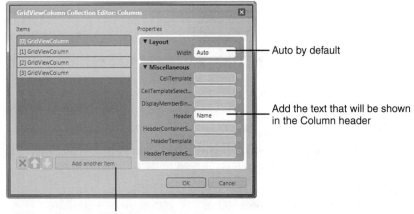

FIGURE 9.15   Control of your view columns.

7. Add three more columns and add the title of the column names in the Header property of each GridViewColumn (see Figure 9.15).

8. As per the Sample.xml file you created, name the columns Name, Age, EyeColor, and Gender. The ListView element should have four columns in the artboard view.

9. With the ListView element still selected, search for the ItemsSource property. Select the Advanced property options (the small square next to the property input box) and select Data Binding... from the context menu.

10. Select the Data Field tab at the top of the dialog box and then select PeopleDS from the Data sources Listbox. "People" should appear in the Fields Listbox with an expander arrow beside it. Expand the Field and select the Person (Array) item in the view (see Figure 9.16).

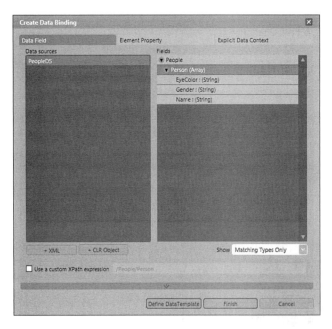

FIGURE 9.16   The Person (Array) is a selected field of the PeopleDS Data source.

11. Click Finish to close the dialog.

On your artboard you now have a ListView control with every field stretched out and showing all the data values for a single person in each field of each column. Why is this?

You defined the view in terms of the columns that you should have, and you specified the data source, but you didn't strictly define which data each column should contain.

If you switch to XAML view, your markup should look similar to that shown in Listing 9.14, which shows the GridViewColumn collection (inside a GridView element) with only the Header property defined.

LISTING 9.14   The ListView Showing Four Columns

```
<Window.Resources>
    <XmlDataProvider x:Key="PeopleDS" d:IsDataSource="True"
Source="D:\Sample.xml" />
</Window.Resources>

<Grid x:Name="LayoutRoot" >
    <ListView Margin="50,50,50,50" HorizontalAlignment="Center"
➥VerticalAlignment="Center" Width="350" Height="350" ItemsSource="{Binding
➥Mode=Default, Source={StaticResource PeopleDS}, XPath=/People/Person}">
        <ListView.View>
            <GridView>
                <GridViewColumn Header="Name"/>
                <GridViewColumn Header="Age"/>
                <GridViewColumn Header="EyeColor"/>
                <GridViewColumn Header="Gender"/>
            </GridView>
        </ListView.View>
    </ListView>
</Grid>
```

In order to see the data, you must specify a Data template for each column. You learn more about data binding in Chapter 13, but for now, understand that the GridViewColumn requires a template that sets out how to show the data it gets, which is set to a property named CellTemplate.

Listing 9.15 shows the markup used to define the template for each GridViewColumn in the GridViewColumn collection. An element type of TextBlock is the element used to show the data, but you may choose to use a button or a label element if you wish.

LISTING 9.15   Data Templates Defined for All Required ListView Columns

```
<GridView>
    <GridViewColumn Header="Name">
        <GridViewColumn.CellTemplate>
            <DataTemplate>
                <TextBlock Text="{Binding XPath=Name}"
➥TextAlignment="Left" />
            </DataTemplate>
        </GridViewColumn.CellTemplate>
    </GridViewColumn>
    <GridViewColumn Header="Age">
        <GridViewColumn.CellTemplate>
            <DataTemplate>
```

```
                            <TextBlock Text="{Binding XPath=Age}"
➥TextAlignment="Center" />
                        </DataTemplate>
                    </GridViewColumn.CellTemplate>
                </GridViewColumn>
                <GridViewColumn Header="EyeColor">
                    <GridViewColumn.CellTemplate>
                        <DataTemplate>
                            <TextBlock Text="{Binding XPath=EyeColor}"
➥TextAlignment="Right" />
                        </DataTemplate>
                    </GridViewColumn.CellTemplate>
                </GridViewColumn>
                <GridViewColumn Header="Gender">
                    <GridViewColumn.CellTemplate>
                        <DataTemplate>
                            <TextBlock Text="{Binding XPath=Gender}"
➥TextAlignment="Left" />
                        </DataTemplate>
                    </GridViewColumn.CellTemplate>
                </GridViewColumn>
            </GridView>
```

Listing 9.15 can be inserted between the <ListView.View> and </ListView.View> tags of Listing 9.14.

With any luck, you should now be able to run your application and you will have a multi-column ListView control, showing the Sample.xml data as required. The DataTemplate element is very powerful in the functionality that is offers, allowing you to specify exactly how you want to present your data, regardless of its source or parental confines.

PasswordBox Control

The inclusion of the PasswordBox control allows you to quickly create password input dialogs or panels that require the user's entered values to be hidden from the screen.

The control's use is almost identical to that of a TextBox control, except that the TextBox control has AutoWordSelection and spell-checking properties. You can set the password property programmatically, specifying a string value only. You may also change the symbol that represents the typed characters by supplying the PasswordChar property with a specified char type. See Figure 9.17.

A change within the Password property also raises the PasswordChanged event. To access the value entered into the Password type control, call the Password property to retrieve the value.

FIGURE 9.17   A simple application using the PasswordBox and displaying an @ symbol as the PasswordChar value.

Add Listing 9.16 to a new project in Blend. View the Properties for the btnRevealPassword button and double-click on the Click event, adding the code shown in Listing 9.17.

LISTING 9.16   Setting Up the PasswordBox Example

```
<Grid x:Name="LayoutRoot">
    <Grid.RowDefinitions>
        <RowDefinition Height="0.206*"/>
        <RowDefinition Height="0.224*"/>
        <RowDefinition Height="0.273*"/>
        <RowDefinition Height="0.297*"/>
    </Grid.RowDefinitions>
    <Label HorizontalAlignment="Center" VerticalAlignment="Center"
Content="Enter Password" FontSize="18"/>
    <Button HorizontalAlignment="Center" x:Name="btnRevealPassword"
➥VerticalAlignment="Center" Content="Reveal Password" Grid.Row="2"
➥Click="btnRevealPassword_Click"/>
        <TextBox HorizontalAlignment="Center" x:Name="txtPasswordRevealed"
➥VerticalAlignment="Center" Width="200" Grid.Row="3" Text="" TextWrapping="Wrap"/>
        <PasswordBox HorizontalAlignment="Center" x:Name="passEntry"
➥VerticalAlignment="Center" Width="200" Grid.Row="1" PasswordChar="@"/>
    </Grid>
```

LISTING 9.17   Revealing the Password Entered

```
private void btnRevealPassword_Click(object sender, RoutedEventArgs e)
{
    this.txtPasswordRevealed.Text = this.passEntry.Password;
}
```

You could now save and run the application in Visual Studio.

ProgressBar Control

As with previous ProgressBar controls available in the CLR, the ProgressBar control shows a visual position of a Value property in relation to the Maximum and Minimum property values. What is vastly different is the designer's ability to change the styling of the control to produce nice visual indicators for the user.

The IsIndeterminate property is an interesting property that is accessible from the Properties panel, Common Properties category. If you add the standard ProgressBar control to your artboard and check this property, the progress values begin to marquee across the length of the control's progress and then reset and begin again. This functionality represents the application equivalent to, "I have no idea how long this will take."

It's better to have this functionality, in which the user sees that something is happening with the application rather than sees nothing and closes the application in belief that it has simply stopped working.

The Brushes category of the Property panel enables you to uniquely present the control. To truly customize it, you need to dig into the Control Template. Buried deep in the template is a Rectangle type element that represents the Fill property of the control parent. Here you can create your own styling preferences, including adding animations to the fill (see Figure 9.18) as it changes value using the ValueChanged event. (See Chapter 12, "Templates," for more detail on Template editing.)

FIGURE 9.18   A modified ProgressBar control template, exploiting the WPF styling functionality.

Setting the values of the ProgressBar in code is just as simple as markup, with calls to the Maximum, Minimum, and Value properties being primary. You can also see in the Listing 9.18 how to set the IsIndeterminate property to true, though you would usually set a value or set the ProgressBar to IsIndeterminate but not both.

LISTING 9.18   Setting the Required Values of a ProgressBar with a Button Click Handler Method

```
private void btnBeginProgress_Click(object sender, RoutedEventArgs e)
{
    this.myProgressBar.Minimum = 0;
    this.myProgressBar.Maximum = 100;
    this.myProgressBar.Value = 69;
  //Set the control to show a scrolling progress
    this.myProgressBar.IsIndeterminate = true;
}
```

RadioButton Elements

The RadioButton control provides your application with a method of allowing mutually exclusive selection. When grouped with other RadioButtons, the control grouping programmatically ascertains which RadioButton should show as checked, and consequently, all others should show as unchecked. Unlike a Checkbox control, the user can't uncheck the RadioButton by clicking on it several times.

The RadioButton derives from the ToggleButton control, which itself is derived from ButtonBase, so the control does allow you to specify Content, be it text, panels, or even another button.

To create a group of RadioButtons, simply embed them as children to a panel-based control (see Figure 9.19). Listing 9.19 shows three RadioButtons that allow the user to "check" only one button at a time.

FIGURE 9.19   The multiple RadioButton group.

LISTING 9.19   RadioButton Autonomy in a Group

```
<StackPanel HorizontalAlignment="Center" Margin="0,0,0,0"
VerticalAlignment="Center" Width="168" Height="106">
    <RadioButton Height="35" Content="RadioButton" IsChecked="True"/>
    <RadioButton Height="35" Content="RadioButton"/>
    <RadioButton Height="35" Content="RadioButton"/>
</StackPanel>
```

The functionality of the ToggleButton, which is a separate control, is different from that of a standard button because it allows a user to maintain a fixed state, that being either an On or Off, In or Out type state.

RichTextBox Control

The RichTextBox control has a long history with Windows form development. When you need to either display or allow the user to display more complex text formatting, the RichTextBox is a powerful control to use.

The content of the RichTextBox is more complicated than a standard text-based control to either set or retrieve, but the formatting options are endless so don't let this put you off. Listing 9.20 shows the code used to add a RichTextBox control.

LISTING 9.20   The Standard XAML Used to Add a RichTextBox Control to the Artboard

```
<RichTextBox HorizontalAlignment="Right"
         Margin="0,35,20,0"
         VerticalAlignment="Top"
         Width="169"
         Height="161">
            <FlowDocument>
                <Paragraph>RichTextBox</Paragraph>
            </FlowDocument>
         </RichTextBox>
```

The RichTextBox (RTB) element available in Blend is similar to the RTB controls that developers used previously in .NET Framework 1.0 and 2.0 but with some added features for pagination, layouts, and a few other nice features.

The RTB supports copy and paste of images, text, and all the usual additions. Although the control itself is quite mature and will accept several input formats, as of this writing, it is recommended that only the PNG, JPG, and GIF image types be used in cut-and-paste scenarios. I can find no explanation for this, so perhaps it is just one of those recommendations until such time as the control is deemed released.

One thing to note about the text that you place within the control is that it always wraps. Several workarounds exist for this, but even they don't always work, so keep this in mind when writing the next mind-blowing text editor.

Take a quick look at the XAML markup in Listing 9.20, and you will note the declaration of Horizontal and Vertical alignment, which does not set the content alignment. For this you must use the HorizontalContentAlignment and VerticalContentAlignment properties, respectively. If left undeclared, the content defaults to Left Aligned.

Note the FlowDocument element, which contains a Paragraph element by default. The FlowDocument element is the only supported child element of the RichTextBox control, but the subelement children of the FlowDocument can contain several useful elements.

The content model of the FlowDocument states that the Top Level child element must be derived from type BLOCK, as Table 9.3 shows.

TABLE 9.3   Element Types Used in Constructing the RichTextBox Content

Element Type	Description
BlockUIContainer	This lets you embed a single UIElement into the container, which could be a Button (as shown in the sample generated by Listing 9.21) or Grid, which would then allow you to add multiple UIElements.
List	You must provide ListItem elements, which provide you with numbered or bulleted lists.
Paragraph	This default element lets you group text and other content. The Paragraph element allows you to declare several other child elements pertaining to the formatting of content such as Bold, Italics, and Underlines. You may also declare content as Hyperlinks and floaters or insert LineBreak elements.
	A special element called an InlineUIContainer works similarly to the BlockUIContainer. You may host a UIElement within the content of the Paragraph, for example, a Button.
Section	A Section allows you to group other Block types or additional Section elements.
Table	The Table allows you to present content in a row- and column-based layout. Several child elements are supported, including TableCell, ListBoxItem, ListViewItem, and FlowDocument.

To get a better understanding of the Block types and properties discussed in Table 9.3, a simple application is provided in Listing 9.21. The end product is shown in Figure 9.20.

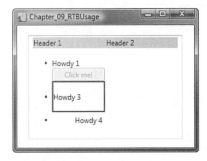

FIGURE 9.20   Complex content is simple with XAML.

Create a new application project in Expression Blend and enter the markup shown in Listing 9.21. Don't forget to add a terminating Grid tag.

LISTING 9.21   Creating a FlowDocument for Use in a RichTextBox Control

```
<Grid x:Name="LayoutRoot">
    <RichTextBox FontSize="12"
Margin="18.8000000000003,17.2000000000005,20.0000000000001,14.4000000000001"
x:Name="RichTextBox" >
      <FlowDocument>
        <Table>
          <TableRowGroup>
            <TableRow>
              <TableRow.Background >LightGray</TableRow.Background>
              <TableCell>
                <Paragraph>
                  <Run>Header 1</Run>
                </Paragraph>
              </TableCell>
              <TableCell>
                <Paragraph>
                  <Run>Header 2</Run>
                </Paragraph>
              </TableCell>
            </TableRow>
          </TableRowGroup>
          <TableRowGroup>
            <TableRow>
              <TableCell>
                <TableCell.BorderBrush>
                  <SolidColorBrush>Red</SolidColorBrush>
                </TableCell.BorderBrush>
                <List Block.TextAlignment ="Left">
                  <ListItem>
                    <Paragraph>Howdy 1</Paragraph>
                    <BlockUIContainer>
                      <Button>Click me!</Button>
                    </BlockUIContainer>
                  </ListItem>
                  <ListItem>
                    <Section>
                      <Section.BorderBrush>
                        <SolidColorBrush Color ="Blue"></SolidColorBrush>
                      </Section.BorderBrush>
                      <Section.BorderThickness>2</Section.BorderThickness>
                      <Paragraph>Howdy 3</Paragraph>
                    </Section>
                  </ListItem>
                  <ListItem>
```

```
              <Paragraph Margin ="5" TextAlignment ="Right" >Howdy 4</Paragraph>
            </ListItem>
          </List>
          </TableCell>
        </TableRow>
      </TableRowGroup>
    </Table>
  </FlowDocument>
</RichTextBox>
</Grid>
```

The RTB has protected mouse events, so custom mouse handlers will not work. Instead you need to use tunnelled events (see Chapter 8, "An Example Control Using Just the Tools Palette," to learn how to add Routed Events) and PreviewMouseUp and PreviewMouseDown events to allow content interaction.

The RichTextBox UIElement is extremely flexible in what it allows as content while at the same time being cumbersome to code from within the .NET environment. The reality is that things don't always work, like cutting and pasting certain image types, but this is a marked improvement on the control that was previously available within .NET.

Using XAML to declare the various requirements of the RTB is by far an easier route to getting what you want in your RTB, but sleep easy with the knowledge that you can code it in .NET if necessary.

Slider Element

The Slider control is one of those controls that is everywhere but often goes unnoticed in its functionality, because of its simplicity.

You increment or decrement the Sliders value by moving what is known as the *thumb*. You can also modify the value in code, as shown in Listing 9.22. The Slider can be shown in either a horizontal or vertical position, controlled by an enumerated value to the Orientation property.

A Minimum and Maximum value is set to contain the range of values applicable to the Value property.

LISTING 9.22   Changing Slider Values

```
private void ControlSlider()
{
    this.mySlider.Minimum = 0;
    this.mySlider.Maximum = 10;
    this.mySlider.Value = 7;
}
```

The Slider has a few obscure properties that allow finite control of its functionality, as shown in Table 9.4.

TABLE 9.4   Unique Slider Control Properties

Property Name	Description
IsDirectionReversed	Set to false (unchecked in the Blend UI interface, which is a checkbox), this self-describing property makes the Slider control value position move downward on increment. This is right to left for Orientation Horizontal and Top to Bottom for Orientation Vertical.
LargeChange	Determines how far the thumb value should increment when the user clicks on the slider track.
SmallChange	Determines how far the thumb value should increment when the user drags the thumb on the slider track.
TickFrequency	When TickPlacement has a valid value, the TickFrequency value indicates at what intervals a tick mark should be drawn on the control.
TickPlacement	Has four enumerated value choices: None, Top Left, Bottom Right, and Both.
IsSnapToTickEnables	Default is false, but when enabled it forces the thumb position to snap to the next Tick mark when the user drags the thumb on the track.

A Look at the New WPF Controls in Blend

As each release of the .NET Framework supersedes the previous version, it's usually the control set that has stayed relatively the same. Sure, there were incremental difference to some controls and much requested functionality added to others, but not since the very first version of the .NET Framework have developers seen such a huge change in the way controls fundamentally work and allow you to work with them. The content model of WPF controls is by far the biggest change that migrating developers need to come to terms with, but it is a welcome change and one that opens up a myriad of possibilities instead of a construct of restriction as was previously the case.

ContentControl

A lot of confusion about templates and styles is attributed to the terminology chosen throughout the Blend application's history from CTP. It was considerably more confusing during the CTPs, where you had different types of templates and styles available on the right-click of an element. You would look at certain controls and see that they had a Content element, which could only accept one child element, and the confusion grew even stronger.

My first thoughts were, "What sort of moron is designing this stuff? One child element is about as handy as an ashtray on a motorcycle!"

Then it occurred to me—and others before me—that you could add a Grid or any panel-based construct element as the child and, therefore, add as many children to that. Now I was feeling like the moron, because someone had obviously thought about it... a lot. (See Chapters 5, "UIElement: Control Embedding," and 6, "Panel-Based Containers," for more detail about Panel types and embedding child controls.)

The ContentControl is a strange control (at first) and one that takes a bit of getting used to, because this level of sophistication was never before available in CLR controls. It could have been explained a whole lot better by Microsoft, which included it in the Fabrikam examples that came with the Blend CTPs, because the use was spread out over two tutorials, and they kept going in and out of explanations, so it got a little confusing. The Microsoft help file writers described the ContentControl as a picture frame, which is a little limiting in its true capabilities but simple enough to at least intrigue you.

The ContentControl allows you to store content (amazing, I know). But more than just content as far as control elements are concerned, ContentControl allows you to style the element and then transfer that style to other areas of your application without having a specific type requirement.

Picture this if, you will. You have a Grid element on your work surface, and you divide that Grid into five rows and five columns. Within each cell of the columns and rows, you want to display a control that could be another Grid, a ListBox, or even a MediaElement control playing a motion video. The only thing is that you want to provide a certain style of border and a specific Datacontext to each one of those cells without limiting what can be added to the cells as far as a control element is concerned.

This is the purpose of the ContentControl, because it allows you to create your style and then transfer that style to other ContentControls, which allow you to add your Grid, Listbox, MediaElement, and so on as a child of the ContentControl, therefore presenting different types with the same visual styling.

The following steps create a simple example application that will give you a better understanding of the ContentControl by using style templating as it was intended. When you are ready, open a new project in Blend.

1. With the LayoutRoot active, find and double-click the Grid element located within the panel-based tools in the ToolBox palette. (See Chapter 7, "Using the Blend Toolbox: Tools and Common Controls," for a detailed look at the Toolbox.)

2. Resize the Grid so that it takes up about three-quarters of the work surface and then double-click the Grid element in the Object and Timelines panel to activate the Grid.

3. Move the mouse over the top of the Grid frame to split the Grid into two columns. You could also use the Properties panel to do this, if you prefer, by typing **defi** into the property search box, revealing the Row and Column definition collection properties. (Chapter 5 shows this in detail.)

4. Open the Asset Library and then locate and select the ContentControl.

5. With the ContentControl selected, manually add the control to fit the majority of the left column of the Grid, as shown in Figure 9.21.

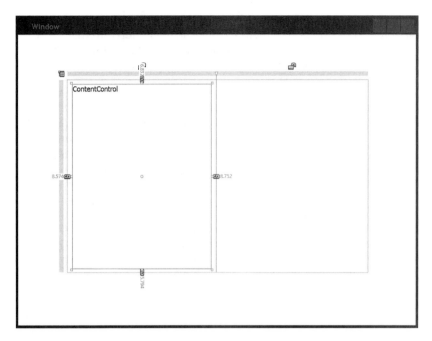

FIGURE 9.21   The Grid divided into two, with a ContentControl added to the first Grid Column.

The ContentControl already has some content, that being the string ContentControl. As soon as you add the next control item, this content will be replaced. Remember that the ContentControl only allows you to have one child element.

6. Select and activate the ContentControl.

7. From the common controls ToolBox palette, select the ListBox control. Double-click it to add it to the ContentControl, where it should automatically fill the entire area.

8. Open the properties panel and select the Brushes category, changing the Background Brush to any color you choose, maybe a red or even a gradient if you're feeling adventurous.

9. With the ContentControl activated in the Objects and Timeline panel, right-click on the element and select Edit Control Parts (Template). Select Edit a Copy to open the Create Style Resource dialog.

10. Within the Resource name (Key) field, enter DemoTemplate1 as the name and click OK.

You are now in template editor mode. As shown in Figure 9.22, the Objects and Timeline panel shows only a ContentPresenter as the child of the template.

But where is the ListBox? Why is it displayed on the screen but not present in the Objects and Timeline panel?

The question is, where does this ContentPresenter come from if you didn't add it as an element?

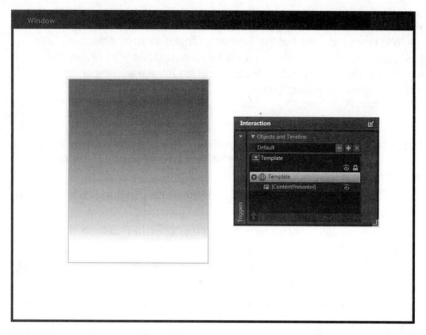

FIGURE 9.22   The current Objects and Timeline panel with the ContentPresenter as the child element and the current template.

ContentPresenter

The ContentPresenter is the real magician of the ContentControl, because it is what Microsoft was referring to when it called ContentControl a picture frame. The ContentPresenter shows the current child element(s) of the ContentControl, allowing you to Style your template or add additional control items to fit with the overall requirement for the control.

Continuing on with the example, go ahead and select the ContentPresenter in the Objects and Timeline panel. Then right-click on the element and select Delete from the menu.

So the ContentPresenter is gone, but it is gone only from the template presentation layer. Open the Assets Library panel and find the ContentPresenter control. Double-click it on the ToolBox palette, and you're the ListBox returns.

Clearly, the ContentPresenter control is not a copy of the child control element(s) but rather a visual representation of the Control Template.

1. Select and delete the ContentPresenter control once more from the Objects and Timeline panel.

2. Find and double-click a Grid element within the ToolBox to add it as a Child of the Template.

ContentControl Child Items Versus Template Child Items

Any elements you add now as the child of the Template transfer as part of the template to any other ContentControl to which you apply this template. As you will see, the child elements of the ContentControl (not its template, which you are working on now) do not transfer, but *all* template elements do.

By default, the Grid element should fill the entirety of the template. Later, you can do whatever you please with this Grid by way of Row and Column definitions, but for now you will just settle with the default.

3. Double-click the Grid element in the Objects and Timelines panel to activate it. This is very important, because you can use only one child element.

4. Find and select the Rectangle control from the Shapes control family in the ToolBox palette.

5. Manually draw the element on the screen so that it fills almost all of its parent Grid, leaving a small but noticeable margin around the Rectangle.

6. Open the Properties panel. In the property search box, type **margin**. Set each of the margin values to 5.

7. Enter the word **radius** into the property search box. The RadiusX and RadiusY properties display. You could always just use the mouse to set these properties on the Rectangle by moving your mouse to the top-left corner of the rectangle, but to be accurate, you enter the values manually. This examples uses the value 15, but you can adjust it to suit your taste and style.

8. Enter the text **brush** into the property search box. Select the fill brush and add a Gradient Brush type (Linear Gradient Mode). Use the Brush Transform tool to rotate the Gradient, showing a dark color on top of a lighter bottom color (see Figure 9.23).

   Not to get caught up in styling, you now get back to the ContentControl.

9. Select and activate the Grid element in the Objects and Timeline panel. Remember that if you activate the Template element, the next control you add replaces the Grid as the only allowable child element, and along with it goes your hard work and master Rectangle styling.

10. You should now be able to find the ContentPresenter control in the last-used controls section at the bottom of the ToolBox palette. Double-click it to again show the ListBox control representation.

11. Resize the ListBox so that it fits nicely within the Rectangle element that you previously added (see Figure 9.24).

That is it for the styling of the template for now (see Figure 9.25). Click on the Scope Up button to return to your artboard with the ContentControl and its child ListBox control showing in the Objects and Timeline panel.

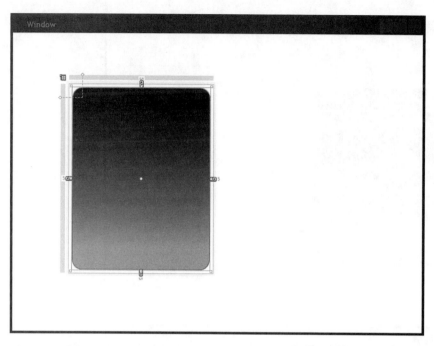

FIGURE 9.23   The Styled Rectangle element with Black/Yellow Linear Gradient applied.

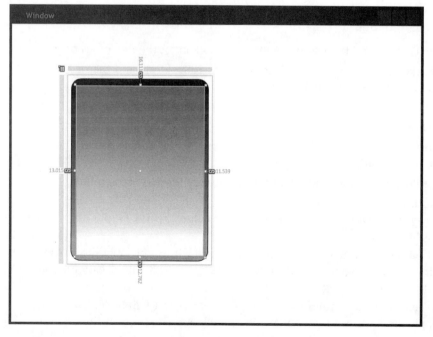

FIGURE 9.24   The ContentPresenter and its representation of the ContentControl's child.

FIGURE 9.25   The result of ListBox styling.

The following steps demonstrate clearly the implications of applying your styled template to another ContentControl:

1. Select the ListBox, and then open the Brushes category of the Properties panel.

2. Set the Background Brush to a Solid Color Brush, 100% white and then reduce the opacity to 20% by setting the Alpha value.

3. Select the Border brush property and set it to No Brush.

4. Double-click the Grid element in the Objects and Timeline panel to activate it.

5. Select the ContentControl from the common controls ToolBox items and manually draw the control within the second column of the Grid.

6. Open the Properties panel and type **margin** into the Property Search box.

7. Set each value to a value higher than normal to create a noticeably smaller ContentControl than what is shown in the first column of the Grid. This example uses 50 for the values.

8. Double-click and activate this new ContentControl within the Objects and Timelines panel. (If you were diligent enough to name the controls, it will be easy for you to find the right one.)

9. Choose the Object menu from the top of the screen, select Edit Style, and then select Apply Resource. Your template—DemoTemplate1—appears in the list. Select the template now.

Is this what you were expecting, or did you expect to see the ListBox in there as well?

Remember that all you did was style the template of the ContentControl. By applying this template to the new ContentControl, just the Rectangle element displays (see Figure 9.26).

FIGURE 9.26   The result of Template styling.

But what if you want to have the ListBox element transfer with the template? Then you need to go back and add it as a child of the Grid element that you added to the template.

The following steps take you through adding the ListBox to the template and, in the process, you see an interesting side effect of editing the Template at this stage of the project development:

1. Select and cut the ListBox element that shows as the Child of the first ContentControl.

2. Double-click to activate the first ContentControl and then right-click to access the context menu. Again select Edit Control Parts (Template), but this time, select Edit Template.

3. Double-click the Grid element to activate it, and then right-click and paste the ListBox into the tree as child element of the Grid.

6

What you should notice as soon as you do this is that the template updates immediately on the second ContentControl. If you were to manipulate or change the properties with this template now, you would see them reflected at the same time.

So why didn't you do this first? Remember that you cannot refer to the Template child elements in code (at least, not very easily), so adding a ListBox (unless prefilled with items) becomes an unusable solution. If you want to Style the ListBox and show that same styling within two ContentControls (or any other control), you need to edit the Style of the ListBox, store it, and apply that styling to the additional ListBox control(s).

There are many instances in which the power to create your own generic styling of a very generic Container control is a fantastic advantage. One of the big areas of benefit is within application skinning, which requires different styles be applied to typed objects. (See Chapter 16, "Using Resources for Skins," for an example in application skinning.)

Now that you understand the ContentControl and the difference between Template and Control styling, you will better understand the requirements for customizing a standard control that features a ContentControl as the containing element.

HeaderedContentControl

Building from your newly acquired knowledge on ContentControls, the concept of HeaderedContentControls is not dissimilar. A HeaderedContentControl contains two Content properties, namely a Header and a Content (referred to as the Primary Content) property.

Both properties can contain only a single child, but as per "Content" rules, you can use a Grid as the single child to enable further embedding of controls. Generally, the header is a way to label the primary content, for example, a TabControl where the TabItem (Tab page, or the primary content) displays the content (usually a panel-based control such as a Grid element) and the Tab (or the Header) displays the name of the page. The Expander control also contains this formula: a Header and Content.

TabControl

The TabControl is an ItemsControl that allows you to deliver "page" items (the collection) to the user interface in a clean and efficient manner. The control (or at least variations and imitations) were widely used in previous Windows Forms applications and, depending on the circumstances, it helped to either provide fantastic user experience or absolutely rubbish screen management by the developer(s) responsible.

Listing 9.23 represents the default markup added to the XAML file when a TabControl is added to the artboard from the Asset Library.

LISTING 9.23   The Base TabControl and TabItems as Created by Expression Blend

```
        <TabControl HorizontalAlignment="Left" VerticalAlignment="Top" Width="100"
Height="100" IsSynchronizedWithCurrentItem="True">
            <TabItem Header="TabItem 1">
                <Grid/>
```

```
    </TabItem>
    <TabItem Header="TabItem 2">
        <Grid/>
    </TabItem>
</TabControl>
```

You can clearly see in Listing 9.23 that two TabItems are added to the content of the TabControl. Inside each TabItem is a Header property with the value "TabItem" assigned, and a Grid element exists as the content container for the TabItem's primary content.

Table 9.5 lists some of the properties that help define the visual layout of the TabControl.

TABLE 9.5   TabControl Common Properties

Property Name	Description
Items(Collection)	The collection of TabItems that the items collection contains. You can add new items to the collection directly from the property in Blend.
SelectedIndex	The default value is –1, which represents that no item should be selected. When a user selects a tab, either via keyboard or mouse, the SelectionChanged event is raised as well as this property value equating to the index of the selected item.
TabStripPlacement	Accepts an enumerated value, one of the following four: Top, Bottom, Left, or Right.

You can use these properties and many others in code to modify an instance of a TabControl, as is shown in Listing 9.24.

LISTING 9.24   Applying TabControl Properties in Code

```
private void CreateNewTabControl()
    {
        TabControl myTabControl = new TabControl();
        myTabControl.TabStripPlacement = Dock.Top;
        myTabControl.FlowDirection = FlowDirection.RightToLeft;

        this.LayoutRoot.Children.Add(myTabControl);

    }
```

The code in Listing 9.24 creates and adds a new TabControl to the LayoutRoot elements child collection, but what about TabItems? This discussion is about HeaderedContentControls after all.

You can create an instance of a TabItem just as easily in code and then add it to the TabControls items collection. This method is shown in the modified Listing of 9.25.

LISTING 9.25   Adding a New TabItem to a New TabControl, Then Adding the TabControl to the Parent Items Collections

```
private void CreateNewTabControl()
{
    TabControl myTabControl = new TabControl();
    myTabControl.TabStripPlacement = Dock.Top;
    myTabControl.FlowDirection = FlowDirection.RightToLeft;

    //Define a TabItem for the items collection of the TabControl
    TabItem newTabItem = new TabItem();
    newTabItem.Header = "Tab Name 1";

    //Make a Grid element for the TabItems content
    Grid TabItemGrid = new Grid();
    TabItemGrid.Background = new SolidColorBrush(Color.FromRgb(255, 0, 0));

    newTabItem.Content = TabItemGrid;

    //Add the TabItem to the TabControl
    myTabControl.Items.Add(newTabItem);

    this.LayoutRoot.Children.Add(myTabControl);
}
```

I don't know about you, but using Blend to create TabControls and TabItems is my method of choice.

HeaderedItemsControl Element

"What is the difference between HeaderedContentControls and HeaderedItemsControls?" Is that the first thing you thought of when you saw the subtitle?

It's not a silly question, but you need to remember what was previously stated about the HeaderedContentControl put in context beside the HeaderedItemsControl to understand this concept. The differences are shown in Table 9.6.

TABLE 9.6   The Difference Between the Two Header Control Types

Type	Description
HeaderedContentControl	The content of the control can only contain a single child item.
HeaderedItemsControl	The control's item collection can contain many items of type content.

An example of elements that are HeaderedItemsControls are MenuItems and TreeViewItems, because they both contain a Header property and an Items collection.

The TreeView control (which is an Items Control—no header) demonstrates this concept clearly. This next example goes through the process of creating a TreeView and then adding the TreeViewItems.

TreeView

TreeView controls have been around in Windows for a long time (Windows 95 was the first, I think). The control plays an important part in showing hierarchical data, the most common example being that of the Windows Explorer application.

Expression Blend allows you to use this element and effectively manage the information that is shown in it, directly in the user interface.

Add the markup from Listing 9.26 to create the TreeView control and its child elements, as shown in Figure 9.27.

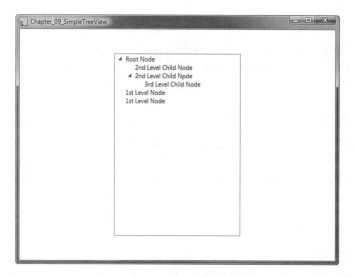

FIGURE 9.27   The simple Node levels.

LISTING 9.26   A Simple TreeView Control

```
        <TreeView HorizontalAlignment="Center" x:Name="myTreeView" VerticalAlign-
ment="Center" Width="250" Height="350">
            <TreeViewItem Header="Root Node" IsExpanded="True">
                <TreeViewItem Header="2nd Level Child Node"/>
```

```
            <TreeViewItem Header="2nd Level Child Node" IsExpanded="True">
                <TreeViewItem Header="3rd Level Child Node"/>
            </TreeViewItem>
        </TreeViewItem>
        <TreeViewItem Header="1st Level Node"/>
        <TreeViewItem Header="1st Level Node"/>
    </TreeView>
```

TreeViewItem

While you can edit a TreeViewItem control by right-clicking on the TreeView control in the Object and Timeline panel, you will add them in code, which demonstrates the child collection more clearly.

With a new project in Blend, add a Button (name it btnAddItems) and an empty TreeView control (name it tvSampleTree) to the artboard.

Select btnAddItems, set the properties you wish, and then select the Event viewer or the Properties panel. Double-click on the Click event to automatically create the Click handler code in Visual Studio.

The code in Listing 9.27 shows not only how a TreeViewItem element is instantiated in code but also how additional TreeViewItem elements are added to the first element's Items Collection.

LISTING 9.27   Creating and Adding Child TreeViewItem Controls

```
    private void btnAddItems_Click(object sender, RoutedEventArgs e)
    {
        //Make the first TreeViewItem which will contain all the others as
        children
        TreeViewItem RootLevel = new TreeViewItem();
        RootLevel.Header = "Root Level";

        //Create the first Child
        TreeViewItem FirstChild = new TreeViewItem();
        FirstChild.Header = "First Child";

        //Create the second Child
        TreeViewItem SecondChild = new TreeViewItem();
        SecondChild.Header = "Second Child";

        //Create the third Child
        TreeViewItem ThirdChild = new TreeViewItem();
        ThirdChild.Header = "Third Child";
```

```
        //Create the fourth Child
        TreeViewItem FourthChild = new TreeViewItem();
        FourthChild.Header = "Fourth Child";


        //Add all the children to the parent items collection
        RootLevel.Items.Add(FirstChild);
        RootLevel.Items.Add(SecondChild);
        RootLevel.Items.Add(ThirdChild);
        RootLevel.Items.Add(FourthChild);


        //Add the root level to the treeview
        this.tvSampleTree.Items.Add(RootLevel);
    }
```

Just because the parent control is a TreeView doesn't mean that the child elements need to be TreeViewItems. You may create an instance of any child element to add to the parents Items Collection, such as a user control.

Two of the properties that are available for the TreeViewItem in the Blend Properties panel are IsSelected and IsExpanded, both self-describing in their functionality. See Table 9.7 for a description of these properties.

TABLE 9.7   Usability Properties Help with Design Time

Property Name	Description
IsSelected	The individual TreeViewItem element appears selected in the view.
IsExpanded	Forces the node to reveal and Child nodes, by default displaying an arrow to indicate the Node is expanded.

Expander Control

The Expander control provides an effective way of controlling screen real estate by allowing you to store other controls grouped by a "common" scenario, so it has a Header and Content area. The visual difference between the Expander control and a combo box, for example, is that the Expander's panel also takes up screen space when expanded. This expansion forces the parent to apply layout logic to any children occupying the same controlled space—for example, in a Row or Column of a parent Grid control—or as shown in Figure 9.28, the other child items in a StackPanel are moved.

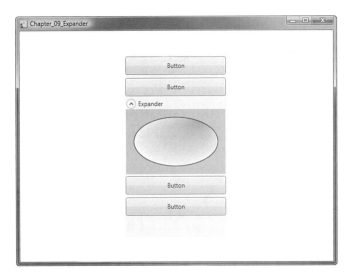

FIGURE 9.28   The Grid element of the Expander, taking up its own physical space.

The Expanders content Window (which is the expanded area) can contain another single control. As you would expect, that could be a Grid (a Grid element is placed by default) or another panel-based control to enable further parent-child control embedding. Listing 9.28 provides some markup for creating an expander that contains multiple child items. See Figure 9.29.

FIGURE 9.29   A simple Expander created with the markup from Listing 9.28.

LISTING 9.28   An Expander Control with Multiple Child Item Elements

```
        <Expander HorizontalAlignment="Center" VerticalAlignment="Top" Width="200"
➥Grid.Row="1" IsExpanded="False" Header="MyExpander">
            <Grid Height="161">
                <Grid.Background>
                    <LinearGradientBrush EndPoint="0.5,1.115" StartPoint="0.5,
➥-0.115">
                        <GradientStop Color="#FF898989" Offset="0"/>
                        <GradientStop Color="#FFFFFFFF" Offset="1"/>
                    </LinearGradientBrush>
                </Grid.Background>
                <StackPanel HorizontalAlignment="Stretch" Margin="0,0,0,0"
➥VerticalAlignment="Stretch">
                    <Button Opacity="0.45" Margin="0,5,0,5" Height="40"
➥Content="Option 1"/>
                    <Button Opacity="0.45" Margin="0,5,0,5" Height="40"
➥Content="Option 2"/>
                    <Button Opacity="0.45" Margin="0,5,0,5" Height="40"
➥Content="Option 3"/>
                </StackPanel>
            </Grid>
        </Expander>
```

Listing 9.29 shows how you can effect the expand and collapse methods in code by calling the appropriate methods of the Expander control. The descriptions of these properties are shown in Table 9.8.

TABLE 9.8   Specific Expander Properties

Property Name	Description
ExpandDirection	You may control the direction in which the Expander's Content appears by setting the enumerated value of the ExpandDirection property.
IsExpanded	Set to false by default, this property determines the current state of the elements view.

LISTING 9.29   Controlling the Expander in Code

```
private void btnExpand_Click(object sender, RoutedEventArgs e)
    {
        this.expMyExpander.ExpandDirection = ExpandDirection.Down;
```

```
        this.expMyExpander.IsExpanded = true;
    }

    private void btnCollapse_Click(object sender, RoutedEventArgs e)
    {
        this.expMyExpander.IsExpanded = false;
    }
```

GridSplitter Control

The GridSplitter control allows you to "resize," or change, the amount of space between Rows or Columns inside of a Grid. The control should always be given its own space, however, in terms of a Row or a Column so that it remains visible on the Grid. You can provide this area by declaring additional RowDefinitions or ColumnDefinitions as needed. The functionality of the control is simple enough, but in some scenarios it is invaluable for allowing your user to control the screen layout of a Grid and its children.

Listing 9.30 creates a simple grid with Columns and a GridSplitter to control the width of each adjacent column. Figure 9.30 shows the Grid with two controls side by side (purposely exaggerated). The GridSplitter gives the illusion of modifying the control widths when, in fact, the HorizontalAlignment properties of these two controls are set to Stretch and the GridSplitter modifies the ColumnDefinition positions.

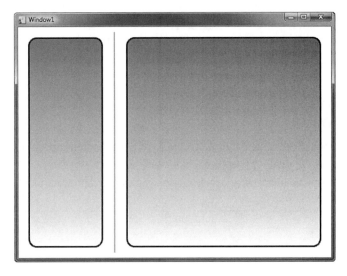

FIGURE 9.30   A GridSplitter controlling the LayoutRoot ColumnDefinitions.

LISTING 9.30   Demonstrating GridSplitter Functionality

```
<Grid.ColumnDefinitions>
            <ColumnDefinition Width="0.28*"/>
            <ColumnDefinition Width="0.01*"/>
            <ColumnDefinition Width="0.71*"/>
        </Grid.ColumnDefinitions>
        <Rectangle Stroke="#FF000000" StrokeThickness="3" RadiusX="15" RadiusY="15"
➥HorizontalAlignment="Stretch" Margin="20,20,20,20" VerticalAlignment="Stretch"
➥Height="Auto">
            <Rectangle.Fill>
                <LinearGradientBrush EndPoint="0.486,1.002" StartPoint="0.487,0">
                    <GradientStop Color="#FF797979" Offset="0"/>
                    <GradientStop Color="#FFFFFFFF" Offset="1"/>
                </LinearGradientBrush>
            </Rectangle.Fill>
        </Rectangle>
        <Rectangle Stroke="#FF000000" StrokeThickness="3" RadiusX="15" RadiusY="15"
➥Height="Auto" Margin="20,20,20,20" Grid.Column="2">
            <Rectangle.Fill>
                <LinearGradientBrush EndPoint="0.486,1.002" StartPoint="0.487,0">
                    <GradientStop Color="#FF797979" Offset="0"/>
                    <GradientStop Color="#FFFFFFFF" Offset="1"/>
                </LinearGradientBrush>
            </Rectangle.Fill>
        </Rectangle>
        <GridSplitter HorizontalAlignment="Stretch" Margin="2,10,2,10"
➥VerticalAlignment="Stretch" Width="Auto" Height="Auto" Background="#FF06A7FF"
➥Grid.Column="1" DragIncrement="1" ShowsPreview="False"/>
```

Table 9.9 discuses some obscure properties, which can change the experience that your user receives from your GridSplitter implementations.

TABLE 9.9   GridSplitter Specific Properties

Property Name	Description
ResizeDirection	Enables you to control whether the GridSplitter can resize only Rows or Columns, or both. Default is Auto (Both).
ShowsPreview	When enabled, the user will see the GridSplitter's position when modi-fied by dragging the mouse. When the selection button is released, the Layout logic is applied to the Rows or Columns of the Grid affected. When set to false, the user sees a real-time view of the affect the GridSplitter has to the Rows and Columns.
DragIncrement	By default the value of this property is set to 1. Modification of the property value changes the spacing that the GridSplitter position takes when moved by the user.

Popup Control

The Popup control appears simple in its functionality, in that as its name would describe, it pops up!

The Control has myriad properties to allow you to be specific with its positioning, animation, and mouse-controlled functionality, such as staying open or disappearing automatically when the mouse moves off the control.

You have no doubt witnessed a Popup in action before. Whenever you right-click on a control in a Windows form, and a context menu appears. That is the Popup control at work.

You can specify absolute coordinates for the Popup position when rendered, or you can attach it to a parent control, specifying the PlacementTarget property value. You may also set the Placement property and specify its visible position when activated with the giant list of associated enumerated values.

The Popup control is slightly different from others you may use in Blend in that it does not contain its own children. You need to name and access the contained controls directly if you wish to modify or use them in some way. You also need to set the AllowsTransparency property to true if you wish to modify the opacity setting of the control itself or change the shape of the popup appearance. In fact, the AllowsTransparency property was added specifically so you could do this. But again, because the Popup control has parent ownership of the contained controls, this has no effect on them in terms of their opacity or transparency.

Listing 9.31 provides for simple markup of a button control and an associated Popup control. Although the functionality can be made to imitate a tooltip or context menu, you are advised to use a tooltip or a context menu for that specific purpose.

What you will notice in the listing is that the ContentPresenter (Text) of the button is now added to a StackPanel, because the Button has a Content property, meaning that only the button text or the Popup control could be the Content property value. So by using a StackPanel, you are able to have both.

LISTING 9.31   Defining a Popup Control

```
        <Grid x:Name="LayoutRoot">
            <Button Margin="228,142,229,0" x:Name="btnPopupButton"
➥VerticalAlignment="Top" Height="36" Click="btnPopupButton_Click">
                    <StackPanel Width="Auto" Height="Auto">
                        <Label Content="This is the Button" Width="101.693"
➥Height="25.96"/>
                            <Popup Placement="Right" x:Name="popButton">
                                <Grid Width="100" Height="100"
➥Background="#FFD2D2D2">
                                    <TextBlock TextWrapping="Wrap"
➥Language="en-gb">
```

```
                                               This is the Popup Grid element set
to display on the Right side of the attached element.
                                   </TextBlock>
                              </Grid>
                         </Popup>
                    </StackPanel>
               </Button>
          </Grid>
```

The code in Listing 9.32 demonstrates the button click handler setting the Popup control's property IsOpen to true, which displays the popup (see Figure 9.31).

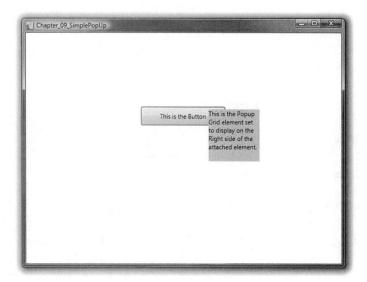

FIGURE 9.31   The Button with attached popup control.

The code also sets the StaysOpen property to False, which forces the control to close when it loses mouse capture, by the user clicking elsewhere on the applications form or another control receives focus.

LISTING 9.32   Forcing the Popup Control to Close After Losing Focus

```
private void btnPopupButton_Click(object sender, RoutedEventArgs e)
     {
          this.popButton.IsOpen = true;
          this.popButton.StaysOpen = false;
     }
```

Table 9.10 shows the properties you will most likely be using most of the time to control how your Popup control(s) function in your application.

TABLE 9.10   Popup Control Properties That Modify the End User Experience and Functionality

Property Name	Description
PopupAnimation	Controls the way in which the Popup control is presented through animation: None (Default) Fade Slide Scroll
HorizontalOffset	Sets the offset amount that the Popup control presents from the left of the original position of the control.
VerticalOffset	Sets the offset amount that the Popup control presents from the top of the original position of the control.
Placement	Enumerated property value that sets the position of the Popup control, relative to the parent: Absolute Relative Bottom Center Right AbsolutePoint RelativePoint Mouse MousePoint Left Top Custom
IsOpen	Determines whether the popup is visible.
StaysOpen	Determines whether the control should stay open when the IsOpen property is set to True.

ScrollViewer Control

It is not unusual for your interface to have resizing capability according to the user's screen resolution, which sometimes inhibits the ability to use screen space effectively. The ScrollViewer control allows you to overcome this by embedding a child control (usually a panel based-control) and providing for a scrollable region that effectively provides more screen space on the panel.

An example of this is visible in most applications, such as word-processing programs where, in normal usage context, one could expect the text or image objects to take up more than one page; yet you as the interface developer still need to provide an effective means of allowing the user to scroll in both horizontal and vertical directions in order to view the content.

That may be a bad example because in WPF you would use a DocumentViewer control, which has built-in pagination functionality. The usage example, however, is the important piece to get across.

The markup in Listing 9.33 demonstrates the ScrollViewer by placing a Grid panel (whose size is greater than the parent ScrollViewer dimensions) inside a ScrollViewer. A further control (an Ellipse) is added as the Gird child and also set to be larger in dimensional size to that of the Grid's parent. The results are shown in Figure 9.32.

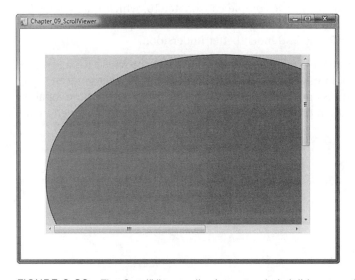

FIGURE 9.32   The ScrollViewer allowing extended visible area of a Grid control.

LISTING 9.33   Creating the Sample ScrollViewer

```
        <ScrollViewer HorizontalAlignment="Stretch" Margin="50,50,50,50"
➥VerticalAlignment="Stretch" Width="Auto" Height="Auto"
➥HorizontalScrollBarVisibility="Auto">
            <Grid Width="800" Height="600" Background="#FFDADADA">
                <Ellipse Fill="#FF808080" Stroke="#FF000000" Margin="0,0,107,113"/>
            </Grid>
        </ScrollViewer>
```

The two most common properties of the ScrollViewer control are detailed in Table 9.11.

TABLE 9.11   ScrollViewer Scroll Bar Control

Property Name	Description
HorizontalScrollBarVisibility	Set to Disable by default, you must set the property to Auto or Visible for it to become active.
VerticalScrollBarVisibility	Set to Visible by default, you can set the property to Auto to hide the scrollbars when its content no longer exceeds the bounds of the control.

Summary

This has been a long chapter, but it was all about getting used to the WPF controls and their types accessible with Expression Blend. You may want to revisit a few of the controls and elements of this chapter after you have completed Chapter 10, which is all about writing code in Visual Studio. Any of the concepts shown in this chapter's code that may have confused you will be re-enforced and much better understood.

These WPF controls are highly flexible compared with control sets provided for in previous .NET Frameworks. You should now have a good understanding of what you can achieve when using these controls and understanding that always using the functionality of an existing control is better than trying to write your own and implement functionality that already exists.

CHAPTER 10

Visual Studio: C# Primer

The subject of designers needing to know a little code to enhance user interfaces created in Blend is a pretty contentious issue among certain groups, because Blend has been sold as the collaborative piece for designers and Visual Studio as the piece for developers.

My belief is that while XAML is a dream scripting language in a lot of ways, XAML alone is not enough to allow complete freedom in design implementation, much the same as really complex Flash pieces often rely on some level of ActionScript.

In saying all this, I also strongly believe it is unreasonable to expect a designer to be able to simply "just learn to code." There is a particular mindset and logic process to being able to code well, and while a lack of these traits would never suggest an unintelligence of designers, it points out that, for the most part, designers think and work one way, and developers do the other.

In this chapter you learn some important coding concepts, which are shown in blocks. Considering that "how to code .NET" books are rarely fewer than 500 pages, be sure to keep the expectation of what you learn in perspective. This chapter shows you only what I consider to be absolute *must* understand concepts. Should you need to know more (which in all probability you will), you will at least have a conceptual understanding of what it is that you need to learn and limit the amount of time you waste getting up to speed.

Data Types

Several data types are commonly used in most applications. When developers talk about a "type," they are referring to the type of data that resides within and is ultimately retrievable from a variable of that type.

You declare a variable in C# using the following syntax:

```
datatype identifier;
```

An example using the *int* datatype would, therefore, be as follows:

```
int myInt;
```

After you declare a variable, you can assign a value to it:

```
myInt = 10;
```

Initializing a variable with a value is good practice so, technically, you should write the code as follows:

```
int myInt = 10;
```

So what is an int? An int is a datatype that represents whole numbers. If you needed to create an object that represented a car, for example, you would use an int type variable to store the amount of wheels that the car would have, seeing as it is unlikely that a car would have half a tire.

You use different datatypes to store values that you use within your application and to ensure performance and accuracy. You should always choose a datatype that best suits the object (such as a tire) it describes.

Eight Flavors of int

In the C# language, you can use eight different types of int. They all refer to the range value (that is, the minimum and maximum) that the given type can hold. The standard int is of type Int32, which means it is a 32-bit signed integer that can contain a value in the range of −2,147,483,648 to +2,147,483,647.

If you require a larger value, or need to save memory and increase performance, you can opt for a smaller int type. Please see other sources of information for the specifications of data types used in the C# language and the .NET Framework.

Primitive Data Types

Table 10.1 shows the most common types (which are referred to as primitives), a brief description of the data types, and an example of the syntax used with the data type.

TABLE 10.1   A Description of C# Primitive Types

Type Name	Description	Syntax Example
Int	Integer values represent whole numbers. Examples: 9 99 726,494	int MyInt = 12;
double	A decimal value that allows greater precision when working with numbers. Examples: 16.9 123.87489	double MyDouble = 12.9828;
Bool	The Boolean value represents a True or a False. Example: A button's IsEnabled property is suited to using a bool data type.	bool MyBool = false;
Char	Represents a single Unicode character.	char MyChar = 'T';
String	Holds a collection of character, symbols, and numbers and is always quoted. Example: "this is a string"	string MyString="Hello";
Object	This is the base of all types and can hold different types to be parsed to other objects.	object MyObject = 2; object MyObject = "a String" ;

While these data types represent the most commonly used data types, it is not uncommon to need to create your own types, which are generally made up of the types shown in Table 10.1 or collections of other user-defined types.

By following the steps described below in Visual Studio, you will attain some valuable experience at defining variables and assigning values to them.

1. Open Blend and create a new application.
2. Add a Button element called btnShowResult to the artboard.
3. Save the application.
4. Open the Properties panel and select the Event icon (the icon at the top, with the lightning bolt)
5. Search for the ClickEvent, which should be near the top.
6. Double-click in the input field to launch Visual Studio and automatically add a click event handler.

10

Add the code shown in Listing 10.1 to the click handler. Try changing the values as well as defining new types.

LISTING 10.1   Combining Strings and ints to Make a Message

```csharp
private void btnShowResult_Click(object sender, RoutedEventArgs e)
{
    string FirstName = "Brennon";
    string LastName = "Williams";
    string CompleteName = FirstName + " " + LastName;

    int MyRealAge = 34;
    int AgeIFeel = 54;

    MessageBox.Show(FirstName);

    MessageBox.Show(MyRealAge.ToString() );
}
```

After you enter the code, click on the File menu in Visual Studio and then click Save All. If a dialog box pop ups, prompting you to save the solution file, agree. Press F5 to run the application and then click the Show Result button.

Notice that you added .ToString() to the variable MyRealAge when you used it in the MessageBox. You did this because the MessageBox requires a value of type String to display.

As you can see in Listing 10.1, the string type variable CompleteName uses the mathematic symbol "+" to concatenate (join together) values of the same type (two string variables).

In the case of numeric data types, you can apply calculations, as follows:

```csharp
int TrueAge = (AgeIFeel /2) + MyRealAge;
```

Joining two types (concatenation) is generally fine as long as they are the same type. But if you want to join two numeric types—for example, a variable of type int with the value 3 assigned and another with the value of 4—you need to first convert these two variables to a string. Look at the following differences to understand this well:

```csharp
int Value1 = 3;
int Value2 = 4;

//Equals 7
int AddedValues = Value1 + Value2;

//Equals "34"
string JoinedValues = Value1.ToString() + Value2.ToString();
```

Now, what if you want to display "my age" in a sentence, using the strings and the ints declared?

You can use the "+" symbols to concatenate the string types (don't forget to add the spaces between the words by adding "") and join the string version of the int to the sentence being assigned to the variable:

```
string MyStatement = CompleteName + " " + "feels " + Convert.ToString(TrueAge);
```

Add a textbox element to your application and name it **txtResult**. Then enter the code into the Click handler block, as shown in Listing 10.2.

LISTING 10.2   Showing the Correctly Formatted Message

```
private void btnShowResult_Click(object sender, RoutedEventArgs e)
{
    string FirstName = "Brennon";
    string LastName = "Williams";
    string CompleteName = FirstName + " " + LastName;

    int MyRealAge = 34;
    int AgeIFeel = 54;
    int TrueAge = (AgeIFeel / 2) + MyRealAge;

    string MyStatement = CompleteName + " " + "feels " +
Convert.ToString(TrueAge);
    this.txtResult.Text = MyStatement;


}
```

In this code you removed the MessageBox calls and instead directed the variable value of MyStatement to the TextBox (txtResult) in the user interface. Notice that you added a .Text part after txtResult, which says that you want to assign a value to the Text property of the txtResult TextBox.

This is no different from opening the UI in Blend, selecting the txtResult TextBox, and finding the Text property in the Common Properties category of the Properties tab.

Think about the following carefully:

1. The txtResult TextBox that you created in Blend has a Text property in Blend.

2. The same txtResult object in code, which represents the TextBox you created in Blend, also has a Text property to which you can assign a value.

So the same must be true for a button? Correct.

How to Find Types in Blend

The Button element in Blend has a `Content` Property that you specify the label shown in the Button. If you named the Button in Blend, for example, you can type the Button name in code, type **.Content =**, and then type the value you want shown.

Simple stuff, right?

In Listing 10.2, you also called a Convert method and asked to convert the value to a string. There is no difference in calling the Convert method to using the .ToString() method, but it's important to note that there is a way to convert between specific types.

You can convert many types to other types, but it needs to be a valid conversion. Otherwise, an exception results (that is, a big ugly message box appears, or your application may even crash).

An example of a valid string to int conversion is shown in the following code:

```
int MyValue = Convert.ToInt32("192");
```

An example of an invalid string to int conversion is shown in the following code:

```
int MyValue = Convert.ToInt32("A192");
```

This string is invalid because the compiler cannot convert the letter A into a number.

The compiler in .NET is very sophisticated, so most of the time, it will tell you what is wrong with your code. In the case of conversions, however, you won't know it's wrong until you run your application (runtime).

Where Are the Data Types Expected in Blend?

Select any UIElement in the Objects and Timeline panel and then open the Properties panel. When you move your mouse over a label of any of the properties, the Tooltip describes what the type is, as shown in Figure 10.1. There are a few exceptions to this rule, however, and they relate to static method calls to set values on an objects parent. The Rows, Columns, RowSpan, and ColumnSpan properties are good examples of this, where the object does not actually contain the property Rows, RowSpan, and so on. The value is stored with the parent (Grid, in this example) and applied against its child. This is called an *Attached Property*.

Property name   Property Type

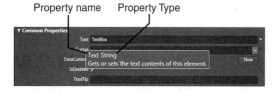

FIGURE 10.1   The property expected type in the ToolTip.

To rehash data types, take a moment and review the following:

▶ Data types store particular types of data, specific for certain types of values.

▶ You can convert between the data types if the conversion will result in a valid value, such as the whole number of a string converted to an int.

▶ You can perform mathematical operations on numeric types using standard mathematic symbols.

▶ The "+" mathematic symbol allows you to concatenate (or join) string types.

▶ You can assign variable values to an objects' properties (such as Text, Content, and so on) just the same as you can enter values in element properties in Blend.

Classes

A class is an awesome concept in coding. Without it, you would not be able to perform some of the complex scenarios required in applications today.

The .NET Framework contains thousands of classes that are ready for you to use in your own code, but it does take some time to get to know them and the purposes for which they are best used.

There are different types of classes, such as base classes and abstract classes. This chapter covers the public, non-static classes that you can use anywhere in your application.

Concept

In design time, you can build a class in Visual Studio by using the correct syntax and by providing public methods and properties that a user of the class can access in order to set or get information held within the class. During runtime, the class becomes an object when a new instance (called instantiation) occurs. This generally takes the following format:

```
ClassName InstanceName = new ClassName();
```

Similar to when you created a variable of the type int, you first specify the type (ClassName), then an identifier (InstanceName), and then you assign a new instance of the type to the identifier: = new ClassName();.

The concept of a class is similar to that of a blueprint, whereby you design an object to be a generic description of something.

A car is a pretty simple example.

You create a class that describes a car, which means that it needs to have properties that refer to the number of wheels on the car, the number of doors, or even an engine size.

When creating your class, create a generic blueprint of a car. When you have a separate instance of the blueprint, you can then create a specific type of car.

Creating a Simple Class

The following steps take you through creating a simple class:

1. In Visual Studio, right-click on the project file and select the Add menu item.

10

2. From the submenu that appears, at the bottom, select the Class menu item.

3. The Add New Item dialog appears, prompting you to enter a name for the class. Name the class Car.cs.

4. Visual Studio creates a new class for you, with syntax similar to the following:

```
class Car
    {

    }
```

Visual Studio May Cause an Error When Adding a Class

Occasionally, Visual Studio 2008 will add a "using directive" for Linq in your new class which will cause your application to fail if you don't have a reference to this particular namespace in your solution. The easiest way to correct this is to check your new class at the top of the file where other using directives have been added, and if you see one that says

```
using System.Linq;
```

delete it.

Scope

The concept of scope is one that either you get or you don't. In coding terms, something that is "public" means that everything else in the code (other classes and so on) has access to that public item. The opposite to this is "private," which means that only items that have a direct level of ownership can access the item.

To demonstrate this, the following sample creates a public and a private variable, similar to what you did with Data types.

1. Inside the class you just created, add the code shown in Listing 10.3.

LISTING 10.3   A Basic Class Declaration

```
class Car
    {
        public int Wheels = 4;
        private int Doors = 4;
    }
```

2. Save All in Visual Studio and then return to Blend. You may be prompted to update the solution, as shown in Figure 10.2, because you added a new class file.

3. Blend will probably close your current screen, but you should switch to the Project tab and then make sure that it shows the new file addition: Car.cs. If this file isn't present, shut down the solution and then open it again.

4. Double-click on the Window1.xaml file to open it again in Blend.

5. Create a new button called btnMakeCar.

FIGURE 10.2   Blend recognizes the change in the solution.

6. Add a Click handler for this new button by double-clicking in the input field for the Click event.

7. Add the code in Listing 10.4 to create a new instance of the generic Car type.

LISTING 10.4   Instantiate a New Car

```
private void btnMakeCar_Click(object sender, RoutedEventArgs e)
        {
            Car MyCar = new Car();
        }
```

You can see how the new Car is created. Now it's time to see the effects of scope.

In Listing 10.3 you can see that a variable with the type "public" and an another one with the type "private" have been declared. Under the new instance of MyCar, type the word **MyCar.** (be sure to include the dot after it) to view the IntelliSense output (see Figure 10.3).

FIGURE 10.3   The IntelliSense for the MyCar object only displays "Public" member variables.

You should see that the member variable Doors is not present but Wheels is. This is because Wheels is public and Doors is not. The only way Doors can have a value is to set inside its own class. How can you get around this?

Properties

Properties allow you to give controlled access (make it read-only or read and write) to any member variable. There are a number of ways to make a property, but this section looks at two specific types. This section also explains the advantages of using one over the other.

CLR Properties

CLR (Common Language Runtime or .NET) properties are really very simple, but this simplicity comes at the cost of reduced functionality. Still, the following example shows the concept of Properties clearly:

1. If you typed MyCar. in Window1.xaml.cs, remove it.

2. In the Solution Explorer, find the Car.cs class file and double-click to open it again.

   Consider this for the concept: The property should have a private backing member and a public accessor method allowing the user to get and set values.

3. Add the code from Listing 10.5.

LISTING 10.5   Creating CLR Properties

```
class Car
{
    private int Wheels = 4;
    public int NumberOfWheels
    {
        get { return this.Wheels ;}
        set { this.Wheels = value;}
    }

    private int Doors = 4;
    public int NumberOfDoors
    {
        get { return this.Doors ; }
        set { this.Doors = value; }
    }

}
```

Breaking this down, you can see that the int Wheels member is now private. This is called the private backing field. Being private now means that the member variables can only be assigned a new value by either the "set" of the public property accessor NumberOfWheels or somewhere else internally in the code of this class only.

If you remove the "set" altogether, the property effectively becomes read-only, because your user can get the value but can't set it. If this is your intention, make sure you define a default value of the private backing field.

Go back to the code point where you created an instance of the Car class and again type **MyCar**. (Be sure to include the ending dot.) This time you should see both the properties to which you can assign values, as shown in Listing 10.6.

LISTING 10.6   Assigning Values to Your Defined Properties

```
private void btnMakeCar_Click(object sender, RoutedEventArgs e)
    {
        Car MyCar = new Car();
        MyCar.NumberOfDoors = 2;
        MyCar.NumberOfWheels = 4;
    }
```

There you have it, nice and simple! You can now create properties of an object and control how the user of the object can interact with it using scope.

Dependency Properties

A DependencyProperty (DP) is not that dissimilar from a CLR property. In fact, a DP is an extension of the CLR property concept, allowing for much greater flexibility in control over the values contained by the property.

I explain the DP concept in two parts, the first being the "public" accessor (CLR wrapper) for the property, as shown in Listing 10.7.

LISTING 10.7   Public Property Wrappers for Dependency Properties

```
public int NumberOfSeats
{
    get { return (int)GetValue(NumberOfSeatsProperty); }
    set { SetValue(NumberOfSeatsProperty, value); }
}
```

Listing 10.7 shows you the slight changes to the "public" property interface compared with the CLR property.

You still have the get/set, which means that if you want to work with this property, you call it using exactly the same method as shown in Listing 10.6.

Internally, the get/set instances call the WPF property API by using GetValue/SetValue, as shown in Listing 10.7.

The second part is about the backing field. DPs also have a backing field, but instead of the field being a private member variable, the DependencyProperty type is the field, as shown in Listing 10.8.

LISTING 10.8   The Static DependencyProperty Declaration

```
    // Using a DependencyProperty as the backing store for NumberOfSeats. This
enables animation, styling, binding, etc...
```

10

```
public static readonly DependencyProperty NumberOfSeatsProperty =
    DependencyProperty.Register("NumberOfSeats", typeof(int), typeof(Car));
```

This code contains quite a few changes and added complexity compared with the "private" backing field member used in CLR events. But the complexity is worth it considering the additional benefits, such as support for binding, animation, styling, property inheritance (the parent supplies the value), and the ability to modify or create your own metadata for the property.

Listing 10.8 shows the bare minimum code required to create a DependencyProperty to which the naming convention NumberOfSeatsProperty is very important, because it is the name of the property that is looked up by the WPF property system.

On creation you can also see that you are required to register the DependencyProperty details. As shown in Listing 10.8, at the minimum, three values are required:

1. The name of the property: NumberOfSeats
2. The data type of the property: typeof(int)
3. The owner class type: typeof(Car)

To implement this property, as shown in Listings 10.7 and 10.8, you are required to also add a using statement at the top of the class file:

```
using System.Windows;
```

Remember how I mentioned previously that the .NET Framework has thousands of classes? DependencyProperty is one of those classes, and it lives in the System.Windows namespace.

How Would You Know Which Namespace to Add?

Visual Studio knows that you probably won't remember or know which namespace the class belongs. Whenever you can't remember (as long as you spell it absolutely case-sensitive correctly), you can place your cursor on the last letter of the object type. Visual Studio puts a small red underscore in place. Put your mouse on this, and a drop-down menu is displayed, enabling you to select the using statement to add, which Visual Studio places the top of the file, as shown in Figure 10.4.

Place your cursor on the last letter to reveal
the little red underscore. Mouse over the
underscore and click to reveal this menu.

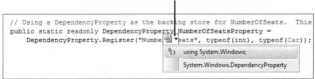

FIGURE 10.4   Visual Studio offers a hand.

Your class must also be a DependencyObject, so you need to inherit from this type to enable the functionality DependencyObject provides, which happens to be the GetValue() and SetValue() methods in the public accessor. You will also want this class to be publicly accessible for other areas of the application to work, so please take note that the scope changes here as well.

Modify your class declaration to look like the following:

```
public class Car : DependencyObject
```

Until you add the using directive for System.Windows, your class will not know about the DependencyObject type either. Again, place the cursor at the end of the word (on the *t* in DependencyObject) and then select the small red underscore to add the using directive as required.

Back in the Window1.xaml.cs file, you can now set the property, as shown in Listing 10.9.

LISTING 10.9   Assigning Values to CLR or Dependency Properties Are the Same

```
        private void btnMakeCar_Click(object sender, RoutedEventArgs e)
        {
            Car MyCar = new Car();
            MyCar.NumberOfDoors = 2;
            MyCar.NumberOfWheels = 4;
            MyCar.NumberOfSeats = 7;
        }
```

As shown in Listing 10.9, the code is no different from when you use a CLR property.

Using the properties in markup is a different scenario, however. For XAML you can only set a property if it is a DependencyProperty. If you want to include an instance of your Car in XAML, you need to convert all your properties to DPs to have access to them.

For more information on properties, especially WPF property types, visit http://msdn2. microsoft.com/en-us/library/ms753192.aspx or do a search on the web for DependencyProperties.

Conditional Coding

Without the capability to conditionally branch code logic, you would be unable to react to different interactions from users. Conditional coding happens many times within an application. C#, like most languages, provides a number of ways to test conditions. Probably the most ubiquitous method is the humble if-else, which allows you to test "if" something equals x, then do y; "else" do z.

if-else

The generalized concept of the if-else is the following:

10

```
if(CONDITION)
... //do this
else
... //do this
```

The CONDITION is an evaluation that can either be true or false, so it is a Boolean evaluation.

Consider the following three variables:

```
int a = 5;
int b = 5;
int c = 10;
```

Now consider the following:

▶ a is equal to b

▶ a + b is equal to c

▶ a is not equal to c

These are all true statements that in code are written as follows:

```
if (a == b)
{
    //do something here
}

if ((a+b) == c)
{
    //do something here
}

if (a != c)
{
    //do something here
}
```

Notice that not a single equals (=) sign is present.

a = c would mean that "a" would then contain a value of 10 (or as some people say "a gets c")

whereas

a == c is a statement asking if "a" is equal to "c"

The second example shows that a mathematic equation should be contained within a set of parentheses, so the addition is performed to get a value to then compare against c.

The last example also shows that you can query if something is not equal to something else, using the != symbols.

You can also use additional mathematic notation for conditional determinations, such as < or > or even <= and >=.

You don't have to rely on local values within variables for these conditional tests, however. You can also call methods that return a value that would then be tested. Imagine a method called GetNumberOfWheels exists in the Car class and returns the value of 4. To use this method in the if statement, you would write something like the following:

```
if (MyCar.GetNumberOfWheels() == 4)
        {
            //Do this is the car has 4 wheels
        }
```

At the moment you don't have this method in the car class, but because the DependencyProperty NumberOfWheels does exist, you could also just call the property value for a return such as the following:

```
        if (MyCar.NumberOfWheels == 4)
        {
            //Do this is the car has 4 wheels
        }
```

The else statement allows you to deal with the scenario that a CONDITION is either a true or a false, or vice versa.

```
        if (MyCar.NumberOfWheels == 4)
        {
            //Do this if the car has 4 wheels
        }
        else
        {
            //Do something here if the car has more or less than 4 wheels
        }
```

The preceding example also raises additional questions, such as, "What if there are three or five wheels?"

You can use the else statement with additional if conditional testing to deal with multiple scenarios, as demonstrated in the following code:

```
if (MyCar.NumberOfWheels == 3)
        {
            //Do this if the car has 3 wheels
        }
        else if (MyCar.NumberOfWheels == 4)
```

```
    {
        //Do this if the car has 4 wheels
    }
    else if (MyCar.NumberOfWheels == 5)
    {
        //Do this if the car has 5 wheels
    }
    else
    {
        //Do something here if the car has
        //less than 3 or more than 5 wheels
    }
```

Within your code you can use numerous other conditional statements, such as do while loops and switch logic (which is discussed shortly). Each method has its positives and negatives, but essentially all are about allowing you to determine what should occur "if" something happens.

Enums

Enums are wonderful in that you get to provide a specific set of scenarios to which a data type can be equal. An example of where you can use enumerations is when you need to know the day of the week.

A week has only seven days, so by putting these into an enum type, the code using the type is constrained to using one of these types, thereby reducing the chances of errors in the code logic.

This does not mean that an enum type must contain a specific number of known values. It means that you are free to specify what you want the known values to be, which you will see shortly.

Simple Enums

Starting simple here, consider the example of the days of the week as a concept of how to declare an enum type.

A day-of-the-week enum would be declared similarly to Listing 10.10.

LISTING 10.10   A Simple Enum Declaration

```
enum DayOfTheWeek
{
    Sunday,
    Monday,
    Tuesday,
    Wednesday,
    Thursday,
    Friday,
```

```
        Saturday
    }
```

Except for the last value, notice that all the values have a comma after them.

Now that the enum is defined, elsewhere in your code you could create a member of this type.

Recall that you previously added private members for use as the backing fields in the CLR property types. Now you can create a member using this enum as the data type as well.

The last paragraph should now have you thinking about properties. You should now understand that the enum is a type, just the same as a string, an int, or a bool (just specific about the values that can be set to it). You use the type in exactly the same way.

Consider an int type declared as a global member variable:

```
private int MyIQ = 64;//Oh dear...
```

Notice the similarities of using your enum as the data type, as shown in the following:

```
private DayOfTheWeek CurrentDay = DayOfTheWeek.Saturday;
```

The difference is that with the int member, you are free to set its value at whatever valid integer you please, whereas with the DayOfTheWeek type member, you must set its value to one of the values as defined within the enum.

Moving back to the Car class, create the enum type, as shown in Listing 10.11.

LISTING 10.11   An Effective Enum Is Self-Describing

```
public enum CarModel
    {
        Mustang,
        Bronco,
        Escort,
        Fairlane,
        Mondeo
    }
```

Now add the code shown in Listing 10.12 to create a DependencyProperty of type CarModel. Pay close attention to how the default value of the property is set.

LISTING 10.12   Creating the CarModel DependencyProperty

```
    public CarModel Model
    {
        get { return (CarModel)GetValue(ModelProperty); }
        set { SetValue(ModelProperty, value); }
```

10

```
        }

        public static readonly DependencyProperty ModelProperty =
                DependencyProperty.Register("Model", typeof(CarModel), typeof(Car), new
        PropertyMetadata(CarModel.Fairlane)));
```

Return to the Window1.xaml.cs file. Set this new property using the following syntax:

```
MyCar.Model = Car.CarModel.Mustang;
```

Switch Statement

The switch statement is really another form of conditional coding and is extremely well suited to the use of enums because the value required for a switch must be a constant, which enum values are. You can't add more values to an enum in runtime, so the ones you declare are implicitly constant.

The switch statement looks like a really fancy if statement, and the logic reads similarly. The following is a sample to demonstrate the concept, using a member variable CurrentDay, which is of enum type DayOfWeek as previously shown in Listing 10.10.

```
        switch (CurrentDay)
        {
            case DayOfTheWeek.Sunday:
                //Should be asleep
                ... do something here
                break;
            case DayOfTheWeek.Monday:
                //Get up early :-(
                ... do something here
                break;
            case DayOfTheWeek.Tuesday:
                //Feel ok, getting used to being up early
                ... do something here
                break;
            case DayOfTheWeek.Wednesday:
                //Hump day.. looking forward to weekend
                ... do something here
                break;
            case DayOfTheWeek.Thursday:
                //Start winding down.. can't overdo it now
                ... do something here
                break;
            case DayOfTheWeek.Friday:
                //Pretty much a standard holiday day.. don't tell the boss
                ... do something here
```

```
                break;
        case DayOfTheWeek.Saturday:
                //Hangover from Friday
                ... do something here
                break;
        default:
                //Should never get here
                ... do something here - log or throw an error
                break;
    }
```

The code is a little sarcastic, but the idea is that you test for the current value in the case and exit from the switch logic by using a break; at the end of each case.

Add another button to your test application, calling it btnCarDetails (see Figure 10.5).

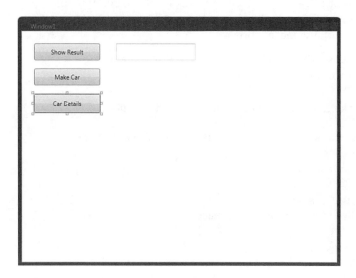

FIGURE 10.5   The application layout.

Add a Click event handler for the new button to return to Visual Studio.

In the previous button click handler, you created a new instance of the Car class (MyCar) and set its property values. While doing this, you created an instance that was only local to that particular handling method, so now that you have a new click handler, you will be unable to access the MyCar instance.

To change the scope of the declared MyCar instance from local to global, take out the declaration of the previous handler and place it above the click handler, as shown in Listing 10.13.

10

LISTING 10.13   Making an Object Instance Global in Scope

```
//Make the MyCar instance global in scope
private Car MyCar = new Car();

private void btnMakeCar_Click(object sender, RoutedEventArgs e)
{
    MyCar.NumberOfDoors = 2;
    MyCar.NumberOfWheels = 4;
    MyCar.NumberOfSeats = 7;

    MyCar.Model = Car.CarModel.Mustang;
}
```

Note that the scope declaration of private was added to the front of the declaration. Although this is not required (by default, all global member variables are private in .NET C#), it is good practice to declare the scope, as shown.

Now add the code in Listing 10.14, which makes use of the MyCar instance now being accessible as a global and demonstrates a usage of the switch statement.

LISTING 10.14   Switch and Case Statements Make Code Readability Simple

```
private void btnCarDetails_Click(object sender, RoutedEventArgs e)
{
    switch (this.MyCar.Model)
    {
        case Car.CarModel.Mustang:
            MessageBox.Show("The car is a Mustang");
            break;
        case Car.CarModel.Bronco:
            MessageBox.Show("The car is a Bronco");
            break;
        case Car.CarModel.Escort:
            MessageBox.Show("The car is an Escort");
            break;
        case Car.CarModel.Fairlane:
            MessageBox.Show("The car is a Fairlane");
            break;
        case Car.CarModel.Mondeo:
            MessageBox.Show("The car is a Mondeo");
            break;
        default:
            MessageBox.Show("Error.. the car model is not set");
            break;
    }
}
```

Note that the value being tested is written like so:

```
switch (this.MyCar.Model)
```

The this. says that the MyCar instance is a member of this class. This is not required, but it can make readability a lot better in complex code because you can instantly tell that MyClass is local to the class.

The case statements cover every possible combination of the enum type that the member variable Model also represents. It is quite easy to follow the code through when reading it.

Enums have other benefits and are quite often used to track the state of objects and where the user is within the application. Enums are great and reduce the potential for logical errors, so I advise that you use them as often as possible.

Methods

Some old-school programmers probably remember methods being called functions. I am unsure as to why the name changed, but no doubt it kept someone in a job at Microsoft and the marketing department busy for another year.

You already used a method when you called the MessageBox object and asked it to show some information in a dialog box:

```
MessageBox.Show(FirstName);
```

The Show() is the method, and as the IntelliSense in Visual Studio describes, the Show() method "Displays a message box in front of the specified window."

Actually, the name *method* is much better suited than *function* (sorry Microsoft people; you were right), because two blocks of code can provide the same functionality but each can contain completely different code in order to achieve the same thing, as shown in Listing 10.15.

The code in both methods performs the same functionality, but achieves that functionality with differing methods. They return the same value.

LISTING 10.15   The Same, But Different

```
private int DoCalculation_Divide()
{
    return 100 / 10;
}

private int DoCalculation_Multiply()
{
    return 100 * 0.1;
}
```

10

A method is a block of code that is written to perform a certain function in a certain way. It can specify a returning value (as shown in Listing 10.15) and can accept values to work with, which are referred to as parameters (or arguments), as shown in Listing 10.16.

Parameters are not required, however it is not uncommon to simply branch code because a block of code is becoming very large and harder to manage. Branching code in this fashion is continually being carried out on a large application to improve readability and understanding and, in some cases, performance. The process is known in the industry as "refactoring."

You can name two methods the same as long as their parameters differ in either the number or the types of parameters. This is called *method overloading*, as shown in Listing 10.16.

LISTING 10.16   Two Ways to Add Two Numbers

```
public int AddTwoNumbers(int NumberOne, int NumberTwo)
{
    int Result = NumberOne + NumberTwo;
    return Result;
}

public int AddTwoNumbers(string NumberOne, string NumberTwo)
{
    int Result = Convert.ToInt32(NumberOne) + Convert.ToInt32(NumberTwo);
    return Result;
}
```

How to Call a Method

In code, you use what is called a dot (or period) notation to call a method. A method belongs to the object where it is written in, so in the case that you added the methods shown in Listing 10.16, you could call them from a button click handler like the following:

```
this.DoCalculation_Divide();
```

Alternatively, the second method would be called as follows:

```
this.DoCalculation_Multiply();
```

If these methods were written inside a different class object, for example, the Car class, you would call them either as

```
this.MyCar.DoCalculation_Divide();
```

or

```
this.MyCar.DoCalculation_Multiply();
```

Why Use "this." Before the Object or Method() Call?

In the previous method examples, you should note that the use of the keyword "this." is optional. I use it for clarity, to remind me that the object or variable is global and resides in the class that I am working in (as opposed to being declared locally inside the method where "this." is not allowed. A lot of other developers don't use it at all. It's a personal preference issue.

Looking at the following code (the first method from Listing 10.16), you see a simple yet well defined method.

```
public int AddTwoNumbers(int NumberOne, int NumberTwo)
{
    int Result = NumberOne + NumberTwo;
    return Result;
}
```

Let's start with the first line of this method:

```
public int AddTwoNumbers(int NumberOne, int NumberTwo)
```

The word *public* represents the scope of the method, or who can use it. This again means that if this method was inside the Car class, it would need to be public—the same as the properties—in order to use it outside of the code of the class.

Next you see that an int is declared. This states that this method *must* return a value of type int.

The method has a name to be referred by: AddTwoNumbers. This is an ideal name for the method because, just by looking at the name, you know what the method does. You should try to implement meaningful names to every area of your code, because anyone else looking at it might otherwise find it difficult to understand what you are trying to achieve.

Next is an open parenthesis, followed by a parameter declaration (int NumberOne), a comma separating the first parameter from the second (int NumberTwo), and then a closing parenthesis.

The next line creates the opening brace, or {, for which you will see a closing brace, or }, at the end of the method listing. These braces tell the application that this is a block of code. When the execution path of the application enters this "block" of code, every line should be executed until the ending brace is met or an instruction is given to exit the code block.

10

This is the same as the click handler blocks of code. In fact, the click handler is just another method.

When to Return?

You can return out of a method at any point as long as you return with the required value type. If the method requires an int as the return type, you must supply an int value or variable after the return statement.

It is quite common for a method not to require a returning type, so the method becomes what is known as a void method. You can stop executing lines of code in this block at any point by simply using the return statement with no value after it, just the semicolon:

```
return;
```

The next line declared a variable (int Result) and at the same time initialized the variable and assigned (=) the resulting value by performing the addition of the two supplied parameters (NumberOne + NumberTwo).

Finally, you use the keyword return to fulfill the requirement to return a value of int: return Result;

In the situations where you want to perform an action but don't want the method to have to return a value, you use a special type called void, so the first line of the method becomes the following:

```
public void AddTwoNumbers(int NumberOne, int NumberTwo)
```

Methods get very complex at times, and there are many different ways to parse values into them using parameters.

Add another button called btnCallMethods to your application.

Try adding the code for Listing 10.17, modifying the original button click handler you added for the btnShowResult button. Run the application and click the new button to try and follow the code logic.

LISTING 10.17   Method Calling Example

```
private void btnCallMethods_Click(object sender, RoutedEventArgs e)
{

    int MyNumber1 = 25;
    int MyNumber2 = 50;
```

```
    int AdditionResult = AddTwoNumbers(MyNumber1, MyNumber2);

    this.txtResult.Text = AdditionResult.ToString();
}

public int AddTwoNumbers(int NumberOne, int NumberTwo)
{
    int Result = NumberOne + NumberTwo;
    return Result;
}

public int AddTwoNumbers(string NumberOne, string NumberTwo)
{
    int Result = Convert.ToInt32(NumberOne) + Convert.ToInt32(NumberTwo);
    return Result;
}
```

Did you notice that you didn't have to specify which of the two methods should be used? The compiler is very clever; it works it out based on the types that you are parsing to the method as parameters.

How Many Methods Can You Have?

You can have as many methods as you need, and you should use them as often as you need to ensure that specific blocks of code run as required. Another benefit of creating a method is that you can call the method throughout multiple areas of your remaining code with much less risk of errors creeping in. Essentially, if you need to change the functionality of the code and are doing the same thing in lots of different places throughout your code, you only need to change it in one place if all those areas are calling the same method, which also reduces the chances of defects in your code.

The principle is the same as creating a Style Template for a Button element. If you need to change the Style, do it in its template once, and every button that uses that particular style will automatically update.

It is good practice to comment your methods so that other people who read your code or use your code in theirs can understand exactly what it is you are asking them to parse and what you are going to give them back. Code comments are also very handy for the person writing the code, as inevitably most developers look back over their code, find comments, and think, "What was I thinking when I wrote this?"

The IntelliSense in Visual Studio uses the information that you add, so it becomes a handy instruction to others who use your code (see Figure 10.6). These special comments can also be used to generate help files and so on.

10

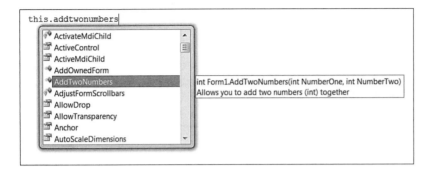

FIGURE 10.6   The IntelliSense presents the comments to the user when he or she calls the method.

In Visual Studio C#, you achieve this by placing three forward slashes on the line just before the method declaration. Visual Studio then puts in a special comment block for you; you just need to fill it out.

The following code shows the comments completed for the first method:

```
/// <summary>
/// Allows you to add two numbers (int) together
/// </summary>
/// <param name="NumberOne">The first number to add</param>
/// <param name="NumberTwo">The second number to add</param>
/// <returns>The two numbers added together</returns>
public int AddTwoNumbers(int NumberOne, int NumberTwo)
{
    int Result = NumberOne + NumberTwo;
    return Result;
}
```

You will now practice creating and calling a method that relates to the controls of the user interface: the txtResult TextBox and the btnShowResult Button elements. For this, remove the code previously added to the btnCallMethods click handler method and add the code in Listing 10.18.

LISTING 10.18   Validating User Input in Code
```
private void btnCallMethods_Click(object sender, RoutedEventArgs e)
{
    try
    {
        //Take the number given and make the textbox width
        //change
        int WidthIn = Convert.ToInt32(this.txtResult.Text);
```

```
        this.txtResult.Width = ValidateWidth(WidthIn);
    }
    catch (Exception x)
    {
        MessageBox.Show("There is an error : " + x.ToString());
    }

}

private int ValidateWidth(int NewWidthValue)
{
    //Make sure the number entered is minimum 100, maximum 250
    if (NewWidthValue < 100)
        return 100;
    if (NewWidthValue > 250)
        return 250;
    //Number supplied is valid
    return NewWidthValue;
}
```

When you run this application, enter different values in the textbox and click the Call Methods button. What happens?

The TextBox width changes. You can now see how referring to objects you add in Blend (as long as you give them a name) are accessible in code, and you can set values to them, just as you would in the Blend property panel.

In Listing 10.18, there is a new keyword called try, which has the code brace { directly under it. If you follow the code down in the click handler method, the code also includes the closing brace }. A separate code block below it reads as follows:

```
catch (Exception x)
{
    MessageBox.Show("There is an error : " + x.ToString());
}
```

Collectively, this is called a try-catch statement, which means that you can protect the integrity of the application by capturing any error that occurs during the execution of the code with the first block.

Why put it there? Because the user must enter a number into the textbox, and you cannot be 100% certain that the value entered will be a number. For example, the value might be a letter or symbol. You want to catch the error, if it occurs, and relay the information back to the user.

If you do not catch errors like this, your application will either crash or hang, neither a particular confidence booster to your end user.

The first line of code is as follows:

```
catch (Exception x)
```

This code states that you want to catch any Exception that occurs. The x will be used later as a reference to that error. You can specify a number of different types of Exceptions, which allow you to fully understand any issues that have occurred during execution. For now, understand that the Exception keyword means that you are not discriminating; you wish to catch any and all errors that occur.

You entered a code block with braces and then added the following line:

```
MessageBox.Show("There is an error : " + x.ToString());
```

The code is pretty descriptive in that you are calling the Show() method of the MessageBox object, discussed previously, designed to display for the user a message in a standard message box dialog. Note also the concatenation of the string value and the x.ToString() statement, again, so that the details of the error can be shown to the user.

What Information Does the Exception Contain?

At the end of this sample, when you run the application, put some characters in the textbox instead of numbers. Clicking the Show Result button should yield a dialog box similar to that shown in Figure 10.7.

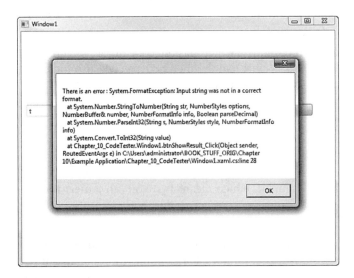

FIGURE 10.7   The Exception dialog.

Figure 10.7 shows the volume of information given back about the error, including the line number where the error occurred.

The information shown may be somewhat cryptic at the moment, but eventually most of the information becomes recognizable and is invaluable when determining where errors have occurred and why.

Most importantly, the try-catch statement has handled any potential errors gracefully. The user can click the OK button and give it another go. Without the try-catch statement, things would be a lot more unpredictable for the end user, and he or she certainly wouldn't be able to continue using the application.

Now on to the next two lines of code, as follows:

```
int WidthIn = Convert.ToInt32(this.txtResult.Text);
this.txtResult.Width = ValidateWidth(WidthIn);
```

You should be able to tell that you created a variable of int type (WidthIn) and assigned the value of the number entered into the textbox (txtResult.Text).

The next line may appear somewhat more cryptic. You are assigning a value to the Width property of the textbox, but the value is returned by a method call:

```
ValidateWidth(WidthIn);
```

The Width property shown here is exactly the same property that you manipulate in Blend in order to change the width of the TextBox element as it appears on the artboard—the same as the Text property.

It is good practice to validate the input that users make, so in this case, you created a new method—ValidateWidth—that took a parameterized value of type int and checked that it was within the correct range, returning a value to be assigned to the textbox's Width property. Let's examine the new method:

```
private int ValidateWidth(int NewWidthValue)
```

You can see that the first line of the new method sets the scope (private), the returning type (int), the identifier (ValidateWidth), and the parameter requirements (NewWidthValue, which is of type int).

The code inside the method does a number of things with the int value (NewWidthValue) that is parsed into the method. The code validates the value of NewWidthValue by checking it against certain rules that are put in place with the if statements.

```
//Make sure the number entered is minimum 100, maximum 250
if (NewWidthValue < 100)
    return 100;
if (NewWidthValue > 250)
    return 250;
//Number supplied is valid
return NewWidthValue;
```

Understanding the mathematical symbols for greater than (>) and less than (<) help you to follow what is happening in this method. You can also see that the code simply returns out of the method with a valid returning data type (an int) after a rule is met. If none of the rules is met, it is declared that the value initially parsed meets the requirements, so the original value is returned as the result.

This last part is probably a lot to take in if you are new to coding. Getting errors in methods and compilers about missing lines and more is all part of the steep learning curve associated with coding. The important thing here is to keep trying to use the correct syntax. Coding is a repetitive task, which you soon get good at by repetition (hence the term *code monkey*). Methods are a big key to creating a complex application. The more you start moving toward complex interactions in WPF, the more code you need to understand.

Events

Events are a common concept in the vast majority of modern coding languages. The name is self-explanatory in that you know this particular area of coding is based around the idea of "something has happened that something else might need to know about."

Concept

As with most areas of .NET development, there are many ways to achieve the same thing. They all have pros and cons, so the more you understand the different options, the better your chances of making the right decision on which method to implement.

The two methods this book covers are the CLR event and the new RoutedEvent. The simple process of events is described in Figure 10.8.

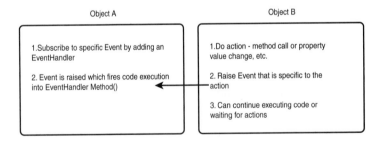

FIGURE 10.8   A high-level overview of an event scenario.

CLR Events

The CLR event model works on a concept of "publishers and subscribers." At any point in an object that you declare an event, that object becomes the event publisher, and any other object that needs to listen for the event becomes a subscriber.

CLR events require an understanding of delegate objects, which in detail is beyond the scope of this chapter, but the concept of the event is the same for both CLR and RoutedEvents.

What Is a Delegate?

A delegate object allows you to create a "pointer" to any other method that matches the declaration of the delegate signature.

The delegate is declared as follows:

delegate result-type identifier (parameters);

The delegate signature in the preceding example is made up of the return-type and the parameters (which are not required).

Consider the following delegate:

```
public delegate void MyDelegateObject(string Message);
```

This means that you can point the delegate toward any Method() in any other class, which takes a string as a parameter and returns void.

For a detailed overview on MSDN, see http://msdn2.microsoft.com/en-us/library/ms173172(VS.80).aspx.

As Figure 10.9 shows, the CLR event travels through to the parent object by way of publicly declared members in each parent object.

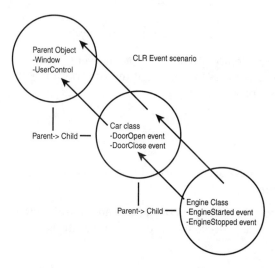

FIGURE 10.9   A CLR event flow.

Think of this as a "bubble" solution.

Parent-to-Child Event Notification

What happens, however, if you want to raise an event from the parent through to the child? Things start to get messy.

RoutedEvents, as discussed in the next section, have a much more elegant way of handling this type of scenario, so don't panic just yet.

You now learn how to implement the DoorOpen CLR event, which makes understanding the RoutedEvent much easier.

1. Open the Car.cs file in Visual Studio so that you are working in the Car class again.

2. Add the code shown in Listing 10.19.

LISTING 10.19   A Simple CLR Event

```
public delegate void DoorOpenDelegate(bool IsOpen);
public event DoorOpenDelegate DoorOpen;

public void OpenTheDoor()
{
    this.DoorOpen(true);
}
```

The first line in Listing 10.19 shows the delegate object declaration for the event. This declaration says that whichever method() or event uses this object, it returns nothing (void), but a bool value must be provided as a parameter.

The next line declares the actual event:

```
public event DoorOpenDelegate DoorOpen;
```

The scope is set to public so that other objects have access to it and then the keyword event is used to describe what is being declared.

Next you are declaring an instance of the DoorOpenDelegate object and an identifier for it. Think of this being similar to a member variable declaration, such as public string MyString.

Next, is the public method:

```
public void OpenTheDoor()
{
    this.DoorOpen(true);
}
```

In the OpenTheDoor() method, you call the identifier of the event DoorOpen. Because it is of type DoorOpenDelegate, you need to parse to it a parameter of type bool. This is called *raising the event*.

Now that your event is declared and will be raised when the OpenTheDoor() method is called, you need to subscribe to this event in both the object that declared the event (the publisher) and any other objects that want to subscribe to it.

You have not yet added a constructor to your Car class. A constructor is one of the best places to add your subscription declaration.

A constructor is a special method that gets called when a class is first instantiated. The constructor is public in scope and has no return type, but it may have parameters. A constructor with no parameters is called a *default constructor*.

Add the code for the default Car constructor method, as shown in Listing 10.20.

LISTING 10.20   Implementing an Event Handler

```
public Car()
        {
            this.DoorOpen += new DoorOpenDelegate(Car_DoorOpen);
        }

        void Car_DoorOpen(bool IsOpen)
        {
            throw new NotImplementedException();
        }
```

The first line is the default constructor declaration.

The next line is interesting:

```
            this.DoorOpen += new DoorOpenDelegate(Car_DoorOpen);
```

This code shows that the event is handled (+= is a sign for addition) by a method (Car_DoorOpen) that is parsed as a parameter to a new instance of a DoorOpenDelegate.

The method declared below the constructor (known as the EventHandler) has the exact signature of the DoorOpenDelegate object, being that it is void and takes a bool type as a parameter.

Why Is It OK to Write Void Without a Scope in Front of It?

By default in Visual Studio C#, any variable or member, such as public or private, that is, declared without a scope is automatically assumed to be private.

Use the IntelliSense to Help with Events

As Figure 10.10 shows, the IntelliSense makes the entire process simple by asking you to press Tab after you add the += sign. This completes the rest of the EventHandler code for you. If you press Tab again, the IntelliSense creates the EventHandler method() as well.

FIGURE 10.10   Press Tab to complete the EventHandler.

1. Inside the method Car_DoorOpen, remove the following line of code:

   ```
   throw new NotImplementedException();
   ```

   This method gets called each time your event is raised. By not removing this code, you would receive and error.

2. Open Blend. To the UI, add another button called btnOpenDoor and set the IsEnabled property to false.

3. Add a Click handler for the button, returning you to Visual Studio.

4. Find the original method you used to create the car, called btnMakeCar_Click.

5. At the end of the code that creates and instance of the Car, add the following line of code:

   ```
   this.btnOpenDoor.IsEnabled = true;
   ```

   Now you can only try to open the door of the car after the Car is created.

6. The Car now has the event that you previously created in the Car class, which you can add a handler for now using almost the same syntax. (Remember to use the IntelliSense). Figure 10.11 shows how the IntelliSense knows that you added the event to the object. Notice the small lightning bolt icon? The same icon is used in Blend when you need to add a click handler event.

   ```
   this.MyCar.DoorOpen += new Car.DoorOpenDelegate(MyCar_DoorOpen);
   ```

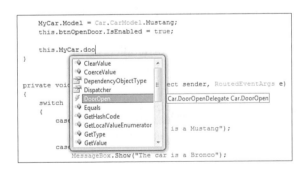

FIGURE 10.11   The DoorOpen delegate object details.

7. If you used the IntelliSense, method called MyCar_DoorOpen should appear. However, you could call this method anything as long as the signature is the same as the Delegate object.

8. Add the following line to the event handler method:

```
MessageBox.Show("The Car Door was opened");
```

9. The last thing to do is hook up the btnOpenDoor click handler, which you added from Blend after you created the button.

   Because the MyCar instance of the Car class is global, you can now call the method that opens the car door directly from the click event handler, as shown below:

```
private void btnOpenDoor_Click(object sender, RoutedEventArgs e)
    {
         this.MyCar.OpenTheDoor();
    }
```

10. Run the application by pressing F5 and then click on the button to create your car. The button to open the door becomes enabled, and you can now click it to open the car door.

Now that you have this event in place, you could add a state handler in the Car class to maintain whether the door is opened or closed, using enums and properties. The event that you added takes a bool, so you could always parse in a false for when the door is not opened. Alternatively, you could really go to town and add an enum for the door states and then use a switch statement to determine which message box to show based on the state of the door in the Car class instance.

RoutedEvents

RoutedEvents were introduced back in Chapter 8, "An Example Control Using Just the Tools Palette," when working with the event trigger system in Blend for a button that you had created. The RoutedEvent you create now allows you to subscribe to event notifications in Blend and, therefore, trigger an animation or some other action you desire.

As mentioned in Chapter 8, a RoutedEvent has three different routing strategies that can be employed:

▶ Bubble: The event notification travels up the visual tree of elements.

▶ Tunnel: The event notification travels down the visual tree of elements.

▶ Direct: Acts similar to a standard CLR event.

You are going to be adding a Bubbling event in the following code, but as you will see, to employ any of the other two strategies, it is a simple matter of changing a parameter value.

RoutedEvents are generally used in visual elements, such as user controls, because they require the owning object to be derived from the type UIElement to enable a call to the RaiseEvent() method. When working with custom classes that contain no design surface, continue to use CLR events as previously shown.

Compare Figure 10.9 with Figure 10.12 to see the high-level differences between CLR events and RoutedEvents.

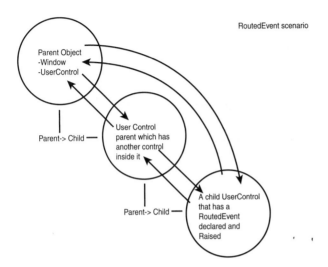

FIGURE 10.12   A RoutedEvent can raise notifications to which any object can subscribe.

1. Open the solution again in Blend.
2. Add a relatively large grid element to your Window's LayoutRoot and name it Child. Figure 10.13 shows the layout and positioning.

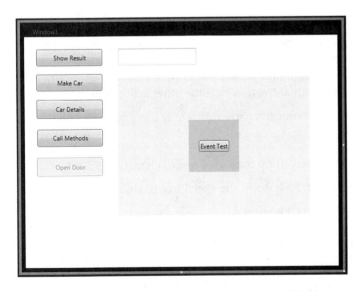

FIGURE 10.13   The grid elements layout and the added button.

3. Set the background to a light yellow SolidColorBrush.
4. Double-click the Child grid and add an additional grid in the center of its parent, setting the background to a light pink and naming the grid GrandChild.

5. Double-click to activate the new grid element (GrandChild) and add a Button element to its center, calling the button btnEventTest.

6. Select the GrandChild grid element in the Objects and Timeline category, right-click, and then select the Make Control menu item.

7. A warning Make Control dialog displays (see Figure 10.14) to let you know that if you modified code or references to the elements inside and including the GrandChild grid, you may need to make changes to get all the references worked out again. This happens because the Make Control feature takes the grid and makes it into a UserControl, but it cannot copy any code or animations. What is also important to note here is that the name of your element (GrandChild) automatically gets the word "Control" appended to it, so from here on out, it will be called GrandChildControl in code.

   Click OK.

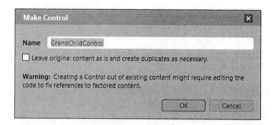

FIGURE 10.14 The Make Control dialog prompts you to understand that references are not carried over to the new control (which includes animations).

8. You should now see a new user control that contains a pink background with your btnEventTest button element already added to it, which is a real time-saving workflow on large UIs.

9. Note that the UserControl is automatically given the name of the element that is used as the root element for the control, which in this case was GrandChild, and as previously stated the word "Control" has been appended to the name.

10. Save your solution in Blend before continuing.

11. Select the button element and add a Click handler for it from the event viewer in the Properties panel. An error dialog appears, as shown in Figure 10.15.

FIGURE 10.15 An error dialog appears because of inconsistencies in the solution makeup between Visual Studio and Blend.

This issue is raised because the new user control(s) is not added to the solution that Visual Studio currently has open. Switch to Visual Studio. A dialog prompts you that the project has been modified and asks if you want to reload it. Click on Reload.

12. Your solution reloads in Visual Studio, and your new user control is added to the Solution Explorer dialog. Return to Blend. Again, add the Click handler event for the btnEventTest button element.

13. In the generated Click handler method, add the code to raise the event after you have created it.

14. Add a the code shown in Listing 10.21, which is a RoutedEvent declaration.

LISTING 10.21   Declaring the TestButtonClicked RoutedEvent

```
public static readonly RoutedEvent TestButtonClickedEvent = EventManager.Register-
RoutedEvent(
          "TestButtonClicked",
          RoutingStrategy.Bubble,
          typeof(RoutedEventHandler),
          typeof(GrandChildControl));

    // Provide CLR accessors for the event
    public event RoutedEventHandler TestButtonClicked
    {
        add { AddHandler(TestButtonClickedEvent, value); }
        remove { RemoveHandler(TestButtonClickedEvent, value); }
    }
```

Move through the RoutedEvent declaration one line at time, starting at the declaration:

```
public static readonly RoutedEvent TestButtonClickedEvent =
```

This instance is created as a static read-only RoutedEvent. Being static enables you to add handlers for this event when an instance of the Engine class has not been made, which is covered shortly. You can also see that the type is RoutedEvent.

What Is "Static"?

You can create Static classes—members, methods, and so on—which allow the data and the methods of the class to be accessed without needing to instantiate an instance of the class.

When would you want to do this? Anytime your object contains data that doesn't depend on any specific instance data.

Now onto the next line:

```
EventManager.RegisterRoutedEvent(
```

This is a call to a method (of a static object called EventManager) that registers your event with the WPF event system and then returns your RoutedEvent object.

Next is the name of the Event, which is of type string:

```
"TestButtonClicked",
```

Next is the Routing strategy that you wish to employ:

```
RoutingStrategy.Bubble,
```

The required value is an enum type of RoutingStrategy.

Next is the event handler type:

```
typeof(RoutedEventHandler),
```

As a default you should use a RoutedEventHandler. In more advanced scenarios, however, you can create your own types of event handlers.

Next is the owner of the event:

```
typeof(GrandChildControl));
```

This parameter is important, as you will see when adding a handler. Generally, the owner type should be the class in which the event is created.

Below this you see the CLR accessors that are provided for the event:

```
public event RoutedEventHandler TestButtonClicked
{
    add { AddHandler(TestButtonClickedEvent, value); }
    remove { RemoveHandler(TestButtonClickedEvent, value); }
}
```

You could think of this as being the same as the public CLR assessors that you added for the Dependency Property example at the start of the chapter. This "wrapper" is what lets you add Handlers for the event in code.

1. Now that you have declared the event and the CLR accessors, you can create an instance of a RoutedEventArgs object and raise the event, as shown in Listing 10.22.

LISTING 10.22   Raising the TestButtonClicked Event

```
private void btnEventTest_Click(object sender, RoutedEventArgs e)
    {
        RoutedEventArgs newEvent = new RoutedEventArgs(GrandChildControl.Test-
BottonClickedEvent);
        RaiseEvent(newEvent);
    }
```

10

The method text should be familiar to you now, so this disucssion starts with the next line of interest:

```
RoutedEventArgs newEvent = new RoutedEventArgs(GrandChildControl.TestBut-
tonClickedEvent);
```

The WPF event model is flexible and so allows you to mash the event in a way that best suits your application. Generally speaking, the .NET event model parses two parameters to the event handler, the first being the object that raised the event and the second being an object that derives from the EventArgs type, as you will see when you create a handler for this event.

In this line, you create an instance of a specific EventArgs type made for the RoutedEvent type, called RoutedEventArgs. In the constructor(s) of the RoutedEventArgs type, you can specify what event your RoutedEventArgs object is for, which is a static call to the owner and specific event (in this case, your GrandChildControl.TestButtonClicked event).

```
RaiseEvent(newEvent);
```

This final line of your method is what Raises the Event.

2. Go back to the Window1.xaml.cs code file.

3. Find the constructor for the Window class and add the code shown in Listing 10.23.

LISTING 10.23   Creating the RoutedEvent Handler Method

```
public partial class Window1
{
    public Window1()
    {
        this.InitializeComponent();

        // Insert code required on object creation below this point.
        this.AddHandler(GrandChildControl.TestButtonClickedEvent, new
RoutedEventHandler(OnTestButtonClickedEvent));
    }

    void OnTestButtonClickedEvent(object sender, RoutedEventArgs e)
    {
        MessageBox.Show("Event Worked!");
    }
```

The line that you are first interested in is as follows:

```
this.AddHandler(GrandChildControl.TestButtonClickedEvent, new
RoutedEventHandler(OnTestButtonClickedEvent));
```

The method AddHandler is built in to the Window type. As you see, this parses in a reference to the static event in the GrandChildControl, which you created previously. The new parameter allows you to declare a method() that will be called when the event is raised.

Because the event handler type you declared in the RoutedEvent declaration is a RoutedEventHandler, you now create a new instance of this type of handler and specify a method name in its constructor, which you do by using the name OnTestButtonClickedEvent. You can name this whatever you like as long as the method signature is the same as what is shown in Listing 10.23 for the method handler void OnTestButtonClickedEvent.

Next is the event handler method:

```
void OnTestButtonClickedEvent(object sender, RoutedEventArgs e)
{
    MessageBox.Show("Event Worked!");
}
```

As previously mentioned about the WPF event model, the event raised is expecting to parse two parameters: object representing the object that raised the event and the parameters that can be parsed through with the event.

Test the application now by clicking F5 in Visual Studio. With any luck, you should see a message box when you click the Event Test button.

The Proof
So far, so good. But what you really have here is the same scenario as shown in the CLR example, in which you have a child control referenced in the main Window. The following pushes this further by deepening the levels of children.

1. Return to Expression Blend and open the Window1.xaml file.
2. This time, find the Child grid control in the Objects and Timeline category. Again, right-click on the control and select Make Control from the context menu.
3. Another dialog warns you about the modification of the code. Again, remember that it will be renamed to ChildControl. When you are satisfied, click OK.

Now you have the same scenario shown in Figure 10.12, where you have a control (button) embedded in a control (GrandChildControl) with a RoutedEvent raised from the Click handler. You also now have the GrandChildControl embedded inside another UserControl (ChildControl), which has no event handlers declared. The ChildControl is now embedded as a UserControl of the main Window1.xaml.

You should be able to just run the application by clicking F5 in Blend. Upon clicking the element, you should again get the message box that tells you it worked!

10

How easy was that? The really big benefit to that also is that now you could create a story-board in your Window (or ChildControl and GrandChildControl controls) that listens for the TestClickedEvent to be raised. You can't this do with a CLR event.

For further information on the RoutedEvent object or any of the supporting objects, please see the MSDN library at http://msdn2.microsoft.com/en-us/library/ms742806.aspx.

Collections

You've no doubt heard the term *arrays* before. But in case not, an array is a group of objects that are put together in a stack, one after the other, where the new item added to an array always goes on the bottom of the pile.

In .NET you have had the ability to create all sorts of weird and wonderful arrays of objects from day one. I believe that every modern development language supports the concept of arrays in one shape or another. It appears that we need this facility regardless of what we are doing with a development language.

Collections (specifically, generic collections) were introduced properly into the .NET Framework 2.0. They were created as a way of improving performance and efficiency over arrays, especially over arrays that contained large sets of objects that were of differing types.

Consider the following array:

```
object[] MyArray = new object[3];
MyArray[0] = "hello";
MyArray[1] = new Car();
MyArray[2] = 45;
```

Why Is the First Item Always a Zero?

The short answer to the reason why collections and arrays are zero-based is because way back when compilers were as complex as rocks in a box, and programmers wrote in Assembler, everything done on a computer (in terms of processing and calculating) was expensive. Starting an array at zero saved on some of that calculating, which in those days was very important. It just stuck from there.

In .NET you always work with what is known as a zero-based system. This means that the first item in a collection (or array) will always be known as item index 0. This is not to say that you can't change this, but it is taken as a standard among developers, so you should not try to reinvent the wheel here. It may appear unnatural at first, but it all starts to feel normal after time.

You can see that there are three different types being added to the array, which doesn't appear to be a bad thing, but where it becomes an issue is when you start recalling the array elements:

```
Car MyNewCar = MyArray[2] as Car ;
```

The problem here is that the compiler won't complain because it does not understand what type is inside the array element. Worse still is that, if there is an issue and the number 45 can't be converted to a Car instance won't be picked up until runtime.

A whole host of other issues called *boxing* and *un-boxing* play a specific role in the performance issues of arrays. Be sure to "Google" these terms in the context of C# to better understand them.

What is different about a generic object collection is that it is, first and foremost, type safe, so if you create a collection of ints, that collection can contain only ints.

The compiler also understands that your generic collections must be type specific, so the following will certainly generate an error before you even get to runtime:

```
List<int> NewList = new List<int>();
NewList.Add("testing");
```

There exist quite a few generic collection types that I encourage you to research, but for the purposes of simplicity and practicality, this chapter looks at two specific types of generic collections (Lists and Dictionaries) that, given some understanding, make it easier to deal with a third type (ObservableCollection), which is used in CLR data binding and explored in Chapters 12, "Templates," and 13, "Data Binding."

Open your solution in Blend. Add another button called btnListMaker and then add a Click event for it, opening Visual Studio.

Before you begin using generic collection types, you need to indicate to the compiler that you are "using" this functionality by adding a using directive at the top of your code page. For Generics, you add the following:

```
using System.Collections.Generic;
```

List<T>

What is so special about generics is that you specify the type values that are contained within them, so the collection becomes "strongly typed." That is why you are reading the term List<T>, where the T represents the type. Strongly typed generic collections speed up code performance dramatically when compared with trying to cast or convert objects from arrays.

You declare a List<T> generic using the following syntax:

```
scope List<T> Identifier;
```

A valid List of int values would be declared and look something like the following:

```
private List<int> myIntCollection = new List<int>();
```

Several methods included with the List type help you to manage the List. In this section you see the most commonly used methods.

List.Add(T);

The code in Listing 10.24 shows how to add a new int value to a List collection.

LISTING 10.24   Adding int Values to a Global List<int> Object

```
private List<int> myIntCollection = new List<int>();


        private void btnListMaker_Click(object sender, RoutedEventArgs e)
        {
            this.myIntCollection.Add(1);
            this.myIntCollection.Add(4);
            this.myIntCollection.Add(5);
            this.myIntCollection.Add(Convert.ToInt32("19"));
        }
```

In Listing 10.24 a global member List is declared (myIntCollection) as a collection of Ints. That is the only type of object that can be added to the list, as you can see in the method calls:

```
            this.myIntCollection.Add(5);
```

The List, or indeed any other Generic collection, does not need to just hold primitive data types, such as int or string. You can create your own objects (such as your Car class) and create a collection of those types of objects as well.

In .NET, when you are thinking about collections or arrays, you need to remember that all collections or arrays are termed as zero-based. This means that the first item in a collection or an array will hold the position 0 in the collection. This is called the *item index*, or just *index*, which is important when you start dealing with the collection in terms of finding a specific object.

The following line retrieves the number of items in the collection:

```
int CollectionCount = this.myIntCollection.Count;
```

Even though the value returned by the property Count will be 4, in the case of the List created and filled in Listing 10.24, the int object with the value of 1, will be located at position 0 in the collection.

Several methods used by Generic collections require you to know the index of the object that you wish to work with.

This is confusing at first, if you have never counted this way, and it will throw you out at some stage. But hopefully you will see the error of your ways soon enough!

In the situation where you want to specify the position of an object when you are adding to a generic collection, call the insert() method of the collection, specifying the required index position and the object:

```
int myInt = 8;
    this.myIntCollection.Insert(1, myInt);
```

You can also remove objects from the collection by calling the RemoveAt() method and specifying the index of the object to remove:

```
this.myIntCollection.RemoveAt(0);
```

In this method call, the object at index or position 0 is being removed, not the object with a value of 0 (if one exists).

Sometimes you may want to remove all the items from the collection, so instead of calling the RemoveAt() method for each item, a call to the Clear() method is all that is required:

```
this.myIntCollection.Clear();
```

Using the objects stored in the collection is not terribly difficult, but you need to know the index position of the object. The following line of code shows how an object at index position 2 is assigned to a variable of the same type—int:

```
int IntAtPosition2 = this.myIntCollection[2];
```

Notice that square brackets, [ ], are used at the end of the collection to retrieve the object. This assigns the object to the variable IntAtPosition2. This is not a reference, however, so changing the value of the IntAtPosition2 member has no effect on the object stored in the collection.

Generally, working with a List<T> is very simple and very fast, and the methods for adding and removing items are always the same.

Dictionary<T,T>

Not terribly distant from the List<T> in terms of functionality and methods that are available, the Dictionary is a key pair collection. This means you specify a type to be used as a key and a type to be used as the corresponding value for the item.

Listing 10.25 shows you how to create a simple Dictionary<T,T>, in much the same way as you previously created a List<T>.

LISTING 10.25   Declaring a Global Dictionary<T,T> Is Simple

```
private Dictionary<int, string> myDictionary = new Dictionary<int, string>();


        private void btnListMaker_Click(object sender, RoutedEventArgs e)
        {
```

```
        this.myDictionary.Add(4, "The number 4");
        this.myDictionary.Add(14, "The number 14");
        this.myDictionary.Add(24, "The number 24");
        this.myDictionary.Add(34, "The number 34");
    }
```

What is important to understand from Listing 10.25 is that the key of the Dictionary<T,T> should not be confused with the concept of the item index.

Can you add the same objects to a list and a dictionary?

You can always add the same instance of an object at anytime—and as many times as you want to both a List<T> and a Dictionary<T,T>. What you can't do in the case of a dictionary is create and add the same Key value.

Before you add a new item to your collection (List or Dictionary), you can call a method to check whether it already exists:

```
        if (!this.myIntCollection.Contains(62))
            this.myIntCollection.Add(62);
```

For the Dictionary you can check whether the key exists:

```
if (!this.myDictionary.ContainsKey(15))
                this.myDictionary.Add(15, "The number is 15");
```

You can also check the value:

```
        if(!this.myDictionary.ContainsValue("The number 34"))
            this.myDictionary.Add(34, "The number 34");
```

As previously mentioned, the types used in the collection do not have to be primitive types, such as int and string., You may decide to use your own custom object such as the Car class you worked on in this chapter.

```
public Dictionary<int, Car> CarsInStock = new Dictionary<int, Car>();
```

In the preceding code, you can see that the key is specified as an int type and the value is specified as a Car type.

"What is the purpose of this?" you may ask.

Pretend that you have a collection of 100,000 cars, and you need to find the one that Mr. Jones ordered, custom designed to his specifications. You could iterate through the entire list, but this would be time consuming (even more so with complex objects), because you would need to check the properties of each car until you matched the specs.

If you know the key of the object, for example "5552125" (which might be Mr. Jones's phone number), you could ask the Dictionary to return this value directly, without having to go through every object until you find it, as shown in Figure 10.16.

```
Car ClientCar = CarsInStock[5552125];
```

```
Car ClientCar = CarsInStock[
                Car Dictionary<int,Car> [int key]
                key:
                   The key of the value to get or set.
```

FIGURE 10.16   The IntelliSense asking for the key of the collection, which is specifically an int in the CarsInStock collection.

Foreach

The foreach statement allows you to loop through a type-specific collection at high speed. For example, if you have several objects stored in your Generic collection, you can traverse the collection, changing the value of every object each time the loop works through the collection.

Because the foreach statement allows you to retrieve type-specific references within a collection, you get the entire object back from a collection every time the loop cycles in the statement.

```
foreach (Car CarObject in this.CarsInStock.Values )
{
}
```

Note that you need to specify the Values property of the collection if you are iterating a Dictionary<T,T>. The Car object is the class that you previously created; the concept is that a Car object contains details about an instance of the Car—how many wheels, how many doors, engine size, and so on—and it also contains an enum variable type for Manufacturer.

Continuing with the car yard example, this car yard has all the same vehicles from the same manufacturer, safety checked at the same time. Broncos are done on a Tuesday, and Mustang's are done on a Wednesday.

1. Open Blend and add yet another button called btnMakeCars.

2. Add another button called btnUpdateServiceStatus is setting its IsEnabled property to false.

3. If you have been following the application layout, you probably have quite a few buttons down the left side of your UI. Select all the buttons by holding down the Ctrl key before drawing the selection rectangle on the artboard.

4. You should see all the buttons are selected in the Objects and Timeline category, right-click on one of the selected buttons and then select Group Into from the context menu, selecting Stack Panel from the child menu that appears from there.

10

5. Add a small Grid and embed inside it two RadioButton elements.

6. Name one RadioButton radBronco and the other radMustang.

7. Save the project in Blend.

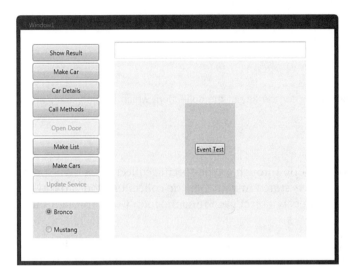

FIGURE 10.17   The final layout of the UI.

8. Add a Click handler for both of the new buttons, which should return you to Visual Studio.

9. Open your Car class and add a new DependencyProperty called IsServiced of type bool.

10. Return to Window1.xaml.cs.

The code in Listing 10.26 shows a new method being called. This method creates a new instance of the Car class from a set of provided parameters. The method returns the Car instance, which is then added to the Car's global collection for use in Listing 10.27.

LISTING 10.26   Creating the Stock List

```
        //Global Dictionary created for the car yard
        public Dictionary<int, Car> CarsInStock = new Dictionary<int, Car>();

        private void btnMakeCars_Click(object sender, RoutedEventArgs e)
        {
            //Simple list of Client references that will be used as a Key in the
collection
            int ClientRef_1 = 5552129;
            int ClientRef_2 = 5553241;
```

```
        int ClientRef_3 = 5555481;
        int ClientRef_4 = 5553197;
        int ClientRef_5 = 5558724;

        //Building the collection of clients in the collection
        this.CarsInStock.Add(ClientRef_1, this.MakeNewCar(4, 4, 3,
Car.CarModel.Bronco));
        this.CarsInStock.Add(ClientRef_2, this.MakeNewCar(2, 4, 2,
Car.CarModel.Mustang));
        this.CarsInStock.Add(ClientRef_3, this.MakeNewCar(2, 4, 4,
Car.CarModel.Mustang));
        this.CarsInStock.Add(ClientRef_4, this.MakeNewCar(4, 4, 4,
Car.CarModel.Escort));
        this.CarsInStock.Add(ClientRef_5, this.MakeNewCar(4, 4, 3,
Car.CarModel.Bronco));

        //Allow the cars to be serviced now
        this.btnUpdateServiceStatus.IsEnabled = true;


    }


    /// <summary>
    /// Makes the new car.
    /// </summary>
    /// <param name="NumberOfDoors">The number of doors.</param>
    /// <param name="NumberOfWheels">The number of wheels.</param>
    /// <param name="NumberOfSeats">The number of seats.</param>
    /// <param name="CarModel">The car model.</param>
    /// <returns></returns>
    private Car MakeNewCar(int NumberOfDoors,
        int NumberOfWheels,
        int NumberOfSeats,
        Car.CarModel CarModel)
    {
        Car NewCar = new Car();

        NewCar.NumberOfDoors = NumberOfDoors ;
        NewCar.NumberOfWheels = NumberOfWheels   ;
        NewCar.NumberOfSeats = NumberOfSeats ;

        NewCar.Model = CarModel ;

        return NewCar;

    }
```

10

LISTING 10.27   The Finishing Touches

```
/// <summary>
      /// Handles the Click event of the btnUpdateServiceStatus control.
      /// </summary>
      /// <param name="sender">The source of the event.</param>
      /// <param name="e">The <see cref="System.Windows.RoutedEventArgs"/>
instance containing the event data.</param>
      private void btnUpdateServiceStatus_Click(object sender, RoutedEventArgs e)
      {
          //Determine which car should be serviced
          Car.CarModel ServiceType;

          if (this.radBronco.IsChecked == true)
              ServiceType = Car.CarModel.Bronco;
          else
              ServiceType = Car.CarModel.Mustang ;


          foreach (Car item in this.CarsInStock.Values)
          {
              if (item.Model == ServiceType)
                  item.IsServiced = true;
          }

          MessageBox.Show("All " + ServiceType.ToString() + "'s are now
serviced.");
      }
```

The code in Listing 10.27 enables the iteration of the collection using a foreach loop, setting the IsServiced status of the Car type as selected by the user with the RadioButtons.

This is a simple enough example, but using foreach is invaluable in data binding management and various other areas of an application. You can use a foreach loop for many other types of collections, not just Generic Lists and Dictionaries. This example showed you how suited the foreach is to a scenario that occurs often in applications.

Summary

By this stage you can see just how much functionality you can add to your application, just by knowing a little about these concepts. Coding can be as simple or as complex as you like, and while performance and elegance should always be a primary concern, readability of code to understand the intended actions takes an even higher precedence.

The concepts of creating classes and using those classes with your UI are at the core of creating complex WPF applications. After all, the humble Button is a class, as are all the control elements you use in your user interface. Understanding how their properties are created and how you may extend these objects will be shown in Chapter 18, "Creating a Custom Control," with modifying an existing control type being the subject of the chapter.

If you are interested at learning how to code with a much greater explanation of .NET concepts and C#, I recommend *Sams Teach Yourself C# in 21 Days* by Bradley L. Jones. He starts from the beginning and leads you to some more advanced uses of the language in a very nice way.

10

PART IV

Extended Graphic Tools

IN THIS PART

CHAPTER 11

Graphic Items

Microsoft Expression Blend has been sold to the masses as a designer's tool first rather than explaining the concept of a XAML architect, and then trying to make people fit the role who might be designers or, in some cases, visual developers. Several tools exist in the application to assist you as a graphic designer in creating visual assets and in creating a functioning prototype that you could then leverage as production code, cutting the development lifecycle time dramatically.

Understandably, you might already be comfortable with another application that you have spent a great deal of time learning, so you're hesitant about just how much of this tool you want to use for graphic design purposes. The good news is that it's all relatively simple, and in Blend you are sure to leverage the knowledge you already gained in other applications. The difference is that you might never before have had to script or code for graphic assets, and teaching you to do so is a goal of this chapter. Together with your newfound coding knowledge from the preceding chapter, you will learn how to define and apply colors to the Stroke and Fill properties of objects. In this chapter, you will look at these tools in detail, in both the Blend UI and in XAML (Extensible Application Markup Language), and you will learn how to create the code instances that also will be inevitably required.

Sample Application

The markup in Listing 11.1 is represented in Figure 11.1. It contains a basic rectangle that has no fill or stroke applied

and two buttons that you will add Click handlers to so that you can then perform the
required coding.

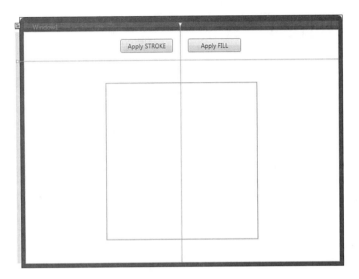

FIGURE 11.1   The basic application.

LISTING 11.1   Setting Up the Example

```
<Grid x:Name="LayoutRoot">
    <Grid.ColumnDefinitions>
        <ColumnDefinition Width="0.5*"/>
        <ColumnDefinition Width="0.5*"/>
    </Grid.ColumnDefinitions>
    <Grid.RowDefinitions>
        <RowDefinition Height="0.126*"/>
        <RowDefinition Height="0.874*"/>
    </Grid.RowDefinitions>
    <Rectangle Fill="{x:Null}" Stroke="{x:Null}" StrokeThickness="0"
➥HorizontalAlignment="Center" Margin="0,0,0,0" x:Name="recDemo"
➥VerticalAlignment="Center" Width="300" Height="300" Grid.ColumnSpan="2"
➥Grid.Row="1"/>
    <Button HorizontalAlignment="Right" Margin="0,15,15,15" x:Name="btnApplyStroke"
➥Width="105" Content="Apply STROKE"/>
    <Button HorizontalAlignment="Left" Margin="15,15,0,15" x:Name="btnApplyFill"
➥Width="105" Content="Apply FILL" Grid.Column="1"/>
</Grid>
```

You are now going to learn how to first create and then apply a *stroke* (which is property
of some control types that takes a brush type) as well as to create different brushes and

apply them to the rectangle's `Fill` property in Blend and then in code. The concepts shown here in code and XAML markup are similar in usage to many other property and object interactions involving brush painting, so you will be able to apply these concepts further.

Different Strokes

Blend provides for a well featured "painting" environment inside the Brushes category of the Properties panel as described in Chapter 3, "Expression Blend Panels."

In the following steps, you are going to be taking a closer look at the advanced properties of the Appearance category, as shown in Figure 11.2, and how the values you apply determine your result.

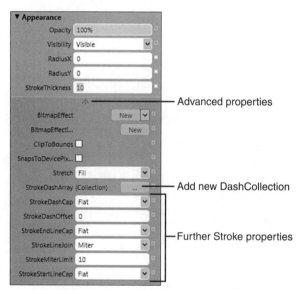

FIGURE 11.2   The array of properties available in the advanced properties section of the Appearance category.

1. Select the recDemo Rectangle element in the Blend UI and then open the Properties panel and Brushes category.

2. Select the `Stroke` property and apply a `SolidColorBrush` in whichever color you choose. By default, the stroke is black for a Rectangle element and has a `StrokeThickness` property value of 1.

3. For this example, you need to be seeing the stroke as you are making changes to the properties, so set the `StrokeThickness` to 10.

4. The remaining advanced properties have no bearing on the stroke's appearance unless a `DoubleCollection` is specified because all the properties pertain to the

appearance of stroke dashes and the caps of such dashes. Click the Add Another Item button shown in Figure 11.2 to add a new DoubleCollection.

5. Figure 11.3 shows the Double Collection Editor and where to add new Double values to the collection. In this sample, you should add two Double items, setting the Double at index position 0 to 5 and the Double at index 1 to 2.

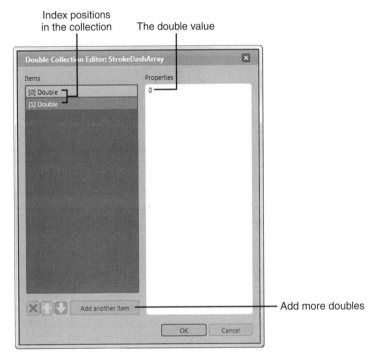

FIGURE 11.3   How to determine the index position of an item in the collection.

Listing 11.2 shows the resultant XAML markup that Blend creates for the DoubleCollection applied to the StrokeDashArray of the Rectangle element.

LISTING 11.2   The Applied StrokeDashArray Shown Bolded

```
<Rectangle Fill="{x:Null}"
Stroke="#FFC51313"
StrokeThickness="10"
HorizontalAlignment="Center"
Margin="0,0,0,0"
x:Name="recDemo"
VerticalAlignment="Center"
Width="300"
Height="300"
Grid.ColumnSpan="2"
```

```
Grid.Row="1"
StrokeDashArray="5 2"
/>
```

6. You should now have a well defined dash pattern on your stroke. The previous values entered into the Double items created the pattern. Bearing in mind that the StrokeThickness is set to 10, imagine a single unit being a 10×10 block. So, setting the first Double item to 5 makes the dash appear five times wider than it is high. The second value specifies the width of the gap.

   The following list details the enumerated values possible for the StrokeDashCap property, which you should set to Round:

   Property Value

   Flat (default)

   Square

   Round

   Triangle

7. Set the StrokeDashOffset property value to 3. You should note that this changes the appearance of the stroke pattern (see Figure 11.4), but what it actually does is allows you to specify the point in the dash pattern at which the dash should start.

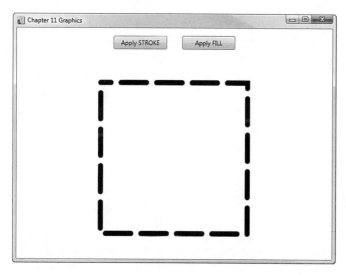

FIGURE 11.4   The end result of creating a dash pattern on the stroke.

Try the remaining properties. You will need to add a line to the artboard to see them because they only apply to a line that has a start and a finish.

1. Select the Pencil tool and draw a wave type horizontal line across the center of the artboard as shown in Figure 11.5.

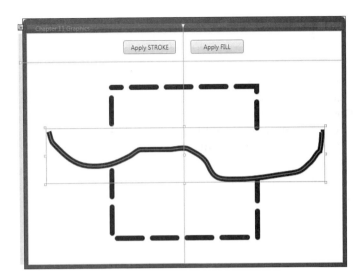

FIGURE 11.5   The described view.

2. Modify the property values of the StrokeEndLineCap, StrokeLineJoin, StrokeMiterLimit, and StrokeStartLineCap to see the effect that these properties have on a path.

The Stroke property plays an important part in how an element can be perceived visually. It can add depth or projection and with the right combination of color and GradientBrush applied, you can even create shadow.

To continue with this chapter, you can remove the path and Rectangle element, create a new rectangle back in the center of the artboard named recDemo, or simply remove the path and reset the Stroke properties for the rectangle. Remember to remove the Double items in the StrokeDashArray! You are now going to learn how to create and apply brushes and strokes in code.

Brushes Category

The Brush class object is concealed in many ways inside the Blend UI. Each time you use the Brushes category of the Properties panel, you are creating instances of brushes that are assigned to the various background, fill, border, opacity mask, stroke, and endless other Brush type properties.

You have already used several classes derived from the Brush class: SolidColorBrush, LinearGradientBrush, and RadialGradientBrush. I am sure you can see where I am going with this.

Using the sample application described previously, you will now create some brushes in code, which should solidify further understanding of properties, classes, and objects:

1. Starting with the Button element btnApplyStroke in Blend, add a Click handler through the Properties panel, Event Viewer to launch Visual Studio.

2. The Rectangle element in the application is named recDemo, so you should call the object and view the properties you want to use. Figure 11.6 shows the list of Stroke properties you are going to work with first.

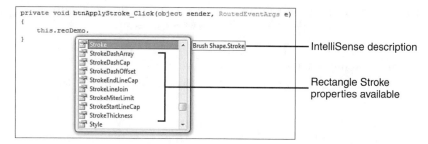

FIGURE 11.6   The IntelliSense view of the various Stroke properties of the Rectangle element.

3. In Figure 11.6, you can see the IntelliSense description of the object property, which shows the type expected for this property—that of a brush. Add the code in Listing 11.3 to the btnApplyStroke Click handler code to create a SolidColorBrush object.

LISTING 11.3   Creating a Simple SolidColorBrush in Code

```
private void btnApplyStroke_Click(object sender, RoutedEventArgs e)
{
    SolidColorBrush SimpleBrush = new SolidColorBrush();
    SimpleBrush.Color = Colors.Red;
    this.recDemo.Stroke   = SimpleBrush;
    this.recDemo.StrokeThickness = 3;
}
```

Even though the *type* expected by the Stroke property of the rectangle is Brush, you must use an object that is derived from the Brush type directly because the Brush class is an abstract class. That means you can't call a brush in the following way:

```
Brush WrongBrush = new Brush();
```

You need to use a class that inherits from the Brush *type,* and thankfully the names of such classes aren't too hard to remember. Along with SolidColorBrush are also the following descriptively named Brush objects:

RadialGradientBrush

LinearGradientBrush

ImageBrush

DrawingBrush

VisualBrush

You will note that you have had to assign values to two Stroke properties. You must supply a StrokeThickness value, otherwise it (the stroke) won't show up.

Another Stroke property is StrokeDashArray, which can only have a Collection (a DoubleCollection to be accurate) assigned to it. In the previous coding chapter, you learned about generic collections and saw how to add items to a collection. The same principles apply here.

Listing 11.4 shows how to create a dash pattern in the stroke by creating a DoubleCollection. The final property assigned defines how the cap of the dash should look in the stroke by assigning a PenLineCap-enumerated value. (You learned about enumerations in Chapter 10, "Visual Studio: C# Primer.")

LISTING 11.4   Creating a Simple DashCollection in Code

```
DoubleCollection DashCollection = new DoubleCollection(4);
        DashCollection.Add(6);
        DashCollection.Add(3);
        DashCollection.Add(9);
        DashCollection.Add(3);

        this.recDemo.StrokeDashArray = DashCollection;
        this.recDemo.StrokeDashCap = PenLineCap.Round;
```

The Double values added to the DoubleCollection define how the dash should appear. The value 6, which is the first item, specifies that the first part of the dash should be six units long. The second part, number 3, says that the gap in the dash at this point should be three units. The next value specifies the dash again, this time nine units long, and last, the number 3 again specifies a gap value. The result is shown in Figure 11.7. You can play around with the different values and see how the effects render.

Applying a fill is similar to applying a stroke in real terms. You already know how to create a derived Brush object, which is pretty much all you need to do in code to assign your choice to the Fill property of the Rectangle element. Add a Click handler for the btnApplyFill button and then add the code shown in Listing 11.5.

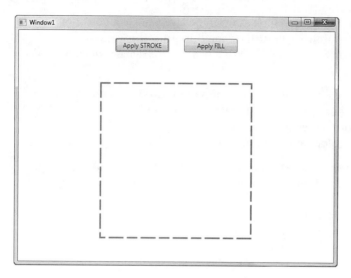

FIGURE 11.7   The dash-gap stepping of the `DoubleCollection`.

LISTING 11.5   Creating Gradient Brushes in Code

```
private void btnApplyFill_Click(object sender, RoutedEventArgs e)
{

    GradientStopCollection GradientStops = new GradientStopCollection(3);

    GradientStop FirstStop = new GradientStop();
    FirstStop.Color = Color.FromRgb(0, 143, 255);
    FirstStop.Offset = 0.0;

    GradientStops.Add(FirstStop);
    GradientStops.Add(new GradientStop(Color.FromRgb(0, 0,0), 0.8));
    GradientStops.Add(new GradientStop(Colors.White,1.0));

    RadialGradientBrush RectRadial = new RadialGradientBrush();
    RectRadial.GradientStops = GradientStops;

    //Additional properties
    RectRadial.Center = new Point(0.2, 0.2);
    RectRadial.RadiusX = 0.5;
    RectRadial.RadiusY = 0.5;

    RectRadial.Freeze();

    this.recDemo.Fill = RectRadial;
}
```

Listing 11.5 adds some interesting areas to look at when creating a Brush object in code. You are not creating a Brush first, but are creating some things (in this case GradientStops) as a bit of preparation for using with a RadialGradientBrush later in the code.

When creating a GradientStop object, the two most important properties are the Color and the Offset (or position in percentage terms) that the GradientStop should be. You can see that you created a color by specifying the method FromRgb(), which allowed you to enter a red, green, and blue color value up to 255.

Because the GradientStops are the type used in the GradientStopCollection, you then call the familiar Add() method to supply the created object as an item to the collection:

```
GradientStop FirstStop = new GradientStop();
FirstStop.Color = Color.FromRgb(0, 143, 255);
FirstStop.Offset = 0.0;

GradientStops.Add(FirstStop);
```

You added the next two GradientStops directly and they are no different from the previous explicit creation of the GradientStop. All you have done here is write a shorter version of the same thing, specifying different Color and Offset values:

```
GradientStops.Add(new GradientStop(Color.FromRgb(0, 0,0), 0.8));
GradientStops.Add(new GradientStop(Colors.White,1.0));
```

Finally you created and instantiated a new RadialGradientBrush object:

```
RadialGradientBrush RectRadial = new RadialGradientBrush();
```

You then assigned the GradientStopCollection to the Brush's property with the following:

```
RectRadial.GradientStops = GradientStops;
```

Then you went about setting some more properties on the Brush itself.

A new method named Freeze() was called. This makes the Brush unable to be modified and improves the performance of the underlying drawing routines that actually paint with this brush.

Lastly, you supplied your new Brush to the Fill property of the rectangle with the following:

```
this.recDemo.Fill = RectRadial;
```

You should have ended up with a display similar to that shown in Figure 11.8.

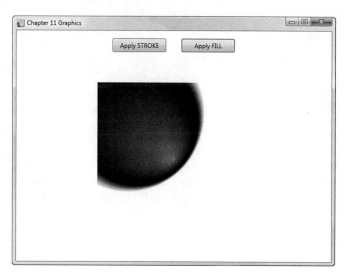

FIGURE 11.8   The resultant `RadialGradientBrush` applied to the Rectangle element.

Creating the same result in XAML is simple. It's even easier if you use Blend to do all the magic for you. Listing 11.6 contains the XAML markup required to achieve a similar effect.

LISTING 11.6   A Transformed `RadialGradientBrush` Applied to the Rectangles Fill Property

```
<Rectangle Stroke="{x:Null}" StrokeThickness="0" HorizontalAlignment="Center"
➥Margin="0,0,0,0" x:Name="recDemo" VerticalAlignment="Center" Width="300"
➥Height="300" Grid.ColumnSpan="2" Grid.Row="1">
          <Rectangle.Fill>
              <RadialGradientBrush GradientOrigin="0.179,0.809">
                  <RadialGradientBrush.RelativeTransform>
                      <TransformGroup>
                          <ScaleTransform CenterX="0.5" CenterY="0.5"
➥ScaleX="0.995" ScaleY="0.995"/>
                          <SkewTransform AngleX="0" AngleY="0" CenterX="0.5"
➥CenterY="0.5"/>
                          <RotateTransform Angle="-90.412" CenterX="0.5"
➥CenterY="0.5"/>
                          <TranslateTransform X="-0.311" Y="-0.288"/>
                      </TransformGroup>
                  </RadialGradientBrush.RelativeTransform>
                  <GradientStop Color="#FF008FFF" Offset="0"/>
                  <GradientStop Color="#FFFFFFFF" Offset="1"/>
```

```
            <GradientStop Color="#FF000000" Offset="0.768"/>
        </RadialGradientBrush>
    </Rectangle.Fill>
</Rectangle>
```

Transformations

Transformations is a generic term used to describe the scaling, rotating, resizing, reposition-ing (translating), skewing, and flipping of objects on your artboard. These functions are all available from within the Blend UI under the Transform category of the Properties panel (see Figure 11.9), and can be applied to almost any object that appears on the artboard, even text controls!

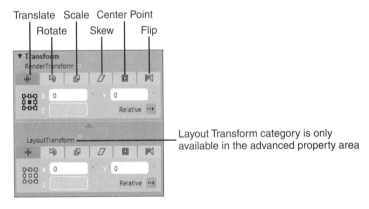

FIGURE 11.9   The Transform category with the two transformation property types (render and layout transforms) available in WPF (Windows Presentation Foundation) as well as each of the property tabs.

So, what's the difference between the two?

▶ **RenderTransform**—Transformations are applied to the element after the parent layout logic is applied, therefore giving a performance benefit to the application.

▶ **LayoutTransform**—Transformations applied to an element through this property are applied to the element before the parent of the element applies layout logic to position the element.

In most cases, you should strive to apply transformations to an object through the RenderTransform property, mostly because of the performance benefit but also because sometimes parent layout logic can reposition an element to a point that was not intended, thus giving you and your user an unexpected result. For that reason, the following information will focus on the `RenderTransform` property of the Transform category.

Working with Blend provides excellent visual feedback as to the result of any transformations that you apply to objects. The artboard in most cases shows you what effect a transformation has by applying it to your element, but it also shows you the original positioning and state of the element before such transforms are applied.

Create a new application in Blend and add a single Rectangle element to the center of the artboard, with an approximate size of 100 wide by 100 high. It's probably best to set the `Fill` property to an arbitrary color so that you can see the rectangle as well.

Translate

Translating the element is simply giving instructions to move the element from one position to another in the coordinate space of the element. By default, the top-left corner of an element is position 0 on the x-axis and position 0 on the y-axis. In the `RenderTransform` property category in the Blend UI, you can see that the z-axis is disabled because you are not working with 3D objects in 3D space, although this does have the same effect only with a third axis (Z) when working in 3D.

Enter the values 100 into the `TranslateX` property and 100 into the `TranslateY` property. You can see that the element has now been repositioned on the screen, but if you open the Layout category and view the `Alignment` and `Margin` properties, you will see that the layout logic applied to the element remains unchanged.

Why is this important? When you animate an element, you are indeed animating properties on the element, nothing more. In a Timeline-Storyboard, when you reposition an element on the artboard, you are modifying the `RenderTransform` property values and not the Layout properties such as margin, alignments, and so on. You still could modify them if you wanted to, however.

The following example demonstrates this. Make sure that you have a new application with a Rectangle element, 100×100 located in the center of the artboard, using the Layout properties.

1. Click on the Create New Timeline button. (See Chapter 3 for more information on the Interaction panel if required.)
2. Leave the default name of Timeline1 (it is not important at the moment).
3. With the Rectangle element selected and the Playhead position at 0:00.000, record a new KeyFrame with the rectangle in its current position.
4. Advanced the Playhead position to 0:01.000 and record a new KeyFrame.
5. With the Selection (V) tool, move the mouse to slightly off center and select the rectangle, dragging it to a new position. Figure 11.10 shows you the dots that indicate

the transformation process line of the element, and Figure 11.11 shows you the values that have been added to the RenderTransform, TranslateX, and TranslateY properties.

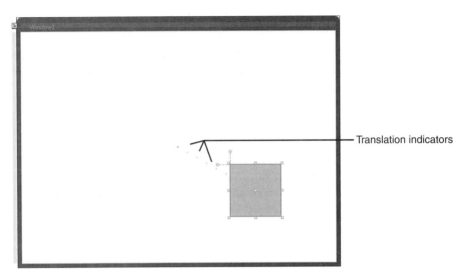

FIGURE 11.10   The visual cues Blend provides for translations.

FIGURE 11.11   The changes applied in the RenderTransform category.

Rotate

A self-explanatory title, this property allows you to rotate the element around its current center point, which is indicated by a dot (see Figure 11.12).

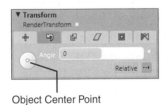

FIGURE 11.12   The rotation transform.

While Timeline recording is still on (indicated by a red border around the window, with a label at the top left of the window), ensure that the Playhead is still at position 0:01.000. Switch to the Rotate tab of the RenderTransform property panel and set the angle to 75. You can move your mouse over the circle indicator, but I find it much easier and more accurate to type the value in manually.

Rewind the animation and play it in the Timeline. Was this the effect you were expecting? The rotation is applied to the element of the period from KeyFrame to KeyFrame, so the rotation transformation is animated from the first to the last KeyFrame. (There's more on animation in Chapter 14, "Animations with Storyboards.")

If you select the Playhead indicator with your mouse and drag it between the two KeyFrames, you can see the Angle property of the Rotation transformation increase and decrease accordingly.

Scale

I am sure that you have had some experience with scaling objects (maybe visual assets) at some stage. Blend allows you to perform scaling on an element on a per axis basis giving you finite control of the result. With the Playhead position remaining at position 0:01.000, modify the ScaleX and ScaleY values to an arbitrary value for each. You will notice that the default value in both properties is 1. This means that the scale of the element is currently 1:1 or full size. If you enter the value 2, you double the scale of the element on that axis, and likewise on any other axis you modify.

Again, when playing the animation, the value is animated or "tweened" between the two KeyFrames.

Skew

To demonstrate the effect of skew on an element in Blend, you are advised to set the element rotation value back to 0 while the Playhead is at position 0:01.000.

Skew is applied to an axis direction of an element while locking the element at its current position. In this example, the rectangle's center position is still 50,50 (X,Y). The skew is applied to the element along an axis, based on the center point of the element. A value of 20 in SkewX moves the top edge 10 pixels to the left and the bottom edge 10 pixels to the right, leaving the center position of the element intact (see Figure 11.13). The same applied in a vertical fashion when the SkewY value is modified.

Play with skew; animating the skew values certainly can give you some wild results as well.

Center Point

When you first look at the CenterX and CenterY properties in the Center Point tab, you will note that both values are 0.5. This indicates that by default the center point of the object is half the width and half the height (see Figure 11.14).

Right-click on the last KeyFrame in the Timeline and delete it. This should remove all the transformations that you might have applied to this point in the chapter.

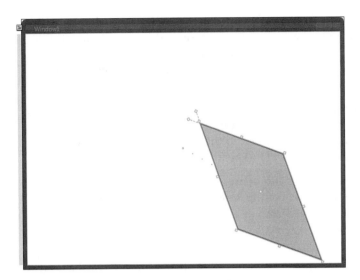

FIGURE 11.13   The result of a skew transformation applied to both SkewX and SkewY.

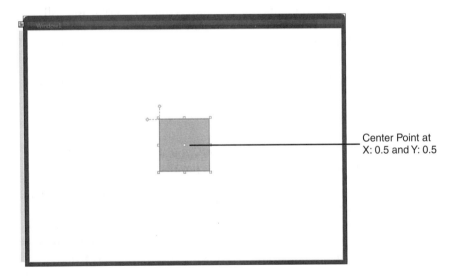

Center Point at
X: 0.5 and Y: 0.5

FIGURE 11.14   The current default position of the center point of the element.

Keep a close eye on the dot as you modify the CenterX and CenterY property values. Setting both properties to 0 will make the center point of the element the top-left corner, and the value 2 applied to both properties will make the center point appear at twice the width and twice the height of the element's position.

Create a new KeyFrame at Playhead position 0:01.000 again, quickly skip back to the Rotation property tab, and apply an Angle property value of 35. Move the Playhead position with the mouse and you will clearly see the path that the element now rotates around the center point.

Flip

The flip transformation is easy to understand: You have a choice of three axes (only two are available in 2D) and you can simply "flip" the element's location on the specified axis.

Delete the KeyFrame at position 0:01.000 to reset the transformations applied, and make sure that the center point transformation property values are set back to 0.5 for both.

The easiest way to see the flip transformation effect is to apply a LinearGradientBrush to the Rectangle element's Fill property, which you should do now. Open the Flip Transform tab and click on the Flip X Axis button. Nice and simple!

Motion Paths

You might recall Chapter 7, "Using the Blend Toolbox: Tools and Common Controls," where you went through using the Path tools to create that exciting egg cup? (Yeah, I know...just kidding.) A fantastic feature of Blend is the ability to declare any Path element as a motion path for other objects to follow during an animation. The scenario where you would use a motion path is pretty much up to your own imagination; one of the first of such scenarios that comes to mind could be that a lens flare type effect could be created to highlight an item to the user.

The following example shows you how to use the motion path in an animation to do just that and after it, you will be surprised at just how little amount of effort it takes to create the effect. Add the XAML markup in Listing 11.7 to a new project in Blend.

LISTING 11.7   Creating the Simple Ellipse Sample

```
<Grid x:Name="LayoutRoot">
    <Ellipse Stroke="#FF0055FF" HorizontalAlignment="Center"
VerticalAlignment="Center" Width="250" Height="200">
        <Ellipse.Fill>
            <RadialGradientBrush GradientOrigin="0.724,0.095">
                <GradientStop Color="#FF0031FF" Offset="1"/>
                <GradientStop Color="#FF00F9FF" Offset="0"/>
            </RadialGradientBrush>
        </Ellipse.Fill>
    </Ellipse>
</Grid>
```

In the center of the artboard, you should have a simple Ellipse element, around which you will attempt to add a glow orbit by following these steps:

1. Select the Ellipse tool and draw a single Ellipse element as shown in Figure 11.15. This ellipse will serve as the path for the Glow element to travel on during the animation. Name the element MotionPath.

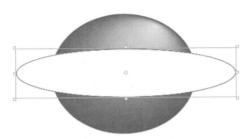

FIGURE 11.15   The placement of the MotionPath ellipse.

2. In the Properties panel, select the `Fill` property of the new ellipse and set it to No Brush.

3. You are now going to create the glow effect using another Ellipse element. Select the Ellipse tool, draw your glow similar to the depiction in Figure 11.16, and then name it GlowEllipse.

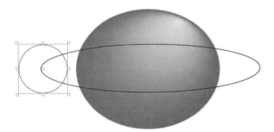

FIGURE 11.16   The placement of the GlowEllipse element.

4. Set the `Stroke` property of GlowEllipse to No Brush.

5. Select the `Fill` property and assign a `RadialGradientBrush`, setting the `GradientStop` at position 1 to an alpha value of 0. Figure 11.17 shows the settings that you might also try.

6. Select the original Ellipse element that you created for the motion path (MotionPath) and set the `Stroke` property to No Brush.

7. Keeping the MotionPath element selected, select the Object menu from the top of the Blend UI; find the Path menu item and then select Convert to Motion Path from the resulting pop-up menu items. You should see the Convert to Motion Path dialog box as shown in Figure 11.18.

8. The dialog is asking which element you want to move on the motion path, so you should select GlowEllipse and click OK.

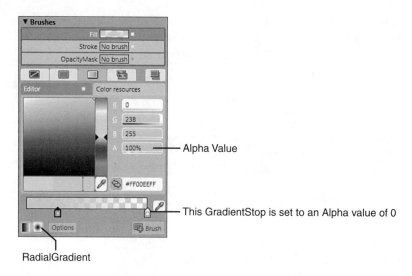

RadialGradient

FIGURE 11.17   The Brush setting applied to GlowEllipse.

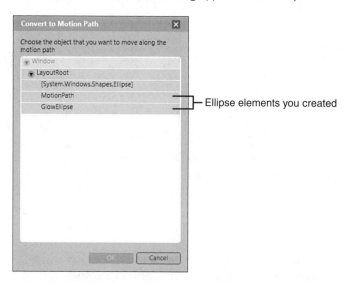

FIGURE 11.18   The Convert to Motion Path dialog box.

9. You should now note that a default timeline called Timeline1 has been created and in the Objects and Timeline category of the Interaction panel. GlowEllipse now has a purple border around it with an arrow indicating that child levels are available for the element.

10. Click on the drill-down arrow of GlowEllipse, each element that it contains, and so on until you can drill down no deeper. You should now have three animation elements present under GlowEllipse, with the last being Motion Path.

11. Even though no KeyFrames have been created, GlowEllipse is now attached to the motion path, which has an animation sequence embedded in the Storyboard, as indicated by the block shading on the Timeline as shown in Figure 11.19.

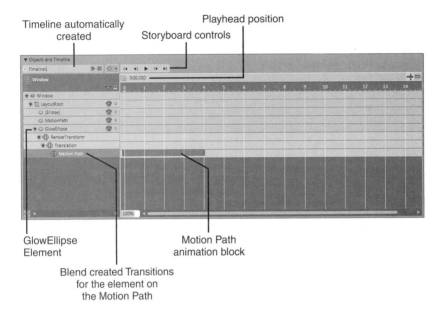

Timeline automatically created

Storyboard controls

Playhead position

GlowEllipse Element

Blend created Transitions for the element on the Motion Path

Motion Path animation block

FIGURE 11.19   The newly created animation elements.

12. You can click Play on the Storyboard controls to view the animation. The time taken for the animation to complete is by default 2 seconds, but you can modify this by dragging the beginning and/or the end of the animation block to a new time point on the Storyboard.

13. The animation looks almost correct except for the fact that the glow still appears when it is supposed to be moving around behind the Globe type element. You need to perform two additional tasks to give some authenticity to this animation. First you need to change the scaling of the glow to give the image some depth, and then you need to control the opacity of the glow to simulate dimensional perception of the elements.

14. Figure 11.19 also pointed out on the Storyboard where the Playhead's position is, which should be a small, yellow, downward-pointing triangle. You will need to click and hold this to move GlowEllipse to certain positions that you need.

15. Selecting the Motion Path animation block, stretch the time in which the animation completes from 2 to 4 seconds as shown in Figure 11.20.

16. Move the Playhead to position 0 on the Timeline and add a new KeyFrame.

17. Open the Transform category of the Properties tab and select the Scale tab. You should notice that the values for X and Y are both 1.

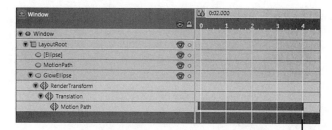

Motion Path animation stretched to position 4 in the timeline

FIGURE 11.20   The stretched Motion Path animation block.

18. Move the Playhead to position 1 and add a new KeyFrame. Now set the values of both X and Y in the Scale tab to 1.5.

19. Move the yellow Playhead to position 2 on the timeline. Considering the start and end of the animation depict the Glow beginning at the far right side, position 2 should position your glow element to the far left of the sphere.

20. Because the glow should be moving around the element from this point, you want to scale down the glow element slightly until it reaches the center point directly behind the sphere in the middle. Double-click the GlowEllipse element so that it becomes the selected element, and then add a new KeyFrame at position 2, setting the X and Y values in the Scale tab back to 1.

21. Move the Playhead position to 3 and add another KeyFrame as GlowEllipse is in the center of the Sphere.

22. Set both the X and Y values to 0.5, which should reduce the size of the GlowEllipse element.

23. Move the Playhead position to 4 and again add a new KeyFrame. Now set the X and Y values in the Scale tab of the Transform category back to 1.

24. Play the animation using the Storyboard controls and you should now have a better-looking GlowEllipse element that gives the perception of depth to your animation. Your animation won't be 100% smooth at this point, but you will learn more about controlling the EaseIn and EaseOut values of KeyFrames in Chapter 14. During the previous steps, you should have noticed that modifying the Scale values automatically created a scale animation element.

25. Now you need to control the opacity levels of the glow as it moves around the sphere. Again using the Playhead positions starting at 1 and then moving around the sphere, you will set the opacity to give the appearance that the GlowEllipse element has gone behind the sphere.

Figure 11.21 shows the point at which you should add a KeyFrame to the GlowEllipse element and set the Opacity value to 100% in the Appearance category of the Properties tab.

Add a new KeyFrame at this point and set the Opacity value to 100%

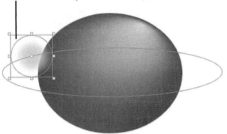

FIGURE 11.21   The start of the GlowEllipse element's fade.

Figure 11.22 shows the point at which you should set the opacity of the GlowEllipse element to 0%.

With the Opacity value set to 0, the glow Ellipse element is invisible.

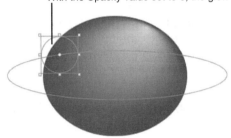

FIGURE 11.22   The point at which the GlowEllipse element should be completely invisible.

26. Moving the Timeline further toward the end, you will see the points where the GlowEllipse is behind the sphere and where it should reappear. Using the same techniques as previous, add new KeyFrames and set the opacity of the GlowEllipse element accordingly to complete the effect. Check each existing KeyFrame to ensure the opacity is set to 0 for the GlowEllipse if it is behind the sphere.

That is a simple effect that now you know how to achieve, and will take you no time to implement in your own interfaces if it is required. You can spend a lot of time perfecting the effect, getting the glow just right, and the fade out and the scaling exactly as they should be. It's all up to you just how perfect you want it to be.

Motion paths don't have to be around only an Ellipse though; you can convert any Path element to a motion path by selecting it and then making selections in the Object menu and subsequent menu choices.

Bitmap Effects

For sometime now I have been yelling and screaming at anyone who will listen about the evil that bitmap effects are. In case you are new to the scene, have been living in a cupboard, or have just ignored me (the latter is probably the case if you came across my ramblings previously), you might be wondering why I am so against their use.

Bitmap effects are a serious performance degrader in WPF because they are software-rendered at runtime, and any visual object they are attached to also becomes a software-rendered object. This is also the case for objects that contain children, such as a panel. The bitmap effect is applied to the container and then down through the visual tree to all the child objects contained within it. Bitmap effects work by analyzing a visual, pixel by pixel, and applying various changes to the pixel structure, returning the entire collection as a `BitmapSource` for output, so the process on large visuals can be very time-consuming in computational terms.

The other downside to bitmap effects is that they require full trust execution to run, so any application that has even the smallest visual with a bitmap effect applied will fail partial trust execution. Therefore it cannot be deployed via a web browser in such a case as an XBAP (XAML browser application) or Silverlight application.

Will this change in the future? YES!!!

Microsoft has now committed to fixing this issue in .NET Framework 4 release due at the end of 2008 (well, in Microsoft time scale, that is).

Beware the Hidden Bitmap Effect

Bitmap effects can sometimes be hiding in assets given to you by other designers, most notably the effects included in Expression Design. When using these vector assets, you need to be sure that the asset is not your downfall in performance terms of your application. Blend is a good testing stick as far as this is concerned. Because the artboard is live, you will notice Blend's own performance degrade substantially when a bitmap effect is applied to the wrong asset. Search the XAML and be on the lookout!

So, that is the bad side of things, and even though bitmap effects offer fantastic visual effects, I strongly advise against using them until the hardware accelerated functionality comes in. But if using them is a must, do so sparingly on small assets and objects.

WPF provides five bitmap effects inside Blend (see Table 11.1), but you can create your own (very nasty experience involving C++) or purchase a library of effects from a third party. It was rumored at some stage that Microsoft's WPF team was working on a substantial release of bitmap effects. Some 40 odd bitmap effects were in development, but strangely enough, very little has been mentioned since 2005.

TABLE 11.1   The Current Supplied Set of Bitmap Effects in Blend

Bitmap Effect Name	Description
BevelBitmapEffect	Creates the appearance of a raised surface on an object, based on the curvature of a bevel
BlurBitmapEffect	Creates a blurred result similar to an out-of-focus photo
DropShadowBitmapEffect	Places a shadow effect behind an object
EmbossBitmapEffect	Gives depth perception to an image
OuterGlowBitmapEffect	Creates a glow pattern, or halo, around an object's extremities

Bitmap effects usually also contain various properties that allow you to modify the effects that they produce. For example, the Blur effect allows you to specify both a radius of the effect as well as the kernel type, Gaussian or box, used to create the effect.

Bitmap effects can be applied in the Blend UI and XAML as well as code. Figure 11.23 shows the result of all five bitmap effects applied against the same image (JPEG image) of the letter A.

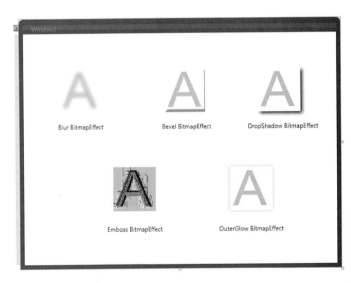

FIGURE 11.23   All singular bitmap effects applied to the same image for comparison.

BitmapEffectGroup

Bitmap effects can also be applied one on top of the other inside a BitmapEffectGroup, which is a collection of bitmap effects. The order of application is important as Figure 11.24 demonstrates, with two bitmap effects reversed to show the difference.

FIGURE 11.24   The results of `BitmapEffectGroups`.

To apply a bitmap effect using Blend, select the target element and then open the Advanced Properties tab of the Appearance category of the Properties panel. As Figure 11.25 shows, you have a choice of six enumerated values to choose from in the Bitmap Effect drop-down list. (Table 11.1 details the choices, except for `BitmapEffectGroup`.) Simply select your choice to apply it.

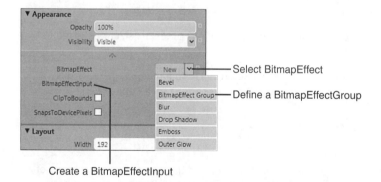

FIGURE 11.25   The bitmap effect choices available.

There you will also see any additional properties that the effect offers, which allows you finite control of your effect results.

BitmapEffectInput

Figure 11.25 also points out an additional bitmap effect–based property called `BitmapEffectInput`. `BitmapEffectInput` allows you to specify what portion of an image a bitmap effect should be applied to, giving you precise control over exactly how your end result should use the effects.

After you have selected your bitmap effect, you can then specify the effect area using the `BitmapEffectInput` property, which (when you click New) gives you three additional properties.

AreaToApplyEffect

This property's input value is dependent on the next property (`AreaToApplyEffectUnits`) choice. If you specify `Absolute` for the `AreaToApplyEffectUnits` property, you need to input four values separated by commas and representing X, Y, width, and height (see Table 11.2).

TABLE 11.2   The `AreaToApplyEffects` Values

Value	Description
X	The position the bitmap effect should start from on the x-axis, based on position 0,0 (X,Y) being at the top-left corner of the target
Y	The position the bitmap effect should start from on the y-axis, based on position 0,0 (X,Y) being at the top-left corner of the target
Width	The width in pixels that the effect should span
Height	The height in pixels that the effect should span

Sample input value: 50,50,100,100

This will create a bitmap effect on the target image, 100×100 pixels in size, positioned at X50,Y50 as shown in Figure 11.26.

If the `AreaToApplyEffectUnits` property is set to `RelativeToBoundingBox`, the values entered refer to percentage portions of the target image element (see Table 11.3).

TABLE 11.3   The `AreaToApplyEffectsUnits` Values

Value	Description
X	The position the bitmap effect should start from on the x-axis as a percentage of the target image source. This is a Double value between 0 and 1.
Y	The position the bitmap effect should start from on the y-axis as a percentage of the target image source. This is a Double value between 0 and 1.
Width	The width the bitmap effect should apply as a percentage of the target image source. This is a Double value between 0 and 1.
Height	The height the bitmap effect should apply as a percentage of the target image source. This is a Double value between 0 and 1.

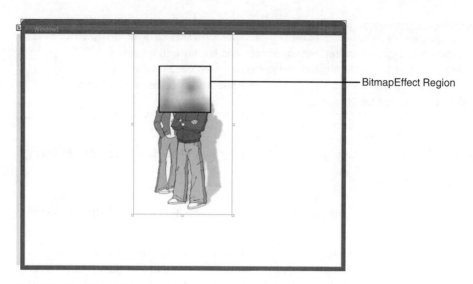

FIGURE 11.26   A Blur effect applied to a specific image area.

Sample input value: 0.25,0.25,0.5,0.5

The preceding example shows a different result, as Figure 11.27 shows, using an Emboss effect.

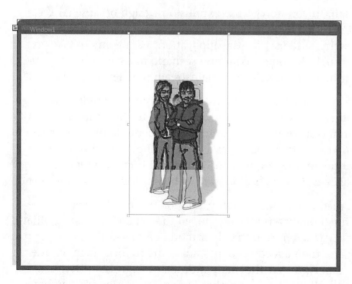

FIGURE 11.27   The BitmapEffectInput result.

Order of Importance with `BitmapEffectInput`

You can chop and change between bitmap effects and not have to reapply a
`BitmapEffectInput` because of the change. You can even decide to add a
`BitmapEffectGroup` and it will be applied to the input area specified without needing a
change in the `BitmapEffectInput` properties.

AreaToApplyEffectUnits

This property can be set to one of two values, `Absolute` and `RelativeToBoundingBox`, as
described previously.

Input

The Windows SDK states that this property "Gets or sets the `BitmapSource` that is used for
the input for the object."

Bitmap effects do have a lot of functionality and use, so it is unfortunate that the performance hits can make a big difference with the end user's experience of the application.
When the software-rendering issues are sorted out, you can be sure that I will be advocat-
ing the use of bitmap effects. But until such a day comes, using them for the purposes of
writing this book is as far as I am willing to go with them. Make of them what you will...

Workflow: Import a Vector Object from Expression Design

I am not going to try and explain to you how to use Expression Design because far greater
resources available on the Internet (http://www.learnexpressionstudio.com) can give you a
better insight into the best practices and uses for the application. I am going to take you
through a process though that might become a common scenario in usage terms as time
goes on and WPF development becomes more of the mainstream preference.

Expression Design is a product purchased by Microsoft to give its suite a standalone design
application that could focus purely on "screen art" in comparison to the "print art" that
some other design packages from companies, such as Adobe, are better known for. There is
nothing wrong with continuing to use these packages as long as they have a compatible
XAML export function, but for my money, Expression Design will become a serious player
in XAML-specific design packages as it matures alongside its big brother, Expression Blend.

Initially the application had a plethora of functionality, and many were dismayed to see
the ritualistic slaying of such functionality as CTP developed to Beta and now on to final
RTM product. Some functionality was removed, fixed, or modified to suit the
Design/Blend workflow better and then added back in. I am going to focus here on one
function that has been vastly improved over the many months of Expression Design
development: the XAML export facility. Please note that Expression Design v2 may have
changed from the following process.

I turned to Stephen Barker to explain it to me before writing this part of the chapter
because there are some gotcha's depending on the specific scenario that you use
Expression Design for. All in all, I am impressed by this "little application that could" and

I will continue to integrate it into my development lifecycle as well as actively nudge the people that work for and alongside me to do the same.

In the following, I am using a simple visual asset developed for me by Steve (I think the screenshots will look better than my efforts!), but you could download and install the trial version (http://www.microsoft.com/expression/products/overview.aspx?key=design) if you don't already have a copy of the application. Create any asset you like, although we are dealing with a single-layer vector graphic in this chapter. You could create something as simple as a single rectangle on a single layer to continue with the examples that follow. Figure 11.28 shows our asset in Design, pointing out the layers that make up the asset which can determine your output scenario.

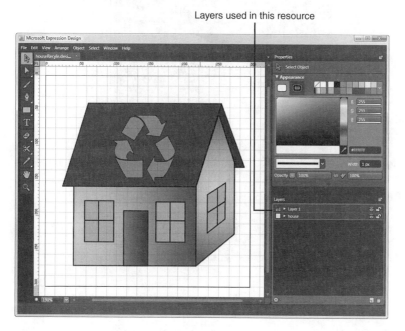

FIGURE 11.28   Steve's house! (Not Steve's actual house...I think.)

Because of the export options available to the user of Design, the graphic artists shouldn't assume which format the asset will be required in by the end user. As the XAML architect, you need to explain in your instructions how the asset will be used in Blend. Do you need to scale the assets or animate it? Do you want to use it as a resource that will be painted on to elements in Blend or do you want the asset in its own element as in a canvas that contains the asset. Does any text in the asset need to be editable inside Blend or should it be a path outline of text letters? Do you need the layers of the asset separated or grouped in a resource? The choices are many, and each determines the positive and negative value of any asset and its perceived use within the Blend application construct.

In this scenario, we want the asset to be supplied in a Resource Dictionary as a single-layer element that we can use to paint onto a Grid element in Blend. In the Expression Design

UI, you will note several menus at the top of the application, similar to that in Expression Blend. After ensuring that your asset is saved as a .design file, select File and then Export. First you will be prompted to give the asset an export filename and importantly a file extension type. Here you want to make sure that .Xaml is selected, give the asset a meaningful name, and save it to a location that you remember. Clicking Save will result in the Export XAML dialog being displayed as shown in Figure 11.29.

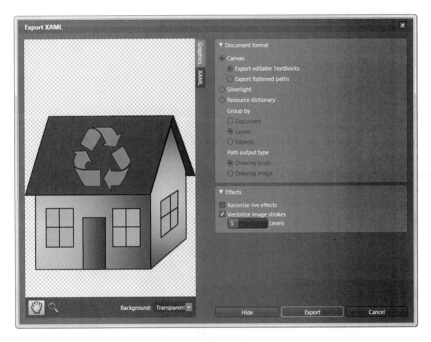

FIGURE 11.29   The Export XAML dialog.

There are essentially two parts to this dialog window: The left allows you to view the asset(s) and the represented XAML, and the right gives you the choices that I wrote about previously and that determine the XAML output.

To demonstrate the differences that the export settings make, select the XAML tab on the left side of the dialog as shown in Figure 11.30. You can clearly see the now familiar syntax of XAML markup.

Select the Document Format category as shown in Figure 11.30, which displays the combination of options available for this asset. By default, the copy I am using is selected to export to a canvas. Click on the Resource Dictionary radio button and keep an eye on the corresponding XAML in the output viewer (or vice versa). Notice the instantaneous change to the output markup?

XAML view tab
Document format selection

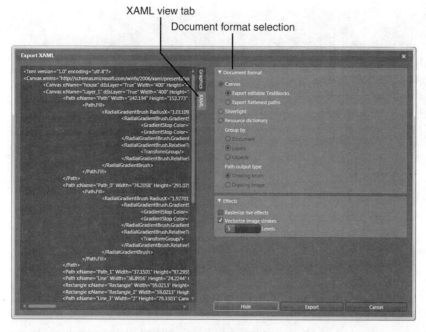

FIGURE 11.30   The output surface tab options and the XAML representations.

TIP

If you are working on the asset yourself, you can shortcut the export import stage simply by making your output choices in the Document Format and Effects category and then selecting, copying, and pasting the XAML markup directly into Blend. You should note that the top line of the markup in the output viewer should not be included in your copied markup (see Figure 11.31) because it is purely XML document formatting structure and to include it would cause a breakage in your Blend application.

You can also see there is a Silverlight output option, and as exciting as that new technology is, we are not going to go there today. Choose Resource Dictionary and then, importantly, make sure that the radio button Layers is also selected. Below that, you can see the Path Output Type, which should be set to Drawing Brush.

Click on the Export button and everything should be taken care of without any additional fuss. You have now created a Resource Dictionary for use in Blend, so you can close Expression Design now if you choose.

Giving the XAML to Blend

Getting your asset into Blend is a relatively simple process as long as you understand what type of asset you are dealing with. In the previous instruction, you created a Resource Dictionary that contains resource(s) split into layers.

1. In Blend, click on the Project menu, Add Existing Item.

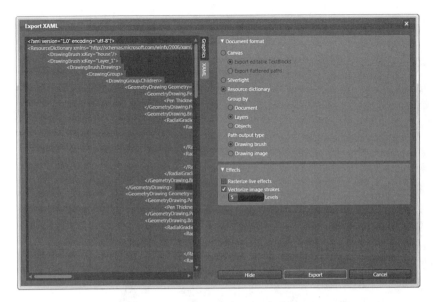

FIGURE 11.31   The markup selected without the XML document format string.

2. Navigate to your exported XAML file in the Add Existing Item dialog and click Open.

3. Immediately you should see your XAML file has been added to your Project panel, as shown in Figure 11.32.

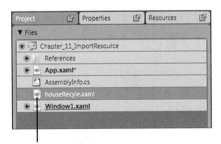

Imported Resource Dictionary

FIGURE 11.32   The imported Resource Dictionary.

4. Click on the Resources Tab and again you should see your exported filename added there also. Important to note is that your project's App.xaml file has become open on the current files list in the UI above the artboard. Click on the file to make it active and select the XAML tab near the artboard to view similar markup as shown in Listing 11.8. You can see the houseRecycle.xaml file linked in bold.

LISTING 11.8   Application-Level Resource Dictionary References

```
<Application
    xmlns="http://schemas.microsoft.com/winfx/2006/xaml/presentation"
    xmlns:x="http://schemas.microsoft.com/winfx/2006/xaml"
    x:Class="Chapter_11_ImportResource.App"
    StartupUri="Window1.xaml">
    <Application.Resources>
        <!— Resources scoped at the Application level should be defined here. —>
        <ResourceDictionary>
            <ResourceDictionary.MergedDictionaries>
                <ResourceDictionary Source="houseRecycle.xaml"/>
            </ResourceDictionary.MergedDictionaries>
        </ResourceDictionary>
    </Application.Resources>
</Application>
```

5. After verifying that your imported Resource Dictionary has been added to your application's merged dictionaries, close the App.xaml file, opting to save the file as prompted by Blend.

6. Now add a Grid element to your application's LayoutRoot or any other element you might have on your artboard that has a suitable background or fill property.

7. Set the Grid Width and Height properties to 400 and the HorizontalAlignment and VerticalAlignment properties to Center.

8. Go back to the Resources tab and drill down on your Resource Dictionary and you should see your exported layer(s). If you named the Layers in Expression Design, that name will also carry over with the Resource Dictionary. In my example, as shown in Figure 11.33, you can see that the exported layers are named house (which is empty) and Layer_1, which contains the image of the house. (I think Steve meant to put the house on the house layer...but you get the point!)

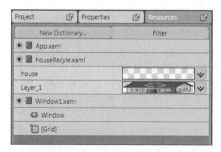

FIGURE 11.33   The Resources tab with the imported resources.

9. Click, hold, and drag the layer until your mouse is over the top of the Grid element you added to the artboard (or your choice of element) and let go of the mouse button.

10. You should get a pop-up menu with the choice of acceptable properties to which you can assign the resource. In this instance, I have selected the Background property of the grid and, as shown in Figure 11.34, my exported asset is now painted on the grid as the Background Brush.

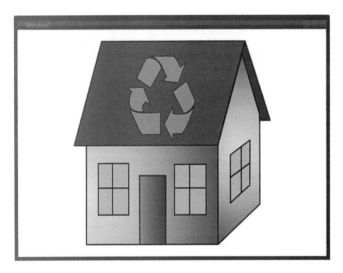

FIGURE 11.34   The finished import and assignment.

Simple stuff when you know how! I encourage you to work with Expression Design and get to know the options available to you as either a designer or XAML architect specifying visual assets. The workflow between Design/Blend/Visual Studio is certainly a smooth process now and with three screens connected to your work machine (four when you are just greedy like me), you can keep all the applications open at once and enjoy an uncompromised view of your application as it is being developed.

Summary

You can see that WPF provides for a substantial array of graphic modification capabilities and those capabilities for the most part are available through the Blend UI. As you become more experienced with WPF, Visual Studio, and Blend, you might want to venture out to creating your own visuals for controls, which is a much more advanced topic and out of the scope of this book.

Hopefully you can also see the benefits of using, or at the very least exporting, visual assets from Expression Design, and how the many export options available allow you to create assets that are flexible and work the way you want and need them to in Expression Blend.

As an applications developer, it certainly is hard to go back to the old way of creating visual assets for forms applications, and as a designer it certainly feels good to see such a vast supporting toolset at such an early stage of the Expression product range development.

PART V

Templates and Data

IN THIS PART

CHAPTER 12

Templates

Templates are a fantastic way of providing standardization for your applications. They also provide you with visual continuity in terms of how your application is going to look with style/data templates for different controls by allowing you to modify all your standard controls to someway adapt to the way your user experienced is intended to be delivered. Data can also be controlled with much more predictable results because of templates. Previously in WinForms, it was often the case that you needed to use a control that could accept or display data. Now you can build controls with templates that look and work a certain way because of the data.

Templates allow you to not only do this within your application, but also you can use the same templates later or send them to another team working on the same application to ensure that styling and design continuity are facilitated. In this chapter you will learn how to modify and create new templates for styles and controls. The next chapter focuses on data binding and will include details of data templates. Your ability to change these templates will directly effect your ability to use the WPF (Windows Presentation Foundation) as an application platform, so you should probably expect to run through some of these concepts a few times to make sure that they are cemented within your mind before moving on. This chapter should really give you a sense of being a god at the end of it because as compared to CLR (Common Language Runtime) controls, XAML (Extensible Application Markup Language) controls are a cinch to work with and to therefore deliver exactly what is required within a design specification and, ultimately, a solution.

Control Templates

At first, the template scenarios in WPF can be quite confusing because they are layered—one template is nested inside another—and indeed, when you start working with more complex templates, additional template references are littered throughout the original template.

What Is a Control Template?

We need to begin this topic by defining what a control is, what an element is, and what a UIElement is. In Blend terms, the differences between a control and a UIElement is described in Table 12.1.

TABLE 12.1   Element and Control Definitions

Type	Example
An element	Label, Path
A singular functioning control	Button, Textbox, Slider
A grouping of individual controls and or elements to create a singular functioning UIElement	Expander, Grid with children

For the most part, the terms *controls* and *elements* are used interchangeably, and you should consider that a control is represented in XAML as a singular, regardless of the internal parts of the control. For example, a Buttons is written in markup as <Button/>. The Expander is a good example of a control that is made up of separate parts (many other elements) to create the singular functioning control. The Expander contains Grids, Borders, ToggleButtons, and ContentControls/ContentPresenters. Therefore some of the individual *parts* of the Expander can have styles applied to modify the appearance and or functionality of it.

For this chapter, you are going to create a new template for a button, modify the existing template of an Expander control, and use your new button template to enhance the Expander so that you can use it in future.

Creating a New Template

Creating a new (control) template is simple and you have already done this several times throughout the book with various exercises. Each time you created a new button, you were creating a new template for the Button element.

A control template is represented in XAML by declaring a ControlTemplate type and a TargetType as shown in the markup following:

```
<ControlTemplate x:Key="ExpanderControlTemplate1" TargetType="{x:Type Expander}"/>
```

The importance of the TargetType is so you don't try to apply a ListBox's control template to an Expander control, for example. The benefit of this is that Blend recognizes the template types and so allows you to assign them interchangeable within single (or groups of) controls that match the target type, without concern that you will apply the wrong template to an incompatible type.

To create a blank template, right click on any element, select Edit Control Parts (Template), and then select Create Empty. From here you can build your own template with various controls to suit. You might lose the functionality of the base control when doing this, though, because the control might have explicit methods, properties, and events that it uses to receive and send input through the control. For example, if you remove the ToggleButton element from the Expander control, you can't expect to automatically have the functionality of the original control based on the events, properties, and methods used by the original ToggleButton. So, be careful!

Where should you start? You could go off and start hand-coding the markup for the given control and fight your way through (which is how we did it in the earliest of days). Or you could use the methods prescribed in the previous paragraph. But my recommendation for people new to XAML and the concepts of the Blend/WPF Templating system is to use what is already there as a base and build on it.

Editing the Control Parts (Template)

When you right-click on a control and select Edit Control Parts (Template), you also see another option: Edit a Copy. By using this option, you are effectively cloning the existing template and giving yourself free rein to modify and enhance (or destroy) the existing template without any real concerns as your original will always be available.

To demonstrate this a little further, you will now modify the ToggleButton control template in a ComboBox control and then apply that to the ToggleButton in an Expander control.

Simple Styles Collection

The control list you see in the Simple Styles collection is in fact a collection of styles and not controls. When you select a simple style, you are creating an instance of a control with a simple style applied to it. Modifying this simple style means that every time you select the Simple Styles version of a given control, it will be created with your modifications already added. This means that if you create a dictionary of different styles, they too will be available in the Asset Viewer for you to choose from. This is a good reason to make sure that you follow a consistent naming convention when you are naming your styles.

Standard Control Styles

You can modify the standard controls as well, but in most cases, special formatting and control styling have been added that presents several levels of added complexity to the base control.

1. Start with a new application in Blend, adding two ColumnDefinitions to the LayoutRoot element to split it down the middle.

2. Open the Asset Library and select a ComboBox element from the Simple Styles collection, placing it on the left side of the artboard, about halfway up.

3. Find the ComboBox element in the Objects and Timeline category of the Interaction panel, right-click to raise the context menu, and select Edit Control Parts (Template), followed by Edit Template.

4. You are now "in" the template editing view and your artboard should have changed to show you a really big ComboBox only. The Objects and Timeline category has also changed, showing you the inner makeup of the ComboBox element as shown in Figure 12.1.

FIGURE 12.1   The Objects and Timeline category of the ComboBox Control template.

5. Double-click the ToggleButton element to activate it. You are now going to edit the ToggleButton element control template, so again go through the process of right-clicking the element, but this time opt to edit a copy instead of the template.

What Is the Difference Between "Edit" and "Edit a Copy"?

To Edit a template, you modify the standard template applied to the control as it appears on your artboard. If you edit the standard template, the changes will be reflected in every other instance of a control that uses the standard template.

If you Edit a Copy of the template applied, you create a new instance of the template and can modify it specifically for the instance. Only when you specifically tell other controls to use this instance of the template will they show the changes you make.

6. The Create ControlTemplate Resource dialog should now be showing. Enter **MyGreenToggleButton** into the Resource Name (Key) edit box, and ensure that the Define radio button for Application is selected.

7. You will now see the Objects and Timeline category shows the individual elements that make up the combo box. Hide some of the elements and you should see that the part that acts as the drop-down button is a Rectangle element that fills the entire space.

8. Select the Rectangle element and change the `Fill` property to show a nice light green SolidColorBrush.

9. If you look in the Triggers category, you should see three Triggers defined that change both the functionality and the style of the element depending on which triggers are raised. (This is the implicit style-editing ability of Blend and will be covered in the next section.) You are looking for the Trigger that is raised when `IsChecked=True`. Select it in the list and you should take note of the Properties When Active area of the Triggers category.

10. Figure 12.2 also shows the style template change that is made when this Trigger is activated and it is this property that we want to change. You will see the style change is also visible in the Rectangle element that you have selected, as you will now see that it has reverted to the silver type PressedBrush resource. Making sure that Trigger Recording is on by verifying the red border around the artboard, you can change the `Fill` property once more to a `SolidColorBrush`, this time choosing a darker green.

11. You have now finished with the ToggleButton template, so you can click on the ScopeUp button to return to the ComboBox template, click on the ScopeUp button again to return to your application scene, or you can use the Template Breadcrumb capability of Blend as described in Figure 12.3. This breadcrumb workflow allows you to move quickly between the layers of templates and the subsequent child controls of parent control templates. After you have specifically opted to edit a ControlTemplate or style template, you no longer need to go through the right-click menu scenarios because you can select the template to edit at anytime on the breadcrumb bar.

12. Press F5 to run the application and click on the drop-down arrow to note the changes that occur with the Trigger activating: The `IsChecked` property is set to true and your Trigger fires to modify the part color to green.

13. What you should have noticed is that the `MouseOver` Trigger is also activated, which again sets the style of the Rectangle. You can go back in and change the style if you really want to!

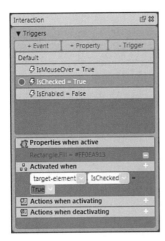

FIGURE 12.2   The Triggers category, specifically the actions applied when the Trigger is activated.

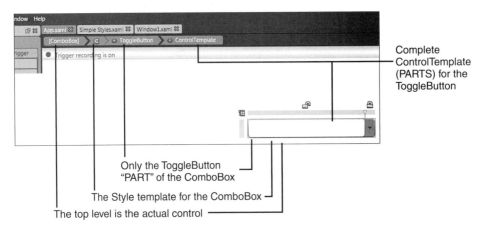

FIGURE 12.3   The Template Breadcrumb workflow facility in Blend attempts to show you the layer makeup of the editable template of the control(s).

Applying to Other UIElements

Applying your template is a very simple process as you will now see continuing with the example. It makes no difference what sort of template you have edited, the *application* of the template is the same as the following procedure.

14. Add a SimpleStyles Expander to your application, setting it to show on the right side of the LayoutRoot grid.

15. When you have finished with your placement of the Expander, double-click on the Expander to activate it, and then continue through to Edit Control Parts (Template) either by right-clicking in the Objects and Timeline category or by using the Template Breadcrumb toolbar. You probably don't see any Style or Template buttons next to the [Expander] button, but you should see a little arrow indicating drop-down features. Click on this button and you will see a shortcut menu appear, giving you same the features as the right-click context functionality. You should be editing the template here, not a copy of the template.

16. As Figure 12.4 shows, the Object and Timeline element tree can be drilled down to show the ToggleButton control—this is the target control you wanted to find.

17. Double-click the ToggleButton element to activate it. Right-click to produce the context menu, again selecting the Edit Control Parts (Template) menu item, and this time moving down to Apply Resource. You should see a new context menu appear, and it should contain the item MyGreenToggleButton. Select the item to apply it. You can also do this from the Template Breadcrumb toolbar.

18. ScopeUp back to your application scene and press F5 to run your application.

When you run your application, you should see the same functionality and style applied to the element as is applied to the ComboBox element. You will notice some other changes that you need to make to complete the correct functionality, which include editing the Expander template (I would advise a copy) and setting the Arrow Path element to point upward when the IsChecked property is true.

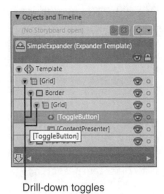

Drill-down toggles

FIGURE 12.4   The drill-down indicators in the Objects and Timeline category.

As you can see, the biggest part of the job is creating the custom template, which is easy thanks to the Blend UI. You can apply the template to your heart's content throughout your application now, ensuring that all ToggleButton elements look the same way.

Style Templates

The Style Template is the top level template of every control and is created at the time of authoring the control.

What Is a Style Template?

When looking at controls in existing pre–.NET 3.0 applications, it's hard to think of them as containing much of any sort of style. The controls are plain in aesthetic terms, conveying very little in the way of user experience or adding much to a good overall user experience.

A style template allows you as a designer to specify how a control should look and function in terms of appearance and animation through property evaluation. As with all templates, you can also store these templates in a resource dictionary if required or just add them to the application's resource collection.

Style animation also has the added benefit of allowing you to define property events. This means that when a given property evaluates to true, an event is raised and you can then execute actions such as starting another animation, setting another property to a desired value, or changing the style to suit the given situation.

An example of this is when you set a Button control's IsEnabled property to false in the Properties panel, Common Properties category. The style template has been designed with a property trigger so that when the IsEnabled property is false, the style changes color to give the user a clear understanding that the control is in a different state. The markup shown in Listing 12.1 is the default style template added by Blend when you edit the template of a button.

LISTING 12.1   The Breakdown of a Style Template

Style Templates are placed by Blend in the Resources collection of the parent control type (which is a UserControl in this case).

```
<UserControl.Resources>
```

Style definition with a Key, a TargetType, and BasedOn property/attribute setting.

```
    <Style x:Key="ButtonStyle1" BasedOn="{x:Null}" TargetType="{x:Type Button}">
        <Setter Property="Template">
            <Setter.Value>
```

This is the ControlTemplate which is editable using the methods described previously in this chapter. The ControlTemplate makes up the parts.

```
                <ControlTemplate TargetType="{x:Type Button}">
                    <Grid x:Name="grid" Background="#FFCEFF00">
                        <ContentPresenter SnapsToDevicePixels="{TemplateBinding
```

```
SnapsToDevicePixels}" HorizontalAlignment="{TemplateBinding
HorizontalContentAlignment}" VerticalAlignment="{TemplateBinding
VerticalContentAlignment}" RecognizesAccessKey="True"/>
                    </Grid>
```

The Trigger declarations allow you to specify what should occur and when.

```
              <ControlTemplate.Triggers>
                  <Trigger Property="IsFocused" Value="True"/>
                  <Trigger Property="IsDefaulted" Value="True"/>
                  <Trigger Property="IsMouseOver" Value="True">
```

In this Trigger, when the IsMouseOver property for the button is true, changes are made to the following element.

```
                      <Setter Property="Background" TargetName="grid"
Value="#FFFF0000"/>
```

This "Setter" requires a property name from a named element (in this case the "grid") and a new value to apply.

```
                  </Trigger>
                  <Trigger Property="IsPressed" Value="True"/>
                  <Trigger Property="IsEnabled" Value="False"/>
              </ControlTemplate.Triggers>
          </ControlTemplate>
      </Setter.Value>
    </Setter>
  </Style>
</UserControl.Resources>
```

Looking through the markup in Listing 12.1, you can see a very simple style template which is a nice and simple example to look at for the distinguishing parts of a style template. Obviously Style templates (and templates in general) can get very complex with multiple trigger scenarios, firing off animations and setting property states. If you can modify an element in your scene and then understand what the XAML is doing to achieve your settings, you will have a better understanding of how and why XAML is so fantastic, and why Blend is the obvious tool of choice (rather than Visual Studio) to make such modifications.

Edit an Existing Style

WPF controls are created with a generic style. This generic style is not dissimilar to the style template shown in Listing 12.1 and is what makes up the markup added to the XAML editor when you do indeed opt to edit or copy a template. The phrase "edit the style template implicitly" means that when you opt to edit the ControlTemplate, you also get the entire style template because as you can also see from Listing 12.1, the ControlTemplate resides within the style template.

When intending to modify styles of existing WPF controls, Blend gives you a baseline series of styles defined for specific controls that are available in the Simple Styles collection available in the Assets panel. Operating system themes are also brought into the mix, and depending on whether you are using Windows XP or Windows Vista, some styles determine how controls should look when in the runtime environment.

An example of the generic base styling and theme-based component styling can be seen with the ProgressBar control. Try adding a standard ProgressBar and a SimpleStyles ProgressBar, one above the other, and then set an arbitrary value to both controls. The difference is dramatic and can be seen in Figure 12.5.

FIGURE 12.5   The two ProgressBar controls and the differences in styling.

If you added the SimpleStyle ProgressBar control to an empty Window or UserControl, you will not see anything in the markup to indicate that a theme is being used to control the visual aspects of the control. If you now edit the template of the control, you should see a new XML namespace added to the top of your Window (or UserControl) declaration. Markup similar to the following:

```
xmlns:Microsoft_Windows_Themes="clr-
namespace:Microsoft.Windows.Themes;assembly=PresentationFramework.Aero"
```

This indicates that the style is using a Windows theme somewhere. And in the ProgressBar's case, deep in the style template, you will see where a Rectangle element has a highlight binding converter, which is what gives the ProgressBar its styled appearance. If you edit a copy of the style template locally with a Simple Style ProgressBar on a new Window or UserControl, you will note that no such theme is used. In addition to the visual differences, when you try to modify the template of the controls you will also see how simple (no pun intended) it is to modify one control against the other.

Style Is Not Functionality Modification

It is important to note that styling the control does not change the base functionality of the control in anyway; the same properties exist in both the SimpleProgressBar and the standard ProgressBar controls, but by modifying the style and adding animations to one, it would appear that the control operates completely different.

Adding or removing controls as control parts (or children) of a UIElement does not constitute a functional change in the code that makes up the control. The functionality still exists regardless of whether or not you use it.

Let's now modify the Simple Styles ProgressBar and, in the process, create a new style template that you can then apply to other ProgressBars that you might want to use later in the same application or a completely different one.

Should You Always Use Simple Styles?

Whenever I am creating a new application there are certain steps I like to take to make life easier down the track. Without fail, people always want changes to the way things look in an application and so I start an application with this in mind. I always only use Simple Styles controls in my applications and I leave them as they are until all the controls for the application are added. This way, I can then create skins for the application and build libraries that allow the people to choose what they like the best instead of me imposing my own visual preferences.

You can spend a long time styling controls in an application, all for the people that sign the checks to turn around and want a completely different style. Save yourself the time and the heartache by getting your controls in place first, even adding the functionality and then changing the visual look and feel after it is all in place. This does not mean that you won't have to rip out a control and start again because, fundamentally, a design change can alter the control type you should be using, so being light during this process in terms of time spent on controls is highly recommended.

This is just my preference, but again I have found this to be the most productive way to work with the fewest number of arguments between designers, developers, and bean counters.

Creating a New Style

The following steps take you through creating a new Style; the same process can be used for all controls:

1. Either add the XAML from Listing 12.2 or start a new empty project and then open the Asset Viewer and type **Progress** into the search box, which should return a single control SimpleProgressBar.

2. Add this control to the center of the LayoutRoot panel and set its height to 15, set the HorizontalAlignment to Stretch, and set the Left and Right Margin to 150.

3. Open the Objects and Timelines panel and navigate through the visual tree to find and select the ProgressBar control.

4. On the top menu, Object, find the option for Edit Style and select Edit Style from the child menu.

LISTING 12.2   A Simple ProgressBar Example

```
<Grid x:Name="LayoutRoot">


    <ProgressBar Margin="150,94,150,0" Style="{DynamicResource SimpleProgressBar}"
VerticalAlignment="Top" Height="15"/>

</Grid>
```

5. Open the Interaction panel if it is not already visible and you should note a default trigger exists called Default. This represents the default property values of the control. By default the Simple ProgressBar contains a property recorded value, setting the Background property of the control.

6. Try changing a visual property such as the Brush applied to the Background property. You will see nothing has changed on the control. Why is this? It's because the SimpleProgressBar is made up of two parts and a Container object, as shown in Table 12.2. The Background property you see in the style template refers to the background of the control as a group and not the individual part shown in the control. The part called Part_Track is a control of type Border and represents what you see as the background panel on the control.

TABLE 12.2   The ProgressBar Control Template

Element Name	Element Type	Description
[Grid]	Grid	The container that operates as the control part's parent control
Part_Track	Border	The background control
Part_Indicator	Border	The progress presentation control

To change the ProgressBar, you need to access the control template and then modify the styles of the individual part components.

FocusVisualStyle

I hesitated about adding this section in this book because the FocusVisualStyle can create a wide range of user experience issues if not used correctly. When you add a Button element to an application and that Button element is focused in runtime, you will note a style is given to the Button to indicate that it does indeed have the keyboard focus. If you add a Simple Styles Button element and run the application, you will note that the appearance of a Focus style is much less prominent.

You will also note at this point that you are modifying the `SimpleStyles.xaml` resource dictionary directly (you should see this file at the top of the artboard in the list of open files).

7. While in the style template, click on the XAML viewer tab and you will see the entire Simple Style file. Open the Asset Library panel and you will see that the Simple Styles button in the Controls category has changed and now shows a combo box control with the word Custom in it. When you click on the combo box, you now have the option to remove your custom styles and reset the Simple Styles dictionary back to its default as shown in Figure 12.6.

Click to reset the Simple Styles library

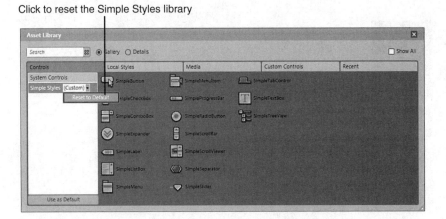

FIGURE 12.6   You can reset your Simple Styles back to their default.

The FocusVisualStyle is a little deceptive in how you are meant to work with it in a solution design sense. You are not meant to change the FocusVisualStyle of individual controls; doing so could lead to a confusing user experience because one control would show a certain focus style and a different control would show a different focus style. You are meant only to work with the FocusVisualStyle when creating a theme to be used across all controls in your solution.

What If I Only Want to Modify One Control's FocusVisualStyle?

Editing the FocusVisualStyle is a heavy handed approach to achieving this and you are advised to edit the control's style template and create a style modification when the `IsFocused` property evaluates to true. This way, you are not modifying every control's FocusVisualStyle.

A FocusVisualStyle is a ControlTemplate element that targets the Control.Template property of the intended target; in this case, a Button element. The following is the easiest way

I have found to create a FocusVisualStyle ControlTemplate, so you will now go through creating a new border for the button when it receives focus.

1. Start a new application in Blend.

2. Add a Border element to the artboard, leaving it at its default position and size in the top left of the artboard.

3. Style the Border element anyway you choose, using the Properties panel to set the Background and Stroke properties. In the example, I have created a red LinearGradientBrush with a bright red SolidColorBrush for the Stroke.

4. Set the BorderThickness property to 2.

FIGURE 12.7   The Border element prepared.

5. Switch to the XAML view and add the listing shown in Listing 12.3 above the LayoutRoot Grid element, which creates the Style and ControlTemplate element you are going to assign to your control.

LISTING 12.3   An Empty Generic Style Template and ControlTemplate

```
<Window.Resources>
    <Style x:Key="NewFocusVisualStyle">
      <Setter Property="Control.Template">
        <Setter.Value>
          <ControlTemplate>

          </ControlTemplate>
        </Setter.Value>
      </Setter>
    </Style>
</Window.Resources>
```

6. You should also be able to see your Border element in the XAML. Select the entire markup for the element and put it between the <ControlTemplate> markup tags in the style you just created in Window.Resources.

7. Your entire markup should look similar to that of Listing 12.4.

LISTING 12.4   Building Out the ControlTemplate

```
<Window.Resources>
    <Style x:Key="NewFocusVisualStyle">
      <Setter Property="Control.Template">
        <Setter.Value>
          <ControlTemplate>
                <Border HorizontalAlignment="Left" VerticalAlignment="Top"
Width="100" Height="100" BorderBrush="#FFFF0000" BorderThickness="2,2,2,2">
                    <Border.Background>
                        <LinearGradientBrush EndPoint="0.502,1"
StartPoint="0.498,0">
                            <GradientStop Color="#FFFF0000"
Offset="0"/>
                            <GradientStop Color="#FFFFFFFF"
Offset="1"/>
                        </LinearGradientBrush>
                    </Border.Background>
                </Border>
          </ControlTemplate>
        </Setter.Value>
      </Setter>
    </Style>
</Window.Resources>
        <Grid x:Name="LayoutRoot">
        </Grid>
```

8. You need to make some final modifications to your Border element that pertain to the size, layout, and positioning of the Border. The Border will take its position from its target element, so you can remove the following markup from your Border element:

```
HorizontalAlignment="Left" VerticalAlignment="Top" Width="100" Height="100"
```

9. Finally, add a new Margin property to the element because you want the Border to appear just outside the bounds of the target control when the focus is on it, just so the user will instantly notice the change in focus. Add the following markup to the Border element:

```
Margin="-3"
```

10. Return to the Design artboard and you should have a clean space to work with. Open the Asset panel and select a Button element from the Simple Styles collection.

11. Place the Button on the artboard at any position and size you choose.

12. With the Button element selected, type the word **foc** into the property search box and you should find the property **FocusVisualStyle** in the Miscellaneous category.

13. You will note that you can't edit the property directly in the property edit box. But don't worry, all is not lost. To the right of the property edit box, you will see a small box that allows you to open the advanced properties options.

14. Click on the small box, and select the Custom Expression menu option, which opens a small pop-up as shown in Figure 12.8.

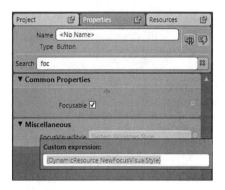

FIGURE 12.8   The small pop-up box used to edit the FocusVisualStyle property directly.

15. Enter the following into the box:

```
{DynamicResource NewFocusVisualStyle}
```

and press Enter to close.

16. Now run your application and press the Tab button to send the focus to your button. It should turn red. Perhaps a little too red?

17. Okay, I was just making a point, albeit a very ugly one. Change the GradientStop color values to something similar to the following and try again:

```
<GradientStop Color="#3FFF0000" Offset="0"/>
    <GradientStop Color="#3FFFFFFF" Offset="1"/>
```

Applying the Style Across the Project

The markup in Listing 12.5 shows that the FocusVisualStyle has been applied to three items in the scene as shown in Figure 12.9. But using the method of applying the style to each individual element could be quite time-consuming to say the least, especially in a large application that contains many screens and/or UserControls.

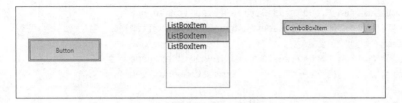

FIGURE 12.9   The FocusVisualStyle applied to all the elements.

LISTING 12.5   Applying the FocusVisualStyle

```
<Grid x:Name="LayoutRoot">


        <Grid.ColumnDefinitions>
                <ColumnDefinition/>
                <ColumnDefinition/>
                <ColumnDefinition/>
        </Grid.ColumnDefinitions>
        <Grid.RowDefinitions>
                <RowDefinition/>
                <RowDefinition/>
                <RowDefinition/>
        </Grid.RowDefinitions>

        <Button FocusVisualStyle="{DynamicResource NewFocusVisualStyle}"
HorizontalAlignment="Stretch" Style="{DynamicResource SimpleButton}"
VerticalAlignment="Stretch" Width="Auto" Height="Auto" Content="Button"
Margin="35,55,35,55" Grid.Row="1"/>

        <ListBox FocusVisualStyle="{DynamicResource NewFocusVisualStyle}"
HorizontalAlignment="Center" Margin="0,20,0,20" Style="{DynamicResource
SimpleListBox}" VerticalAlignment="Stretch" Width="100" Grid.Column="1"
Grid.Row="1" IsSynchronizedWithCurrentItem="True">
                <ListBoxItem FocusVisualStyle="{DynamicResource
NewFocusVisualStyle}" Style="{DynamicResource SimpleListBoxItem}"
Content="ListBoxItem"/>
                <ListBoxItem FocusVisualStyle="{DynamicResource
NewFocusVisualStyle}" Style="{DynamicResource SimpleListBoxItem}"
Content="ListBoxItem"/>
                <ListBoxItem FocusVisualStyle="{DynamicResource
NewFocusVisualStyle}" Style="{DynamicResource SimpleListBoxItem}"
Content="ListBoxItem"/>
        </ListBox>
        <ComboBox FocusVisualStyle="{DynamicResource NewFocusVisualStyle}"
HorizontalAlignment="Stretch" Margin="15,25,15,0" Style="{DynamicResource
SimpleComboBox}" VerticalAlignment="Top" Grid.Column="2" Grid.Row="1"
IsSynchronizedWithCurrentItem="True" SelectedIndex="0">
```

```
            <ComboBoxItem FocusVisualStyle="{DynamicResource
NewFocusVisualStyle}" Style="{DynamicResource SimpleComboBoxItem}"
Content="ComboBoxItem"/>
            <ComboBoxItem FocusVisualStyle="{DynamicResource
NewFocusVisualStyle}" Style="{DynamicResource SimpleComboBoxItem}"
Content="ComboBoxItem"/>
            <ComboBoxItem FocusVisualStyle="{DynamicResource
NewFocusVisualStyle}" Style="{DynamicResource SimpleComboBoxItem}"
Content="ComboBoxItem"/>
        </ComboBox>

</Grid>
```

There has to be an easier way to apply the FocusVisualStyle across the application, right? Well, if you have heeded my advice and have chosen to use only SimpleStyle elements in your application, you will be able to open your version of the `SimpleStyles.xaml` file and add your FocusVisualStyle directly to the elements that you use.

Open the file and search for each component's element markup or do the following:

1. Right click on a SimpleStyle element in your artboard.
2. Select Edit Control Parts (Template) and then Edit Template.
3. In the Objects and Timeline category of the Interaction panel, select the Template item, right click, and select View XAML.

You should see above the element's markup there will be either a style defined or a reference to a FocusVisualStyle that the element uses. You can modify this style directly or replace it entirely at your discretion.

It's interesting to look through the file and see how the certain existing styles have been created. You could even use those as a template and simply modify the colors and or stroke values as required.

Data Templates

Data templates are a powerful tool in your arsenal, enabling you to control and deliver data exactly as is required by your end user(s). Because you are working with a template, you can store that template in a Resource Dictionary or simply keep it in the application markup source.

You have the ability, with data templates, to change the number, definition, and property values of any control you add to the template, which means that you are free to mold data visualization assets with unprecedented ease.

Setting the Data Source

You should create a new project and add the markup from Listing 12.6. The listing creates a simple ListBox, an XMLDataProvider, as well as a basic DataTemplate for displaying an

Internet RSS (Really Simple Syndication) feed from CNN.com. The process to create Listing 12.6 is identical to the steps you took in Chapter 2, "Welcome to the New World," to connect the twitter RSS feed.

LISTING 12.6   A ListBox with DataProvider Attached

```
<Window.Resources>
    <XmlDataProvider x:Key="rssDS"
Source="http://rss.cnn.com/rss/si_topstories.rss">
        <XmlDataProvider.XmlNamespaceManager>
            <XmlNamespaceMappingCollection>
                <XmlNamespaceMapping Prefix="feedburner"
Uri="http://rssnamespace.org/feedburner/ext/1.0"/>
                <XmlNamespaceMapping Prefix="atom10"
Uri="http://www.w3.org/2005/Atom"/>
            </XmlNamespaceMappingCollection>
        </XmlDataProvider.XmlNamespaceManager>
    </XmlDataProvider>
    <DataTemplate x:Key="rssTemplate">
        <StackPanel>
            <TextBlock Text="{Binding Mode=OneWay, XPath=@version}"/>
            <StackPanel>
                <TextBlock Text="{Binding Mode=OneWay, XPath=channel/title}"/>
                <TextBlock Text="{Binding Mode=OneWay, XPath=channel/link}"/>
                <TextBlock Text="{Binding Mode=OneWay, XPath=channel/description}"/>
                <TextBlock Text="{Binding Mode=OneWay, XPath=channel/copyright}"/>
                <StackPanel>
                    <Image Source="{Binding Mode=OneWay,
XPath=channel/image/url}"/>
                </StackPanel>
                <ItemsControl ItemsSource="{Binding Mode=OneWay,
XPath=channel/item}">
                    <ItemsControl.ItemTemplate>
                        <DataTemplate>
                            <StackPanel>
                                <TextBlock Text="{Binding Mode=OneWay,
XPath=title}"/>
                            </StackPanel>
                        </DataTemplate>
                    </ItemsControl.ItemTemplate>
                </ItemsControl>
            </StackPanel>
        </StackPanel>
    </DataTemplate>
</Window.Resources>
```

```
<Grid x:Name="LayoutRoot">
    <ListBox HorizontalAlignment="Center" VerticalAlignment="Center"
Width="457" Height="334" ItemTemplate="{DynamicResource rssTemplate}"
ItemsSource="{Binding Mode=Default, Source={StaticResource rssDS}, XPath=/rss}"
IsSynchronizedWithCurrentItem="True"/>

</Grid>
```

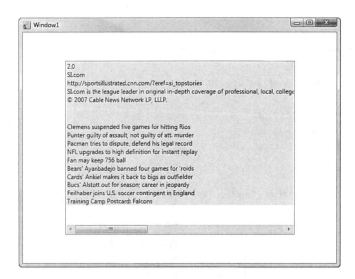

FIGURE 12.10   The resulting basic application.

The main point you should understand here is that it doesn't matter what type of data source you have, be it RSS, XML files, or CLR objects; the DataTemplate doesn't care. Its job is to take data and display it using the controls that you think are best suited for that purpose for each piece of data. If you think about that a little more, you will then realize that because you are specifying control elements to display the data, you can style those elements using templates as well!

Creating a Data Template

The markup in Listing 12.6 already contains a basic data template; well, it contains two, actually. You are now going to edit one of those templates to move things around and add some style to the output.

1. You will note that the Objects and Timeline category looks pretty bare and this is because the data template is referenced by the ListBox and not part of its items collection. Right-click on the ListBox and look for the menu item Edit Other

Templates, or use the Template Breadcrumb toolbar at the top of the artboard. You can choose Edit Generated Items (Item Template) and then select Edit Template.

2. The DataTemplate is now visible in the Objects and Timeline category of the Interaction panel, as shown in Figure 12.11. Technically it is actually the ContentPresenter template, but it represents the DataTemplate and the controls that defined within it. Walk through the visual tree, double clicking to activate the individual control elements, and you will see on the artboard where those controls are located.

FIGURE 12.11   The DataTemplate definitions.

3. Activate the top most StackPanel element and you will see that this control stretches way to the right of the bounds of the ListBox. Pan the artboard to the direction of the outer bounds of the control. Resize the control so that it fits neatly inside the ListBox and you should see an image come into view as shown in Figure 12.12.

4. Working down the Objects and Timeline tree, you can resize the elements and change fonts and colors to start to give your data some distinctive styling. You should realize by now that all these control elements are inside the parent StackPanel control, so you could change the Panel type if the stacking of the elements does not suit your layout ambitions.

5. With the second element activated (the TextBlock with "2.0"), open the Common Properties category of the Properties panel and you should see the Text property has an orange border around its value input box (see Figure 12.13) and the advanced property options square is also orange. This indicates that the value present is the result of a data binding.

6. Click on the advanced property options button (little orange square) and you will be presented with a context menu that has an option at the bottom for data binding, as shown in Figure 12.14.

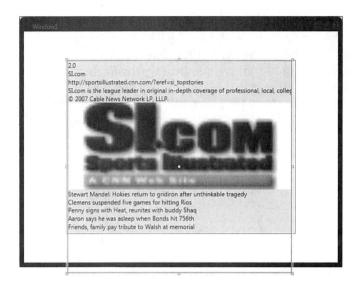

FIGURE 12.12   The StackPanel resized to fit the ListBox.

FIGURE 12.13   The databound indicator of the Text property.

FIGURE 12.14   The Data Binding option of the advanced property options context menu.

7. The Create Data Binding dialog is presented, which should automatically show you the Explicit Data Context tab with the field list that the control is currently bound to, as shown in Figure 12.15.

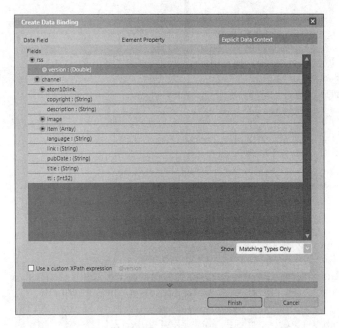

FIGURE 12.15   The dialog control and the fields available for binding.

8. You could change the field here that the element is bound to using either the Fields selector or you could add a custom XPath expression.

9. Click Cancel to close the dialog or Finish if you selected a new Field.

10. Begin moving, resizing, and changing the properties of the control elements as you see fit. When you get to the TextBlock element that contains the starting text "SI.com is the league leader in...", you will notice that the text extended out past the bounds of the ListBox. In the property search box, enter the word **Wrap** and you should then change the property to Wrap, which will resize the control for you.

11. Set the Top Margin property value to 10 to give a little space between this element and the previous element (see Figure 12.16).

12. You should now be looking at the distorted image, which is clearly incorrectly sized. The Image element also sits inside a StackPanel for no obvious reason. Drag the element in the Object and Timeline visual tree so that it becomes a child of the StackPanel parent element and not inside its own StackPanel. This should move the image to the very bottom of the screen.

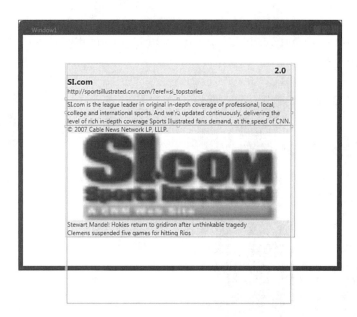

FIGURE 12.16 The element formatting in progress.

13. Remove the empty StackPanel element now—it is no longer needed. Right-click on the Image element and select Order and then Send to Back from the subsequent context menus. Hopefully you should now have something similar to Figure 12.17 and your Objects and Timeline category should look like Figure 12.18.

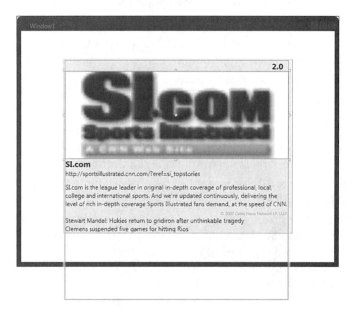

FIGURE 12.17 The element positioning.

FIGURE 12.18   The DataTemplate elements.

14. Now the image placement is where you want it (or where I want it), you now need to do something about the size of the image. Because this image is from an RSS feed, there is no guarantee that the image will be the same every time or indeed the same dimensions, so you should really bind the Width and Height properties of the Image element to the field properties (if present) inside the data source.

15. With the Image element selected, find the Width and Height properties in the Layout category of the Properties panel. Starting with the Width property, select the advanced property option button and then select Data Binding.

16. Select the Explicit Data Context tab, drill down through the list of fields until you find the image, and then select the width: (Int32) field. Click Finish to apply this binding.

17. Do the same for the Height property. If all is well, you should end up with the correctly formatted image in your template, as shown in Figure 12.19.

    You will notice that the last element at the bottom of the visual tree is called ItemsControl. When you activate it, it appears that the ItemsControl element contains the rest of the fields being shown. The ItemsControl is showing a collection of items from the data source (the feed, in this case), so it could dynamically change both the number and the content of each item and the data template would handle it without error.

18. Double-click the ItemsControl element to activate it if you have not already done so and right-click the element in the Object and Timeline visual tree. Again you need to select Edit Other Templates, Edit Generated Items (Item Template), and then Edit Template.

19. You can now see the template in the Objects and Timeline category, which contains a single StackPanel and child TextBlock element. This confirms that the ItemsControl is a template for each item shown, so any change you make to this template is propagated to each item in the collection.

20. You should select and delete the TextBlock element. All the items will disappear but you are going to put it all back in a short while.

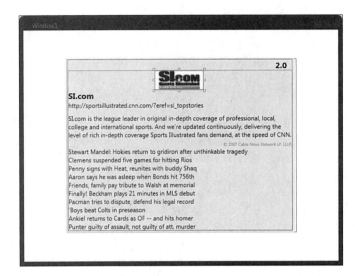

FIGURE 12.19   The correct Image formatted dimensions are shown.

21. Double-click to activate the StackPanel element.

22. Find the Button control in the toolbox and add a single button as the child element of the StackPanel. You will now see quite a few buttons back on the artboard as shown in Figure 12.20.

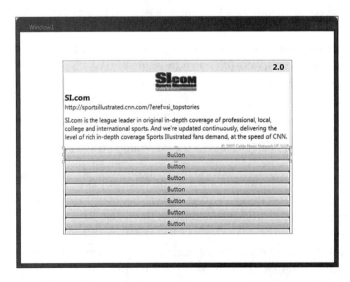

FIGURE 12.20   All the buttons that represent items in this collection.

23. Looking at Figure 12.20, you can see that there are many more buttons than space. Obviously a scrollbar needs to be implemented somewhere so that the user can see all the items, but you can't do it in this template because the template represents just one item. You will change this shortly.

24. With the Button element activated, find the Content property, again selecting the advanced property options button and selecting Data Binding.

25. Inside the Explicit Data Context tab, you need to remember that you are looking for the Item Array (because this is the Item collection you are working with). Find the appropriate field, which in this case is title: (String). Select it and click Finish.

26. You should now have some more meaningful content inside each of the Button element items. You can go ahead now and style the button to your requirements. My efforts are shown in Figure 12.21.

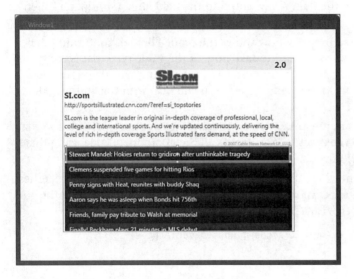

FIGURE 12.21   The Button elements with the bound title field as content.

27. You changed the DataTemplate to have buttons instead of TextBlock elements, and there was a reason for that. You want users to be able to click on a headline shown in the button and launch a browser taking them to the selected story. So, how do you achieve this? You can add a click handler for each button because the data template only defines one button. In addition, the content is dynamic, so you need to somehow parse the correct information though the button so that the application can act on it.

28. With the Button element activated, enter the word **Tag** into the property search box. You should see only one property, which is (funnily enough) called **Tag**.

What Is a Tag?

The Tag property can be found in most, if not all control elements. Its data type is that of Object so you can store anything you want in there to be used with the attached control.

Tag is a useful place to store arbitrary information and is ideal for parsing extended values with the object in data binding as you are doing in this exercise. There is no limit to the type of object you can place in the field, so you could attach the entire data source object if you wanted to, but in this case you are just parsing the URL link string, contained inside an XmlElement.

---

29. Using the advanced property options, Data Binding menu, navigate inside the Explicit Data Context, to the Item Array, and find the field Link: (String), and then click the Finish button.

    You will note that the Tag property now shows the orange border, confirming that the value is databound, but you need to take note of the value type that is contained in the property. Even though you bound directly to the string type field Link, you are actually binding to an XmlElement object. You will deal with this in the code when the object is used.

    Each Button item now has the link for its corresponding headline embedded so that now all you have to do is extract that link and call the appropriate code using that information, as you will now do.

30. With the Button element still activated, open the Event Viewer list in the Properties panel, looking for the Click event. Add the click handler by double-clicking the Handler field box to open Visual Studio.

```
private void Button_Click(object sender, RoutedEventArgs e)
{

}
```

31. The parameters available through this event handler are very handy. You can see the first one (object sender) is of type Object and it represents the object that made the call to this event. In this case, it is the Button element that represents the item. Using this information, you can first of all test that the Tag property does contain something and then you can begin to use the information as you please.

32. Complete the method by adding the code shown in Listing 12.7. You will notice that there is a call from an object called Process. You will need to add a using statement at the top of the code page to enable this:

    ```
    using System.Diagnostics;
    ```

    You will also need to add the following using statement for the XmlElement type used:

    ```
    using System.Xml;
    ```

LISTING 12.7   Reading the Tag Value an Element

```
private void Button_Click(object sender, RoutedEventArgs e)
{
    if ((sender as Button).Tag != null)
    {
        XmlElement Target = (XmlElement)(sender as Button).Tag;
        Process.Start(Target.InnerText);
    }
}
```

12

33. Ridiculously simple? You can see in the code in Listing 12.7 that you are casting the object parameter sender to its original type, a Button element, which then allows you to retrieve the Tag property. First you check to make sure that the property object does not equal null, and then you convert the Tag property (which was of type Object, remember) to an XmlElement type. Process.Start() does all the rest, firing up the user's default browser and loading the page given the URL link contained in the InnerText property of the XmlElement object.

34. Save the solution in Visual Studio and select OK to save the .sln file where Visual Studio suggests.

35. Back to Blend and the editing of the ItemsControl template is complete, so scope up to return to the first DataTemplate.

36. With the ItemsControl activated, you should see that the border of the control extends well beyond the visible area of the ListBox, as shown in Figure 12.22, and as you will remember, previously you noted the amount of Button elements generated by the ItemsControl.

37. Right-click on the ItemsControl in the Object and Timeline category and select to cut the element.

38. Find the parent StackPanel (which contains most of the fields) and double-click it to activate it.

39. In the Panel Based Control collection in the toolbox, or the Asset Library, find the ScrollViewer element and add it as a child of the StackPanel.

40. It should be placed at the bottom of the StackPanel automatically as new items are stacked from the bottom. Stretch the ScrollViewer element so that it now reaches the bottom of the ListBox control.

41. Double-click the ScrollViewer element to activate it, and then right-click and select Paste to put the ItemsControl element inside it.

42. Ensure that the Width of the ItemsControl is set to Auto and the HorizontalAlignment is set to Stretch. (Make sure the Property search box is cleared to find the properties.) The ItemsControl should now extend the ScrollViewer to show a scrollbar vertically, as shown in Figure 12.23.

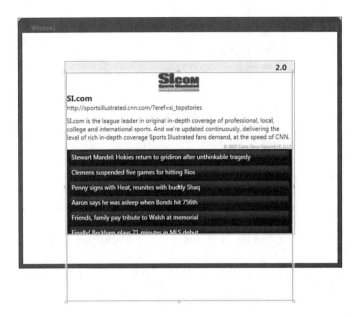

FIGURE 12.22   The issues with the ItemsControl.

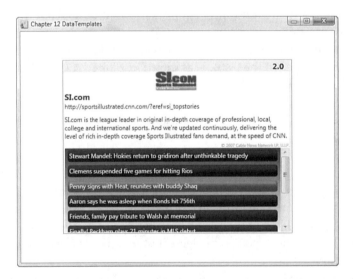

FIGURE 12.23   The completed application with the ItemsControl now scrollable.

You are now ready to test the application by pressing F5. Click on any of the HeadLine buttons to launch your browser to that page.

Summary

In this chapter, you learned to change the makeup of a control by modifying and replacing the elements in it, while at the same time using this specification to create a reusable template. You also learned about styles and how changes to the style template can dramatically change the way the control looks to the end user.

There are a few gotchas, such as not being able to use Color Resources in style templates (which is a Framework defect and not Blend, apparently). Designers could find it particularly difficult to modify templates stored in external Resource Dictionaries as apposed to in-control editing because they will have no visual context to work with—only the template is visible on the artboard and not the surrounding controls of a Window or UserControl, for example. Aside from these issues, templating in Blend is very good and you can expect it only to become even easier to use in future versions.

Data templates are very specific to the controls they will be applied to, but as you have seen, you can create and modify these templates just as easy as you can a standard ControlTemplate.

Remember that the naming of your templates is very important as well as the location that you choose to create your template and the scope that you give it for others to use within the application framework.

12

Data Binding

One of the areas that can sometimes be frustrating for new users is that of data binding. There are some conceptual hurdles to get over when working in Blend and until you understand the flow of objects and how they can be bound, you will most likely run around in circles, at the very least where binding to a CLR (Common Language Runtime) object is concerned.

Data binding in Expression Blend is for the most part quick and simple, made possible by the excellent wizards that Blend provides, taking most of the hassles out of even thinking about your source details. Where most people tend to struggle naturally is the CLR-level bindings, so this chapter will be focused toward providing you the skills to understand a process that can be used.

Data Sources

Data sources can and do come in all varieties from XML (Extensible Markup Language) files, RSS (Really Simple Syndication) web feeds (XML streams), CLR objects, system classes, and even other controls in your Blend application. Throughout the chapter, we will look at some specific requirements for some of these sources to be recognized.

Binding to an Element

Data binding in Expression Blend is not just limited to finding a file, stream, or object to find some form of bindable data. A feature of XAML (Extensible Application

Markup Language) is that you can specify binding sources and targets of other UIElements that are within the scope of your current workspace.

The only catch is that the properties of the UIElements you use to be either a binding source or target must be dependency properties, and the element must be a dependency object. That said, you will find the ability to bind properties of UIElements very handy, and a process that could save you a lot of time.

In the sample application shown in Figure 13.1, you are going to template bind a number of slider controls to properties of the Ellipse as well as to the values in the text boxes shown. Doing so will enable you to change the color and the size of the Ellipse by using the sliders as well as entering values into the text boxes. A simple enough example, but one worth your while to do to get the feel of template binding.

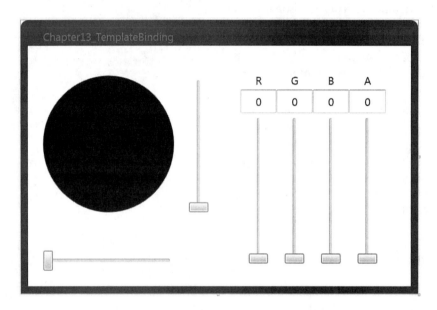

FIGURE 13.1   The sample application used for template binding.

Create a new application, resizing the Window element to 450 px wide by 300 px high and then enter the XAML markup shown in Listing 13.1.

LISTING 13.1   Setting Up the Example Application

```
<Grid x:Name="LayoutRoot" Width="Auto" Background="{x:Null}">
<Grid.ColumnDefinitions>
        <ColumnDefinition Width="0.5*"/>
        <ColumnDefinition Width="0.5*"/>
    </Grid.ColumnDefinitions>
    <Grid HorizontalAlignment="Stretch" x:Name="PART_Ball"
VerticalAlignment="Stretch" Width="Auto" Height="Auto">
```

```xml
    <Grid.ColumnDefinitions>
        <ColumnDefinition Width="0.832*"/>
        <ColumnDefinition Width="0.168*"/>
    </Grid.ColumnDefinitions>
    <Grid.RowDefinitions>
        <RowDefinition Height="0.818*"/>
        <RowDefinition Height="0.182*"/>
    </Grid.RowDefinitions>
    <Ellipse Stroke="#FF000000" x:Name="myBall" Fill="#FF000000"
Width="150" Height="150"/>
    <Slider Height="30" Maximum="150" Value="{Binding Path=Width,
ElementName=Ellipse, Mode=Default}" HorizontalAlignment="Stretch"
x:Name="slidWidth" VerticalAlignment="Center" Width="150" Grid.Row="1"/>
    <Slider Maximum="150" Value="{Binding Path=Height, ElementName=Ellipse,
Mode=Default}" Orientation="Vertical" HorizontalAlignment="Center"
x:Name="slidHeight" VerticalAlignment="Stretch" Width="30" Height="150"
Grid.Column="1"/>
  </Grid>
  <Grid Margin="25,25,25,25" x:Name="PART_Color" Grid.Column="1">
    <Grid.ColumnDefinitions>
        <ColumnDefinition Width="0.25*"/>
        <ColumnDefinition Width="0.25*"/>
        <ColumnDefinition Width="0.25*"/>
        <ColumnDefinition Width="0.25*"/>
    </Grid.ColumnDefinitions>
    <Grid.RowDefinitions>
        <RowDefinition Height="0.107*"/>
        <RowDefinition Height="0.123*"/>
        <RowDefinition Height="0.77*"/>
    </Grid.RowDefinitions>
    <Slider Orientation="Vertical" Width="Auto" Maximum="255" Value="{Binding
Path=Fill, ElementName=Ellipse, Mode=Default}" HorizontalAlignment="Center"
x:Name="slidR" VerticalAlignment="Stretch" Grid.Row="2" Grid.RowSpan="1"/>
    <Slider Orientation="Vertical" HorizontalAlignment="Center" x:Name="slidG"
Grid.Column="1" Grid.Row="2" Grid.RowSpan="1" Maximum="255"/>
    <Slider Orientation="Vertical" HorizontalAlignment="Center" x:Name="slidB"
Grid.Column="2" Grid.Row="2" Grid.RowSpan="1" Maximum="255"/>
    <Slider Orientation="Vertical" x:Name="slidA" HorizontalAlignment="Center"
Grid.Column="3" Grid.Row="2" Maximum="255"/>
    <Label HorizontalAlignment="Stretch" VerticalAlignment="Stretch"
Height="Auto" Content="R" FontSize="12" HorizontalContentAlignment="Center"
VerticalContentAlignment="Top" Grid.RowSpan="1"/>
    <Label Content="G" FontSize="12" HorizontalContentAlignment="Center"
VerticalContentAlignment="Top" VerticalAlignment="Stretch" Height="Auto"
Grid.Column="1" Grid.RowSpan="1"/>
```

13

```
        <Label Content="B" FontSize="12" HorizontalContentAlignment="Center"
VerticalContentAlignment="Top" VerticalAlignment="Stretch" Height="Auto"
Grid.Column="2" Grid.RowSpan="1"/>
        <Label Content="A" FontSize="12" HorizontalContentAlignment="Center"
VerticalContentAlignment="Top" VerticalAlignment="Stretch" Height="Auto"
Grid.Column="3" Grid.RowSpan="1"/>
        <TextBox HorizontalAlignment="Stretch" x:Name="txtRed"
VerticalAlignment="Stretch" HorizontalContentAlignment="Center"
VerticalContentAlignment="Center" Grid.Row="1" Text="0" TextWrapping="Wrap"/>
        <TextBox HorizontalContentAlignment="Center"
VerticalContentAlignment="Center" Text="0" TextWrapping="Wrap" x:Name="txtGreen"
Grid.Column="1" Grid.Row="1"/>
        <TextBox HorizontalContentAlignment="Center"
VerticalContentAlignment="Center" Text="0" TextWrapping="Wrap" x:Name="txtBlue"
Grid.Column="2" Grid.Row="1"/>
        <TextBox HorizontalContentAlignment="Center"
VerticalContentAlignment="Center" Text="0" TextWrapping="Wrap" x:Name="txtAlpha"
Grid.Column="3" Grid.Row="1"/>
    </Grid>
</Grid>
```

The following steps will take you through template binding two Sliders to the Ball that is now in your application:

1. Locate the slider named slidWidth in the Objects and Timeline category and then open the Properties tab.

2. In this scenario, you want to bind the Value property of the slider element to the Width property of the Ellipse element named myBall. Locate the Value property of the slider and next to the property input box you will find a little box that has the ToolTip Advanced Property Options when you mouse over it. Clicking on this box will raise the context menu shown in Figure 13.2.

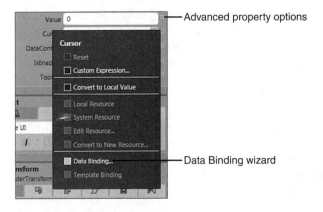

FIGURE 13.2 The Advanced Property Options context menu and the Data Binding menu item.

3. Selecting the Data Binding menu option shows the Create Data Binding dialog, which is discussed in detail throughout this chapter and shown in Figure 13.3.

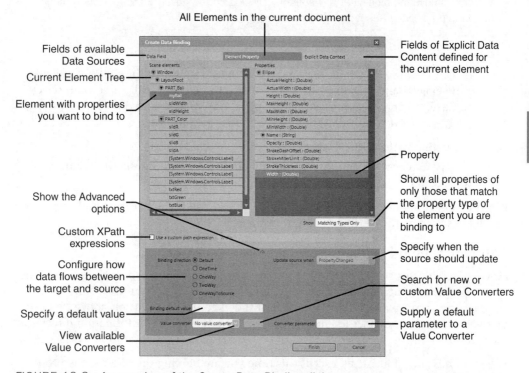

FIGURE 13.3   An overview of the Create Data Binding dialog.

4. Select the middle tab, Element Property, which provides on the left pane a list of UIElements available in this document. The list is identical to that of the visual tree shown in the Objects and Timeline category of the Interaction panel.

5. Drill down through the element list until you see the UIElement myBall, and then select it.

6. On the right side of the dialog, you should now see a list of properties that are available for the selected element. You should note that, by default, only matching property types are shown. This means that because you are binding the Value property of the slider element which is of type Double, the properties shown are all of type Double. I know what you are thinking: You can see the property Name: (String) in the list. A number of built-in type converters exist in Blend, so properties that can be automatically converted to type are also shown.

7. Select the Width property from the list and then click Finish.

8. You should now see that the property Value has an orange border around it, which is a visual indicator that this property is bound.

How to Unbind a Property Value

You can remove the binding at any stage by clicking on the Advanced Properties Option button and selecting Reset from the context menu.

9. You can view the XAML for the binding by right-clicking on the slidWidth element in the Objects and Timeline category and selecting View XAML, or you can select the Custom Expression context menu option from the advanced property options, which will show you the XAML directly which looks like this:

```
{Binding Path=Width, ElementName=myBall, Mode=Default}
```

10. Now try to repeat the actions of template binding by binding the slidHeight value property to that of the Height property of the myBall element.

When you have completed this, you should be able to run the application and move both the sliders to adjust the width and height of the ball.

Two-Way Binding

Moving on with this simple example: You have previously template bound the Width and Height properties, but you can adjust only one element to change another. Now we are going to "two-way" template bind the vertical sliders to the text controls above them so that you can move the slider to effect a change, but can also enter information directly in the text box to move the slider.

The process is almost identical, except this time you are binding the slider Value property to the textbox text property.

You can perform the binding from either the slider or the text box. It doesn't matter in this scenario because we are going to use two-way binding, but in different circumstances, you might need to be more aware of which element represents the target and which one is the source.

The following steps show you how to implement two-way data binding on your TextBox and Slider elements:

1. Select the Value property of the slidR element and again select the Advanced Property Options, Data Binding context menu item.
2. Remembering to select the Element Property tab, search for the correct text box, txtRed, and then find the text property in the right panel of the dialog box.
3. Before clicking Finish, select the Advanced Options button as shown in Figure 13.3, which should present the lower part of the dialog as shown in the figure.
4. Table 13.1 discusses the different values of the binding directions that you should familiarize yourself with. Select the TwoWay radio button and ensure that you have selected Property Changed for the Update Source When option.
5. Click Finish.

TABLE 13.1   Binding Directions

Value	Description
OneTime	Initializes the target only with a value from the source. Any additional changes to the target or the source are not reflected.
OneWay	Only changes made to the source value will be propagated to the target.
TwoWay	Properties made to either the source of the target are reflected in each other.
OneWayToSource	The source value is changed on when the target value changes. This is in effect the reverse of OneWay.

Run the application now and test this first vertical color slider by moving the slider up and down as well as entering values into the text box. You will note that dragging the slider results in an overflow of text in the text box. This occurs because the slider is showing a very high precision Double value in the text box.

To remedy this, select the slidR element and locate a property called IsSnapToTickEnabled. You can find this in the advanced properties of the Common Properties category or you could use the search box feature. You will find that by default it is unchecked, so you should check it, which will make the slider move by whole units of 1 which is defined by the TickFrequency property. Try the application again and this time you should find only whole numbers only appearing in the text box.

You should also note that the Maximum property for the slider is set to 255, which is the maximum value of a color that we will set shortly. Typing a larger number into the text box doesn't cause an error, but just shows the slider at the maximum position. You will fix this in code shortly, so the maximum value shown in the text box is 255.

Work your way through the remaining sliders, two-way binding them to their corresponding text boxes. Don't forget to change the IsSnapToTickEnabled property for each of the sliders. Test the application and each slider to ensure that they are the same.

A Change of Color

The following steps introduce some code to validate the data that is being applied by both the sliders and the text boxes. When everything is set, you will build and apply the new color setting to the ball.

1. Select the txtRed element in the Objects and Timeline category.
2. Open the Properties panel and select the lightning bolt icon to show the events view.
3. At the bottom of the Events list, you should find a property called TextChanged. Double-click the input box to launch Visual Studio.
4. The quickest workflow here is to immediately move back to Blend, selecting the next text box and again double-clicking the property input box for TextChanged. On completing this, you should have four event handlers in Visual Studio, as shown in Listing 13.2.

LISTING 13.2   Adding TextChanged Event Handlers

```
private void txtRed_TextChanged(object sender, TextChangedEventArgs e)
{

}

private void txtGreen_TextChanged(object sender, TextChangedEventArgs e)
{

}

private void txtBlue_TextChanged(object sender, TextChangedEventArgs e)
{

}

private void txtAlpha_TextChanged(object sender, TextChangedEventArgs e)
{

}
```

5. Because we are going to be validating the same type of information from all four text boxes, it would make sense to write a validation method that all four event handlers can call. Create the method shown in Listing 13.3 and then modify each of the four event handlers to call the method shown in Listing 13.4.

LISTING 13.3   Validating Color Values

```
/// <summary>
/// Validates the provided string number and converts it to an byte
/// </summary>
/// <param name="InputValue">The value to validate</param>
/// <returns></returns>
private byte ValidateColorValue(string InputValue)
{
    byte ValidateValue = Convert.ToByte(InputValue);

    if (ValidateValue < 0)
        return 0;

    if (ValidateValue > 255)
        return 255;

    return ValidateValue;
}
```

The method shown in Listing 13.3 first converts the string value to a Byte type that we can then perform validation on using mathematical equations. You are using a Byte type here because an ARGB color data type is made up of four byte values representing each piece of the color structure.

Because the individual color value must be between 0 and 255, the method ensures that this rule is adhered to, and if the value is between 0 and 255, it simply returns the value supplied.

LISTING 13.4   Global Byte Types

```
private byte RedValue = 0;
private byte GreenValue = 0;
private byte BlueValue = 0;
private byte AlphaValue = 0;

private void txtRed_TextChanged(object sender, TextChangedEventArgs e)
{
    this.RedValue = this.ValidateColorValue(this.txtRed.Text);
    this.txtRed.Text = this.RedValue.ToString();
}
```

The code in Listing 13.4 shows some new global Byte variables that have been created to store the individual color values. The event handler for the txtRed text box then calls the validation method (which returns a Byte) and stores the validated value in the correct global value. Next the code assigns the validated value back to the text box by converting the global value to a string. The logic behind storing the validated value in a global will become apparent shortly.

1. Modify the code in all four event handlers to validate their respective text box values as well as to assign the validated value to the correct global value.

2. A new method is created in Listing 13.5 that takes the global values, creates a Solid Color Brush object, and assigns the color to the Brush. The Brush object is then assigned to the Fill property of the myBall element.

LISTING 13.5   Creating a New SolidColorBrush

```
/// <summary>
        /// Create the new Brush object using the global values
        /// </summary>
        private void CreateBackgroundColor()
        {
            SolidColorBrush NewColorBrush = new SolidColorBrush();
            NewColorBrush.Color = Color.FromArgb(this.AlphaValue, this.RedValue,
this.GreenValue, this.BlueValue);
```

```
//Assing the Brush to the correct proeprty
this.myBall.Fill = NewColorBrush;
}
```

3. The last task is to modify each of the event handlers to call the method added in Listing 13.5. Add the following code to each of the event handlers:

```
//Create the color and assign it to the ball
this.CreateBackgroundColor();
```

Build your solution in Visual Studio and run the application. You should be able to now create a color value with both the sliders and the text boxes and it should apply to the ball object (see Figure 13.4). If you don't see any color, make sure that you have the A slider value set to at least 100.

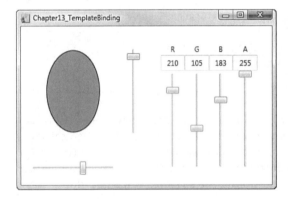

FIGURE 13.4   The finished application.

This has been a simple example of template binding and how using it can dramatically reduce the code you have to enter. How much code? Without template binding, to achieve the same sample in code only, you would need several event handlers for each element and the subsequent code to sequence all the methods. This would easily add up to a few hundred lines of code!

Using ValidationRules

There exist several powerful mechanisms within WPF (Windows Presentation Foundation) data binding to perform functioning validation and resultant error handling during object data updating. The ValidationRule class allows you to create custom validation objects that implement a Validation method. For more information on this advanced data binding topic, please consult the MSDN library found at http://msdn. com.

Using Data Context

Moving to a slightly more complex form of data binding now, we are going to take a swift look at creating a Data Context. You have used XML feeds throughout this book to perform some form of data binding previously, but the Data Context concept provides a means of binding a single parent item (such as a Grid element) and then allow all child items to bind to the single binding source.

This is what is typically used to create simple Master-Detail data-bound forms where you typically select items from a list (the master) and then the relevant information is shown next to it (the details). As you will see, several WPF controls are uniquely set up to take advantage of a Data Context by allowing the synchronization between item collections, so a change of one bound element affects other elements bound to the same context.

This sample is relatively simple in its design, but after performing the following steps, you will be able to create a Data Context for other areas of you applications with ease:

1. Create a new application in Blend.

2. In the Projects tab, Data category, select the +XML button.

3. Add the following URL to the URL for XML data input box:

   http://api.flickr.com/services/feeds/photos_public.gne?tags=fractal&lang= en-us&format=rss_200

   As you can tell from the URL, you are going to create a very simple fractal viewer from an RSS feed provided by the good people of flickr.com.

4. Click OK and after a short period, your Data category should contain the data source shown in Figure 13.5.

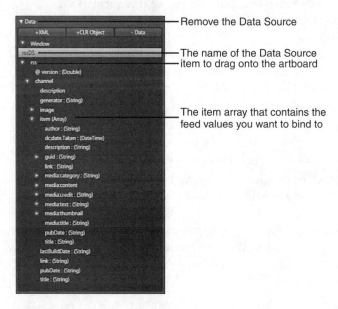

Remove the Data Source

The name of the Data Source item to drag onto the artboard

The item array that contains the feed values you want to bind to

FIGURE 13.5   The data source is now available.

13

5. Double-click the LayoutRoot element to make it activated and select a Grid element from the toolbox.

6. Set the Grid to stretch both horizontally and vertically, with the Width and Height properties both set to Auto. Set the Margin property for all four sides to 25.

7. Return to the project menu and drag the item rss from the Data category (as shown in Figure 13.5) on to the new Grid element you just added.

8. You will see a context menu appear as shown in Figure 13.6, which gives you several binding options. In this scenario, you want to bind the data source to the Grid, so select the first menu item: Bind rss to Grid.

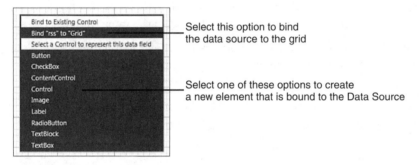

FIGURE 13.6   The Binding context menu.

9. A small dialog called Create Data Binding appears, and should already have the value DataContext in the Select Field field. Click OK.

What you have just done is assign the data source to the Grid element's Data Context property so that all child items will now have access to the data source through this explicit data context.

10. With the Grid element still selected, open the Properties tab, Common Properties category, and you should now see the Data Context property is encircled by an orange border, which is the visual indicator that the property is bound.

11. Click on the small box to the right of the property to display the Advanced Property Options context menu, and then select Data Binding.

12. You should see the Create Data Binding dialog. If it is not already selected, choose the Data Field tab at the top, which shows the data sources available to this document.

13. rssDS should be shown in the Data Sources pane along with rss selected in the Fields pane. As shown in Figure 13.7, you should drill down through the fields and select the Item: (Array).

14. Click Finish to close the dialog. In this process, you have now set the Data Context to be bound directly to the Items array so that you can access the Items collection with child elements.

15. Double-click to activate the new Grid.

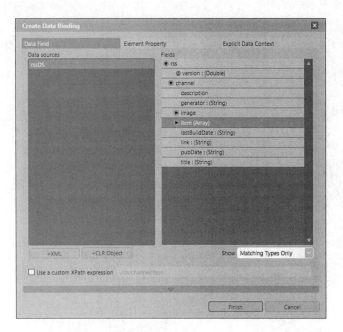

FIGURE 13.7   The fields to select.

16. With the selection tool, create a Column definition and set the Column width to 0.4 Star.

17. Select a ListBox element from the Common Controls toolbox item and add it as a child to the Grid, setting it to fill the first column.

18. With the ListBox still selected, locate the ItemsSource property in the Common Properties category of the Properties panel.

19. Once again select the Advanced Property Options context menu and then select Data Binding.

20. This time in the Create Data Binding dialog, you want to select the Explicit Data Context tab. The Fields pane will show you the data source that is available through the Data Context, which should be rss. Figure 13.8 shows the location of the Define Data Template button, which you should select *after* you have drilled down through the fields and selected the Item (Array) field.

21. You are now defining the data template for the Items collection, so you should be able to see every field available. In this scenario, you want to define a new template with only the title: (String) field selected. As you can see in Figure 13.9, you should also change the templated element type to a Label for the title field.

22. When completed, you should now see the application ListBox element has gained some content as shown in Figure 13.10. You should now locate an Image element (in the Asset Library—use the search functionality), and add it as a Child element of the Grid as also shown in Figure 13.10.

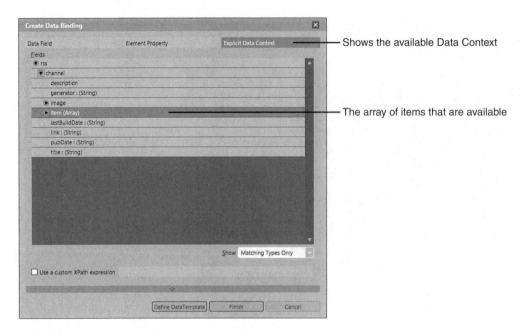

FIGURE 13.8   The location of the Item array field.

You may have created several templates in your application which you can access here

The default styling is only appropriate when displaying single items and not items in a collection

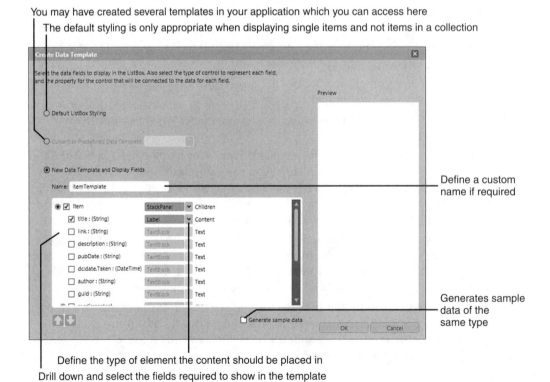

FIGURE 13.9   The data template settings in this scenario.

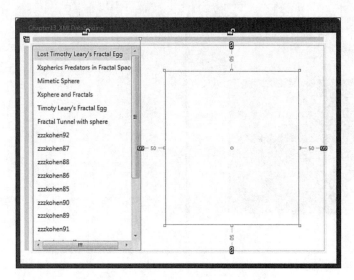

FIGURE 13.10   The application coming together.

23. Set the Image element's horizontal and vertical alignment properties to Stretch as well as the Width and Height properties to Auto. Set the Margin values for all four sides to 50 pixels.

24. With the Image element selected, locate the Source property inside the Common Properties category of the Properties panel. Again select the Data Binding menu option from the Advanced Property Options context menu.

25. Selecting the Explicit Data Context tab, you will this time note that the Define Data Template button is missing. This is because you are binding directly to the Image element, so there is no need to customize the display element used. This time, you need to drill down through several properties until you find the (String) field located inside the mediacontent field. When you select it, click Finish at the bottom of the dialog.

After several seconds (depending on your Internet connection speed), you should see an image appear. Why did this happen? This is because the ListBox element has a property called IsSyncronizedWithCurrentItem that basically dictates to the Data Context which Item from the array is currently being viewed. Because the Image element is bound to this data context, it automatically displays the field it is bound to, which in this case is the source URL for the image.

Run the application and select through the items in the ListBox, and you should see most items contain a fractal image (see Figure 13.11). Be patient with the load speed coming back from the API, though.

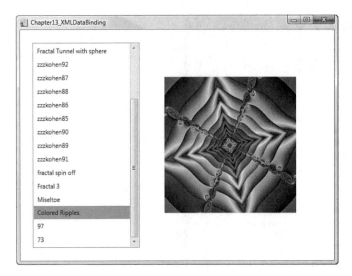

FIGURE 13.11   The application running.

CLR Data Binding

The most complex form of data binding in WPF is CLR (Common Language Runtime) data binding, and this is not because the act of binding is any more complex, but because the creation of the source is a manual process. At this point in the book, I need to assume that you have read Chapter 10, "Visual Studio: C# Primer," on the introduction to coding, and that you have been experimenting with code to some extent. I particularly hope you understood the sections on classes, properties, and generic collections because these three topics are the crux of the matter when it comes to CLR data binding.

You are about to create two objects in Visual Studio, one being the binding source collection, the other being the data object.

CLR data binding works by allowing you to select an ObservableCollection<T> (generic collection type similar to List<T> and Dictionary<T,T>) as the binding source. This collection contains a data type that you also design and create.

The Scenario

In this scenario, you are going to create the data object first, which will contain simple string-based properties. You can always expand this example later to include property types that you require.

When you have completed that, you are going to then create the collection. You are going to fill it with some objects that also have test data inside them.

The following steps show you how to create the test data and binding CLR object:

1. Create a new project in Blend.

2. Add a ListBox element as a child of the LayoutRoot.

3. Set the ListBox horizontal and vertical alignment properties to Stretch and the Width and Height properties to Auto. Set all four Margin property values to 30 pixels.

4. Save the application.

5. Select the Project panel. Right-click at the top of the solution (on the Solution item), and select Edit in Visual Studio from the context menu.

6. Inside Visual Studio, you should see your application visible in the Solution Explorer dialog. If this dialog is not visible, select the View menu item—the Solution Explorer should be second from the top.

7. Right-click on the Project (not the solution) inside Solution Explorer, select Add from the context menu, followed by Class from the subsequent context menu. This entire process is shown in Figure 13.12.

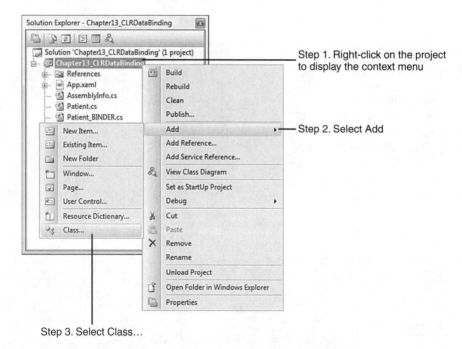

FIGURE 13.12   How to quickly add a new class to the project.

8. Now the Add New Item dialog appears with the class preselected. You should change the Name field to Patient.cs and click Add to complete the process.

As with Chapter 10, adding a .NET Framework 3.5 class tends to add a using directive to Linq. Remove the using directive to avoid a build error.

9. Visual Studio quickly creates your new class outline for you.

Because this class represents the data object that will be exposed through the
binding collection, all public properties that you add to this object will be available
as fields to bind to.

This data object is going to be nice and simple, featuring just three String type
properties.

10. Add the code as shown in Listing 13.6 to the Patient class, also defining your class
as "public" if required.

LISTING 13.6   Creating the Patient Class Properties

```
public class Patient
{
    public Patient()
    {
        //Constructor
    }

    private string _firstName;

    public string FIRST_NAME
    {
        get { return _firstName; }
        set { _firstName = value; }
    }

    private string  _lastName;

    public string  LAST_NAME
    {
        get { return _lastName; }
        set { _lastName = value; }
    }

    private string _notes;

    public string NOTES
    {
        get { return _notes; }
        set { _notes = value; }
    }
}
```

11. As previously shown, add another new class to the project, this time calling it `Patient_BINDER.cs`.

Why Call It Patient_BINDER?

If you work on larger projects, you could find that there will be lots and lots of `Class` objects all throughout the solution. When it comes time to find the classes that you can bind to with CLR binding, you need to find the correct classes. This naming convention enables you to know just from the name what the data object class is (`Patient`). And because it has `_BINDER` attached, you know that this class is an ObservableCollection that you can use for binding.

---

12. The Patient_BINDER object will be what you select in Expression Blend to be the binding source. For this object to be recognized, you need to expose it as an ObservableCollection.

    To do this, you need to make the `BINDER` class inherit from the ObservableCollection and contain the correct data object that exposes the properties you just created.

13. Modify the `Patient_BINDER` class as shown in Listing 13.7. You will also need to add the following using statement at the top of your class file:

    ```
    using System.Collections.ObjectModel;
    ```

LISTING 13.7   Inheriting from ObservableCollection<T>

```
public class Patient_BINDER : ObservableCollection<Patient>
{
    public Patient_BINDER()
    {
    }
}
```

Make sure that you spell ObservableCollection exactly as shown. You can also see how this collection is now strongly typed to contain your data object Patient.

14. Because Expression Blend has a live artboard, you can take advantage of this unique feature by creating some test data in your binding class. This means that after you have successfully added this class as a binding source in Blend, you can then go off and define the data template using actual data. To achieve this, you use the default Constructor method that you added from Listing 13.7. This method is what is called by Blend when it first creates an instance of the binding source object.

15. Create a new method as shown in Listing 13.8.

LISTING 13.8   Creating the Test Data Objects and Adding to the Objects Collection

```
private void BuildTestData()
{
    Patient TestPatient = new Patient();
    TestPatient.FIRST_NAME = "Tom";
    TestPatient.LAST_NAME = "Jones";
    TestPatient.NOTES = "Tom has a problem with his throat, caused by smoking too
much.";

    //Add this test object to the collection
    this.Add(TestPatient);

    //must null out the object now
    TestPatient = null;

    TestPatient = new Patient();
    TestPatient.FIRST_NAME = "Pamela";
    TestPatient.LAST_NAME = "Anderson";
    TestPatient.NOTES = "Pam has an injured back. She is unaware of what might be
causing this problem.";

    //Add this test object to the collection
    this.Add(TestPatient);

}
```

You can see that in Listing 13.8, you are first creating an instance of your Patient data object. You then assign some test data to the public properties and then you see that calling this.Add(TestPatient) adds the object to the collection that this class now is.

It is at this point that you could be calling a live web service or a back end database and retrieving real data. All you need to do is build the data object with the public properties you want to allow, and then fill the collection with as many instances as you like.

16. Add the following line of code into the constructor to call the test method:

```
public Patient_BINDER()
{
    this.BuildTestData();
}
```

17. Save the solution (at which point Visual Studio might prompt you to save the `.sln` file) and then build the solution from the Build menu item.

18. Return to Expression Blend where you should be prompted to reload the project. Click Yes. When it appears to have reloaded, open the Project tab and verify that both of your new classes are visible. If they are not, close the project and then navigate to the solution file you just saved and open it in Blend.

19. Open the Window1.xaml file if not already open. You can now open the Data category of the Project tab and select the +CLR Object button, which will open the Add CLR Object Data Source dialog as shown in Figure 13.13.

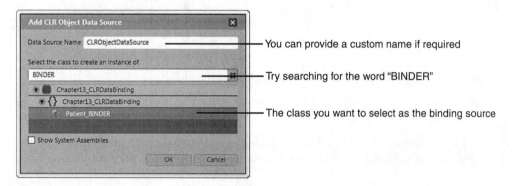

FIGURE 13.13   The clarity of a good naming convention.

20. The naming convention should have come in handy right about now because you can clearly see which class is the BINDER. Select the `Patient_BINDER` class and click OK.

21. You should now see that the Data category is populated with the data source. With the LayoutRoot element activated, select and drag the Patient_BINDER (Array) element from the Data category over to the ListBox element you added at the start of this sequence.

22. Select the first option and bind PatientBINDER to ListBox.

23. Leave the field ItemsSource as displayed in the next dialog that shows and click OK.

24. You should now see the Create Data Template dialog, which I am hoping is now familiar to you. You should be able to see some information in the Preview pane of this dialog, and when you are happy with the binding elements being added to the template, click the OK button.

25. If all has gone well, you should now see the two test data items that you created in the `Patient_BINDING` class as shown in Figure 13.14.

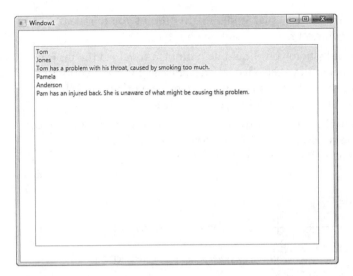

Tom
Jones
Tom has a problem with his throat, caused by smoking too much.
Pamela
Anderson
Pam has an injured back. She is unaware of what might be causing this problem.

FIGURE 13.14   The two test items added to the collection.

You should be starting to feel comfortable enough to now go through and modify the item templates as required. That process was shown in detail in the previous chapter.

Summary

This chapter has been about using Expression Blend to bind values from a variety of sources to elements within the user interface. Don't let the complexities of code frighten you away from attempting to use CLR object data binding. The process of binding doesn't get much more complicated than what has been shown.

Remember to try and use the Data Context where possible—it can improve performance by not having multiple binding objects throughout the application, and when trying to use bound elements in a navigation sense, it simply is a must.

The best thing to try with Expression Blend data binding is experimentation. Try to hook up as many RSS feeds as you can, and get used to the workflow within the binding dialogs. Have a look at the XAML markup and see how the binding is put together because this can sometimes aid in teaching you the process.

PART VI

Controlling Controls

IN THIS PART

Animations with Storyboards

Events and properties are usually taught as two separate areas of development skill when learning how to author software. But when dealing with Expression Blend, there are three areas in the application where you will be working with events and two areas where you will be working with properties. You will come to see how they are related to each other loosely, how calling or setting a property can raise an event and, conversely, how raising an event can set a property evaluation to true.

Why is this so important to know? You use these events and property states to trigger certain actions and re-actions in your applications. In particular, you use event triggers and property triggers to perform tasks such as executing a Storyboard animation.

In this chapter, you are going to learn how to use the RoutedEvents and DependencyProperties talked about in Chapter 10, "Visual Studio: C# Primer," (the ones in code), how to connect your elements (or controls) to react to an event being raised or property state being changed, as well as how to record object property states.

Storyboards and Timelines

One of the first pieces of software that I used with what I would call a successful timeline implementation was Flash. To me it appeared natural in its flow in terms of making an application run sequentially by calling different segments of time to run new functions within my application.

This works fine for a lot of scenarios, but when you need to provided a scaled implementation of a large object orientated project, it soon becomes unmanageable to a large degree. However, many skilled Flash developers have improved the methods they use when dealing with an object-oriented architecture and certainly ActionScript has also advanced to allow application architecture to improve. The one overriding issue with Flash is that the timeline output is based on frame rates, meaning you can set your Flash movie to play at 30 frames per second, which is all great if the target machine is capable of maintaining a consistent frame rate, but it can all fall down if you are not careful.

Expression Blend works with object orientation naturally, as opposed to a sequential application, and this probably creates significant confusion to new users of the application. Having a timeline is about the only thing in terms of application functionality that Blend has in common with Flash. Blend's time is based on actual time, which means if you want a visual control to move from point A to point B over a 5-second period, it will occur. The transition in between is what is modified to achieve this.

Timelines in Blend are used for object property animation. Notice I specifically said *property*? In the XAML (Extensible Application Markup Language) markup, when you add an animation as a result of manipulating an object's timeline, you will see something similar to the bolded markup in Listing 14.1.

LISTING 14.1   An Animation Type of DoubleAnimation Applied to an Object Property

```
<Window
    xmlns="http://schemas.microsoft.com/winfx/2006/xaml/presentation"
    xmlns:x="http://schemas.microsoft.com/winfx/2006/xaml"
    x:Class="Chapter14_AnimationSample.Window1"
    x:Name="Window"
    Title="Window1"
    Width="640" Height="480">

    <Window.Resources>
        <Storyboard x:Key="Timeline1">
            <DoubleAnimationUsingKeyFrames BeginTime="00:00:00"
                Storyboard.TargetName="rectangle"
                Storyboard.TargetProperty="(UIElement.Opacity)">
                <SplineDoubleKeyFrame KeyTime="00:00:00" Value="1"/>
                <SplineDoubleKeyFrame KeyTime="00:00:01" Value="0.25"/>
            </DoubleAnimationUsingKeyFrames>
        </Storyboard>
    </Window.Resources>
    <Window.Triggers>
        <EventTrigger RoutedEvent="FrameworkElement.Loaded">
            <BeginStoryboard Storyboard="{StaticResource Timeline1}"/>
        </EventTrigger>
    </Window.Triggers>

    <Grid x:Name="LayoutRoot">
```

```
        <Rectangle HorizontalAlignment="Center"
x:Name="rectangle"
VerticalAlignment="Center"
Width="100"
Height="100"
Fill="#FF000000"/>
    </Grid>
</Window>
```

For now, take note of the properties set in the animation shown in Listing 14.1 and you will note first that the entire animation resides inside a Storyboard tag, which has the name Timeline1. Then you see the animation type, which in this instance is a type of DoubleAnimationUsingKeyFrames.

So, as you might have guessed, because an animation is a type, you can create an instance of an animation in code and apply that to object properties dynamically during runtime. We will look at this scenario at the end of this chapter.

We will now break down the Storyboard XAML to understand the parts that it contains.

```
<DoubleAnimationUsingKeyFrames BeginTime="00:00:00"
```

The first property being set is BeginTime, which is a TimeSpan value telling the animation to begin from a set time after the Storyboard has been called. In this case, the value of "00:00:00" means start immediately.

```
Storyboard.TargetName="rectangle"
```

The TargetName property is the element that is going to have a property modified.

```
Storyboard.TargetProperty="(UIElement.Opacity)">
```

Now we see the property type being set, which is the Opacity property.

```
<SplineDoubleKeyFrame KeyTime="00:00:00" Value="1"/>
```

This is the first KeyFrame set which shows the value that the property (Opacity) should be at the given time in the Storyboard.

```
<SplineDoubleKeyFrame KeyTime="00:00:01" Value="0.25"/>
```

Now we see a second KeyFrame and the new value that it should be by the time the Storyboard time has elapsed.

```
</DoubleAnimationUsingKeyFrames>
```

Now the enclosing tag to end the animation settings.

This is the essence of animation in XAML and how properties are set at specific time intervals. Now you could sit there all day writing XAML markup to achieve animation nirvana, but why would you when you have such a simple way of doing this with Blend?

1. Create a new application in Blend.

2. Add a Rectangle element as the child to the LayoutRoot element. You can make it of arbitrary size but for ease of use you should center the element in the LayoutRoot and keep it to approximately 200 wide by 200 high.

3. Create a new storyboard by clicking the create new Storyboard button as shown in Figure 14.1, which will provide a dialog for you to name your storyboard. When you have entered a name, your storyboard will be opened automatically for you to work with.

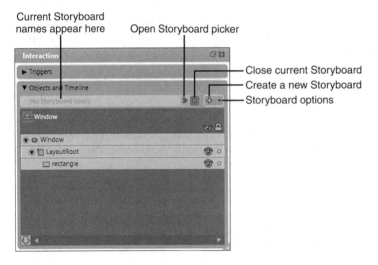

FIGURE 14.1   Some points of interest on the Object and Timeline category.

KeyFrames

Those that have used KeyFrames previously will be familiar with their usage, which Blend implements in typical fashion. A KeyFrame's purpose is to ensure that the property value of a given object or element is maintained at specific points in time.

As shown in Figure 14.2, each element in the visual tree has a corresponding line of time where KeyFrames are added.

The workflow is that you select the element you want to work with and then move the Playhead position to the location that you want to add the KeyFrame, click the Record KeyFrame button (as shown in Figure 14.2) or change an element's properties directly to automatically create a new KeyFrame.

4. With the Playhead position at 0:00.000, select the Rectangle element.

Click here to add a new KeyFrame

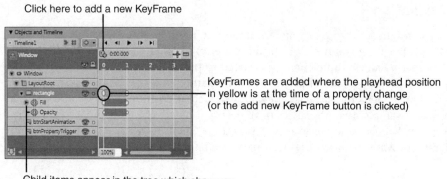

KeyFrames are added where the playhead position
in yellow is at the time of a property change
(or the add new KeyFrame button is clicked)

Child items appear in the tree which show you
which properties have been modified

FIGURE 14.2 A KeyFrame being added for the element.

14

5. Open the Properties panel and then the Brushes category.

6. Modify the Fill property to a new color.

7. Move the Timeline Playhead to a new position (which might be an increment or
   decrement of time), perhaps 1 second, and again add a KeyFrame to the Timeline for
   the selected Rectangle element.

8. In the Properties panel, modify the Opacity and Fill properties. Figure 14.3 shows
   the Timeline as it should have recorded.

A red dot here indicates that recording is on

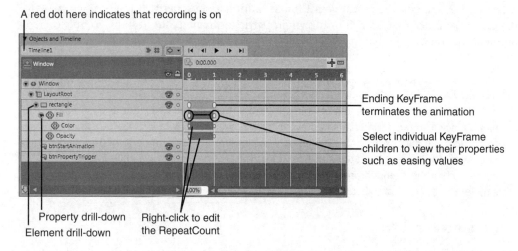

Ending KeyFrame
terminates the animation

Select individual KeyFrame
children to view their properties
such as easing values

Property drill-down   Right-click to edit
Element drill-down   the RepeatCount

FIGURE 14.3 The simple Timeline KeyFrames, properties, and other points of interest.

9. You should be able to now drag the Playhead position between the KeyFrames and
   see the effect that you have created.

Repeat Animation

Quite often you might want to repeat an animation and although it is possible to do so, accessibility to this setting is not easy to find for the uninitiated. Because you have animated a property value of an element, you need to perform the repeat count on a specific animated property value of the selected element. Figure 14.3 demonstrates this by showing a Rectangle element that has a KeyFrame added at position 0:00.000 and again at 0:01.000. In this example, two properties have been animated: the Fill property and the Opacity property. You can also see in Figure 14.3 the element now has a level of drill-down available showing the properties that have been animated under the selected element.

Figure 14.3 shows the area of the animated property that you must right mouse click to see the context menu item Edit Repeat Count. You will then see the Edit Repeat dialog as shown in Figure 14.4. You can key in the number of specific repeats for the property or click the Infinity symbol button to set to repeat forever.

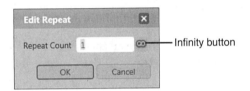
Infinity button

FIGURE 14.4   The simple Edit Repeat Dialog with Infinity button.

It is either fantastic flexibility or extremely poor design when you take into consideration that you need to edit the repeat count for each animated property. It might not appear to be much hassle at present with only two properties animated, but in more complex animation, you can find yourself right-clicking and setting repeat values for quite some time.

TIP

In large animation sets with lots of animated properties on each element, it is sometimes quicker to raise the completed event for a timeline and then call the storyboard again from the code-behind file. This is not the preferred method to perform a repeat, but given the Blend UI limitations at this stage, it might be worth your while investigating this when the scenario presents itself. At the end of this chapter, you will see how simple it is to call a storyboard in code.

KeyFrame Easing

Ease In and Ease Out (also called *easing*) are the common terms used to describe the interpolation of values between two KeyFrames. Easing allows you to control the speeds that values change from KeyFrame to KeyFrame, but where would you use this?

In real life, often when an object (such as a ball) moves from one point to another, it does so starting slowly, and then reaching a certain speed or velocity. Or it could be the other way, such as a car driving along at a constant speed but needing to slow down before stopping, not just coming to a sudden stop.

The Blend Objects and Timeline panel will allow you to set three different types of easing interpolation, although four types are supported in XAML (see Table 14.1), the fourth being the default interpolation rate on creation of the KeyFrames.

TABLE 14.1   Interpolation Values

Interpolation Name	Description
Ease In	Slows the rate of incremented change between the selected KeyFrame and the next defined KeyFrame.
Ease Out	Slows the rate of incremental change when time has passed the selected KeyFrame and before time reaches the next KeyFrame.
Hold Out	The effect of Hold Out is that no interpolated changes will take place on the property until the next KeyFrame is reached. In other words, the selected object will switch from one property state to another when the next KeyFrame is reached.
Linear	The standard interpolation rate between two KeyFrames. The property will increment equally across the time/space difference.

Unlike the repeat count, you can set the interpolation rate to apply to all properties in a selected object by selecting the top KeyFrame of the object (the Rectangle, for example) or individually by selecting KeyFrames one at a time (the opacity KeyFrames) as shown in Figure 14.5.

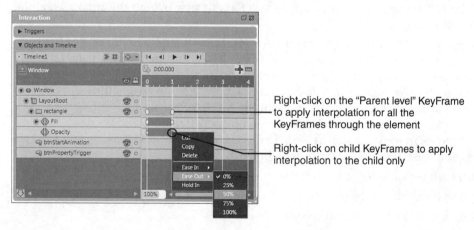

FIGURE 14.5   One method of applying interpolation settings.

Expression Blend 2 has added visual support for editing the easing values of KeyFrames, but unless you understand the concept of easing from a XAML point of view, it can be rather strange at first.

To demonstrate the use of easing, the following steps continue on with the current project containing the Rectangle object:

1. Close the current Storyboard (if it is still open) by clicking the x button near the Storyboard picker. Or you can also enter the Storyboard picker and click on the Close Storyboard button as shown in Figure 14.6.

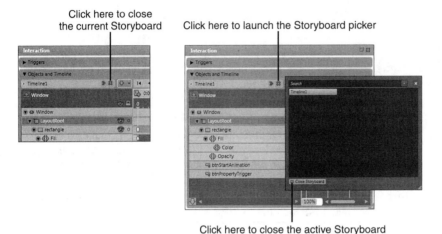

FIGURE 14.6   The close actions of the Storyboard picker and the Objects and Timeline panel.

2. You will notice that the Objects and Timeline panel should now just show your Rectangle element again without any child entries and so forth.

3. Press F11 as many times as you need to get a split view of both the artboard and the XAML editor.

4. What you will notice is that Blend has added quite a large amount of XAML to your markup file. Take a minute to walk through it and look for the name of the storyboard in tags and so on to try and get an understanding of what is being referenced by what in order to deliver the animation. When you are satisfied, you can either start a new project or remove all the XAML between the <Window.Resources> and </Window.Resources> declarations and the <Window.Triggers> section as well. This is the part of the XAML you should be paying close attention to from here on out.

5. Go back through the process of creating a new storyboard, naming it ShowEasing.

6. Select the Rectangle in the Objects and Timeline category.

7. Add a KeyFrame at position 0:00.00.

8. Move the Playhead position to the 1 second mark again.

9. Select the Rectangle on the artboard and move it to an arbitrary position on the artboard.

10. You should note that a KeyFrame has been created for you. Test your animation using the Rewind and Play buttons near the Playhead position label.

11. Your <Window.Resources> XAML should look something similar to that in Listing 14.2.

LISTING 14.2   Storyboard with Easing Values Applied

```
<Window.Resources>
    <Storyboard x:Key="ShowEasing">
        <DoubleAnimationUsingKeyFrames BeginTime="00:00:00" Storyboard.Target-
Name="rectangle" Storyboard.TargetProperty="(UIElement.RenderTransform).(Transform-
Group.Children)[3].(TranslateTransform.X)">
            <SplineDoubleKeyFrame KeyTime="00:00:00" Value="0"/>
            <SplineDoubleKeyFrame KeyTime="00:00:01" Value="-218"/>
        </DoubleAnimationUsingKeyFrames>
        <DoubleAnimationUsingKeyFrames BeginTime="00:00:00" Storyboard.Target-
Name="rectangle" Storyboard.TargetProperty="(UIElement.RenderTransform).(Transform-
Group.Children)[3].(TranslateTransform.Y)">
            <SplineDoubleKeyFrame KeyTime="00:00:00" Value="0"/>
            <SplineDoubleKeyFrame KeyTime="00:00:01" Value="-152"/>
        </DoubleAnimationUsingKeyFrames>
    </Storyboard>
</Window.Resources>
```

12. The XAML markup that you should now play particularly close attention to is the four lines that look similar to this:

```
<SplineDoubleKeyFrame KeyTime="00:00:01" Value="-218"/>
```

13. In the Objects and Timeline category, click on the last KeyFrame added at the 1 second mark for the Rectangle element, making sure that you have the Properties panel visible.

14. You should now see the Easing category being displayed with a KeySpline editor, as shown in Figure 14.7.

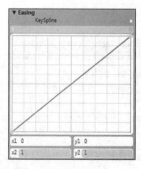

FIGURE 14.7   The new Blend 2 KeySpline editor.

I am going to explain what a KeySpline is shortly, but first I want you to see it and its effects because I think this makes it easier to understand.

15. Don't touch the KeySpline editor just yet.

16. Right-click on the KeyFrame at the 1 second position for the Rectangle element, select Ease In, and then select 100%.

Two things have happened that I hope you are aware of here: The KeySpline editor has changed and a new attribute has been added to the <SplineDoubleKeyFrame> A KeySpline! The specific markup should look something similar to this:

```
<SplineDoubleKeyFrame KeyTime="00:00:01" Value="-218" KeySpline="0,0,0.5,1"/>
```

The KeySpline editor has also changed to look something similar to Figure 14.8.

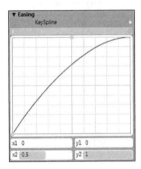

FIGURE 14.8   The KeySpline modification made with setting the easing values.

If you match this value to what is showing in the KeySpline editor, you can see that the first two values shown in the XAML (0,0) represent the x1 and y1 properties in the KeySpline editor and the second two values (0.5,1) represent x2 and y2.

Rewind and run the animation to see the effect, and you should see the rectangle animate to your chosen point at a rapid speed at first before slowing down at the end of the animation.

What Is a KeySpline?

A KeySpline is essentially a concept wherein a changing value is mapped against a period of time. Because that spline can be a curve, the value can change at different rates over the said period of time.

As shown in Figure 14.9, you can expect that with a steeper curve at the start of the KeySpline shown, and then a very gradual flattening of the spline toward the position 1,1, the animated change would result in a very fast value change at the start with a gradual slowdown at the end of the interpolation.

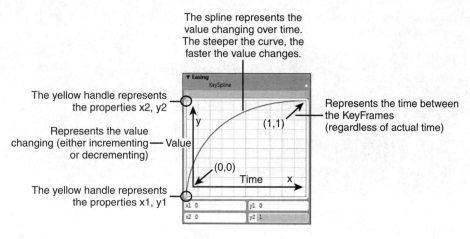

FIGURE 14.9   The time/value principle.

In XAML, a KeySpline always contains four values. The first two values (x1,y1) represent a point in time and a value, as do the second two. Each value can be a value between 0 and 1, inclusive.

Play with the KeySpline editor to better understand the animated effects that you can achieve with it, mapped against the XAML output.

Triggers

Within Blend, the concept of triggers is prominent with the usage of storyboards. A *trigger* is an action that occurs due to an event being raised or a property (that you have assigned to a trigger) evaluating to true (as in the condition being satisfied). Typically an event trigger is a single action that occurs when an event is raised where property triggers have both a starting and ending action, so they represent greater flexibility.

You should always try to use property triggers where you can, and use event triggers only when you need to. Property triggers can only be defined in a template or style (such as a Button), with the quoted best practice being to put them in a template where possible.

Event Triggers

By default, when you create a timeline in a new application or user control, Blend adds an event trigger called Windows.Loaded. If you look on your XAML editor (continuing from the last example), you will see the Window.Loaded trigger defined in the <Window.Triggers> region. This is an event trigger that you can see in the Triggers category of the Interaction panel, and is explained in Figure 14.10.

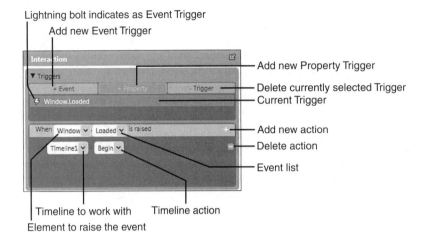

FIGURE 14.10   The areas of interest in the Trigger category for an event trigger.

If you close the current storyboard now and run the application, you will see that the animation starts as soon as the Window is loaded (visible on screen); the corresponding `Window.Loaded` event is raised, which this trigger is listening for.

In the following steps, you will add a Button element to your application. This button will call the same timeline (`ShowEasing`) by assigning the storyboard to the trigger's actions. These actions are started on raising the `Click` event of the button.

1. Ensure that you have no current storyboard active.

2. In the Triggers category of the Interaction panel, select the `Window.Loaded` trigger, and then click the -Trigger button to remove this trigger.

3. Double-click the LayoutRoot element to activate it.

4. Add a new Button element at an arbitrary point and of a size of your choice.

5. Name the Button element btnStartAnimation and set the `Content` property to Start Animation.

6. Make sure that the Button element remains selected.

7. In the Triggers category, click on the +Event button to add a new trigger.

8. By default, it will again say `Window.Loaded`. In the Element drop-down control (shown in Figure 14.10 as "Element to raise the Event"), you will see that only two elements are available: the Window and the Button element. Select the Button element.

Why Didn't the Rectangle Element Show in the Drop-Down List?

The Element drop-down list shows the topmost element being the Window and the currently selected element from the Objects and Timeline category. If you select the Rectangle element, it will, along with the Window element, be the only two items displayed.

9. The next drop-down control (Event list) shows the available events for the selected element. The events are categorized by their Base class event listing, so you will see the Click event is under the ButtonBase heading because this is the class that provides the event to the Button element.

10. Select the Click event from the list in the drop-down.

11. Click on the Add New Action button as shown in Figure 14.10.

12. By default the ShowEasing timeline should be automatically placed for you, but in the case it isn't, you should open the drop-down containing all timelines (you have only one now). This also gives you an option to create a new timeline. If it is present, select ShowEasing.

13. Next to this is a drop-down with a list of options for timeline actions (see Figure 14.11). These actions are described in Table 14.2. You want to start your animation when this event is raised, so select Begin.

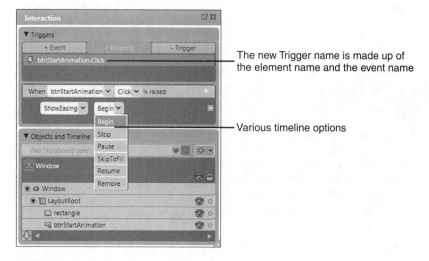

FIGURE 14.11   The event trigger completed with the new name and the timeline action options.

TABLE 14.2   Timeline Actions

Value	Description
Begin	Starts the animation from the beginning.
Stop	Stops the animation at the current point in time. The completed event is not raised.
Pause	Pauses the animation.
SkipToFill	Forces the animation to complete.
Resume	Resumes a paused animation.
Remove	Removes the animation completely.

Run the application and click the button, which should result in your animation starting.

As previously mentioned, event triggers are limited because they offer only one action, but you can work around this most of the time because events are usually paired, such as MouseDown and MouseUp. You just need to create two triggers to perform the required effect(s).

Timeline States

As shown in Figure 14.11, the Timeline action option provides six choices. These choices are discussed in Table 14.2.

There are additional methods available for storyboards that aren't supported in the Blend UI, such as Seek and SetSpeedRatio. Please consult the Windows SDK for further information on such methods.

Property Triggers

Property triggers have two actions, an Enter action and Exit action, as well providing property setters to enable even more functionality. Table 14.3 defines these topics further.

TABLE 14.3   Property Trigger Actions

Name	Description
Property setters	Property setters allow you to specify the value of an element property when a particular trigger is executed. An example of this is when a Button's IsMouseOver property becomes true, you can change the color of the background of the Button element. The Property setter allows you to define these values when trigger recording is on.
Enter actions	Allows you to control one or more timelines.
Exit actions	Allows you to control one or more timelines.

As Table 14.3 shows, you can use property setters to effect changes to elements when a property condition is satisfied. What you must remember with this is that the property setter remains in place only while the property condition is satisfied. The following example demonstrates this and the Property Trigger actions:

1. Add another new Button element to your application. (Keep the old one there as well because you will be using it shortly.) Name the button btnPropertyTrigger.

2. Select the btnPropertyTrigger Button element in the Objects and Timeline category, select Edit Control Parts (Template), and then select Edit Copy.

3. The Create Style Resource dialog should appear. Here you can name the style template as you please and store it in this document. Click OK to finish.

4. Now you are in Template-Editing mode, you should have noticed the appearance of three triggers predefined in the Triggers category of the Interaction panel. If you

click on one of these to select it, you should also notice that the artboard gets a red border and "Trigger recording is on" displays in the top-left corner of the artboard.

What Is Trigger Recording?

You can turn trigger recording on or off by clicking on the red dot beside the recording label on the artboard. Or if you select a predefined trigger, you will also notice a red dot appears next to the lightning bolt event icon. When trigger recording is on, any changes you make to an element (if you have a property trigger selected) will also be recorded as the state of that property.

Turning recording off allows you to modify a given property and the change will not be recorded against the element properties.

5. You might have also noticed that the +Property button is now enabled in the Triggers category, so now you can define property triggers.

6. Click on the +Property button and select the "MinWidth = 0" trigger. The resulting actions should look familiar to you, but they are slightly different from event triggers, as shown in Figure 14.12.

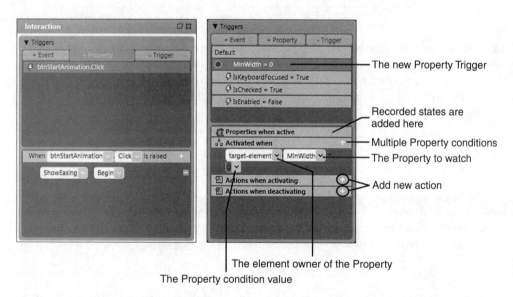

FIGURE 14.12   The property trigger has many more options than its less interesting relation, the event trigger.

7. Define the trigger by first selecting the element in the Activated When area. Leaving it set to target-element means that it will be listening across the entire element tree of children.

8. Now find the property that you want to listen to. In this case, select `IsMouseOver` from the combo box.

9. You should see the Property Condition value box changes from showing a 0 to True, which you should leave for this example.

10. You can take advantage of the property setters here and record a property value that will be set as soon as this property condition (`target-element.IsMouseOver == true`) is true.

11. Set the `Opacity` property value to 55%.

12. As soon as you change the value, you should see the description of the action in the Properties When Active area. You should also see that you could remove this setter at anytime by selecting the – (minus sign) button to the right of the information.

13. Now you can click on Add New Action for the Actions When Activating area (shown in Figure 14.12), and you should receive a dialog telling you that no timelines exist.

Where Is the Timeline that Moves the Rectangle Element?

You need to remember that you are inside the template of the Button at present, so anything you do here is attached to the template. Just as the timeline you previously created is not available here, this new timeline will not be available outside of the Button template.

14. Click OK to create a new timeline. You will see that it defaults to being called Timeline1. You can edit this by selecting the value in the timeline drop-down combo and typing a new name for it or use the Storyboard drop-down menu, which has an option to rename a storyboard on it. Try this now and call this timeline `DoMouseMove`.

14. Select Chrome in the Objects and Timeline category.

16. Without adding a KeyFrame at position 0:00.000, move the Playhead position to 0:01.000.

Setting the Playhead Position

You can either drag the orange Playhead position guide into the desired position or you can enter the information directly into the time label by clicking on it.

17. You are going to change the color of the Chrome now, so open the Brushes category of the Property panel. If you can't find these properties in the Brushes category, try using the Property search box to locate them.

18. You will notice that quite a few of the properties have orange borders around them, which is the result of the template bindings of the theme that is applied at present. You should select the advanced properties options button from the little orange box beside the `Background` property, and then select Convert to Local Value.

19. You should now see the property is unbound.

20. Modify the color properties by selecting the gradient stops and changing their values. There are four gradient stops: two are in the center, one on top of the other.

21. You should note now that a KeyFrame has been added to the timeline.

22. You can now go back and select the IsMouseOver property trigger from the Triggers category. You will note that the Actions When Activating area now has your timeline (correctly renamed) set to begin.

23. You can go through the same process when adding an action to the Actions When Deactivating area, but typically you just want to stop the timeline that is running. Click on the Add New Action button in the Actions When Deactivating area.

24. You will see that your DoMouseMove timeline is shown by default. Select the combo box showing the name DoMouseMove and you should see the New Timeline option second in the list. Select this option.

25. Name this timeline FinishMouseMove.

26. Again select the Chrome element in the Objects and Timeline category, but this time set the entire Background property color to Red.

27. Select the IsMouseOver trigger again in the Triggers category.

28. You should see your new timeline has been added to the Actions When Deactivating area, but you should also check to make sure that it hasn't been added to the Actions When Activating area. If it has, click the - button to remove it. Figure 14.13 shows the completed Trigger collection.

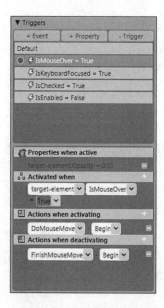

FIGURE 14.13 The completed property trigger.

29. You can click on the Scope Up button located to the left of the label NewStyle (Button Template), which will return you to the application artboard.

Run the application now and move your mouse over the button and you will note the order in which the actions occur:

1. The button opacity fades instantly.

2. The DoMouseOver animation runs.

When you move your mouse off the button, the following actions should occur:

1. The button opacity returns to 100% instantly.

2. The FinishMouseMove animation runs.

So, you now have some of idea of how triggers are "supposed" to work. You used buttons in these examples, but the same principles apply to triggers regardless of the elements that you are working with.

Handoff Animation

Expression Blend allows you to create and run more then one animation at a time, including multiple animations that affect the same element. However, when two separate animations run and modify the same property at the same time, and if you have not specified a KeyFrame at position 0:00.000 on the second animation, this is considered a *handoff animation*. As a result, the second animation will smoothly transition the property value at the point of intersection with the first animation to the end KeyFrame on the second animation.

What happens if you do specify a KeyFrame at position 0:00.000 on the second animation? Consider the following:

▶ Your first animation is tweening the opacity of a rectangle from 0% to 100% over a 5-second period.

▶ Your second animation also has instructions to tween the opacity value of the rectangle but only to 75%.

▶ The first and second animations intersect at the 2.5 second mark, so it would be safe to assume that the opacity value of the rectangle at this point is 50%.

What Happens to the First Animation?

The first animation stops even if it is set to repeat forever.

4. If you specified a 0% opacity value on KeyFrame position 0:00.00 of the second animation, at this point (2.5 seconds) the second animation would switch the rectangle's opacity instantly back to 0%

5. If you didn't specify a KeyFrame at position 0:00.00, the second animation would tween the opacity value of the rectangle as if it had been set to 50% on KeyFrame 0:00.000, and so the resulting animation would be smooth.

Duplicate and Reverse a Timeline

A great new feature added to Expression Blend 2 with the addition of the Storyboard Picker is the ability to reverse an animation. This feature is somewhat different from the Storyboard property AutoReverse, which rewinds the animation after it is completed.

To create the reverse of a specific animation, you first need to duplicate the animation, which is a cool feature in itself. In the following, you are going to take the rectangle animation created earlier and make a reverse:

1. Open the Storyboard Picker and select the ShowEasing animation.
2. From the Storyboard Management drop-down, select the Duplicate option, as shown in Figure 14.14.

FIGURE 14.14   The Storyboard Management drop-down.

3. You will notice that your new Storyboard is generated with the same name, but with a suffix of _Copy1. Select the Rename option from the management drop-down and name this new Storyboard ShowEasingReverse.
4. Again open the Storyboard Management drop-down, but this time, select Reverse.
5. Run the animation to test that it is as you would expect.
6. Close the Storyboard now.
7. Add another Button element to your application, calling it btnReverse.
8. Add a new event trigger, connecting your new button to the newly created reversed animation.

Run the application and click the Start Animation button. When it is complete, you should be able to click the Reverse Animation button to bring the Rectangle element back to the center of the screen. It's interesting to note in the reversed animation is that the easing is also reversed.

I am sure that you will find many uses for this handy workflow which can dramatically reduce your Storyboard creation time.

Controlling the Timeline in Code

In Expression Blend, a storyboard represents a collection of animations contained within a single timeline. If you create a new timeline, you will create a new storyboard. Depending on where you opted to store it, it becomes part of a resource collection that is accessible in the code-behind file. Blend makes working with storyboards quite simple and you should expect to see even greater functionality added to this area of the application in the versions to follow.

You can reference your storyboards in code and listen to the various events that the storyboard object can raise as well. In the following section, you will learn how simple it is to reference and work with storyboards in code.

C# Example

Previously, you added a button that, when clicked, raised an event trigger to change the opacity and color of the rectangle in your project. Instead of starting the animation from the event trigger, you are now going to reference the Storyboard in code and start it from there.

1. Ensure you are no longer in Template-Editing mode. Click on the Scope Up button if you need to return to the scene.
2. Add a new Button element to your application and call it btnCodeAnimationStart.
3. Select Save All from the File menu.
4. Select the btnCodeAnimationStart Button element in the Objects and Timeline category.
5. Open the Properties panel and select the lightning bolt icon to show the event list for the Button element.
6. Locate the Click event and double-click it to add it to the code-behind file.
7. Add the code from Listing 14.3.

LISTING 14.3   Calling a Storyboard from Code

```
private void btnCodeAnimationStart_Click(object sender, RoutedEventArgs e)
{
    Storyboard myTimeline = this.FindResource("ShowEasing") as Storyboard;
    myTimeline.Begin(this);
}
```

As you can see in Listing 14.3, the first line creates a Storyboard type variable and then calls the FindResource() method, parsing in the name of the storyboard when it was created in Blend. Because this method returns an object, you also need to cast it to a Storyboard type for compatibility.

The next line simply calls the Begin() method of the storyboard, parsing in the owner, which happens to be this as the Window.

Whilst the `FindResource()` method does what it says, you are advised to use the
`TryFindResource()` method, which returns a null value if it can't find the storyboard. This
following code shows the preferred method and code to test that the storyboard is indeed
found and assigned:

```
Storyboard myTimeline = this.TryFindResource("ShowEasing") as Storyboard;
if (myTimeline != null)
    myTimeline.Begin(this);
```

Listing 14.4 is the same as Listing 14.3, but modified to reference the `Completed` event
(and add the relevant event handler) so that you can get notification of when your animation has indeed completed.

LISTING 14.4   Adding a Completed Event Handler for a Storyboard Reference

```
private void btnCodeAnimationStart_Click(object sender, RoutedEventArgs e)
{
    Storyboard myTimeline = this.TryFindResource("ShowEasing") as Storyboard;
    //Add the completed event handler
    myTimeline.Completed += new EventHandler(myTimeline_Completed);

    if (myTimeline != null)
        myTimeline.Begin(this);
}

void myTimeline_Completed(object sender, EventArgs e)
{
    MessageBox.Show("Animation complete");
}
```

Listing 14.5 shows some additional code that calls the timeline that you added inside the
Button's (btnPropertyTrigger) control template.

LISTING 14.5   Calling a ControlTemplate Storyboard

```
private void btnCodeAnimationStart_Click(object sender, RoutedEventArgs e)
{
    Storyboard myTimeline = this.TryFindResource("ShowEasing") as Storyboard;

    //Add the completed event handler
    myTimeline.Completed += new EventHandler(myTimeline_Completed);

    if (myTimeline != null)
        myTimeline.Begin(this);

    ControlTemplate CT = this.btnPropertyTrigger.Template as ControlTemplate;
```

```
    Storyboard mouseTimeline = CT.Resources["DoMouseMove"] as Storyboard;

    if (mouseTimeline != null)
        mouseTimeline.Begin(this.btnPropertyTrigger, CT);
}
```

The code in Listing 14.5 shows a slightly different method of referencing the timeline. First you need to get a reference to the Button element's applied template. Then you find the storyboard from the template's resource collection—note that there is no `TryFindResources()` method from a ControlTemplate object. Last you begin the timeline directly from the Storyboard reference, parsing in the owner element and the owner of the element's resource collection.

When you run the application now, and you click on the Start Animation button, you will see both the rectangle animation running as well as the animation that starts when you mouse over the Property Trigger button. Animations are great fun and you can be assured that even more work is continuing on this feature for versions of Blend to come.

Summary

In this chapter, you looked at the principles of storyboards, timelines, and triggers. You learned how to create event and property triggers as well as what the difference between them is. You also learned how to reference Timelines in code and begin these Timelines, giving you even greater flexibility and control of your user interfaces.

There are so many combinations of storyboards and controlling them that you are bound to want to do even more then what has been shown here. Just remember that a storyboard is an object in code, so you can create collections of the objects and use them like any others in your applications.

CHAPTER **15**

Commands

An important area that should be considered by developers is any action that is repetitively performed by an application's input controls, such as buttons and menu items. An example of this is when you add a menu control with a File Open menu item and at the same time, make a button available to the user in the interface that performs the same function. Cut and paste functionality is also often implemented in a menu item as well as a button on a toolbar and, more often than not, it will be implemented in a context menu, too.

Previously in .NET, you would most likely just create a common method that would be called by both the Click event of the menu item and the button. In more complex scenarios, things could quickly get out of hand, especially when you needed to parse parameters to the methods that you were invoking.

Concept of Commands

Although the concept of commands was implemented in the MFC (Microsoft Foundation Class) Library, it has taken a little while for the functionality to move through to the .NET Framework as a simplified implementation. Commands are a powerful edition to the Framework supported by the WPF (Windows Presentation Foundation), providing a much easier method of connecting functionality to control events.

WPF defines a number of commands straight out the box as well as making some functionality specific to certain commands on certain controls. Buttons and MenuItems are just two controls that provide a property called Command, which allows you to set a specific command to be used. To enable controls within your application to take advantage of Commands, you only need to create a CommandBinding and implement its events, and you are then free to attach that Command as often as you please just by specifying the Command name.

To provide support for Commands within your own objects, you need to implement the ICommand interface, which defines three methods that you must implement. Execute, CanExecute, and CanExecuteChanged represent the methods that surround the functionality of almost all actions that you can specify.

The CanExecute method returns a Bool telling subscribers whether the required action is available (this is automatically synchronized by Buttons and MenuItems). As soon as you or your application modifies the Command's availability, the CanExecuteChanged event is fired. So, again, manually synchronizing your control state is a no-brainer.

Execute is the method that you call from within your event (the Click event on a button, for example) and this method either contains or goes off and invokes the methods specific to the Command.

To connect your own custom named Command in Blend, you will need to add a CommandBindingCollection, which requires you to implement the IList interface for generic collections. You can then add the fully qualified Collection.Command name as a value to the Command property of a WPF control.

Table 15.1 shows the four System.Windows.Input classes that provide Command functionality ready for you to use.

TABLE 15.1   WPF Input Commands

ApplicationCommands	CancelPrint	Close
	ContextMenu	Copy
	CorrectionList	Cut
	Delete	Find
	Help	New
	NotACommand	Open
	Paste	Print
	PrintPreview	Properties
	Redo	Replace
	Save	SaveAs
	SelectAll	Stop
	Undo	

TABLE 15.1   WPF Input Commands

ComponentCommands	ExtendSelectionDown	ExtendSelectionLeft
	ExtendSelectionRight	ExtendSelectionUp
	MoveDown	MoveFocusBack
	MoveFocusDown	MoveFocusForward
	MoveFocusPageDown	MoveFocusPageUp
	MoveFocusUp	MoveLeft
	MoveRight	MoveToEnd
	MoveToHome	MoveToPageDown
	MoveToPageUp	MoveUp
	ScrollByLine	ScrollPageDown
	ScrollPageLeft	ScrollPageRight
	ScrollPageUp	SelectToEnd
	SelectToHome	SelectToPageDown
	SelectToPageUp	
MediaCommands	BoostBass	ChannelDown
	ChannelUp	DecreaseBass
	DecreaseMicrophoneVolume	DecreaseTreble
	DecreaseVolume	FastForward
	IncreaseBass	IncreaseMicrophoneVolume
	IncreaseTreble	IncreaseVolume
	MuteMicrophoneVolume	MuteVolume
	NextTrack	Pause
	Play	PreviousTrack
	Record	Rewind
	Select	Stop
	ToggleMicrophoneOnOff	TogglePlayPause
NavigationCommands	BrowseBack	BrowseForward
	BrowseHome	BrowseStop
	DecreaseZoom	Favorites
	FirstPage	GoToPage
	IncreaseZoom	LastPage
	NavigateJournal	NextPage
	PreviousPage	Refresh
	Search	Zoom

Table 15.2 shows the System.Windows.Documents class that provides Command functionality ready for you to use.

TABLE 15.2   WPF Document Commands

EditingCommands	AlignCenter	AlignJustify
	AlignLeft	AlignRight
	Backspace	CorrectSpellingError
	DecreaseFontSize	DecreaseIndentation
	Delete	DeleteNextWord
	DeletePreviousWord	EnterLineBreak
	EnterParagraphBreak	IgnoreSpellingError
	IncreaseFontSize	IncreaseIndentation
	MoveDownByLine	MoveDownByPage
	MoveDownByParagraph	MoveLeftByCharacter
	MoveLeftByWord	MoveRightByCharacter
	MoveRightByWord	MoveToDocumentEnd
	MoveToDocumentStart	MoveToLineEnd
	MoveToLineStart	MoveUpByLine
	MoveUpByPage	MoveUpByParagraph
	SelectDownByLine	SelectDownByPage
	SelectDownByParagraph	SelectLeftByCharacter
	SelectLeftByWord	SelectRightByCharacter
	SelectRightByWord	SelectToDocumentEnd
	SelectToDocumentStart	SelectToLineEnd
	SelectToLineStart	SelectUpByLine
	SelectUpByPage	SelectUpByParagraph
	TabBackward	TabForward
	ToggleBold	ToggleBullets
	ToggleInsert	ToggleItalic
	ToggleNumbering	ToggleSubscript
	ToggleSuperscript	ToggleUnderline

Defining a New Command

The following steps take you through implementing Commands attached to Button elements.

1. Start a new project in Blend.
2. Change the Window Width to 355 and the Height to 108.
3. Replace the XAML (Extensible Application Markup Language) added by default with that shown in Listing 15.1.

LISTING 15.1   Set Up the Test Application

```
<Grid x:Name="LayoutRoot">
      <Grid.ColumnDefinitions>
            <ColumnDefinition/>
            <ColumnDefinition/>
      </Grid.ColumnDefinitions>
      <Button Margin="5,5,5,5" x:Name="btnFireNew" Content="Fire New"/>
```

```
        <Button IsEnabled="True" Margin="5,5,5,5" x:Name="btnFireCustom"
Content="Fire Custom" Grid.Column="1"/>
</Grid>
```

4. Select and activate the Button element showing Fire New as its content.

5. Open the Properties panel. In the property search box, type **com** to reveal the **Command** property options.

6. Type the word **New** and you will see that the Button automatically looks like it is disabled, even though the property is set to enable. This is because in design mode the command is returning false to the **CanExecute()** method that is implemented by the New Command.

7. Save your project and then open the events list in the Properties panel while still having the btnFireNew element selected.

8. Double-click in the Click event input box to launch Visual Studio and create a new Click event handler.

9. You are not going to add any code to the Click event handler at this stage, but you are going to create the CommandBinding so that the Button has the required functionality. In the class constructor, add the code shown in Listing 15.2. You will need to add using directive for System.Windows.Input at the top of the class file to expose the CommandBinding type.

LISTING 15.2   Attaching a Command Binding

```
public Window1()
{
        this.InitializeComponent();

        // Insert code required on object creation below this point.
            CommandBinding cbNew = new CommandBinding();
            cbNew.CanExecute += new CanExecuteRoutedEventHandler(cbNew_CanExecute);
            cbNew.Executed += new ExecutedRoutedEventHandler(cbNew_Executed);

            //The command to attach to
            cbNew.Command = ApplicationCommands.New;

            //Add to our CommandBindings collection
            this.CommandBindings.Add(cbNew);

}
```

10. You should have created two event handlers while adding the code from Listing 15.2. You should now add code similar to that of Listing 15.3 to give the Command some functionality.

LISTING 15.3   Adding Functionality to the Commands

```
void cbNew_Executed(object sender, ExecutedRoutedEventArgs e)
{
    MessageBox.Show("Command New Fired!");
}

void cbNew_CanExecute(object sender, CanExecuteRoutedEventArgs e)
{
    e.CanExecute = true;
}
```

11. By setting CanExecute to true, you are telling the button that this Command is perma-nently available. Save the application in Visual Studio, and then return to Blend. You may need to reload the project at this point if Blend directs you to.

12. Test the application by clicking F5 and then clicking the Fire New button. You should see the appropriate message displayed.

Invoking a Command

If you find yourself in a method that requires you to invoke a command, you can easily query the CommandBindingsCollection for an executable Command.

In the test application you previously created, add a Click event to the btnFireCustom button and add the code from Listing 15.4. Run the application from within Blend to test whether the Command was indeed invoked.

LISTING 15.4   Executing the Command

```
private void btnFireCustom_Click(object sender, RoutedEventArgs e)
{
    if (this.CommandBindings[0].Command.CanExecute(null))
        this.CommandBindings[0].Command.Execute(null);
}
```

So, the result is that now when you run the application, both buttons fire the same event, even though one button (btnFireNew) doesn't have any code in its Click handler and the other button (btnFireCustom) is calling a method defined by a Command.

Simple XAMLNotepad Application

There are two reasons for building this next sample application. The first reason is that it provides a way for us to create and test Command interaction with menus and buttons. The second is because I just think it is awesome. As you will see, at the heart of the application, there really is only several lines of code that provide all the required functionality of the XAMLNotepad main areas.

The following is another step by step approach showing you how to create the XAMLNotepad application, and as always you are free to style your elements as you see fit along the way:

1. Create a new project in Blend, selecting Standard Application exe as the type.

2. Find and add a Grid element to the LayoutRoot.

3. Set the `Width` and `Height` properties of the Grid to Auto and set the `HorizontalAlignment` and `VerticalAlignment` properties to Stretch.

4. Double-click to activate the Grid. Open the Properties panel and in the property search box, type **def** to view the Column and Row definition collection properties.

5. Add three row definitions. Set the `Height` property for each of the definitions, located in the Layout category of the collection editor:

   ▶ RowDefinition[0] = 0.6 Star

   ▶ RowDefinition[1] = 0.3 Star

   ▶ RowDefinition[2] = 0.1 Star

6. Set the Grid `Background` property to a color that pleases you (mine is gray).

7. Clear the property search box.

8. Find and add a RichTextBox control as a child of the Grid and position it in the middle row.

9. Name the RichTextBox element rtbXAMLText.

10. Set the `Background` property to your chosen color. Perhaps a Solid Color Brush should be used because this will be the markup entry panel. I set mine to a sickly pale yellow/gray (#FFF0F5D0).

11. Set the `Row` property located in the Layout category to 1.

12. Set both the `HorizontalAlignment` and `VerticalAlignment` properties to Stretch.

13. Set all the `Margin` properties to 5.

14. Right-click on the control in the artboard and select Edit Text from the context menu.

15. Add the following markup in Listing 15.5 as the text of the RichTextBox control; this will be the markup shown by default in the control when the application runs.

LISTING 15.5   The Default Namespace XAML

```
<Page xmlns="http://schemas.microsoft.com/winfx/2006/xaml/presentation"
      xmlns:sys="clr-namespace:System;assembly=mscorlib"
      xmlns:x="http://schemas.microsoft.com/winfx/2006/xaml">
```

```
</Page>
```

15

16. Click the Selection tool icon to leave Edit Text mode (or press the Esc key).

17. In the property search box, type **spel**, and make sure that the property **SpellCheckIsEnabled** is unchecked. Clear the search box.

18. Change the font to anything that you like, but you might want to set the LineHeight property in order to improve your markup viewing ability. Type **line** into the property search box where you will find this property located on the second tab of the Text category. Clear the search box when completed.

19. Type **tab** into the property search box, which should reveal the **AcceptsTab** property at the bottom of the returned items. You should ensure that this property is checked. Clear the search box as always after use.

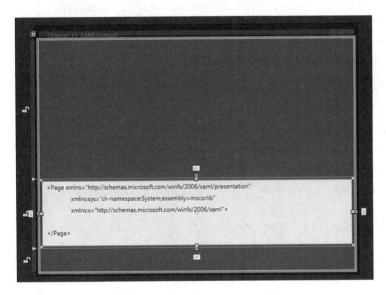

FIGURE 15.1 The current build progress.

20. Select and activate the Grid component again. Find and add a GridSplitter control as a child element.

21. Set the Width property of the GridSplitter to Auto and set the Height property to 3.

22. Set the HorizontalAlignment property to Stretch and the VerticalAlignment property to Bottom. You can choose to color the control.

23. Again select the Grid element in the Objects and Timeline panel, this time finding and adding a TextBox control as a child element.

24. Clear the default text from the control and then name the control txtError.

25. Set the Width and Height properties to Auto if it is not already done.

26. Set the HorizontalAlignment and VerticalAlignment properties to Stretch.

27. Set the Row property value to 2.

28. Set the Margin properties to 1.

29. Again select the Grid element, this time finding and adding a Frame control as the element child. You might need to look in the Asset Library for this one.

30. Name the Frame control frmDocRoot.

31. Set the Background property to a Solid Color Brush, my suggestion being white because this represents the artboard of your application.

32. Set the Width and Height properties to Auto if it is not already done.

33. Set the HorizontalAlignment and VerticalAlignment properties to Stretch.

34. Set all the Margin properties to 5, except for the Bottom margin, which should be set to 8 to take the GridSplitter control into account.

35. Type **cont** into the property search box to find the **Content** property. Clear the text "Frame" from it.

36. Type **nav** into the property search box and set the **NavigationUIVisibility** property to Hidden.

37. Clear the property search box.

15

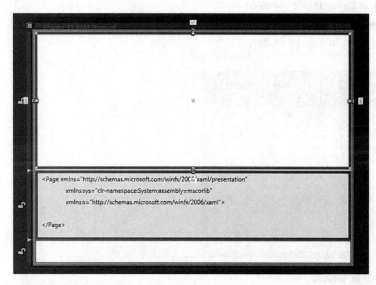

FIGURE 15.2   The shell of the XAMLNotepad application at this point.

You have almost completed the basic design for the application with just the menu items and toolbars to add. When this is all in place, you will move to Visual Studio to look at coding up the application, including the commands.

Building the Menu Items

Anyone can add just plain boring MenuItems, so I thought we would take this opportunity to look at the ToolBarTray control and ToolBar items controls.

We are not going to go all out here and add a million buttons, but I hope that you will see some of the options and build on this in the future. For the present, though, we are just going to add a few built-in command buttons:

Save

Load

Cut

Copy

Paste

Saving the file will constitute a loose XAML file that you can also view in Internet Explorer 7, although you could also use the tool for quick viewing any XAML that someone sends you.

1. Select the Grid control and find the TOP margin property for it in the Properties panel, Layout category. Set it to 34.

2. Select and activate the LayoutRoot element.

3. Open the Asset Library and type **tool** into the search box, which should reveal several controls as shown in Figure 15.3.

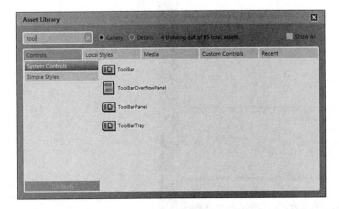

FIGURE 15.3   The plethora of toolbar choices.

4. Select the ToolBarTray control and then add it as a child to the LayoutRoot element.

5. The ToolBarTray allows you to add as many ToolBar controls as you like, so it acts as a panel specific to ToolBar controls. Set the Width property to Auto and the Height property to 32.

6. Set the HorizontalAlignment property to Stretch and the VerticalAlignment property to Top.

7. Open the Brushes category and select the Background property. If it appears to be missing (some preview versions) do a search for "Back" in the Property search box. You will find it in the Miscellaneous category, looking as if it is bound to a resource even though in the XAML it is clearly not.

8. You can change the Background property to suit; I have created a gradient effect as can be seen in Figure 15.4.

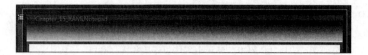

FIGURE 15.4   The gradient applied to the Background property.

9. Set your gradient declaration in XAML to the following:

```
<LinearGradientBrush EndPoint="0.516,1.051" StartPoint="0.516,-0.103">
```

10. Select and activate the ToolBarTray element in the Objects and Timeline panel.

11. Type **toolbar** into the property search box to reveal the **ToolBars** collection property. Click on the ellipses button next to the property to launch the ToolBar Collection Editor dialog.

12. Click Add Another Item to add a single ToolBar control to the tray.

13. In the right side of the dialog (named Properties), scroll down until such time as you find the Common Properties category. You should find a property named Items (Collection) with an ellipsis button next to it. Click this button to launch the Collection Editor dialog.

14. Figure 15.5 shows the Item object types that may be added as ToolBar items. For now, click on the Add Item button to add a single Button item.

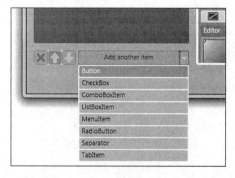

FIGURE 15.5   The myriad ToolBar Item choices available.

15. Again, scroll down the list of properties on the right side of the dialog until such time as you find the Common Properties category. In the Content property, type the word **Save**.

16. Scroll further down the properties until you find the Miscellaneous category where you should be able to find the Command property. Again type the word **Save** (it must be spelled exactly as shown).

17. Next find and select a separator to add from the list of Items available in the Items drop-down. Click on the Add Item to insert it onto the ToolBar.

18. Find and add another Button control, this time adding the word *Open* to both the Content and Command properties.

19. Click the OK button to exit the dialog.

20. Select the ToolBarTray element and navigate to the ToolBars collection property (in the Miscellaneous category). You will see your first ToolBar present, select "Add another item" to add a new ToolBar.

21. Select the second ToolBar in the Objects and Timeline category, then navigate to the Items collection property.

22. In the Items collection dialog, add a Button object followed by a Separator for three items: Cut, Copy, and Paste (see Figure 15.6). Remember to add the value to both the Content and the Command properties of all the Buttons.

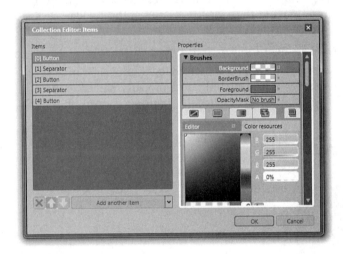

FIGURE 15.6   The Collection Editor shows the three new Buttons with Separator elements.

23. Click OK when you are satisfied, but before clicking OK to exit the ToolBar Collection Editor, check the Background property of both ToolBar items (see Figure 15.7).

If you test the application as is stands, obviously there will not be any functionality. Blend is fantastic for high speed development, but even it can't predict what you intend to do...yet. Note that the ToolBar buttons are disabled; you will recall the previous notes that state the executable status of a command is bound to the subscriber.

Let's put the functionality in place so that you can get on with impressing your friends!

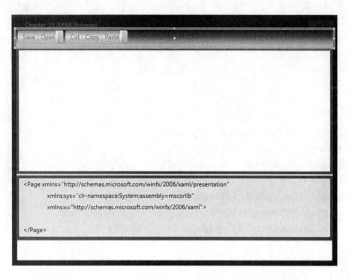

FIGURE 15.7   The progress of our work, which is visually complete.

Save everything in Blend if you have not already done so, and then select the rtbXAMLText element on the Objects and Timeline panel. Switch the Properties panel to Event List view and look for the event named TextChanged. Double-clicking the event should open Visual Studio as predicted.

You will need to add five new using statements to reference the classes we need to use:

```
using System.Xml
using System.Windows.Documents
using System.Windows.Markup
using System.Windows.Input
using Microsoft.Win32
```

Copy the code in Listing 15.6, which creates a UIElement from the user input and then attaches that element to the Frame control's content.

LISTING 15.6   Generating the XAML Element from the XAML Text

```
private void rtbXAMLText_TextChanged(object sender, TextChangedEventArgs e)
{
    //Make sure the app has completed loading first
    if (!this.IsLoaded )
        return;
    //Get all the text in our document
    TextRange DocText = new TextRange(this.rtbXAMLText.Document.ContentStart,
this.rtbXAMLText.Document.ContentEnd);

    //Make sure text is present
```

```
    if (string.IsNullOrEmpty(DocText.Text))
        return;

StringReader stringReader = null;
XmlTextReader xmlReader = null;
try
{
    /*In order to create a UIElement tree from the text
     * in our input pad, we need to push it into a XML
     * format, and then Load that through the XAMLReader object */

    stringReader = new StringReader(DocText.Text);
    xmlReader = new XmlTextReader(stringReader);
    UIElement documentRoot = (UIElement)XamlReader.Load(xmlReader);

    //Add our Element tree to the frame
    this.frmDocRoot.Content = documentRoot;

    //Clean up
    this.txtError.Text = string.Empty;
}
catch (Exception ex)
{
    //Simple error display
    if (this.txtError != null)
        this.txtError.Text = ex.Message.ToString();

}
finally
{
    //Close all
    if (stringReader != null) stringReader.Close();

    if (xmlReader != null) xmlReader.Close();
}


}
```

Now you need to add the Command handlers and provide the functionality that the user is expecting from the ToolBar buttons.

Because you have a few Commands to add, you are going to use a shorthand version of the methods implemented in the previous sample. This involves creating the event handlers by hand for each Command but makes for more manageable code overall.

For the Commands Save and Open, create the four event handler methods shown in Listing 15.7.

LISTING 15.7   A Template for the Command Event Handler Methods

```
void Save_Executed(object sender, ExecutedRoutedEventArgs e)
    {

    }

    void Save_CanExecute(object sender, CanExecuteRoutedEventArgs e)
    {

    }

    void Open_Executed(object sender, ExecutedRoutedEventArgs e)
    {

    }

    void Open_CanExecute(object sender, CanExecuteRoutedEventArgs e)
    {

    }
```

Each Command handler should have the CanExecute method property set to true by default, so within each CanExecute method add code similar to the code shown in Listing 15.8.

LISTING 15.8   Permanent Execution

```
void Save_CanExecute(object sender, CanExecuteRoutedEventArgs e)
{
    //Always available
    e.CanExecute = true;
}
```

For each Command, you need to add the code from Listing 15.9: the CommandBinding methods inside the constructor of our Window class.

LISTING 15.9   Adding the Command Bindings

```
public Window1()
{
    this.InitializeComponent();
```

```
    // Insert code required on object creation below this point.

    this.CommandBindings.Add(new CommandBinding(ApplicationCommands.Save,
Save_Executed,Save_CanExecute));
    this.CommandBindings.Add(new CommandBinding(ApplicationCommands.Open, Open_Exe-
cuted, Open_CanExecute));

}
```

Save and Open a XAML Package

Creating the code to save and open a XAML package is really quite simple and I would suspect that for most part, experienced coders could work it out for themselves. You are using pretty standard .NET code to produce the correct dialog controls. Perhaps the only thing that might throw you off would be the actual retrieval and refreshing of text inside the RichTextBox that you are using as the markup input pad.

For both of these executed methods, you launch a Save As or Open dialog box, returning the filename and either taking the TextRange from the RichTextBox control (to save) or replacing it with file contents (to open).

Listing 15.10 contains the code for the Save operation, whereas Listing 15.11 contains the Open code. Have a look through the code, paying attention to the TextRange class methods that are employed to make the job very simple indeed.

LISTING 15.10   Saving Markup

```
void Save_Executed(object sender, ExecutedRoutedEventArgs e)
{
    // Configure save file dialog box
    SaveFileDialog dlg = new SaveFileDialog();
    dlg.FileName = "Document";
    dlg.DefaultExt = ".xaml";
    dlg.Filter = "XAML Markup file (.xaml)¦*.xaml";

    // Show save file dialog box
    Nullable<bool> result = dlg.ShowDialog();

    // Process save file dialog box results
    if (result == true)
    {
        // Save document
        string filename = dlg.FileName;
```

```
        //Get all the text in our document
        TextRange DocText = new TextRange(this.rtbXAMLText.Document.ContentStart,
this.rtbXAMLText.Document.ContentEnd);

        FileStream sWriter = null;
        try
        {
            using (sWriter = new FileStream(filename, FileMode.Create))
            {
                DocText.Save(sWriter, DataFormats.XamlPackage);
            }

            MessageBox.Show("File save complete.",
                "Save Status",
                MessageBoxButton.OK,
                MessageBoxImage.Information,
                MessageBoxResult.OK);
        }
        catch (Exception ex)
        {
            MessageBox.Show("File save failed with the following error." +
                Environment.NewLine +
                Environment.NewLine +
                ex.Message.ToString(),
                "Save Status",
                MessageBoxButton.OK,
                MessageBoxImage.Error,
                MessageBoxResult.OK);
        }
        finally
        {
            sWriter.Close();
        }
    }
}
```

LISTING 15.11   Open a XAML File

```
void Open_Executed(object sender, ExecutedRoutedEventArgs e)
        {
            // Configure open file dialog box
            OpenFileDialog dlg = new OpenFileDialog();
            dlg.FileName = "Document";
            dlg.DefaultExt = ".xaml";
            dlg.Filter = "XAML Markup file (.xaml)¦*.xaml";
```

```
            // Show open file dialog box
            Nullable<bool> result = dlg.ShowDialog();

            // Process open file dialog box results
            if (result == true)
            {
                // Open document
                string filename = dlg.FileName;

                FileStream  sReader = null;
                try
                {
                    //Clear what is already there
                    this.rtbXAMLText.Document.Blocks.Clear();
                    TextRange DocText = new
TextRange(this.rtbXAMLText.Document.ContentStart,
                            this.rtbXAMLText.Document.ContentEnd);

                    if (File.Exists(filename))
                    {
                        using (sReader = new FileStream(filename,
FileMode.OpenOrCreate))
                        {
                            DocText.Load(sReader, DataFormats.XamlPackage);
                        }
                    }
                }
                catch (Exception ex)
                {
                    MessageBox.Show("File Open failed with the following error." +
                        Environment.NewLine +
                        Environment.NewLine +
                        ex.Message.ToString(),
                        "Open Status",
                        MessageBoxButton.OK,
                        MessageBoxImage.Error,
                        MessageBoxResult.OK);
                }
                finally
                {
                    sReader.Close();
                }
            }
        }
```

So, why have you implemented only Save and Open? Cut, Copy, and Paste commands are built-in functionality of the RichTextBox class (and other such as the standard TextBox element), so as long as the Button objects hook into those supported Commands, they are synchronized to the Commands availability as well as automatically call the functionality provided by the RichTextBox.

After you have added the code to the respective executed methods, the application is complete. You should save your work in Visual Studio and then return to Blend for the grand launch!

With any luck, your application should look similar to that shown in Figure 15.8. More importantly I would hope that it functions the way it should. For a test, add the markup shown in Listing 15.12 to create a simple button.

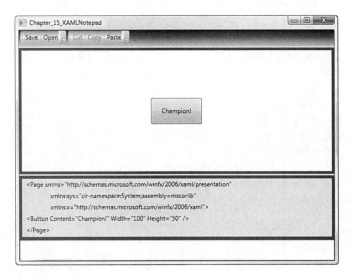

FIGURE 15.8   The completed application.

LISTING 15.12   Test Markup

```
<Page xmlns="http://schemas.microsoft.com/winfx/2006/xaml/presentation"
      xmlns:sys="clr-namespace:System;assembly=mscorlib"
      xmlns:x="http://schemas.microsoft.com/winfx/2006/xaml">

<Button Content="Champion!" Width="100" Height="50" />
</Page>
```

You can now also try the Save and Open methods to ensure that they are working correctly, as well play around with the edit commands you added. You have the chance to modify and extend this application to how it suits you best or maybe even put it into a control for use in other applications. Finally, you could add the markup shown in Listing 15.13, which demonstrates that even styles can be employed in your new creation.

LISTING 15.13   Running Style Demonstration

```
<Page.Resources>
    <Style x:Key="ButtonStyle1"
        BasedOn="{x:Null}"
        TargetType="{x:Type Button}">
        <Setter Property="Template">
            <Setter.Value>
                <ControlTemplate TargetType="{x:Type Button}">
                <Grid>
                    <Ellipse Stroke="#FF000000">
                    <Ellipse.Fill>
                        <LinearGradientBrush
                            EndPoint="0.496,-1.039"
                            StartPoint="0.504,2.039">
                            <GradientStop Color="#FFD5FC1D"
                                Offset="0.003"/>
                            <GradientStop Color="#FF0CC953"
                                Offset="1"/>
                        </LinearGradientBrush>
                    </Ellipse.Fill>
                    </Ellipse>
                    <ContentPresenter
                        SnapsToDevicePixels="{TemplateBinding SnapsToDevicePixels}"
                        HorizontalAlignment="{TemplateBinding
HorizontalContentAlignment}"
                        VerticalAlignment="{TemplateBinding
VerticalContentAlignment}"
                        RecognizesAccessKey="True"/>
                </Grid>
                </ControlTemplate>
            </Setter.Value>
        </Setter>
    </Style>
</Page.Resources>
    <Grid x:Name="LayoutRoot">
        <Button HorizontalAlignment="Left"
            Margin="53,46,0,0"
            Style="{DynamicResource ButtonStyle1}"
```

```
            VerticalAlignment="Top"
            Width="117"
            Height="38"
            Content="Button"/>
    </Grid>
```

Summary

Command bindings are extremely powerful and can greatly reduce the time required to create application functionality. And because the functionality is in many cases controlled internally by the controls themselves, you can be assured of (almost) no defects in that functionality.

Writing the XAMLNotepad application also shows the use of the commands, and how simple it is to use XAML as a scripting language if you really want to. No customized objects or huge coding blocks are required to pull the XAML into your object and return a UIElement.

Explore commands and try to use them as often as possible within your applications. The more you use them, the quicker it is to implement them.

Using Resources for Skins

Expression Blend has a great system for including and using resources within your applications. These resources can be almost anything you want to include with your application, such as images (of varying formats), text files, and even different data templates.

Resource Dictionaries (shown in detail in Chapter 12, "Templates,") are, of course, considered resources. And in this chapter, you will see how to use these in terms of creating a skin for your application and the code logic that enables you to switch the skins during runtime. I should point out that *theming* in the WPF (Windows Presentation Foundation) is considered by Microsoft to be the operating system theme applied to the control types you use in your application, whereas *skinning* refers to changes made to a specific application.

The Power of WPF Resources

The concept of styling applications (or skinning) has been around for a long time, and an application such as Windows Media Player is probably one of the most well known that has this feature included. It's when you start to consider the implications on a large enterprise application that things quickly get out of hand.

In some enterprise applications, it is not unusual to have many tens, hundreds, and sometimes more than a thousand controls that may be loaded up as part of a user interface. Although it might appear to be a daunting task to have to skin all these controls, the good news is that you usually (aside from custom controls) have a set of

10–50 control types (such as text box and button) of which you create a style for. Applying the style across all the user controls, windows, and so on, is a single attribute value, and even quicker to use Blend to point to.

The best practice, I believe, is to implement a very strictly enforced Resource Dictionary naming convention, which means that every control, and PART_ of a control must be connected to a style that you have in your Resource Dictionaries. If you create a style template locally and set your control styles to use it, it becomes very difficult to manage the changing of the skin during runtime.

Changing a Style at Runtime in Code

For the most part, users tend to change the Skin of the application during runtime, so while being able to create skin resources in design time is high on the priority list, enabling Resources interchange is the key to a successful skinning system.

Starting off with a simple example, the following steps take you through applying a new style in code at runtime, using two styles that reside in the same Resource Dictionary.

1. Create a new application in Blend.
2. Add a SimpleStyles ProgressBar control and a Button.
3. Name the ProgressBar pbSimple.
4. Name the Button btnChangeStyle.
5. You might want to make your window smaller and layout similar to that shown in Figure 16.1.

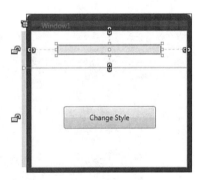

FIGURE 16.1   The simple application layout.

6. Set your ProgressBar element's Value property to 50.
7. Click on the Resources tab and select the New Dictionary button.
8. The default name of ResourceDictionary1.xaml should be shown in the New Item dialog. For this example, please leave this name intact.

   You should now see your ResourceDictionary1.xaml file in the list under Simple Styles.xaml.

9. Locate the pbSimple control in the Objects and Timeline category of the Interaction panel.

10. Right-click and select Edit Control Parts (Template) and then select to edit a copy.

11. Give the Key of PBSimpleStyle1 and make sure to select your ResourceDictionary1.xaml file from the drop-down list next to the Resource Dictionary radio button. Click OK to continue.

12. Begin to modify the style of the template by selecting the PART_Track element in the Objects and Timeline category.

    For this example, I simply changed the Background property in the Brushes category to a SolidColor red brush.

13. Use the breadcrumb control to return back to the application or use the Scope Up button.

14. Go back through the Edit Control Parts (Template) process again, again opting to create a copy. This time call the style PBSimpleStyle2. Remember to add this to your Resource Dictionary.

15. Modify the PART_Track to show a green SolidColor brush.

16. You should be able to see your two styles as children of your ResourceDictionary1.xaml file as shown in the Resource tab.

17. Scope back up to your application.

    So, you now have two styles for the same control in the same Resource Dictionary. Now you are going to go through in code, changing out the Style, which is a very simple process.

18. Save your application in Blend.

19. Select your Button element and then find the Click event in the Properties panel.

20. Double-click the Click event name input box to launch Visual Studio with an event handler added for you.

Because you named your ProgressBar control pbSimple, you can now easily refer to the control to assign a new style to its Style property value. Add the code shown in Listing 16.1.

LISTING 16.1 Finding a Style

```
private void btnChangeStyle_Click(object sender, RoutedEventArgs e)
{
    this.pbSimple.Style = this.TryFindResource("PBSimpleStyle1") as Style;
}
```

Run the application from Visual Studio by pressing F5. Click the button and your style should change from green to red.

This is a simple example of applying a new style to an existing style of an existing control, but what happens when you have many controls and styles and you can't add 10 different ProgressBar styles to one file? This is the job of the Merged Resource Dictionary feature of WPF.

Using MergedDictionaries

MergedDictionaries is a scenario where two or more ResourceDictionaries are merged together in a Resource Dictionary collection. You have already done this without probably knowing and you can see the results of it in your App.xaml file (see Listing 16.2) from the last simple example).

LISTING 16.2   The MergedDictionaries Property from the Simple Sample App.xaml File

```
<Application
    xmlns="http://schemas.microsoft.com/winfx/2006/xaml/presentation"
    xmlns:x="http://schemas.microsoft.com/winfx/2006/xaml"
    x:Class="Chapter_16_SimpleStyleChange.App"
    StartupUri="Window1.xaml">
    <Application.Resources>
        <!— Resources scoped at the Application level should be defined here. —>
        <ResourceDictionary>
            <ResourceDictionary.MergedDictionaries>
                <ResourceDictionary Source="Simple Styles.xaml"/>
                <ResourceDictionary Source="ResourceDictionary1.xaml"/>
            </ResourceDictionary.MergedDictionaries>
        </ResourceDictionary>
    </Application.Resources>
</Application>
```

Usually when you add items to a ResourceDictionary, each item must contain a unique x:Key attribute to identify it, but you will notice in the markup of Listing 16.2 that each Resource Dictionary is specified with a Source value and no Key value. This is a special scenario and the only time it is allowed.

Having to specify unique Key values inside a ResourceDictionary does not mean that, internal to both Resource Dictionaries, items cannot contain the same Key value. It just means that a scope order exists as to which resource will actually be returned to you if two or more items share the same key in different dictionaries.

The resource returned is from the last ResourceDictionary found to contain the required Key value, listed in the Collection. The example being that if both Simple Styles.xaml and ResourceDictionary1.xaml contained the same style with the same Key, the style from ResourceDictionary1.xaml would be the style returned. If a style of the specified Key is not found in ResourceDictionary1.xaml, the application will continue its search back up the list of Resource Dictionaries until it finds a Key (in which case it stops looking) or it doesn't find a Key with the required value (which might result in a null object exception if the designer or developer is not careful).

It is not unusual for an application to contain many Resource Dictionaries, perhaps each one used for a specific purpose such as colors, brushes, common controls, custom controls, or more. Be aware that Blend does not really understand what Resource Dictionaries it is adding to the list and in what order, so you might want to check from time to time to remove duplicate entries from the collection.

Application.Current.Resources

Your application at runtime contains a property that allows you to access the Resources collection as shown in Listing 16.2, including the MergedDictionaries collection; you can either replace the entire set of resources being used or add a new ResourceDictionary to the MergedDictionary collection as is required.

This makes it easy to manage large sets of resource dictionaries or MergedDictionary collections at runtime and the following example leads you through swapping out the current resources for a new Dictionary, which is an extension of the method previously shown:

1. Create a new application in Blend.
2. Set your Window Width to 270 and Height to 375.
3. Replace your LayoutRoot XAML with the markup shown in Listing 16.3.

LISTING 16.3   Setting Up the Sample Application

```
<Grid x:Name="LayoutRoot">
    <Grid.RowDefinitions>
        <RowDefinition Height="75"/>
        <RowDefinition Height="75"/>
        <RowDefinition Height="75"/>
        <RowDefinition Height="*"/>
    </Grid.RowDefinitions>
    <ProgressBar Margin="27.5,19,27.5,35.036"/>
    <Button Margin="27.5,20,27.5,17" Content="Button" Grid.Row="1"/>
    <CheckBox Margin="27.5,22,27.5,26" Content="CheckBox" Grid.Row="2"/>
    <Label Margin="27.5,8,27.5,0" VerticalAlignment="Top" Height="36"
Content="Select your Skin" Grid.Row="3" FontSize="18" FontWeight="Bold"/>
    <ComboBox IsSynchronizedWithCurrentItem="True" HorizontalAlignment="Center"
Margin="0,48,0,0" VerticalAlignment="Top" Width="200" Grid.Row="3"/>
</Grid>
```

You will note that not one of the controls is named in the markup. The result is shown in Figure 16.2.

16

FIGURE 16.2   The layout of the application.

4. Open the Resources panel and create three new Resource Dictionaries called Blue.xaml, Red.xaml, and Green.xaml.

5. You should notice that the App.xaml element in the Resources tab starts to link to your new Resource Dictionaries automatically. Remember where these are because you will need to unlink them shortly.

6. Edit a copy of the Control Parts (Template) for the ProgressBar, naming the style PBStyle and add it to the Blue.xaml ResourceDictionary.

7. You will notice that this is not a SimpleStyles control template, but you should be able to find the same PART_Track as used previously.

8. Set the PART_Track to a SolidColor brush of a blue color.

9. Scope up back to the application level.

10. Edit a copy of the Control Parts (Template) for the Button, naming the style BTNStyle and add it to the Blue.xaml ResourceDictionary.

11. Select the element called Chrome. You will note that the Background brush has an orange square next to it, which indicates its value is currently template-bound. Click on the little square and select Reset from the advanced property options shown.

12. You should now be able to select the SolidColor brush and set the color to the previous blue you used for the ProgressBar.

13. Scope up back to the application level.

14. Edit a copy of the Control Parts (Template) for the CheckBox, naming the style CHKStyle and add it to the Blue.xaml ResourceDictionary.

15. Select the element called [BulletDecorator].

16. You should be able to select the Background property in the Brushes category of the Properties panel and set it to a SolidColor brush using the previous blue you used for the ProgressBar and Button.

17. Scope up back to the application level.

18. Open the Resources panel and find the child elements of the App.xaml file, selecting the Linked To: Blue.xaml item. Right-click and select Delete from the context menu. This will remove only the item from the MergedDictionaries collection, not the Resource Dictionary. You may also receive notices in the Results panel that the specific styles "cannot be resolved" but you should ignore these.

FIGURE 16.3   The resulting Blue.xaml skin on the controls.

Do steps 6–18 for the additional colors for each of the three controls used in this example (ProgressBar, Button, and CheckBox), only this time keep the same name for each of the styles for each particular control regardless of which Resource Dictionary it is going into, as shown in Table 16.1.

TABLE 16.1   Elements to Modify

Resource Dictionary	ProgressBar Style Name	Button Style Name	CheckBox Style Name	Template Element to Modify
Blue.xaml	PBStyle	BTNStyle	CHKStyle	PART_Track
Red.xaml	PBStyle	BTNStyle	CHKStyle	Chrome
Green.xaml	PBStyle	BTNStyle	CHKStyle	[BulletDecorator]

Obviously you need to change the color of each of the elements in the resources you create to match the Resource Dictionary to which you are adding the style template.

Why Delete the MergeDictionary Entry?

You shouldn't have to delete these, but due to an issue that has been reported, Blend will sometimes disable the buttons in the Edit Resources dialogs, not letting you add a Key with the same name as other elements in different Resource Dictionaries.

When you go to create the new style using a name that is already declared in an existing Resource Dictionary, you receive a warning as shown in Figure 16.4. At the time of writing, a defect meant that sometimes the OK button is disabled incorrectly; hence the need for you to unlink the Resource Dictionaries in the App.xaml file.

FIGURE 16.4   The name already exists in the linked Resource Dictionaries.

Skin Logic

Now you have completed creating your three Resource Dictionaries, you need to remove the existing Style attribute from each of the three controls.

19. Select the ProgressBar control in the Objects and Timeline category.

20. Type **Style** into the Property search box and you should see the **Style** property in the Miscellaneous category.

21. You may note that the property value has a green square next to it and the value also has a green border. This indicates that the element is using a resource (static or dynamic) to supply its value.

22. Click on the green square next to it and select Reset from the advanced property options menu.

23. Do this for the other two controls and you should notice them returning to their standard styled state. It should be noted that if all the Resources Dictionaries were unlinked previously, your controls should already be in their standard style state.

24. Activate the ComboBox element in the Objects and Timeline category by double-clicking on it.

25. Add three child ComboBoxItem controls by right-clicking on the ComboBox in the Objects and Timeline category and selecting Add ComboBoxItem from the menu.

26. Change the Content property of each of the ComboBoxItems, setting the first to Blue, the second to Green, and I will let you guess the third one! (Make sure each value contains exactly the same spelling as the title of each Resource Dictionary you created.)

27. Check that you have, at the minimum, one Resource Dictionary linked to the App.xaml file and the styles from that Resource Dictionary applied to each of the three controls.

    If you have removed all styles and have no Resource Dictionaries linked:

    a. In the Resources panel, right-click on the App.xaml element and then select Link to Resource Dictionary, selecting one of your Resource Dictionaries.

    b. For each of the three elements in the application, right-click on the element in the Objects and Timeline category, select Edit Control Parts (Template), select Apply Resource, and then select the PB style you created, as shown in Figure 16.5.

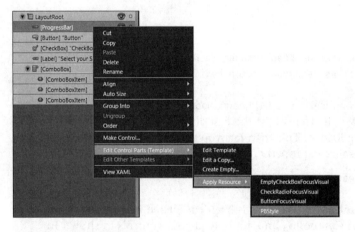

FIGURE 16.5   How to apply the style to your elements.

28. Save the application.

29. Selecting the parent ComboBox again, open the Event Viewer mode of the Properties panel and find an event named SelectionChanged. Double-click the input box to open Visual Studio with the correct event handler code added.

30. Add the code shown in Listing 16.4.

LISTING 16.4   Handling the Selection Changed Event for the ComboBox

```
private void ComboBox_SelectionChanged(object sender, SelectionChangedEventArgs e)
{

    if (sender != null)
    {
```

```
        string ResourceSelected = ((e.OriginalSource as ComboBox).SelectedItem as
ComboBoxItem).Content.ToString();

        ResourceDictionary rd = Application.LoadComponent(new Uri(ResourceSelected
+".xaml", UriKind.Relative)) as ResourceDictionary;

        Application.Current.Resources = rd;

    }
}
```

The following line of code takes the string value from the Content property of the selected ComboBoxItem:

```
string ResourceSelected = ((e.OriginalSource as ComboBox).SelectedItem as ComboBox-
Item).Content.ToString();
```

The next line:

```
ResourceDictionary rd = Application.LoadComponent(new Uri(ResourceSelected
+".xaml", UriKind.Relative)) as ResourceDictionary;
```

This shows a method of the application called LoadComponent(), which allows you to specify the location of a XAML file to load. At the end of that line, you are specifying that a ResourceDictionary is being loaded. This then lets you apply the loaded Resource Dictionary to the current Resources property of your application:

```
Application.Current.Resources = rd;
```

Run your application now, and if everything has been completed in order, you should be able to select a skin from the ComboBox and apply it to your controls as shown in Figure 16.6.

You will also note that this change takes immediate effect and, as long as the naming convention is adhered to, the styles update without incident.

Loading an External Skin File

Inevitably, you will come across a scenario in which you need to provide the ability for other users to create their own skins and your application has to be able to deal with that.

What If I Want to Load a XAML Skin File with Code Behind?

Although the methods talked about here will allow you to load what is termed as a "loose" XAML file, should your skin be any more complex and require code-behind files and so forth, you will need to research alternative methods for loading assemblies. (A hint: Look up "wpf probing privatepath" with Google.)

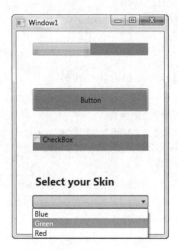

FIGURE 16.6   A new skin being selected from the ComboBox.

The `Application.LoadComponent()` method is great when you have a referenced file or file linked to your application, but in this scenario you are dealing with an "unknown" file. You would need to ensure that your skin provider has matched your naming convention for the styles to be applied correctly. So, given that, the following should correctly load the file and apply the style. This is an extension of the previously built application.

1. Add another Button element to your application and call it btnLoadSkin.

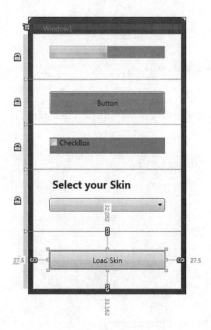

FIGURE 16.7   The new button added to the UI.

2. Find the ComboBox element in the Objects and Timeline category and give the element the name of cmboSkinSelector.

3. Create a new Resource Dictionary called Orange.xaml.

4. Move through the controls, creating a copy of the template(s) into the new Orange.xaml Resource Dictionary.

5. Remember to name the styles exactly as you have done previously.

6. When you have completed all the styles, open the Resources panel and look at the App.xaml children. You should note that Orange.xaml is linked. Right-click and select Delete to unlink the Resource Dictionary.

7. Your controls should go back to the previous style, which is the MergedDictionaries doing their job by applying the last item in the collection!

8. Open the Project tab and find your Orange.xaml file in the project list.

9. Select the file, right-click, and select Remove from Project. You will be asked if you are sure; select Yes. **Do not delete the file!**

10. Save your application.

11. Select your new Button element and add a Click event handler to open Visual Studio.

From here on out, you must make the previous code a little bit more robust in order to make the skin system user friendly. You are asking the user to find the skin file by opening a dialog, but you want the user to have to do this only once, with the relevant style being added to the MergedDictionary collection. You will also want to add a ComboBoxItem so that the users can reselect this style as they please. Add the code shown in Listing 16.5 to the newly created event handler method.

LISTING 16.5   Loading the Resource from File

```
private void btnLoadSkin_Click(object sender, RoutedEventArgs e)
{
    //Create a dialog box so we can search for the Skin file
    Microsoft.Win32.OpenFileDialog newDialog = new Microsoft.Win32.OpenFileDialog();
    newDialog.DefaultExt = ".xaml";
    newDialog.Filter = "XAML Files¦*.xaml";
    newDialog.InitialDirectory = Environment.CurrentDirectory;

    //Show the dialog
    if (newDialog.ShowDialog() == true)
    {
        //Get a stream for the XAMLReader
        Stream newSkin = newDialog.OpenFile();

        //Try and load the loose xaml file
        ResourceDictionary ExternalRD =
System.Windows.Markup.XamlReader.Load(newSkin) as ResourceDictionary;
        if (ExternalRD != null)
```

```
        {
            //Set the Source property
            ExternalRD.Source = new Uri(newDialog.FileName,
UriKind.RelativeOrAbsolute) ;

            //Add this RD as the last one in the list
            Application.Current.Resources.MergedDictionaries.Add(ExternalRD );

            //Add a new ComboBoxItem so the user can reselect the imported skin
            ComboBoxItem newItem = new ComboBoxItem();
            newItem.Content = Path.GetFileNameWithoutExtension(newDialog.FileName);
            this.cmboSkinSelector.Items.Add(newItem);
        }
    }

    //Close the file stream
    newDialog = null;


}
```

The most important lines in Listing 16.5 are

```
ResourceDictionary ExternalRD = System.Windows.Markup.XamlReader.Load(newSkin) as
ResourceDictionary;
```

These lines take a stream (from the file being opened) and use the XamlReader.Load()
method to deserialize the file into the correct object type.

The difference in this example is that you are not clearing out the MergedDictionary
collection when the new skin is selected; you are using the rules of the MergedDictionary
and adding this new object to the bottom of the list as shown with this line:

```
Application.Current.Resources.MergedDictionaries.Add(ExternalRD );
```

Because the code in Listing 16.5 also creates a new ComboBoxItem control for your user
to select from, you also need to change the code in the ComboBox_SelectionChanged event
to deal with the new Resource Dictionary. Listing 16.6 shows the changes made to the
event handler method with two additional methods added to make the code easier to
follow, debug, and ultimately to upgrade.

LISTING 16.6   Modifying the ComboBox selection event

```
private void ComboBox_SelectionChanged(object sender, SelectionChangedEventArgs e)
    {

        if (sender != null)
        {
```

16

```
                //Get the string of the Selected Item
                string ResourceSelected = ((e.OriginalSource as ComboBox).
SelectedItem as ComboBoxItem).Content.ToString();

                //Check to see if the ResourceDictionary already exist in the
merged dictionaries
                int CurrentPosition = this.FindResourceDictionaryByName
(ResourceSelected);

                //Do we need to load up the Resource?
                if (CurrentPosition == -1)
                {
                    //Load up the Resource as specified by the name in the item
selected
                    ResourceDictionary InternalRD = Application.LoadComponent(new
Uri(ResourceSelected + ".xaml", UriKind.Relative)) as ResourceDictionary;
                    InternalRD.Source = new Uri(ResourceSelected + ".xaml",
UriKind.RelativeOrAbsolute);

                    //Add the Resource to the collection
                    Application.Current.Resources.MergedDictionaries.Add(InternalRD);
                }
                else
                {
                    //Using the MergedDictionaries rules, set the dictionary to the
last position
                    this.RepositionRD(CurrentPosition);
                }

            }
        }


        private int FindResourceDictionaryByName(string RDName)
        {
            int LoopCount = 0;
            string FileNameTest = string.Empty;

            //Search the existing collection of Resources for the Dictionary by
name using the Source value
            foreach (ResourceDictionary item in
Application.Current.Resources.MergedDictionaries)
            {
                //Get just the Filename and the extension
                FileNameTest = Path.GetFileName(item.Source.OriginalString);
```

```
            if (FileNameTest == RDName + ".xaml")
                break;

            LoopCount++;
        }

        if (LoopCount <=
Application.Current.Resources.MergedDictionaries.Count - 1)
        {
            //Send back the current position in the Collection
            return LoopCount;
        }
        else
        {
            //-1 indicates that the Name was not found
            return -1;
        }
    }

    private void RepositionRD(int OldPosition)
    {
        //Check that it isnt already the last ResourceDictionary in the list
        if (OldPosition ==
Application.Current.Resources.MergedDictionaries.Count )
            return;

        //Get an instance of the Resource Dictionary
        ResourceDictionary RemovedRD = Application.Current.Resources.MergedDic-
tionaries[OldPosition ] as ResourceDictionary;

        //Remove it from its previous position
        Application.Current.Resources.MergedDictionaries.RemoveAt(OldPosition);

        //Send it to the last item by adding it back to the collection
        Application.Current.Resources.MergedDictionaries.Add(RemovedRD);
    }
```

The first of the two new methods added is responsible for finding the selected skin file by name from the collection. The second enables you to reposition the Resource Dictionaries to the bottom of the list so that the styles contained within are applied to the elements on the screen.

Summary

I hope this chapter has been as much fun for you as it has been for me writing it.

One thing for sure is, when it comes to skinning, a lot of testing and validation needs to be taken care of on loading of skin files. You need to create a skin map if using purely loose XAML files because it is crucial to ensure that your style naming convention is adhered to. Of course, Resource Dictionaries can contain lots of types of resources, so maybe you can adapt and change these methods to allow your users to load different data templates or even animations.

CHAPTER 17

Working with Windows

Window is an element type, just as a Button or ListBox, and has properties and methods that you can call on to control how the user interacts with it. In this chapter, you will learn what the common properties of the Window element do, as well as how to customize the Window to suit your own requirements. Another area that is always requested is how to create more than one Window and have both communicate with each other, so you will also look at an eventing scenario that can help you manage this.

Window Elements

A *Scene* was the original terminology used by Microsoft to describe everything that your application would do with a single Window. I assume that there must have been some sort of communication issue between the development teams creating Expression Interactive Designer (EID) and the Cider extensions for Visual Studio because at the time, neither product married to the other very well and terminology differences were rife. Whereas Visual Studio would create a new Window object for you, EID would create a new Scene.

This terminology gap was filled in with the release of the first Expression Blend Beta, which also marked a move toward using WPF (Windows Presentation Foundation) terminology and therefore tightening the connection between the two products. You decide what terminology works best for you to understand what it is you are talking about, but make sure that you understand a few of the properties that make up a Window as shown in Table 17.1.

TABLE 17.1   Common Window Properties

Property	Type	Description
Allows Transparency	Bool	Set to false by default, this property needs to be true to enable custom form shapes and transparency.
WindowStyle	Enum	None No border at all. This also removes the functionality provided through the taskbar for the Window such as minimize and maximize. SingleBorderWindow (Default) Standard form window with full functionality. ThreeDBorderWindow The Window should contain a 3D border. ToolWindow Used for dialog and tool windows, the window frame shows no icon and displays only a Close button.
Left	Double	Set to Auto by default, this value determines the Window's left edge in relation to the user desktop.
Top	Double	Set to Auto by default, this value determines the Window's top edge in relation to the user desktop.
Icon	Image	Unlike previous WinForms that required a specific icon-formatted image, Blend allows you to select any image to use as the Windows icon that appears in the top left of the Window border as well as on the taskbar when appropriate settings are applied.
ResizeMode	Enum	NoResize Removes the ability for the Window to be minimized and maximized as well as resized. CanMinimize The Window can only be minimized and restored. CanResize (default) The Window can be resized. CanResizeWithGrip Forces the display of a Resize Grip in the bottom-right corner of the application.
ShowInTaskbar	Bool	Set to true by default, this property determines if this Window will be displayed in the taskbar.

TABLE 17.1   Common Window Properties

Property	Type	Description
SizeToContent	Enum	Manual (default)
		The Window will not automatically resize itself based on its content. Other properties of the Window, such as width and height, must be set to determine the size.
		Width
		The Window will automatically resize its width based on its content.
		Height
		The Window will automatically resize its height based on its content.
WidthAndHeight		The Window will automatically resize itself in width and height based on its content.
Title	String	The title to display in the Windows border as well as on the taskbar.
TopMost	Bool	Set to false by default, this property determines whether the Window should remain on top of all other windows.
WindowStartupLocation	Enum	Manual (Default)
		The startup location of the Window is determined by its settings or default location.
		CenterOwner
		If the Window is a child of another Window, its startup location is in the center of the parent Window.
		CenterScreen
		The startup location is in the center of the active screen when the Window is loaded.
WindowState	Enum	Normal (Default)
		The Window should display as its normal properties determine. This is the same as Restore.
		Minimized
		The Window is set to a minimized state.
		Maximized
		The Window is set to a maximized state.

17

Setting a Window to Show as Transparent

There will be occasions where you are required to create a Window of varying shape and or varying levels of transparency. Where people usually come unstuck is when they need to provide a mechanism for allowing the user to move the Window.

1. Create a new application in Blend.

2. Select the LayoutRoot element.

3. Select the Pen or Pencil tool from the toolbox and draw a closed shape as shown in Figure 17.1.

FIGURE 17.1   A cloud path drawn.

4. Set the Path to show a colored fill from the Brushes category of the Property tab.

5. With the Path element selected, hold down the Ctrl key and click on the LayoutRoot element in the Objects and Timeline category of the Interaction panel.

6. You should now have both elements selected. It is important that the Path was selected first. Go to the Object menu at the top of the application, select the Path menu option, and then select Make Clipping Path from the submenu that appears.

7. Your artboard is probably looking blank with just the Window frame, which is fine. You need to select the LayoutRoot element and apply a color to the Background property.

8. You should now see the shape you created previously. Select the Window element in the Objects and Timeline category.

9. Find the AllowsTransparency property (in the Appearance category) and set it to true by checking the box.

10. With the Window still selected, set the Background property to NoBrush.

11. Run the application and you should just have a form in the shape you created previously.

You can't do anything with the form in terms of repositioning or closing it because you have no controls on the form to do this now. You can close the application, though, by right-clicking on the taskbar item representing your application and selecting Close from its menu.

Adding a controller is quite simple, as the following steps show:

1. With the LayoutRoot element activated, add a Grid element at a nondescript position inside your shape as shown in Figure 17.2.

FIGURE 17.2   Grid Placement within the LayoutRoot.

2. Double-click to activate the Grid element.
3. Add an Ellipse element as a child of the Grid and apply a brush to the Fill property so that you can see it.
4. With the Ellipse selected, open the Event Viewer inside the Properties tab and scroll down to find the MouseDown event.
5. Double-click inside the input box to launch Visual Studio.
6. Add the following lines of code to the event that is created for you:

```
private void Ellipse_MouseDown(object sender, System.Windows.Input.MouseBut-
tonEventArgs e)
{
    if (e.ChangedButton == System.Windows.Input.MouseButton.Left)
        this.DragMove();
}
```

You need to make sure that the MouseDown event has been raised by the left mouse button only, as the DragMove() method works only with the primary mouse button.

Save and then run your application in Visual Studio. You should now be able to move the window around by selecting and dragging your mouse on the Ellipse element. Simple, wasn't it?

But what about closing the application with no close button? You could add a button specifically for this and call the following in the event handler:

```
Environment.Exit(0);
```

In this case, you can also just close the application by selecting Stop Debugging from the Debug menu in Visual Studio.

Creating Multiple Windows

When you create a new empty application in Blend, you are by default given an empty Window to play with as the "host" of the new application. I am sure you are aware of this by now, but what happens when you want your application to show more than one Window or you want two Windows to talk to each other?

Creating a new Window is very easy in Blend; you simply select File and then New from the Blend menu at the top of the application. When you see the dialog, just add the name of the Window and you are good to go. You can also create a new Window by right clicking on a project nested in a solution inside the Projects tab, and following the menu system.

The Importance of Naming

In version 1.0 of Expression Blend, a whole host of issues is present with the naming of objects such as Windows and user controls. This issue has been reported many times throughout testing and will hopefully be fixed before the release of the second version of the product. If you are currently using version 1.0, I would advise you to think carefully about the names of your Windows and the like because the name you give it when first creating a new Window will ultimately be its last.

You can go about setting up your Window to the style that you want to achieve, remembering that this Window may indeed be a child of a parent Window in terms of ownership. You can set the WindowStyle property to one of the values shown in Table 17.1.

A Window property that is set to false by default is TopMost. When selected or set to true, this will ensure that your Window will remain at the front of all other windows (and other applications) until such a time as it is minimized, removed, or superseded by another application Window that also has its TopMost property value set to true.

Switching Between Windows in Code

To show a second Window, you need to create an instance of the Window object and call its Show() method. The following takes you through creating a second Window and spawning that Window from a button Click event:

1. Using the application previously created, add a new Grid as a child element of the LayoutRoot. Add a button and Label elements as shown in Figure 17.3. Name the Button element btnSpawnWindow2 and the Label element labNotify.

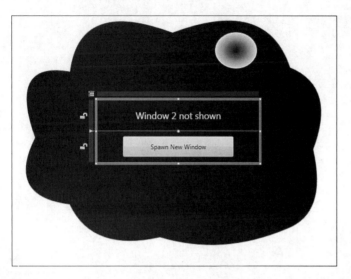

FIGURE 17.3   The new child elements.

2. Add a new Window to the project by selecting File and then New Item from the menu at the top of Blend.

3. By default the Window will be selected in the Add New Item dialog window. You could rename the Window, but for this sample, just leave it as Window2.xaml.

4. Ensure that the Include Code File check box is checked and click OK.

5. Modify this new Window to suit your design terms. As shown in Figure 17.4, I just added a Label element for display purposes.

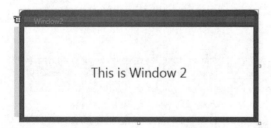

FIGURE 17.4   The new Window with a Label element added to it.

6. With the Window element selected in the Objects and Timeline category of the Interaction panel, open the Event Viewer of the Properties panel.

17

7. Locate the `Closed` event. Double-click on its input box to add the event handlers to the code behind file in Visual Studio. You should get an error dialog box appear as shown in Figure 17.5. Why does this occur?

FIGURE 17.5   The event handler error dialog box.

The solution in Visual Studio does not know that you have added a second Window to the project, so it cannot add event handlers to it just yet. Click the OK button to close the error dialog and reopen Visual Studio. You should now get a dialog, as shown in Figure 17.6, which asks you to reload the solution. Click on Reload.

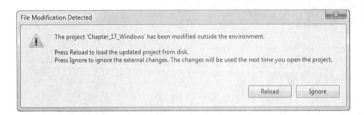

FIGURE 17.6   The Reload notification dialog in Visual Studio.

8. When Visual Studio has reloaded your application, you should see in the Solution Explorer that `Window2.xaml` has been added. Click the Save All button, or select File and then Save all from the main menu. You might be prompted to save the solution (`.sln`) file at which point you can just click Save to complete.

9. You can now go back to Expression Blend and again attempt to add the `Closed` event handler. This time Visual Studio should open up with the correct code event handler added.

What Is the Difference Between the Closing and Closed Events?

When the `Closing` event is raised, you have an opportunity to stop the Window from completing its close instruction(s). You can use this when you want to ask the user to save some changes or other arbitrary requirement, and at the same time you might want to give the user the ability to cancel the close instruction in case it was an accident. To cancel the `Closing` event, you would add code similar to the following inside the `Closing` event handler:

```
private void Window_Closing(object sender, System.ComponentModel.CancelEven-
tArgs e)
```

```
        {
            e.Cancel = true;

        }
```
The Closed event has no such argument options.

---

10. Go back to Blend and locate the Loaded event. Double-click to add this event to the code-behind file as well.

11. You can now add the code as shown in Listing 17.1, which creates a RoutedEvent that the parent Window can subscribe to (for notification when events change), an Enum *type* for the Window state, and a method to make raising the event easy.

LISTING 17.1   Creating a RoutedEvent for the WindowState Change

```
public partial class Window2
        {
                public Window2()
                {
                        this.InitializeComponent();

                        // Insert code required on object creation below this point.
                }

        public static readonly RoutedEvent WindowStateChangedEvent =
EventManager.RegisterRoutedEvent(
        "WindowStateChanged", RoutingStrategy.Bubble,
typeof(RoutedEventHandler), typeof(Window2));

        // Provide CLR accessors for the event
        public event RoutedEventHandler WindowStateChanged
        {
            add { AddHandler(WindowStateChangedEvent, value); }
            remove { RemoveHandler(WindowStateChangedEvent, value); }
        }


        public enum WINDOW_STATE
        {
            Closed = 0,
            Loaded = 1
        }

        private void Window_Closed(object sender, EventArgs e)
        {
            this.RaiseStateChange(WINDOW_STATE.Closed);
```

```
    }

    private void Window_Loaded(object sender, RoutedEventArgs e)
    {
        this.RaiseStateChange(WINDOW_STATE.Loaded);
    }



    private void RaiseStateChange(WINDOW_STATE CurrentState)
    {
        RoutedEventArgs newEvent = new RoutedEventArgs
(Window2.WindowStateChangedEvent, CurrentState);
        RaiseEvent(newEvent);
    }
    }
```

1. Save and Build the application in Visual Studio before switching back to Expression Blend. Open the Window1.xaml file.

2. Select the btnSpawnWindow2 element and add an event handler for Click.

3. You should now be in Visual Studio again with the Click handler method being added just below the previous MouseDown event handler.

4. You must now create an instance of your second Window by using the following code inside your button Click event handler:

   ```
   Window2 NewWindow = new Window2();
   ```

5. Before you can call the Show() method of the Window2 instance, you should add an event subscriber for the RoutedEvent WindowStateChanged that you created inside the Window2 class. Add the following line underneath the NewWindow declaration:

   ```
   NewWindow.WindowStateChanged += new RoutedEventHandler(NewWindow_WindowStat-
   eChanged);
   ```

6. You should either be able to auto-generate the handler method by using the Tab key as directed by the IntelliSense or you can add it manually as shown here:

   ```
   void NewWindow_WindowStateChanged(object sender, RoutedEventArgs e)
       {

       }
   ```

7. When this event is raised, you want to set the notification to the Label element you added to the Window. You can do this using the code shown in Listing 17.2.

LISTING 17.2   Handling the State Change of the Window

```
void NewWindow_WindowStateChanged(object sender, RoutedEventArgs e)
{

        Window2.WINDOW_STATE CurrentState = (Window2.WINDOW_STATE)e.
OriginalSource;
    switch (CurrentState)
    {
        case Window2.WINDOW_STATE.Closed:
            this.labNotify.Content = "Window2 is now Closed";
            break;
        case Window2.WINDOW_STATE.Loaded:
            this.labNotify.Content = "Window2 is now Loaded";
            break;
        default:
            break;
    }
}
```

The first line inside this method creates an instance of the WINDOW_STATE enumerated type and then assigns the `CurrentWindowState` property value to it, which you placed in a copy of the Window2 object as the original source for the event when creating the code to raise the event inside Window2.

The `switch` statement simplifies the notification process as you can see, by reacting to the different state types.

8. Now you need to call the `Show()` method of the NewWindow instance. The complete code for the `Click` handler method is shown in Listing 17.3.

LISTING 17.3   Showing the Window

```
private void btnSpawnWindow2_Click(object sender, RoutedEventArgs e)
{
    Window2 NewWindow = new Window2();

    NewWindow.WindowStateChanged += new RoutedEventHandler(NewWindow_WindowState-
Changed);
    NewWindow.Show();
}
```

What Is the Difference Between Show() and ShowDialog() Methods?

The `ShowDialog()` method opens the instance as a dialog box that takes complete focus of the application. This means that you cannot interact with other parent forms or items until this form is closed. This is handy to use in the case where you need your users to make a decision without allowing them to change previous information.

You should now be able to run the application and you should see the notifications in the Label as you spawn and close the second Window (see Figure 17.7).

FIGURE 17.7   The application with the second Window opened and the correct notification showing in the first custom shaped window.

Summary

This was a simple chapter that has given you the ability to handle the requirements of a Window design as well as enable branching of your application to additional Windows. One area of WPF that does not provide for such a simple experience is when you opt to have no Window borders at all, and you want your user to be able to resize the application. The only functionality provided for by WPF is to set the Windows ResizeMode property to CanResizeWithGrip, which places a small ResizeGrip in the bottom right corner of the Window.

Hopefully these areas will be improved in coming versions.

PART VII

Advanced Topics

IN THIS PART

Creating a Custom Control

When you first start using Expression Blend and the WPF (Windows Presentation Foundation) through Visual Studio, there are a few notable controls and or elements missing from the collection—ones that developers in particular were used to having. The DataGrid is not there, and there are no date and or calendar controls either. What really ate me was the fact that a particular piece of functionality that developers had been wanting for a long time, functionality that was added to .NET 2.0, is not implemented in the .NET Framework 3.0/3.5. This very simple functionality was the ability to build a simple AutoComplete collection for a text box control.

Although DataGrids are available from a few vendors, the calendar controls are still missing. It's a lot of fun creating custom controls, but not much fun when you are under a deadline to get a project complete (which of course is always when you realize that a requirement of the project can't be met with what is provided for you).

In this chapter, you are going to create a custom text box control, which takes a list of potential matches for the text the user types into it, and displays the matches in a drop-down list from the control. This control will not be 100% commercial quality, but it will give you a great insight into what you can do to create your own controls with specific functionality.

Things to Consider

The .NET Framework comes with several thousand classes that belong to varying families of namespaces. Many of these classes are known as base classes, which means they represent the base of a type. Panel is a base class for example, providing functionality to all Panel types used in WPF, such as StackPanel, DockPanel, and so forth.

The following is the hierarchy of inheritance for several Button elements you use in Expression Blend:

```
System.Object
    System.Windows.Threading.DispatcherObject
        System.Windows.DependencyObject
            System.Windows.Media.Visual
                System.Windows.UIElement
                    System.Windows.FrameworkElement
                        System.Windows.Controls.Control
                            System.Windows.Controls.ContentControl
                            System.Windows.Controls.Primitives.ButtonBase

                                System.Windows.Controls.Button
                                System.Windows.Controls.GridViewColumnHeader
                                System.Windows.Controls.Primitives.RepeatButton
                                System.Windows.Controls.Primitives.ToggleButton
```

As you can see in the inheritance hierarchy, all four Button elements derive from the ButtonBase type, which in turn inherits from the ContentControl, and so on down the line.

What is most important to note is that every single class in the .NET Framework inherits from System.Object. Even empty classes you create in Visual Studio inherit from Object. You don't see the syntax showing the inheritance because it is implicitly created along with the class.

It is important to realize that after you start inheriting from classes that are at a much lower level than FrameworkElement, you really are in some very powerful areas. And along with this, you will be losing quite a bit of built-in functionality that Control and ContentControl can provide to your controls.

There are four levels you should look at when you need to create a custom control. Each of these levels represents a level of inheritance as listed in the inheritance hierarchy, which derives from the root of System.Object:

```
System.Object
    System.Windows.Threading.DispatcherObject
        System.Windows.DependencyObject
            System.Windows.Media.Visual
                System.Windows.UIElement
                    System.Windows.FrameworkElement
                        System.Windows.Controls.Control
                            System.Windows.Controls.ContentControl
                                System.Windows.Controls.UserControl
```

Each of the levels are shown this way to enforce the fact that each level inherits from the previous level.

Level 1—FrameworkElement

You certainly need to understand what is going on in WPF to even consider creating a control that sits on this level (well, the level above it, actually). All the existing WPF controls are not even on this level (as you can see, System.Windows.Controls.Control), which means that although basic functionality is available, many of the most desirable attributes of a control (such as templates or a proper content model for children) are left up to you to implement. This level is where base-level controls such as Panel are created.

Level 2—Control

This level implements the ControlTemplate functionality that allows you to modify the appearance of a control by providing a modified or custom ControlTemplate. Most of the WPF control types inherit directly from Control, so although the power of this inheritance level is obvious, the complexity is also much greater.

Level 3—Inherited Control

This is a very powerful method of taking an existing control and extending the functionality that the control gives you in its standard format. You will use this method in this chapter, taking a text box and extending its functionality to suit your requirements. When inheriting a control (such as a Button or Grid, for example), you modify the functionality in the code-behind files and as per normal, you can supply a custom control template or style template to modify the existing appearance.

Level 4—UserControl

The UserControl inherits directly from ContentControl so it makes it easy for you to add existing elements defined by WPF to your customized control. There are a few disadvantages to this in that UserControls do not support templates at all, so any complex customization of the appearance of the control can only be performed directly on each element that you add. Still the UserControl is very common because of its simplicity and is the level that is directly supported by the Blend UI.

Think about what your control needs to do and, at every opportunity, always consider first whether you can modify existing controls to get the job done. This is pretty much what we are going to do in this chapter. Merge the functionality of three existing controls to provide a single UserControl, and at the same time take advantage of the functionality already built in to all the controls.

For a more advanced look at objects and base classes, I direct you to the Windows SDK, which can provide you with the most accurate and intimate details of all classes available to you through the .NET Framework.

18

Where to Start

The remit for this particular control is: Provide a text box type control that, when the user starts typing into it, displays a filtered list of predefined words for the user to select from; if so required.

Figure 18.1 shows the control in action. Similar to an IntelliSense type feature if you will, but a standalone control that can be used as required by the client and its developers.

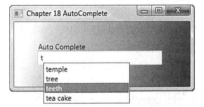

FIGURE 18.1   The list populated by the start of the word added to the TextBox.

On more complex controls, you will most likely (and should) perform a design analysis to make sure that what you are required to build will be the end result based on functionality, appearance, and usability.

The overall functionality and usability were part of the wider project's UI specification; my point here is that even with a very simple control, there was some element of design and validation between the developer and the customer.

Thinking about the control, there are a couple of standout areas that make creating such a control fairly trivial:

▶ You can inherit from the TextBox control and use its functionality in your own class.

▶ Styles and templates could them be applied to the TextBox (not the entire control).

▶ A Popup control could also be employed, which enables the Auto Complete (AC) control to be used inside Grid cells without constriction.

▶ Use of a customized ListBox element inserted into the Popup element will provide the listing functionality.

▶ By using a generic collection of type List<T>, you can store the word match dictionary and use a predicated search delegate.

Building the Control

You are going to create this control in a separate control library so that you can use it later on when required.

1. Start a new project in Expression Blend.

2. Save the project, select the solution inside the Project panel, and right-click to select Edit in Visual Studio from the Project menu.

3. In Visual Studio, open the Solution Explorer panel if it is not already visible by selecting Solution Explorer from the View menu.

4. Right-click on the Solution icon at the top of the Solution Explorer panel, and then select Add and then New Project from the subsequent menu.

What If You Don't Have a Solution Icon at the Top of the Explorer Panel?

For those that are using earlier version of Blend than 2.0 release, Blend only creates a project file instead of a Visual Studio Solution (.sln). For you to add a new project, you can always select the File menu, then Add and then New Project.

---

5. In the resulting Add New Project dialog that appears, you need to navigate to the Visual C# - Windows project types and then select WPF Custom Control Library from the templates as shown in Figure 18.2.

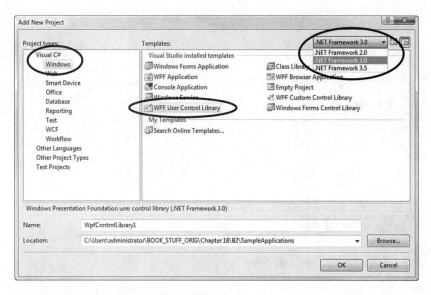

FIGURE 18.2   The new project type.

Figure 18.2 also shows how you can choose the target Framework from the combo box at the top of the dialog. You can choose either Framework 3.0 or 3.5 for this project because we are not using any Framework 3.5–specific coding.

6. Name the project MyCustomControl.

7. Ensure that the project is going to be located where you want it to be, and then click OK to complete the actions.

18

8. Visual Studio will now go through the creation of your new project and add a default control called `UserControl1.xaml` to your project. Sometimes Visual Studio automatically opens the new control as well, which can be painfully slow in Visual Studio 2005 because of the rendering surface initialization. In Visual Studio 2008, you can press the Esc key to stop this from occurring.

9. From the Window menu item at the top of Visual Studio, select Close All Documents.

10. Right-click on the `UserControl1.xaml` file in the Solution Explorer panel and then select Delete from the subsequent context menu. You are not going to be using this control for this project.

11. As Figure 18.3 shows, right-click on the MyCustomControl project inside the Solution Explorer.

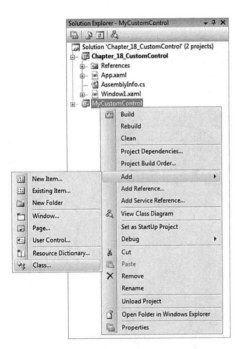

FIGURE 18.3   The mechanism for creating a new class.

12. Select Add from the context menu and then subsequently select Class.

13. Call the class `AutoComplete_TextBox.cs`.

You now have your original project and the new project in the solution. You are now going to continue through coding up the new class, and then adding the project as a reference before returning to Blend to test the control.

14. Modify the class as shown in Listing 18.1 to inherit from the `TextBox` class provided by the Framework.

LISTING 18.1   Inheriting the TextBox Class

```
namespace MyCustomControl
{
    public class AutoComplete_TextBox : System.Windows.Controls.TextBox
    {
    }
}
```

15. You are going to create two constructor methods now. One is a standard constructor and the other allows the user to parse in a predefined List<T> of words to add to the dictionary of words. Listing 18.2 shows the dependency property added to accommodate the List<T> as well as the constructors. Note that the dependency property does not contain any change notification.

LISTING 18.2   Building Out the Dictionary Functionality

```
public class AutoComplete_TextBox : System.Windows.Controls.TextBox
{
    public AutoComplete_TextBox()
    {

    }

    public AutoComplete_TextBox(List<string> WordDictionary)
    {
        this.STORED_LIST = WordDictionary;
    }

    public List<string> STORED_LIST
    {
        get { return (List<string>)GetValue(STORED_LISTProperty); }
        set { SetValue(STORED_LISTProperty, value); }
    }

    public static readonly DependencyProperty STORED_LISTProperty =
    DependencyProperty.Register("STORED_LIST", typeof(List<string>), typeof(Auto-
Complete_TextBox),
    new FrameworkPropertyMetadata(null,
    FrameworkPropertyMetadataOptions.None));
}
```

16. Regardless of how the user instantiates this object, you want to create the Popup control immediately so that it is ready to use as soon as the user starts typing into the TextBox. Before doing this, though, you need to create a customized ListBox

control that enables better handling for the user workflow for this type of control. By this I mean that when the user selects a word from the ListBox and presses the Enter key, you want to assume that he has made his choice. So, you need a way to listen for the events and to ensure that the control then places the selected text into the TextBox part of the control. Listing 18.3 shows the custom class inheriting from the ListBox. It contains a single event that simply instructs the TextBox that the user has made a choice. You can see the overridden methods that allow you to listen for specific actions from which you can then raise the event.

You will also need to add the following using directive for the ListBox:

```
using System.Windows.Controls;
```

LISTING 18.3   Creating the Custom ListBox Control

```
/// <summary>
/// Custom listbox class to allow user actions to act as a click
/// </summary>
class AutoCompleteListBox : ListBox
{
    public AutoCompleteListBox()
    {
        this.EnterKeyPressed += delegate() { };
    }

    public delegate void EnterKeyPressedDelegate();
    public event EnterKeyPressedDelegate EnterKeyPressed;

    protected override void OnKeyUp(KeyEventArgs e)
    {
        base.OnKeyUp(e);

        if (e.Key == Key.Enter)
            this.EnterKeyPressed();
    }

    protected override void OnMouseDoubleClick(MouseButtonEventArgs e)
    {
        base.OnMouseDoubleClick(e);
        this.EnterKeyPressed();
    }

    protected override void OnMouseDown(MouseButtonEventArgs e)
    {
        base.OnMouseDown(e);
        this.EnterKeyPressed();
    }
}
```

17. Now you can create the method that builds the Popup control (inside the AutoComplete_TextBox class) as well as sets up the ListBox you just created. Listing 18.4 shows the method used to create the Popup, and you should add a call to this method from both constructors inside the AutoComplete_TextBox class. Note the event handlers added for both the ListBox and the Popup control. Both the ListBox and the Popup controls are defined as global types.

You will need to add the following using directives for the Popup control, the Rect class, and for the type of event arguments that are generated:

```
using System.Windows.Controls.Primitives;
using System.Windows.Input;

   using System.Windows;
```

LISTING 18.4   Creating the Popup Control

```
private Popup ListPopUp = new Popup();
private AutoCompleteListBox ListDisplay = new AutoCompleteListBox();
private void BuildPopUp()
{
    ListDisplay.MaxHeight = 80;
    ListDisplay.Width = 150;
    ListDisplay.MouseDown += new System.Windows.Input.MouseButtonEventHandler
(ListDisplay_MouseDown);
    ListDisplay.EnterKeyPressed += new AutoCompleteListBox.
EnterKeyPressedDelegate(ListDisplay_EnterKeyPressed);

    ListPopUp.MouseDown += new System.Windows.Input.MouseButtonEventHandler
(ListPopUp_MouseDown);
    ListPopUp.Child = this.ListDisplay;
    ListPopUp.StaysOpen = false;
    ListPopUp.PopupAnimation = PopupAnimation.Fade;
    ListPopUp.Placement = PlacementMode.Relative;
    ListPopUp.PlacementTarget = this;
    ListPopUp.PlacementRectangle = new Rect(10, 20, 300, 300);
}

void ListPopUp_MouseDown(object sender, System.Windows.Input.MouseButtonEventArgs
e)
{
    if (this.ListDisplay.SelectedItem != null)
    {
```

```
        this.Text = this.ListDisplay.SelectedItem.ToString();
        this.ListPopUp.IsOpen = false;
    }
}

void ListDisplay_EnterKeyPressed()
{
    if (this.ListDisplay.SelectedItem != null)
    {
        this.Text = this.ListDisplay.SelectedItem.ToString();
        this.ListPopUp.IsOpen = false;
    }
}

void ListDisplay_MouseDown(object sender, System.Windows.Input.MouseButtonEventArgs
e)
{
    if (this.ListDisplay.SelectedItem != null)
    {
        this.Text = this.ListDisplay.SelectedItem.ToString();
        this.ListPopUp.IsOpen = false;
    }
}
```

18. As you can see, each of the event handler methods simply sets the Popup to close and assigns the selected value from the ListBox to the TextBox control using the this.Text property.

19. Because the user can opt to use the default constructor and provide a List<T> (or different List<T> objects throughout runtime) at a later stage, you need to provide a method that will clear the existing collection, which is simply calling the Clear() method of the STORED_LIST:

```
/// <summary>
/// Clear the store of its current values
/// </summary>
public void ClearStore()
{
    this.STORED_LIST.Clear();
}
```

20. You should also provide a public method that allows the user to add single words to the list at any time, possibly each time a new word is entered in the TextBox, to build a dynamic history dictionary. Listing 18.5 shows the method created.

LISTING 18.5   Adding New Values to the Dictionary

```
/// <summary>
/// Supply a new value to add to the store
/// </summary>
/// <param name="NewValue">A string representing the new value</param>
public void AddNewValueToStore(string NewValue)
{
    //Keep only one copy of the item
    if (!this.STORED_LIST.Contains(NewValue))
        this.STORED_LIST.Add(NewValue);
}
```

21. Now you need to add the methods required to filter the dictionary, which involves supplying a predicate to the List<T>.FindAll() method.

    What is a predicate?

    It is shown like this:

    ```
    NewList<T> = OriginalList<T>.FindAll(Predicate<string> match);
    ```

    In this scenario, the predicate requires the creation of a delegate method that performs the value-matching logic. This means that the original collection will attempt to match a value one at a time in the collection by parsing the string value to the method specified, and with the delegate method returning a Bool value (true for matched), the original collection generates a new collection of the same type with only the matched values.

    Listing 18.6 demonstrates this as you can see the point where the STORED_LIST generic type object has the FindAll() method called, parsing the name of the method to perform the matching.

LISTING 18.6   Filtering the Dictionary

```
private void BuildFilteredList()
{

    if (this.Text.Length > 0)
    {

        List<string> FilteredStore = this.STORED_LIST.FindAll(DoMatch);

        if (FilteredStore.Count == 0)
        {
            this.ListPopUp.IsOpen = false;
            return;
        }
```

```
        else
        {
            this.ListDisplay.Items.Clear();

            foreach (string var in FilteredStore)
            {
                this.ListDisplay.Items.Add(var);
            }

            this.ListPopUp.IsOpen = true;
        }
    }

}

private bool DoMatch(string ValueToTest)
{
    if (ValueToTest.StartsWith(this.Text, true, null))
        return true;
    else
        return false;
}
```

In this line of Listing 18.6:

```
    if (ValueToTest.StartsWith(this.Text, true, null))
```

You are testing the value by calling the StartsWith() method, which has three over-loaded options. The first parameter we are testing for is the text that the user has already entered into the text box, the second true specified whether the method should ignore case sensitivity, and the third parameter is for culture information. A null value tells the method to use the current culture information.

22. The last method you need to create (see Listing 18.7) is an overridden instance of the OnKeyUp event handler for the TextBox, which allows you to control the PopUp control and then call the method you just added to filter the dictionary (List<T>) based on what the user has already entered.

LISTING 18.7   Implementing the OnKeyUp Method Handler

```
/// <summary>
/// Checks to see if the currently entered text is available from
/// the Store. If so, display the popup
```

```
/// </summary>
/// <param name="e"></param>
protected override void OnKeyUp(KeyEventArgs e)
{
    base.OnKeyUp(e);

    if (e.Key == Key.Down)
    {
        if (!this.ListPopUp.IsOpen)
            this.ListPopUp.IsOpen = true;

        this.ListDisplay.SelectedIndex = 0;
        this.ListDisplay.Focus();

    }

    if (this.STORED_LIST.Count > 0)
        this.BuildFilteredList();
}
```

The complete listing of the control will be at the end of this chapter should you need to review its creation.

Testing the Control

That wasn't too hard after all, was it? A very simple and clean control that you can now add to any project, which is what you should now try to do. Before doing this, though, you need to build the new control and then add a reference to it from the testing project you initially created.

1. Click the SaveAll button in Visual Studio or Save All from the File menu.
2. Now select Build Solution from the Build menu in Visual Studio. Hopefully everything builds correctly for you and you are now ready to move on.
3. In the Solution Explorer panel, locate the References folder of the first project you created—*not the control project.*
4. Right-click and select Add Reference. Visual Studio might take a little while to display the Add Reference dialog box, but this is just because it is finding a lot of information in your computer about other available references.
5. As Figure 18.4 shows, select the Projects tab of the dialog box and you should see the MyCustomControl project available.

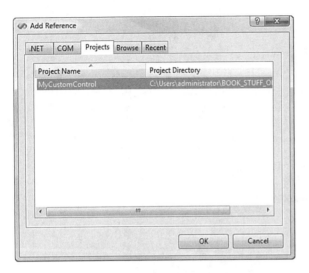

FIGURE 18.4   The Add Reference dialog.

6. Select it and click OK.

You should now be able to see your control in the Reference list under the References folder.

Referencing to Other Files and Controls

Because the .NET Framework creates a specific type of file when you build your project or solution, Visual Studio allows you to reference these files and use them in new projects and or solutions. It doesn't matter if it is a .NET-created `.dll` or `.exe` file.

When you build your projects, you can find the `.exe` or the `.dll` file located in the Bin folder underneath your project location. Sometimes developers will create controls for you and just send you the file instead of the entire project. You can, in those cases, select the Browse tab in the Add Resources dialog to include these controls into your project.

Blend also gives you the ability to add references to projects, but you must navigate directly to the `.dll` or `.exe` file directly after the project has been built.

Please see further information in the Windows SDK or other online resources to learn more about references, the different types of references, and the issues regarding circular references.

Now to the moment of truth: testing your new control.

1. Open the solution in Expression Blend, checking that both projects are available. If you still only have the first project open in Blend, you will need to close the project and then select Open -> Project/Solution (Ctrl + Shift + O) from the File menu, navigating to the .sln file, or check to see if the .sln file is listed in your Recent Projects list (available from the File menu).

2. Make sure that you have Window1.xaml open inside Blend.

3. Open the Asset Library and select the Custom Controls tab.

4. You should see your AutoComplete_TextBox control in the list, complete with the correct icon, thanks to the TextBox you inherited. Add the control to your project. It should look like an ordinary text box at this stage.

5. Open the Properties panel and name the new control actxtTest.

6. Clear out the default text that is populated in your control.

7. Select the Window element inside the Objects and Timeline category of the Interaction panel.

8. Locate and add the Loaded event handler for the Window, taking you back to Visual Studio.

9. You can now define a simple list to parse to the control for testing as shown in Listing 18.8. You will need to add the following using directive for the List<T> type:

```
using System.Collections.Generic;
```

LISTING 18.8   Building a Test Dictionary

```
private void Window_Loaded(object sender, RoutedEventArgs e)
{
    //Create a new list to add to the auto complete control
    List<string> DictionaryList = new List<string>();
    DictionaryList.Add("temple");
    DictionaryList.Add("tree");
    DictionaryList.Add("teeth");
    DictionaryList.Add("tea cake");
    DictionaryList.Add("dog");
    DictionaryList.Add("dilbert");
    DictionaryList.Add("dam");
    DictionaryList.Add("pretty");
    DictionaryList.Add("polly");


    this.actxtTest.STORED_LIST = DictionaryList;
}
```

When you run the application, type the letter **t** into the TextBox. You should get a ListBox showing you the result of the filter. You can click on the down arrow to move through the list and then press the Enter key to make it the text inside the control.

18

Well, that was a pretty simple test and by no stretch of the imagination would it even be considered a commercial test of a control. This control does not support localization in the form of flow direction any more than the individual components inside of it, and then there is the fact that a dictionary could get quite large, so a more efficient way to store and extract a match list would be required. But those were not really the goals of the chapter now were they?

If you had issues with building the control from Visual Studio, Listing 18.9 is a complete listing of the classes inside the control.

LISTING 18.9   The Complete Control Listing

```
using System;
using System.Collections.Generic;
using System.Text;
using System.Windows.Controls.Primitives;
using System.Windows.Controls;
using System.Windows.Input;
using System.Windows;

namespace MyCustomControl
{
    public class AutoComplete_TextBox : System.Windows.Controls.TextBox
    {
        public AutoComplete_TextBox()
        {
            this.BuildPopUp();
        }

        public AutoComplete_TextBox(List<string> WordDictionary)
        {
            this.STORED_LIST = WordDictionary;
            this.BuildPopUp();
        }

        public List<string> STORED_LIST
        {
            get { return (List<string>)GetValue(STORED_LISTProperty); }
            set { SetValue(STORED_LISTProperty, value); }
        }

        public static readonly DependencyProperty STORED_LISTProperty =
        DependencyProperty.Register("STORED_LIST", typeof(List<string>),
typeof(AutoComplete_TextBox),
            new FrameworkPropertyMetadata(null,
            FrameworkPropertyMetadataOptions.None));
```

```
        private Popup ListPopUp = new Popup();
        private AutoCompleteListBox ListDisplay = new AutoCompleteListBox();
        private void BuildPopUp()
        {
            ListDisplay.MaxHeight = 80;
            ListDisplay.Width = 150;
            ListDisplay.MouseDown += new System.Windows.Input.
MouseButtonEventHandler(ListDisplay_MouseDown);
            ListDisplay.EnterKeyPressed += new AutoCompleteListBox.
EnterKeyPressedDelegate(ListDisplay_EnterKeyPressed);

            ListPopUp.MouseDown += new
System.Windows.Input.MouseButtonEventHandler(ListPopUp_MouseDown);
            ListPopUp.Child = this.ListDisplay;
            ListPopUp.StaysOpen = false;
            ListPopUp.PopupAnimation = PopupAnimation.Fade;
            ListPopUp.Placement = PlacementMode.Relative;
            ListPopUp.PlacementTarget = this;
            ListPopUp.PlacementRectangle = new Rect(10, 20, 300, 300);
        }

        void ListPopUp_MouseDown(object sender, System.Windows.Input.
MouseButtonEventArgs e)
        {
            if (this.ListDisplay.SelectedItem != null)
            {
                this.Text = this.ListDisplay.SelectedItem.ToString();
                this.ListPopUp.IsOpen = false;
            }
        }

        void ListDisplay_EnterKeyPressed()
        {
            if (this.ListDisplay.SelectedItem != null)
            {
                this.Text = this.ListDisplay.SelectedItem.ToString();
                this.ListPopUp.IsOpen = false;
            }
        }

        void ListDisplay_MouseDown(object sender, System.Windows.Input.
MouseButtonEventArgs e)
        {
            if (this.ListDisplay.SelectedItem != null)
```

18

```
        {
            this.Text = this.ListDisplay.SelectedItem.ToString();
            this.ListPopUp.IsOpen = false;
        }
    }


    /// <summary>
    /// Clear the store of its current values
    /// </summary>
    public void ClearStore()
    {
        this.STORED_LIST.Clear();
    }


    /// <summary>
    /// Supply a new value to add to the store
    /// </summary>
    /// <param name="NewValue">A string representing the new value</param>
    public void AddNewValueToStore(string NewValue)
    {
        //Keep only one copy of the item
        if (!this.STORED_LIST.Contains(NewValue))
            this.STORED_LIST.Add(NewValue);
    }


    /// <summary>
    /// Checks to see if the currently entered text is available from
    /// the Store. If so, display the popup
    /// </summary>
    /// <param name="e"></param>
    protected override void OnKeyUp(KeyEventArgs e)
    {
        base.OnKeyUp(e);

        if (e.Key == Key.Down)
        {
            if (!this.ListPopUp.IsOpen)
                this.ListPopUp.IsOpen = true;

            this.ListDisplay.SelectedIndex = 0;
            this.ListDisplay.Focus();

        }

        if (this.STORED_LIST.Count > 0)
            this.BuildFilteredList();
```

```csharp
    }

    private void BuildFilteredList()
    {

        if (this.Text.Length > 0)
        {

            List<string> FilteredStore = this.STORED_LIST.FindAll(DoMatch);

            if (FilteredStore.Count == 0)
            {
                this.ListPopUp.IsOpen = false;
                return;
            }
            else
            {
                this.ListDisplay.Items.Clear();

                foreach (string var in FilteredStore)
                {
                    this.ListDisplay.Items.Add(var);
                }

                this.ListPopUp.IsOpen = true;
            }
        }

    }

    private bool DoMatch(string ValueToTest)
    {
        if (ValueToTest.StartsWith(this.Text, true, null))
            return true;
        else
            return false;
    }

}

/// <summary>
/// Custom listbox class to allow user actions to act as a click
/// </summary>
```

```
class AutoCompleteListBox : ListBox
{
    public AutoCompleteListBox()
    {
        this.EnterKeyPressed += delegate() { };
    }

    public delegate void EnterKeyPressedDelegate();
    public event EnterKeyPressedDelegate EnterKeyPressed;

    protected override void OnKeyUp(KeyEventArgs e)
    {
        base.OnKeyUp(e);

        if (e.Key == Key.Enter)
            this.EnterKeyPressed();
    }

    protected override void OnMouseDoubleClick(MouseButtonEventArgs e)
    {
        base.OnMouseDoubleClick(e);
        this.EnterKeyPressed();
    }

    protected override void OnMouseDown(MouseButtonEventArgs e)
    {
        base.OnMouseDown(e);
        this.EnterKeyPressed();
    }
}

}
```

Summary

I hope you have enjoyed creating this handy control and in the process taken in just how powerful inheritance really is by allowing you to maintain functionality that is present in the original control(s). You could do a lot more with this control in terms of providing design-time support for list objects and giving the user better control of the pop-up positioning and so on. I leave it to you to improve the outcome. Please don't be shy and by all means send me a copy of your modifications!

This chapter has been about code though, so although we yell at the top of our voices about the brilliance of XAML, its simplicity and ease of use, you should always keep the thought in the back of your mind about what technologies are best at which types of jobs. If working with code, especially in the areas of creating new controls, you should also think about just how complex you need to go to achieve the desired solution.

As also discussed in the early part of the chapter, making the choice of which level of the inheritance hierarchy your control sits can also make the difference between functionality and simplicity to the end user of your control.

CHAPTER 19

Using 3D in Blend

3D is very exciting to work in, but it can also be extremely frustrating because everything appears clunky and sometimes things just disappear for what would appear to be no reason at all. The fact that you see these ultra smooth demos that have 3D content can usually be put down to the brilliance of those that take the extra time required to actually produce such content.

In this chapter you will be introduced to the controls available to you in Blend to control 3D objects and their associated assets such as materials. You will also see that you have control of such things as the lights and camera that you want to use. Blend is not a tool to create 3D objects, although you certainly can create them using XAML (Extensible Application Markup Language) and code, as time-consuming as it is.

Viewport3D

The Viewport3D element is a 2D document of sorts, specifically built to render 3D content. The element provides a number of properties that are familiar to the standard 2D layout elements, such as Height and Width properties and various events, but unlike standard containers such as Grid and Canvas, the Viewport3D's ClipToBounds property is set to true by default.

The following steps will give you a taste of what the element provides, as you can create a 3D mesh from a 2D image using a built-in Blend tool, Convert Image to 3D:

1. Locate an image on your computer that you would like to use.

2. Create a new application in Expression Blend.

3. From the Project panel, Files category, right-click on your Project file and select Add Existing Item from the context menu.

4. Navigate to your chosen image's location.

5. Your image should now appear in your project's content.

6. Double-click on your LayoutRoot Grid element to ensure that it is the activated control.

7. Right-click on the image file in the Files category and select Insert.

8. Your image should now be on your artboard. With your image selected in the Objects and Timeline category, select the Tools menu and then select Make Image 3D from the menu.

   At first it might appear as if nothing has happened, but if you look at your Objects and Timeline category, you now have a Viewport3D control where the Image element previously was.

   If you drill down into the Viewport3D element, you will see that Blend has added quite a few new items for you (see Figure 19.1), including a camera, a container for the model, as well as two lights (an ambient and directional light). Not bad for one click on a menu item.

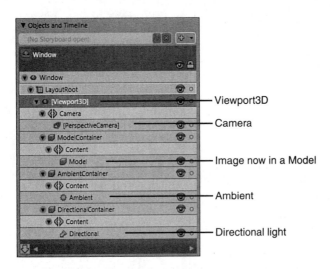

FIGURE 19.1   The effects of Blend's Make Image 3D tool.

   Your original image has not actually been magically converted to a 3D model though; it has now been used as a material for a mesh plane created by the tool.

9. With the Viewport3D element selected, open the Properties panel and set the Viewport3D element to be in the center of your window.

10. When drilling down into the Viewport3D element, find the ModelContainer element, and then locate and select its child, Model, in the Objects and Timeline category.

As Figure 19.2 shows, selecting this 3D model restricts the amount of controls that are available to you in the toolbox.

FIGURE 19.2   The only toolbox items that can be used with a Viewport3D model.

You are already familiar with the Selection and Zoom and Pan tools, so this next section deals with the Camera Orbit tool and the Selection tool.

The Selection Tool

The Selection tool allows you to control the positioning and rotation of the 3D model inside the Viewport3D container by providing a 3D axis transformation tool as shown in Figure 19.3.

FIGURE 19.3   The axis transformation tool.

Each of the colors represents an axis for both transforming the position and rotation as explained in Figure 19.4.

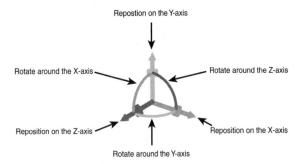

Reposition on the Y-axis

Rotate around the X-axis

Rotate around the Z-axis

Reposition on the Z-axis

Reposition on the X-axis

Rotate around the Y-axis

FIGURE 19.4   The axis transform concept.

Red Arc & Pointer
Allows repositioning and rotation of the object on the x-axis only

Green Arc & Pointer
Allows repositioning and rotation of the object on the y-axis only.

Blue Arc & Pointer
Allows repositioning and rotation of the object on the z-axis only.

The Camera Orbit Tool

The Camera Orbit tool allows you to treat the camera in the Viewport3D similar to a video camera. The tool specifically allows you to zoom in and out and reposition where the camera is pointing.

With your model selected in the Objects and Timeline category, holding down the left mouse button and dragging the tool over the artboard changes where the camera is looking. Holding down the Shift key allows you to control the movement of the camera by snapping its change angle to every 15 degrees in any of the three axes. Holding down the Ctrl key constrains the tool to just the x-axis and y-axis, whereas holding down the Alt key lets you zoom in and out.

At first this action could appear strange and you might mistakenly think that you are moving the 3D model, but alas you are not. This tool changes only the camera's view (see Figure 19.5). You are free to record these movements in a storyboard to bring your 3D image to life the same way as you can record the transformation of any element inside a 2D container such as a Grid element.

FIGURE 19.5   The effects of transforming the orbit on the camera.

Importing 3D Objects

Expression Blend allows you to import 3D .obj-formatted files. You can also import associated files, such as material files, in the .mtl format. Importing these files is the same process that you went through to include your image file previously, and right-clicking on the .obj file in the Files category of the Projects panel gives you the Insert menu option to place your object(s) into a Viewport3D element.

Erain ZAM 3D is an application built to expressly allow you to create 3D content that is exportable in the XAML file format, which like .obj files, allows materials to be placed on the 3D objects. The XAML exported files from ZAM 3D map directly to image resources for the materials, so all the images as well as the exported XAML file must be added to the project. Stephen Barker has courteously provided such a model, shown in Figure 19.6.

FIGURE 19.6   A music player model by Stephen Barker.

One of the big benefits to using ZAM 3D–exported models is that you have the opportunity to name the elements before they are exported to XAML. This means it is very simple then to reference those elements and show a music video on the screen, for example, or modify the element in some other way that suits your requirements.

Materials

Three types of materials are used within the Blend material subproperty editor as shown in Table 19.1.

TABLE 19.1   Material Definitions

Name	Description
Specular material	A specular material allows you to control the level of highlighting that appears on a 3D object. Similar to that used to create reflections or shiny spots on metal-type objects.
Diffuse material	A direct color that results in the 3D object appearing as if illuminated by white light.
Emissive material	A material that gives the appearance that the light is emanating from the object, similar to that of a glow, where the color of the glow is the material color.

To edit the material properties of a 3D object, select the desired model object from the Objects and Timeline category and you will notice that the Properties panel has a Material category added. Two properties, BackMaterial and Material, are available for you to edit.

Click on the property input box and you will see an advanced menu appear as shown in Figure 19.7. Click Edit Resource and the subproperty material editor will appear as shown in Figure 19.8.

FIGURE 19.7   The advanced menu categories.

You can add and remove materials from the collection as well as change the properties of each type using the individual editors. With not too much work, it is easy to completely

Add new material
Remove material
Send material back
Bring material forward

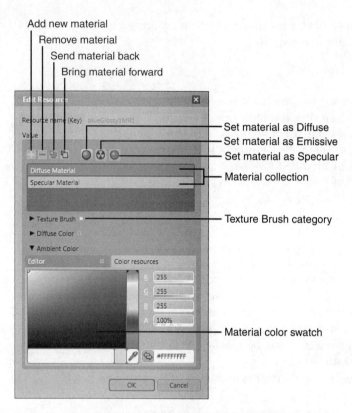

Set material as Diffuse
Set material as Emissive
Set material as Specular

Material collection

Texture Brush category

Material color swatch

FIGURE 19.8   The subproperty material editor dialog.

change the look of an object based purely on the materials applied. When Stephen gave me the music player model, he had set a blue color material onto the housing of the player model. With just a slight modification to the specular and diffuse materials, it is now a hot pink color as shown in Figure 19.9.

FIGURE 19.9   A new housing color for the object, created with material modification.

19

Don't forget that objects can also have a BackMaterial, so you will need to pay close attention to the object's usage and adjust as required.

The Camera

By default, Blend creates a perspective camera for you, which might very well suit your requirements from the start. Given that you have two choices of camera, you might want to modify the settings for scenarios that require a different view. Table 19.2 shows the settings of the camera types and Figure 19.10 shows the Camera category of the Properties panel where such settings can be modified.

TABLE 19.2   Camera Properties

Property Name	Description
Camera Type	Perspective camera (default): Similar to a standard camera, objects appear in a perspective view, meaning they get smaller the further away from the camera they are.
	Orthographic camera: An orthographic view removes the concept of perspective view from the camera lens. Objects are kept in scale and the camera view is determined by a Width property.
Position (x,y,z)	Allows you to define the position of the camera on each of the three axes.
Direction (x,y,z)	Allows you to specify the direction that the camera is pointed at.
Up Vector (x,y,z)	This property allows you to specify which direction is up, where x0,y1,z0 is the default.
Perspective Field of View (POV)	This property is available only when the perspective camera is selected. This allows you to control the amount of distortion that takes place on objects and the amount of objects visible in the viewport. The bigger the number, the more distortion created.
Far Clipping Plane	Similar to clipping on a 2D grid, canvas, and so on, this value controls how far an object can be away from the camera and still be visible.
Near Clipping Plane	Similar to clipping on a 2D grid, canvas, and so on, this value controls how close an object can be to the camera and still be visible.

You have already seen how to change the position of the camera using the Camera Orbit tool, which changes the values in the Camera category directly.

The Lights

As Figure 19.11 shows, the Light category of the Properties panel allows you to set a light to one of four types: Ambient (Table 19.3), Point (Table 19.4), Directional (Table 19.5), or Spot (Table 19.6). Each light has its own property set, each of which is detailed in the following tables.

Perspective camera type

Orthographic camera type

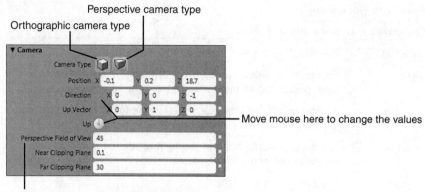

Move mouse here to change the values

Field changes to the Width property if the camera type is Orthographic

FIGURE 19.10   The Camera category.

Ambient light   Directional light

Point light   Spot light

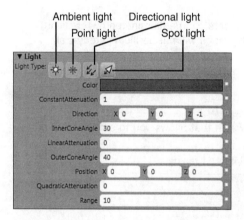

FIGURE 19.11   The Light category of the Properties panel when a light is selected.

TABLE 19.3   Ambient Light Properties

Ambient Light Properties	Description
Color	A simple color swatch that allows you to set the base color of the light

TABLE 19.4   Point Light Properties

Point Light Properties	Description
Color	A simple color swatch that allows you to set the base color of the light.
ConstantAttenuation	A value that specifies how powerful the light should be the further light is away from the source position.

19

TABLE 19.4   Point Light Properties

Point Light Properties	Description
Direction (x,y,z)	The direction the light is facing.
InnerConeAngle	The most powerful starting point of the light (of the cone of light) positioned at the center of the light source position.
LinearAttenuation	A value specifying how much the light reduces in intensity the further away the light is from the source position.
OuterConeAngle	The least powerful point of the light (of the cone of light) positioned at the end of the light.
Position (x,y,z)	The position of the light.
QuadraticAttenuation	The value of which the light should diminish the further away from the source position. The intensity of the light is calculated by a quadratic operation that causes the light to drop quickly in intensity at first.
Range	The range to which objects can be illuminated by this light. Objects outside of the range will not be illuminated at all.

TABLE 19.5   Directional Light Properties

Directional Light Properties	Description
Color	A simple color swatch that allows you to set the base color of the light.
Direction (x,y,z)	The direction the light is facing.

TABLE 19.6   Spot Light Properties

Spot Light Properties	Description
Color	A simple color swatch that allows you to set the base color of the light.
ConstantAttenuation	A value that specifies how powerful the light should be the further light is away from the source position.
Direction (x,y,z)	The direction the light is facing.
InnerConeAngle	The most powerful starting point of the light (of the cone of light) positioned at the center of the light source position.
LinearAttenuation	A value specifying how much the light reduces in intensity the further away the light is from the source position.
OuterConeAngle	The least powerful point of the light (of the cone of light) positioned at the end of the light.
Position (x,y,z)	The position of the light.

TABLE 19.6   Spot Light Properties

Spot Light Properties	Description
QuadraticAttenuation	The value of which the light should diminish the further away from the source position. The intensity of the light is calculated by a quadratic operation that causes the light to drop quickly in intensity at first.
Range	The range to which objects can be illuminated by this light. Objects outside of the range will not be illuminated at all.

Ambient Light

Ambient lights create an even distribution of a light source as in a generalized light source.

Point Light

A point light is a global light source from a single position.

Directional Light

Directional light is light from a specific direction that you can control.

Spot Light

Spot light is a powerful light that distributes light outward in a cone shape.

As Figure 19.12 shows, you can select a light in the Objects and Timeline category and, using the Selection tools, move the position and rotation of the light using the axis transformation tool, the same as when you move/rotate objects.

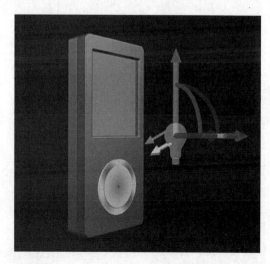

FIGURE 19.12   A directional light about to be repositioned.

19

You can toggle lights to all show at once or turn them all off by selecting on the View menu at the top, and then select Show/Hide 3D lights.

Summary

Use of 3D in WPF application is of course very much encouraged, but you should also be warned that the performance impact on your application can be huge if you start bringing in lots of high polygon models, with large textures and materials.

You should understand how to use the tools in Blend to place your 3D objects in your scene now. The tools are a little limiting, but given that the ability to create 3D objects is not yet in the product, it would appear that any more control would simply be overkill.

Interacting with your 3D models is really the same as using 2D controls. As long you name the elements, you can create storyboards to animate and/or be used in Triggered actions as well as refer to them in code.

I have a feeling that the use of 3D will start to become much wider with WPF when Microsoft implements a much improved DirectX interop with .NET Framework 4, but for now, because of the performance implications, it is a case of "just a little is just right."

CHAPTER 20

Controlling Media (Music or Video)

There are several ways to approach creating a Media Player–type application using Expression Blend as the UI builder. The WPF (Windows Presentation Foundation) provides the MediaElement and you can also incorporate the features of the Microsoft Media Player class if so desired, but it is important to note that only the MediaElement supports the use of XAML to set its properties and so on.

It is because of this XAML support that you will be using the MediaElement control in this chapter.

MediaElement Not Supported in 64-Bit Compilations

The Windows SDK says that application using this element must compile for the x86 architecture only.

Creating the Project

In designing this application, I did contemplate adding the player to a plane in a 3D environment but then I thought this might be just a little too much overkill for what we are trying to achieve, so I have stuck with just creating a basic player with styled controls. The player will allow you to stop, play, and pause the content as well as provide you with the visual duration feedback common with most media players.

The MediaElement supports playback in two different modes (as does the Media Player control), independent and clock mode, with independent being the default and will be active if ever the Clock property is set to null.

The difference between these two modes is playback control and how certain properties are set. One such property is the source media that the player is going to use, which can be set directly as a URI (Uniform Resource Identifier) value to the MediaElement source property when in independent mode. Otherwise, you must set the value through a MediaTimeline if you choose to control the player with a clock.

You can't use the built-in control functions of Play, Stop, and so on when in Clock mode either, because playback control of the media player is controlled by a ClockController object that is derived from the MediaTimeline. The big advantage to using this method, though, is that you can interactively control the Timeline the same way as you control any other animation in a storyboard, allowing triggers to be assigned and fired during playback. We are going to stick with independent mode as the functionality available suits the remit of this chapter.

XAML Requirement

Listing 20.1 shows a single line of markup that will run a media file on the application loading (which I think is just awesome). Add this markup between the Grid tag in a default Blend project and then run the application to test it. You must make sure that you have a .wmv file named Demo at the location shown for this to work; otherwise, add a path to a known audio or video file location and name.

What Formats Are Supported?

WMV 1 through 3 as well as VC-1 video formats, WMA 7 through 9 audio format as well as MP3s in various forms are all supported by the MediaElement. ASX files are also supported but do have some limitations, especially if using the MediaElement in Silverlight applications. For detailed information on the limitations of some media formats, please visit: http://msdn2.microsoft.com/en-us/library/bb980063.aspx.

LISTING 20.1   The Single Line Video Player

```
<MediaElement Source="C:\Demo.wmv"/>
```

You are first going to create a shell of your media player. You will add all your components, lay them out, and then go about styling the player before attaching the controls to some back end functionality.

The following steps take you through this process but you are welcome to modify your elements as you see fit:

1. Create a new Blend application.

2. Find and add a Dock panel element as the child of the LayoutRoot.

3. Set the Dock panel `Width` and `Height` properties to Auto, and `Alignment` property to Stretch, so as to fill the available screen with the Dock panel.

4. Select and activate the Dock panel element in the Objects and Timeline panel.

5. Find and add a Grid element as the first child of the Dock panel.

6. Name this Grid element ButtonControls.

7. Set the ButtonControls element `Width` property to Auto and the `Height` property to 85.

8. Set the `HorizontalAlignment` and `VerticalAlignment` properties to Stretch.

9. You should see the `Dock` property in the Layout category; set it to Bottom.

10. Select and activate the Dock panel again, and then find and add another Grid element as a child.

Remember the `Fill` Property?

You will notice that even though the Grid element's `Dock` property is set to Left by default, the Dock panel property `LastChildFill` is set unchecked by default, meaning that the Grid element will always place left first.

---

11. You should now set the `LastChildFill` property of the Dock panel to true to make the Grid element take up the rest of the available space.

12. Name this Grid PlayerSurface.

13. Select and activate the PlayerSurface element.

14. Locate a Border element from the toolbox and add it as the ButtonControls child.

15. You can now choose to style the Border element any way you choose. Just remember that you can only have a single child element of the Border element, so add a Grid element if you think you are going to be adding more elements.

16. When you are pleased with your styling efforts, add a MediaElement as a child element of the Border and name it mediaMainScreen. Figure 20.1 gives an example.

    The MediaElement has a property category called Media that is specific to the element, and these properties along with the important advanced properties are shown in Table 20.1.

17. Set the MediaElement `LoadedBehavior` to Manual.

18. Set `ScrubbingEnabled` to true.

19. Set `UnloadedBehavior` to Stop.

20

TABLE 20.1   MediaElement Properties (Found in the Media Category of the Properties Panel)

Property Name (a Denotes Advanced Property)	Type	Description
Balance	Double	Get or set the volume ratio between the speakers available. The range is between –1 and 1 with the default being 0.
Clock	MediaClock	A clock can be associated with a Media Timeline that can control media playback.
IsMuted	Bool	Get or set if the audio is muted during playback.
Position	TimeSpan	Get or set the position of the media playback.
Source	Uri	Get or set the source media value.
Volume	Double	Get or set the volume level output of the element. The value range is between 0 and 1 with a default value of 0.5.
LoadedBehavior (a)	Enum	Manual The element waits until the Play() method is called until starting. Play (default) The element automatically plays valid media when loaded. Close Closes loaded media and releases all resources being used by the element. Pause The element queues the media and enters a paused state. Stop The element queues the media but doesn't play it.
ScrubbingEnabled (a)	Bool	Gets or sets a value indicating that the media will continue to update even when in a paused state.
SpeedRatio (a)	Double	The default value is 1 for normal playback speed. All values less than 0 are treated as 0 and all values above 1 make the player speed faster then normal playback speed.

ScrubbingEnabled Has Performance Implications

The ScrubbingEnabled property does have performance implications when set to true and the user tries to interactively seek to a new playback position. This is because the element will continuously try to update itself to show the current playback frame. Setting this property to false disables the update during media playback if the element is in the Paused state.

TABLE 20.1   MediaElement Properties (Found in the Media Category of the Properties Panel)

Property Name (*a* Denotes Advanced Property)	Type	Description
Stretch (a)	Enum	None
		Allows the media to display at its original size.
		Fill
		Removes aspect ratio from the media and allows the element to fill its container.
		Uniform (default)
		The media preserves its aspect ratio while playing allowing the element to fill as much as possible to the parent container.
		UniformToFill
		The media is clipped to fit in the element as it is contained in its parent element, thus preserving the medias aspect ratio.
StretchDirection (a)	Enum	Both (default)
		The content stretches to fit the parent container.
		DownOnly
		When the content is larger then the parent element, it scales down to fit.
		UpOnly
		When the content is smaller then the parent element, it scales up to fit.
UnloadedBehavior (a)		See LoadedBehavior.

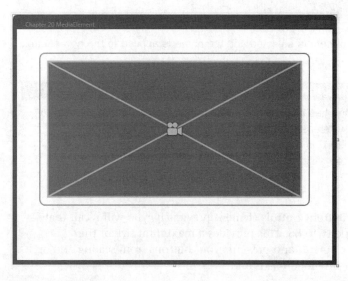

FIGURE 20.1   My simple efforts.

You are now going to add some button controls that will slot right in and act as the player controls for our media player, but in keeping with object-oriented design principles, you should add this control group to a new user control.

Player Controls

If you haven't already done so, save all your work.

You should create a new user control by selecting File, and then New Item to reveal the Add New Item dialog as shown in Figure 20.2.

1. Select the UserControl item and then rename the file to MediaPlayerController.xaml. You should also make sure that the Include Code File check box is also checked.

2. Click OK to create the user control.

3. Select the parent element UserControl in the Objects and Timeline category and then rename the element in the Properties panel to ucPlayerControl.

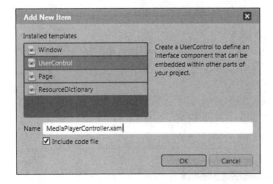

FIGURE 20.2   The UserControl item is selected and the name is applied to the new control.

What Effects Do the Names Have?

This name added to the Properties panel (ucPlayerControl) is the name that you use to refer to the control in code, whereas the name of the file (MediaPlayerController.xaml) is the name of the control as it appears in the Custom Controls collection tab, visible in the Asset Library.

When you created the ButtonControls element previously, you will recall that you set the Height property to 85. This provides a maximum size of the MediaPlayerController element, and prevents your buttons from scaling and or stretching beyond their intended maximum.

You are going to set the LayoutRoot to hold the controls within their own cell position, but because the widths of your form and mine might vary, I am just going to show you an image detailing the row and column definitions that you should add (Listing 20.2 has my XAML for reference).

4. Set the ucPlayerControl element `Height` property to 85, which will give you the indication of the size of real estate you have to play with.

5. Because you have three buttons to add (Play, Stop, Pause), a volume controller (slider), a balance controller (slider), and a current position controller (slider) to add, you need to position the rows and columns accordingly.

LISTING 20.2   Provide Definitions for Columns and Rows

```
<Grid x:Name="LayoutRoot">
    <Grid.ColumnDefinitions>
        <ColumnDefinition Width="0.25*"/>
        <ColumnDefinition Width="0.15*"/>
        <ColumnDefinition Width="0.15*"/>
        <ColumnDefinition Width="0.15*"/>
        <ColumnDefinition Width="0.25*"/>
    </Grid.ColumnDefinitions>
    <Grid.RowDefinitions>
        <RowDefinition Height="0.224*"/>
        <RowDefinition Height="0.776*"/>
    </Grid.RowDefinitions>
</Grid>
```

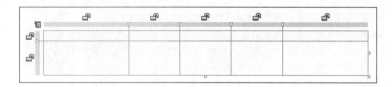

FIGURE 20.3   The row and column definitions that are also available in Listing 20.2.

6. You can now select and activate the LayoutRoot element and add three buttons as shown in Figure 20.4. At this stage of the book, you should be able to take care of the styling of your own controls. You can take the time to style these buttons as you would prefer and I would suggest adding your new styles to a Resource Dictionary for possible future use.

It is extremely important to remember to name all the controls that you add to your MediaPlayerController element because you will need to refer to them in code shortly. I have named the Play button btnPlay, the Stop button btnStop, and I think you can guess the name of the Pause button.

20

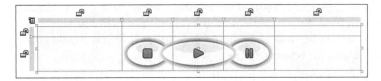

FIGURE 20.4   The location and styling applied by myself.

The entire control set that you need to add is in Table 20.2 and should be referenced against Figure 20.4 for the example.

TABLE 20.2   PlayerControl—Controls Required

Control Type	Control Name	Description	Row Position	Column Position
Slider	slidPosition	The slider to control the playback position of the media	0	0
Slider	slidVolume	The control for playback volume	1	0
Slider	slidBalance	The control for playback speaker balance (left to right)	1	4
Button	btnPause	The pause button	1	3
Button	btnStop	The stop button	1	1
Button	btnPlay	The play button	1	2
Label	Name not required	The volume label	1	0
Label	Name not required	The balance label	1	4

Now to the three final control elements, which are all slider controls. The Volume control slider needs to provide values between 0 and 1 with the default being 0.5 as per the Windows SDK documentation for the MediaElement class.

7. Set the Slider Value property (for your slidVolume element) to 0.5.

8. Set the Maximum property to 1.

9. Set the TickFrequency property to 0.1.

10. Locate the IsSnapToTickEnabled property in the advanced properties and set it to true.

The Balance control slider needs to provide values between –1 and 1 with the default value being 0.

11. Set the Slider Value property to 0.

12. Set the Maximum property to 1.

13. Set the Minimum property to –1.

14. Set the `TickFrequency` property to 1.

15. Locate the `IsSnapToTickEnabled` property in the advanced properties and set it to true.

I will assume that you have followed suit in terms of implementing your own designs and are pleased with your styling attempts. If not, you can always continue on styling at your leisure or maybe get some assistance from any designer friends you have.

An example of a completed design is shown in Figure 20.5.

FIGURE 20.5   The completed user control.

Save and build your project now, and then head back to the Window1 artboard.

Double-click the ButtonControls Grid element to activate it, and then open the Asset Library, selecting the Custom Controls tab. You should see your MediaPlayerController component to which you can now add to the ButtonControls grid.

Make sure that you name this control MediaPlayerController. You might need to modify the Width settings of the user control to suit the ButtonControls container, and you should also take into consideration the possibility of the application being expanded to full screen. For this, you can either change the LayoutRoot element column and row definitions inside your user control, or you can give the user control a fixed size inside the ButtonControls grid and center it. All things being equal and your application should be starting to take shape. Figure 20.6 shows the current view of the application as I have created it.

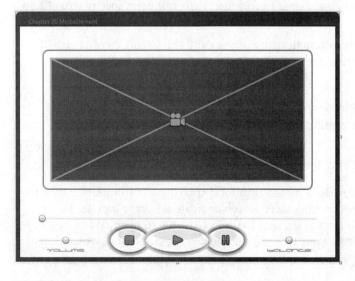

FIGURE 20.6   The application parts in place.

The final piece of the visual puzzle is about giving the user the ability to select the media they want to play. For this, you are going to add a menu item that prompts the user for a file location.

The DockPanel element is currently filling the entire area of the LayoutRoot, so you need to add a new row to the LayoutRoot, fix its height for the menu element, and then specify that the DockPanel should sit in row 1 if your MediaElement is set to fill the entire area of the PlayerSurface grid:

1. Double-click to activate the LayoutRoot element.

2. Add a row at the top of the LayoutRoot and fix it to 30 Pixels high.

3. Locate a Menu element in the Asset Library (I suggest using a SimpleMenu element from the simple styles collection).

4. Add the Menu element and specify it to site in row 0 and set it to stretch both horizontally and vertically.

5. Double-click the Menu element to activate it.

6. You can right-click on the Menu element in the Objects and Timeline category to view the element context menu, where you will see the option to Add MenuItem (or Add SimpleMenuItem if you used the SimpleMenu element).

7. Type the word **Open** into the **Header** property of the MenuItem element.

You are now going to go through and code all the events between the controls and allow for the user to select a media file to play.

Code Requirement

Our media player is quite simple and so it shouldn't take too long to hook up our controls, but we have one important area to consider: How will users specify what file they want to play?

You are going to use the built-in functionality of the .NET Framework to display an OpenFileDialog control and take the user input from it. This is a good place to start coding the application:

1. Save and build the application.

2. Select the Open menu item.

3. Open the Properties panel and click on the Lightning Bolt icon to view the Event list.

4. Locate the Click event and double-click it to launch Visual Studio.

The OpenFileDialog class provides a mechanism for displaying a customizable Open file dialog box. You can set values on the object as well as create an event handler for the FileOk event that notifies you when the user has selected a file to open. When you have completed adding your settings, you then call the ShowDialog() method, which displays the dialog to the user.

You need to add a using reference as shown here:

```
using Microsoft.Win32;
```

Listing 20.3 shows the MenuItem_Click handler method you just created, the code to display a customized Open file dialog, and the relevant FileOk event handler that assigns the file to the MediaElement's source property.

LISTING 20.3   Creating a Custom Open File Dialog (OFD)

```
private void MenuItem_Click(object sender, RoutedEventArgs e)
{
    //Ask the user to specify a media file to play
    OpenFileDialog OFD = new OpenFileDialog();
    OFD.AddExtension = true;
    OFD.Multiselect = false;
    OFD.Title = "Select Media File to Play";
    OFD.DefaultExt = "wmv";
    OFD.Filter = "Windows Media Video (*.wmv)¦*.wmv";
    OFD.InitialDirectory = "c:\\";
    OFD.CheckFileExists = true;
    OFD.FileOk += new System.ComponentModel.CancelEventHandler(OFD_FileOk);
    OFD.ShowDialog();
}

void OFD_FileOk(object sender, System.ComponentModel.CancelEventArgs e)
{
    string FilePath = (sender as OpenFileDialog).FileName;
    this.mediaMainScreen.Source = new Uri(FilePath);
}
```

The MediaElement has a number of events that you might want to make use of; specifically in this project, you should go back to Blend and select the MediaElement. Select the following events in the Properties panel and add the relevant handlers in the Visual Studio code-behind file:

MediaEnded

MediaFailed

MediaOpened

Inside the MediaEnded handler method, you need to add some code that will change the state of the buttons in your player, but before you can do this, you will need to add some public methods in the MediaPlayerController.xaml.cs file.

1. Open the MediaPlayerController.xaml.cs file in Visual Studio. You can open the Solution Explorer and drill down through the file listings until you find it.

2. Add the public methods, events, and enumerations shown in Listing 20.4 to your code.

LISTING 20.4   The MediaElement Event Handlers

```
public MediaPlayerController()
{
    this.InitializeComponent();

    // Insert code required on object creation below this point.
    this.VolumeChanged += delegate(double NewVolume) { };
    this.BalanceChanged += delegate(double NewBalance) { };
    this.PlaybackPostionChanged += delegate(double NewPosition) { };
    this.MediaController += delegate(MEDIA_CONTROL Controller) { };
}

public delegate void VolumeChangedDelegate(double NewVolume);
public event VolumeChangedDelegate VolumeChanged;

public delegate void BalanceChangedDelegate(double NewBalance);
public event BalanceChangedDelegate BalanceChanged;

public delegate void PlaybackPostionChangedDelegate(double NewPosition);
public event PlaybackPostionChangedDelegate PlaybackPostionChanged;

public delegate void MediaControllerDelegate(MEDIA_CONTROL Controller);
public event MediaControllerDelegate MediaController;

public enum MEDIA_CONTROL
{
    Play = 0,
    Stop =1,
    Pause =2
}

public enum ENABLED_STATE
{
    Enabled =0,
    Disabled =1
}

public void SetPlayButtonState(ENABLED_STATE State)
{
}

public void SetStopButtonState(ENABLED_STATE State)
```

```
{
}

public void SetPauseButtonState(ENABLED_STATE State)
{
}

public void SetPlayerControlStates(ENABLED_STATE State)
{
}
public void SetPlayerPostion(Double CurrentPostion, Double TotalTime)
{
}
```

3. You can now fill the methods for the button's states using Listing 20.5 as a guide for all the methods. Don't worry about the last public method (SetPlayerPostion()) at the moment—you will come back to this last.

LISTING 20.5   Example State Handler

```
public void SetPlayButtonState(ENABLED_STATE State)
{
    if (State == ENABLED_STATE.Enabled)
        this.btnPlay.IsEnabled = true;
    else
        this.btnPlay.IsEnabled = false;

}
```

4. The code for the SetPlayerControlState() method should set all the slider control values to the specified state. For example:

```
public void SetPlayerControlStates(ENABLED_STATE State)
{
    switch (State)
    {
        case ENABLED_STATE.Enabled:
            this.slidBalance.IsEnabled = true;
            this.slidVolume.IsEnabled = true;
            this.slidPosition.IsEnabled = true;
            break;
        case ENABLED_STATE.Disabled:
            this.slidBalance.IsEnabled = false;
            this.slidVolume.IsEnabled = false;
            this.slidPosition.IsEnabled = false;
```

20

```
                    break;
                default:
                    this.slidBalance.IsEnabled = false;
                    this.slidVolume.IsEnabled = false;
                    this.slidPosition.IsEnabled = false;
                    break;
            }
        }
```

5. Open Expression Blend and then open the MediaPlayerController user control.

6. Select and add `Click` event handlers for all the button's elements.

7. Select the slider elements and add `ValueChanged` events for each except for the slidPosition element.

8. Set all the `IsEnabled` properties to false for all UIElements in the MediaPlayerController user control.

9. You should now have five new event handlers in your code-behind file. You can continue to move through each, calling the events that you created earlier, which will send notifications through to the window on which buttons were clicked, slider positions changed, and so on.

```
private void slidVolume_ValueChanged(object sender, RoutedEventArgs e)
{
    if (this.VolumeChanged != null)
        this.VolumeChanged(this.slidVolume.Value);
}
private void btnPause_Click(object sender, RoutedEventArgs e)
{
    this.MediaController(MEDIA_CONTROL.Pause);
}
```

10. You will notice the check to see whether the VolumeChanged delegate is null and this is because the slidVolume element value will change during the controls initialization, which is before the delegate events get initialized. If you don't check to see whether it is null, you will probably get an error on application startup. You should also apply this methodology to the other Slider changed event handlers.

The last method to code up is the `SetPlayerPosition()` method. You are taking in two Double values through the parameters for the method and assigning them to the slidPosition UIElement:

```
public void SetPlayerPostion(Double CurrentPostion, Double TotalTime)
```

An issue will arise though when programmatically you are changing the slidPosition element's value using the parameters, and when the user tries to drag the slidPosition thumb to set a new playback position. Why does this occur?

Very shortly, you will see how to update the playback position slider every time your application re-renders itself, which on average will be around 30–60 times per second. This will make for extremely smooth and accurate playback positioning. The trouble with this is that because the position value is being updated so frequently, the application doesn't know when the user has changed the position (by dragging the thumb) or when the position is being set by the `SetPlayerPosition()` method programmatically. The result is that unless you handle this, the position value will be updated so frequently that the user will not be able to drag the thumb on the slider element, therefore removing some vital functionality.

You will recall that previously you were instructed not to add the `ValueChanged` event handler for the slidPosition element. This is because each time the application changed the position of the slider (30–60 times per second) that event would fire, which again means that each time the user would try to drag the slider to a new position, it would have already changed position programmatically.

Open Expression Blend and locate the slidPosition slider element in the `MediaPlayerController.xaml` file. You should be able to find to specific event handlers for the slider called

> `PreviewMouseDown`
>
> `PreviewMouseUp`

You can add both of these handlers now. By studying Listing 20.6, you will see how to prepare the object for user-managed positioning by setting the global, and then how, when the user has chosen the new playback position, the position is raised back through the event process to instruct the MediaElement where to start playing the media file from.

LISTING 20.6   Handling User Playback Position Changes

```
private bool UserUpdatePosition = false;
public void SetPlayerPostion(Double CurrentPostion, Double TotalTime)
{
    if (UserUpdatePosition)
        return;

    this.slidPosition.Maximum = TotalTime;
    this.slidPosition.Value = CurrentPostion;
}
private void slidPosition_PreviewMouseDown(object sender,
System.Windows.Input.MouseButtonEventArgs e)
{
    UserUpdatePosition = true;
}


private void slidPosition_PreviewMouseUp(object sender, System.Windows.Input.Mouse-
ButtonEventArgs e)
```

20

```
{
    this.PlaybackPostionChanged(this.slidPosition.Value);
    UserUpdatePosition = false;
}
```

Listing 20.6 shows the `SetPlayerPosition()` method and it also shows how a global Bool variable called `UserUpdatePosition` is declared. You can see in the code that if this variable is set to true, the method is effectively ignored by returning out of the code execution. The `PreviewMouseDown` event gives the user a chance to move the thumb and set the new position while not disrupting the playback of the media file.

You can add the code shown in Listing 20.6 to your `MediaPlayerController.xaml.cs` code file now, which will complete the control. Now that you have finished coding up the MediaPlayerController class, you have only to add the events that you just created to the `Window1.xaml.cs` file and then there remains a few methods to finish it all off. This is more to do with sequencing then anything else.

When a media file starts to play, you might want to set the Pause button to enable. You might want to handle the Play `Click` event by restarting the playback. I will leave those decisions up to you.

1. Start by opening the `Window1.xaml.cs` code-behind file and adding the public events from the `MediaPlayerController` class to the default constructor as shown in Listing 20.7.

LISTING 20.7   Creating the Event Handlers for the `MediaPlayerController`

```
public Window1()
        {
            this.InitializeComponent();

            // Insert code required on object creation below this point.
            this.MediaPlayerController.VolumeChanged += new
MediaPlayerController.VolumeChangedDelegate(MediaPlayerController_VolumeChanged);
            this.MediaPlayerController.BalanceChanged += new
MediaPlayerController.BalanceChangedDelegate(MediaPlayerController_BalanceChanged);
            this.MediaPlayerController.PlaybackPostionChanged += new
MediaPlayerController.PlaybackPostionChangedDelegate(MediaPlayerController_
PlaybackPostionChanged);
            this.MediaPlayerController.MediaController += new
MediaPlayerController.MediaControllerDelegate(MediaPlayerController_
MediaController);
        }

        void MediaPlayerController_MediaController(MediaPlayerController.
MEDIA_CONTROL Controller)
        {
```

```
    }

    void MediaPlayerController_PlaybackPostionChanged(double NewPosition)
    {

    }

    void MediaPlayerController_BalanceChanged(double NewBalance)
    {

    }

    void MediaPlayerController_VolumeChanged(double NewVolume)
    {

    }
```

2. Now you have the event handlers created for the controller, you can hook these values directly into the MediaElement as shown in Listing 20.8.

You will also notice the following method call in Listing 20.8:

```
    this.TryPlayMedia();
```

This method is implemented in Listing 20.11 and creates a controlled entry point for attempting to play media.

LISTING 20.8   Adding the MediaPlayerController Event Handlers

```
void MediaPlayerController_MediaController(MediaPlayerController.MEDIA_CONTROL
Controller)
{

    switch (Controller)
    {
        case MediaPlayerController.MEDIA_CONTROL.Play:
            this.TryPlayMedia();
            break;
        case MediaPlayerController.MEDIA_CONTROL.Stop:
            this.mediaMainScreen.Stop();

this.MediaPlayerController.SetPlayButtonState(MediaPlayerController.ENABLED_STATE.
Enabled );

this.MediaPlayerController.SetStopButtonState(MediaPlayerController.ENABLED_STATE.
Disabled );
```

```
            if (this.mediaMainScreen.CanPause)
                this.MediaPlayerController.SetPauseButtonState
(MediaPlayerController.ENABLED_STATE.Disabled );

            break;
        case MediaPlayerController.MEDIA_CONTROL.Pause:
            if (this.mediaMainScreen.CanPause)
            {
                this.mediaMainScreen.Pause();

                this.MediaPlayerController.SetPlayButtonState
(MediaPlayerController.ENABLED_STATE.Enabled);
                this.MediaPlayerController.SetStopButtonState
(MediaPlayerController.ENABLED_STATE.Enabled );
                this.MediaPlayerController.SetPauseButtonState
(MediaPlayerController.ENABLED_STATE.Disabled);
            }

            break;
        default:
            break;
    }
}


void MediaPlayerController_PlaybackPostionChanged(double NewPosition)
{
    this.mediaMainScreen.Position = new TimeSpan(0, 0, 0, 0, Convert.ToInt32
(NewPosition));
}


void MediaPlayerController_BalanceChanged(double NewBalance)
{
    this.mediaMainScreen.Balance = NewBalance;
}


void MediaPlayerController_VolumeChanged(double NewVolume)
{
    this.mediaMainScreen.Volume = NewVolume;
}
```

3. You can now deal with the three events that the MediaElement will raise during the load/play/stop process. One event handler that is particularly important is the MediaFailed() event. You will want to display a message to the end user showing what is wrong, so you should consider adding code similar to Listing 20.9.

LISTING 20.9   Handling Media Failure Errors

```
private void mediaMainScreen_MediaFailed(object sender, ExceptionRoutedEventArgs e)
{
    string Message = "A Media error has occured with the following message:" +
        Environment.NewLine + Environment.NewLine + e.ErrorException.Message;

    MessageBox.Show(Message, "Media Failed", MessageBoxButton.OK,
MessageBoxImage.Error);

}
```

4. Now you need to add a way to update the position of the playback, relevant to the length of the overall media playback. The purpose of this is so that you can check the current position of the media playback and update the values accordingly in the MediaPlayerController user control.

5. You will need to add the following event handler to the default constructor of the Window1.xaml.cs file:

```
CompositionTarget.Rendering += new EventHandler(CompositionTarget_Rendering);
```

What Is the CompositionTarget?

The CompositionTarget represents the application's display surface, so by hooking into the Rendering event, you can effectively perform functionality each time your application redraws itself.

A word of caution though: You should perform only minor calculations inside this event because you need to execute code as quickly as possible and get out of there so that the application still draws itself at a reasonable frame rate. If you do anything too intense in here, your application can become unresponsive and any animations or screen updates will appear jerky.

6. Listing 20.10 shows how to check for a duration in the media and, if one is found, how to retrieve the required values to send through to update the slidPosition element in the MediaPlayerController.

LISTING 20.10   Checking the Media Duration

```
void CompositionTarget_Rendering(object sender, EventArgs e)
{
    if (this.mediaMainScreen.NaturalDuration.HasTimeSpan)
    {

        double Total = this.mediaMainScreen.NaturalDuration.TimeSpan.
TotalMilliseconds;
```

20

```
        double Current = this.mediaMainScreen.Position.TotalMilliseconds;

        this.MediaPlayerController.SetPlayerPostion(Current, Total);
    }
}
```

7. Add the code from Listing 20.11 to complete the MediaOpened event actions as well as to create the TryPlayMedia() method. The TryPlayMedia() method provides a safe and convenient way for you to start media playback from several points in your application. You should also add calls the TryPlayMedia() method at the end of the OFD_FileOK event handler.

LISTING 20.11   Safe Media Control in the TryPlayMedia() Method

```
private void mediaMainScreen_MediaOpened(object sender, RoutedEventArgs e)
{
    this.TryPlayMedia();
}
private void TryPlayMedia()
{
    try
    {
        this.mediaMainScreen.Play();


this.MediaPlayerController.SetPlayerControlStates(MediaPlayerController.ENABLED_
STATE.Enabled);

this.MediaPlayerController.SetPlayButtonState(MediaPlayerController.ENABLED_STATE.
Disabled);

this.MediaPlayerController.SetStopButtonState(MediaPlayerController.ENABLED_STATE.
Enabled);

        if (this.mediaMainScreen.CanPause)

this.MediaPlayerController.SetPauseButtonState(MediaPlayerController.ENABLED_STATE.
Enabled);
        else

this.MediaPlayerController.SetPauseButtonState(MediaPlayerController.ENABLED_STATE.
Disabled);

    }
    catch (Exception x)
```

```
    {

        string Message = " The Media Playback process has failed with the following
message:" +
            Environment.NewLine + Environment.NewLine + x.Message;

        MessageBox.Show(Message, "Media Playback Failed", MessageBoxButton.OK,
MessageBoxImage.Error);

    }
}
```

8. When the media file completes playing, you can choose to do several things with your player from the MediaEnded() event handler. In this sample, though, you simply need to call the Stop() method of the MediaElement, which will return the playback position to the start and set the button states again in the MediaPlayerController:

```
private void mediaMainScreen_MediaEnded(object sender, RoutedEventArgs e)
    {
        this.mediaMainScreen.Stop();

this.MediaPlayerController.SetPlayerControlStates(MediaPlayerController.ENABLED_
STATE.Disabled);

this.MediaPlayerController.SetPlayButtonState(MediaPlayerController.ENABLED_STATE.
Enabled);

    }
```

You should now be able to run your application, select a media file, and control its playback positioning as well as general playback functionality through the MediaPlayerController group.

The code in Listing 20.12 represents the Window1.xaml.cs code file and Listing 20.13 represents the MediaPlayerController.xaml.cs code file in their entirety so that you can check your work if required. Figure 20.7 shows the end product in action.

LISTING 20.12   Window1.xaml.cs

```
using System;
using System.IO;
using System.Net;
using System.Windows;
using System.Windows.Controls;
using System.Windows.Data;
```

20

```
using System.Windows.Media;
using System.Windows.Media.Animation;
using System.Windows.Navigation;
using Microsoft.Win32;
using System.Windows.Threading;

namespace Chapter_20_MediaElement
{
    public partial class Window1
    {
        public Window1()
        {
            this.InitializeComponent();

            // Insert code required on object creation below this point.
            this.MediaPlayerController.VolumeChanged += new
MediaPlayerController.VolumeChangedDelegate(MediaPlayerController_VolumeChanged);
            this.MediaPlayerController.BalanceChanged += new
MediaPlayerController.BalanceChangedDelegate(MediaPlayerController_BalanceChanged);
            this.MediaPlayerController.PlaybackPostionChanged += new
MediaPlayerController.PlaybackPostionChangedDelegate(MediaPlayerController_
PlaybackPostionChanged);
            this.MediaPlayerController.MediaController += new
MediaPlayerController.MediaControllerDelegate(MediaPlayerController_MediaController);

            CompositionTarget.Rendering += new EventHandler(CompositionTarget_
Rendering);
        }

        void MediaPlayerController_MediaController(MediaPlayerController.MEDIA_
CONTROL Controller)
        {
            // Based on the event parameter, perform an action on the player and
            //control the buttons that the user can click on etc.
            switch (Controller)
            {
                case MediaPlayerController.MEDIA_CONTROL.Play:
                    this.TryPlayMedia();
                    break;
                case MediaPlayerController.MEDIA_CONTROL.Stop:
                    this.mediaMainScreen.Stop();

                    this.MediaPlayerController.SetPlayButtonState
(MediaPlayerController.ENABLED_STATE.Enabled );
                    this.MediaPlayerController.SetStopButtonState
(MediaPlayerController.ENABLED_STATE.Disabled );
```

```
                    if (this.mediaMainScreen.CanPause)
                        this.MediaPlayerController.SetPauseButtonState
(MediaPlayerController.ENABLED_STATE.Disabled );

                    break;
                case MediaPlayerController.MEDIA_CONTROL.Pause:
                    if (this.mediaMainScreen.CanPause)
                    {
                        this.mediaMainScreen.Pause();

                        this.MediaPlayerController.SetPlayButtonState
(MediaPlayerController.ENABLED_STATE.Enabled);
                        this.MediaPlayerController.SetStopButtonState
(MediaPlayerController.ENABLED_STATE.Enabled );
                        this.MediaPlayerController.SetPauseButtonState
(MediaPlayerController.ENABLED_STATE.Disabled);
                    }

                    break;
                default:
                    break;
            }
        }


        void MediaPlayerController_PlaybackPostionChanged(double NewPosition)
        {
            this.mediaMainScreen.Position = new TimeSpan(0, 0, 0, 0,
Convert.ToInt32(NewPosition));
        }


        void MediaPlayerController_BalanceChanged(double NewBalance)
        {
            this.mediaMainScreen.Balance = NewBalance;
        }


        void MediaPlayerController_VolumeChanged(double NewVolume)
        {
            this.mediaMainScreen.Volume = NewVolume;
        }


        private void MenuItem_Click(object sender, RoutedEventArgs e)
        {
            //Ask the user to specify a media file to play
            OpenFileDialog OFD = new OpenFileDialog();
            OFD.AddExtension = true;
```

20

```
            OFD.Multiselect = false;
            OFD.Title = "Select Media File to Play";
            OFD.DefaultExt = "wmv";

            //Add as many filters as you like using the following format
            OFD.Filter = "Windows Media Video (*.wmv)¦*.wmv";
            OFD.InitialDirectory = "c:\\";
            OFD.CheckFileExists = true;
            OFD.FileOk += new System.ComponentModel.CancelEventHandler(OFD_FileOk);
            OFD.ShowDialog();
        }


        void OFD_FileOk(object sender, System.ComponentModel.CancelEventArgs e)
        {
            string FilePath = (sender as OpenFileDialog).FileName;

            this.mediaMainScreen.Source = new Uri(FilePath);

            this.TryPlayMedia();
        }

        private void mediaMainScreen_MediaEnded(object sender, RoutedEventArgs e)
        {
            this.mediaMainScreen.Stop();

this.MediaPlayerController.SetPlayerControlStates(MediaPlayerController.ENABLED_
STATE.Disabled);

this.MediaPlayerController.SetPlayButtonState(MediaPlayerController.ENABLED_STATE.
Enabled);
        }

        private void mediaMainScreen_MediaFailed(object sender,
ExceptionRoutedEventArgs e)
        {
            string Message = "A Media error has occured with the following
message:" +
                    Environment.NewLine + Environment.NewLine + e.ErrorException.Message;

            MessageBox.Show(Message, "Media Failed", MessageBoxButton.OK,
MessageBoxImage.Error);

        }

        private void mediaMainScreen_MediaOpened(object sender, RoutedEventArgs e)
        {
```

```csharp
            this.TryPlayMedia();
        }

        private void TryPlayMedia()
        {
            try
            {
                this.mediaMainScreen.Play();

                this.MediaPlayerController.SetPlayerControlStates
(MediaPlayerController.ENABLED_STATE.Enabled);
                this.MediaPlayerController.SetPlayButtonState
(MediaPlayerController.ENABLED_STATE.Disabled);
                this.MediaPlayerController.SetStopButtonState
(MediaPlayerController.ENABLED_STATE.Enabled);

                if (this.mediaMainScreen.CanPause)
                    this.MediaPlayerController.SetPauseButtonState
(MediaPlayerController.ENABLED_STATE.Enabled);
                else
                    this.MediaPlayerController.SetPauseButtonState
(MediaPlayerController.ENABLED_STATE.Disabled);

            }
            catch (Exception x)
            {

                string Message = " The Media Playback process has failed with the
following message:" +
                    Environment.NewLine + Environment.NewLine + x.Message;

                MessageBox.Show(Message, "Media Playback Failed",
MessageBoxButton.OK, MessageBoxImage.Error);

            }
        }

        void CompositionTarget_Rendering(object sender, EventArgs e)
        {
            if (this.mediaMainScreen.NaturalDuration.HasTimeSpan)
            {
                double Total =
this.mediaMainScreen.NaturalDuration.TimeSpan.TotalMilliseconds;
                double Current = this.mediaMainScreen.Position.TotalMilliseconds;
```

20

```
                        this.MediaPlayerController.SetPlayerPostion(Current, Total);
                }
            }


        }
    }
```

FIGURE 20.7   The completed media player application.

LISTING 20.13   MediaPlayerController.xaml.cs

```
using System;
using System.IO;
using System.Net;
using System.Windows;
using System.Windows.Controls;
using System.Windows.Data;
using System.Windows.Media;
using System.Windows.Media.Animation;
using System.Windows.Navigation;

namespace Chapter_20_MediaElement
{
    public partial class MediaPlayerController
    {
        public MediaPlayerController()
        {
            this.InitializeComponent();
```

```
    // Insert code required on object creation below this point.
    this.VolumeChanged += delegate(double NewVolume) { };
    this.BalanceChanged += delegate(double NewBalance) { };
    this.PlaybackPostionChanged += delegate(double NewPosition) { };
    this.MediaController += delegate(MEDIA_CONTROL Controller) { };
}


#region"EVENTS"
public delegate void VolumeChangedDelegate(double NewVolume);
public event VolumeChangedDelegate VolumeChanged;

public delegate void BalanceChangedDelegate(double NewBalance);
public event BalanceChangedDelegate BalanceChanged;

public delegate void PlaybackPostionChangedDelegate(double NewPosition);
public event PlaybackPostionChangedDelegate PlaybackPostionChanged;

public delegate void MediaControllerDelegate(MEDIA_CONTROL Controller);
public event MediaControllerDelegate MediaController;
#endregion

#region"ENUMS"
/// <summary>
/// Represents specific Media Control Elements
/// </summary>
public enum MEDIA_CONTROL
{
    Play = 0,
    Stop =1,
    Pause =2
}


/// <summary>
/// Represents object Enabled states
/// </summary>
public enum ENABLED_STATE
{
    Enabled =0,
    Disabled =1
}
#endregion

#region"PUBLIC METHODS"
/// <summary>
/// Set the current state of the Play button.
/// </summary>
```

20

```
/// <param name="State">The state value to set</param>
public void SetPlayButtonState(ENABLED_STATE State)
{
    switch (State)
    {
        case ENABLED_STATE.Enabled:
            this.btnPlay.IsEnabled = true;
            break;
        case ENABLED_STATE.Disabled:
            this.btnPlay.IsEnabled = false;
            break;
        default:
            this.btnPlay.IsEnabled = false;
            break;
    }
}

/// <summary>
/// Set the current state of the Stop button.
/// </summary>
/// <param name="State">The state value to set</param>
public void SetStopButtonState(ENABLED_STATE State)
{
    switch (State)
    {
        case ENABLED_STATE.Enabled:
            this.btnStop.IsEnabled = true;
            break;
        case ENABLED_STATE.Disabled:
            this.btnStop.IsEnabled = false;
            break;
        default:
            this.btnStop.IsEnabled = false;
            break;
    }
}

/// <summary>
/// Set the current state of the Pause button.
/// </summary>
/// <param name="State">The state value to set</param>
public void SetPauseButtonState(ENABLED_STATE State)
{
    switch (State)
    {
```

```
                case ENABLED_STATE.Enabled:
                    this.btnPause.IsEnabled = true;
                    break;
                case ENABLED_STATE.Disabled:
                    this.btnPause.IsEnabled = false;
                    break;
                default:
                    this.btnPause.IsEnabled = false;
                    break;
            }
        }


        /// <summary>
        /// Set the current state of all Slider elements.
        /// </summary>
        /// <param name="State">The state value to set</param>
        public void SetPlayerControlStates(ENABLED_STATE State)
        {
            switch (State)
            {
                case ENABLED_STATE.Enabled:
                    this.slidBalance.IsEnabled = true;
                    this.slidVolume.IsEnabled = true;
                    this.slidPosition.IsEnabled = true;
                    break;
                case ENABLED_STATE.Disabled:
                    this.slidBalance.IsEnabled = false;
                    this.slidVolume.IsEnabled = false;
                    this.slidPosition.IsEnabled = false;
                    break;
                default:
                    this.slidBalance.IsEnabled = false;
                    this.slidVolume.IsEnabled = false;
                    this.slidPosition.IsEnabled = false;
                    break;
            }
        }


        private bool UserUpdatePosition = false;


        /// <summary>
        /// Instruct the player to update the playback position slider element
        /// </summary>
        /// <param name="CurrentPostion">The position on the slider that represents
        /// the current playback position</param>
```

20

```csharp
    /// <param name="TotalTime">The total duration of the current media</param>
    public void SetPlayerPostion(Double CurrentPostion, Double TotalTime)
    {
        if (UserUpdatePosition)
            return;

        this.slidPosition.Maximum = TotalTime;
        this.slidPosition.Value = CurrentPostion;
    }

    #endregion

    #region"PRIVATE METHODS & EVENT HANDLERS"

    private void slidVolume_ValueChanged(object sender, RoutedEventArgs e)
    {
        if (this.VolumeChanged != null)
            this.VolumeChanged(this.slidVolume.Value);
    }

    private void slidBalance_ValueChanged(object sender, RoutedEventArgs e)
    {
        this.BalanceChanged(this.slidBalance.Value);
    }

    private void btnPause_Click(object sender, RoutedEventArgs e)
    {
        this.MediaController(MEDIA_CONTROL.Pause);
    }

    private void btnStop_Click(object sender, RoutedEventArgs e)
    {
        this.MediaController(MEDIA_CONTROL.Stop );
    }

    private void btnPlay_Click(object sender, RoutedEventArgs e)
    {
        this.MediaController(MEDIA_CONTROL.Play );
    }

    private void slidPosition_PreviewMouseDown(object sender,
System.Windows.Input.MouseButtonEventArgs e)
    {
        UserUpdatePosition = true;
    }
```

```
        private void slidPosition_PreviewMouseUp(object sender,
System.Windows.Input.MouseButtonEventArgs e)
        {
            this.PlaybackPostionChanged(this.slidPosition.Value);
            UserUpdatePosition = false;
        }
        #endregion


    }
}
```

Summary

I hope you have enjoyed creating this great little application as much as I did writing about it! You might have thought at the start of the chapter that it was going to be a simple job to hook up all these controls. It wasn't too bad, but I did want you to get the feeling of how complete even a simple application needs to be to cover the possibility of errors, as well as guide the user into being able to use certain functionality at certain times.

The MediaElement is very flexible in what it allows you to achieve very quickly, and I recommend you become familiar with the element because you will find that it is almost identical to the MediaElement control used in Silverlight.

Index

Symbols

A

B

C

D

E

end users, 28-29

workflow, 27-28

design environment, 13

Visual Studio, compared, 17

Expression Design, 6

definition, 350

vector objects, building, 350-356

external skin files, loading, 468, 471-473

code listing, 470

ComboBox selection event, 471-473

Eyedropper tool, 166-167

F

Far Clipping Plane property, 518

File Explorer (Vista), 10

files

external skin, loading, 468, 471-473

code listing, 470

ComboBox selection event, 471-473

media formats, 524

MediaPlayerController.xaml.cs, 548-553

referencing, 502

resources, linking, 204

Window1.xaml.cs, 543-548

Files category (Project panel), 74-75

Fill Property brush, 177

filtering resources, 72

finding Blend data types, 274-275

FindResource( ) method, 434

flipping objects, 339

FlowDocument control (RichTextBox controls), 243-245

FocusVisualStyle, 370-374

fonts, embedding, 84

foreach statement (collections), 315-318

FrameworkElement level, 491

Freeze( ) method, 332

FromRgb( ) method, 332

G

gel button, creating, 176-178

adding to Resource Dictionary, 201-202

animated glow, 191

animation requirements, 194

GlowBase element animation, 196-198

mouse over trigger, 194-196

timeline, adding, 194

animation, 190-191

arrow shape, 179

base, 178

base brush suggestions, 180

brush stroke property settings, 181

brush suggestion tables

one, 176

five, 182

six, 182

seven, 184

eight, 184

nine, 193

brush transforms, 183

Button control listing, 214-215

fill color, 178

Fill Property brush/Linear Gradient brush, 177

Fill Property transform, 184

gradient stops, 178

highlights, 181-182

Make Button tool, 188-190

points, adding, 179

RoutedEvents, 199-201

shading, 178

shapes completed, 179

smoothing, 179

stroke thickness, 178

testing, 203

MouseMove event, 206-207

Resource Dictionary/control template, 204-206

XAML code listing, 185-188

generic collections, 311

I

IAddChild interface, 95

ICollection interface, 95

ICommand interface, 438

Icon property (windows), 476

if-else condition, 281-284

ImageBrush example, 230

images. *See* graphics

implementing DoorOpen CLR event, 300

importing 3D objects, 515-516

    camera properties, 518

    light properties, 518, 521

    materials, 516-517

inheritance hierarchy for button elements, 490

Inherited Control level (custom controls), 491

InnerConeAngle property (3D objects lighting), 520

input commands (WPF), 438-439

Input property, 350

int data type, 270-271

IntelliSense functionality in Visual Studio, 120

Interaction Panel, 65

interfaces

    child, 95

    IAddChild, 95

    ICollection, 95

    ICommand, 438

interpolation values (KeyFrames), 421

invoking commands, 442

IsDirectionReversed property (Slider control), 246

IsDropDownOpen property (comboboxes), 222

IsEditable property (comboboxes), 222

IsExpanded property

    Expander control, 261

    TreeViewItem control, 259

IsIndeterminate property (ProgressBar control), 240

IsMuted property (MediaElement), 526

IsOpen property (Popup control), 266

IsSelected property (TreeViewItem control), 259

IsSnapToTickEnabled property, 246, 397

Items property (TabControl element), 255

ItemsCollection control, 222-225

J–K

KeyFrames (animations)

    adding, 70, 418-419

    erasing, 420-425

    repeat animation, 420

KeySpline editor, 423-425

keywords

    this, 291

    try, 295

L

Label Content property (TreeView control), 125

Label control, 231

    adding to TreeView control, 122

    mnemonics, 231

    names, 121

languages

    programming versus scripting, 21

    selecting, 13, 32

LargeChange property (Slider control), 246

layers

    gel button creation, 176-178

        arrow shape, 179

        base, 178

        base brush suggestions, 180

        brush stroke property settings, 181

        brush suggestions sample one, 176

        brush suggestions sample five, 182

        brush suggestions sample six, 182

        brush suggestions sample seven, 184

        brush suggestions sample eight, 184

U

Y–Z

UNLEASHED

Unleashed takes you beyond the basics, providing an exhaustive, technically sophisticated reference for professionals who need to exploit a technology to its fullest potential. It's the best resource for practical advice from the experts, and the most in-depth coverage of the latest technologies.

ASP.NET 3.5 Unleashed
ISBN: 0672330113

OTHER UNLEASHED TITLES

ASP.NET 3.5 AJAX Unleashed
ISBN: 0672329735

C# 3.0 Unleashed
ISBN: 0672329816

LINQ Unleashed
ISBN: 0672329832

Microsoft Dynamics AX 5.0 Programming Unleashed
ISBN: 0672330105

Microsoft Dynamics CRM 4.0 Unleashed
ISBN: 0672329700

Microsoft Exchange Server 2007 Unleashed
ISBN: 0672329204

Microsoft ISA Server 2006 Unleashed
ISBN: 0672329190

Microsoft Office Project Server 2007 Unleashed
ISBN: 0672329212

Microsoft SharePoint 2007 Development Unleashed
ISBN: 0672329034

Microsoft Small Business Server 2003 Unleashed
ISBN: 0672328054

Microsoft SQL Server 2005 Unleashed
ISBN: 0672328240

Microsoft Visual Studio 2008 Unleashed
ISBN: 0672329727

Microsoft XNA Unleashed
ISBN: 0672329646

System Center Operations Manager 2007 Unleashed
ISBN: 0672329557

VBScript, WMI and ADSI Unleashed
ISBN: 0321501713

Windows Communication Foundation Unleashed
ISBN: 0672329484

Windows PowerShell Unleashed
ISBN: 0672329530

Windows Server 2008 Unleashed
ISBN: 0672329301

Silverlight 1.0 Unleashed
ISBN: 0672330075

Windows Presentation Foundation Unleashed
ISBN: 0672328917

SAMS

informit.com/sams